I0661504

Key West Hemingway

UNIVERSITY PRESS OF FLORIDA

Florida A&M University, Tallahassee
Florida Atlantic University, Boca Raton
Florida Gulf Coast University, Ft. Myers
Florida International University, Miami
Florida State University, Tallahassee
New College of Florida, Sarasota
University of Central Florida, Orlando
University of Florida, Gainesville
University of North Florida, Jacksonville
University of South Florida, Tampa
University of West Florida, Pensacola

Edited by Kirk Curnutt
and Gail D. Sinclair

University Press of Florida

Gainesville

Tallahassee

Tampa

Boca Raton

Pensacola

Orlando

Miami

Jacksonville

Ft. Myers

Sarasota

Key West

Hemingway

A Reassessment

Frontis: Ernest and Pauline Hemingway, outside 907 Whitehead Street, mid-1930s. Ernest Hemingway Collection/John F. Kennedy Presidential Library and Museum, Boston.

Copyright 2009 by Kirk Curnutt and Gail D. Sinclair
Copyright 1993 by Carol Hemingway with permission for *907 Whitehead Street*
Copyright 1994 by Patrick Hemingway for the Introduction to "A Key West Girl"
Copyright 1994 "A Key West Girl" by Ernest Hemingway. Permission for domestic use by the Hemingway Foundation/Society and the Hemingway Copyright Owners. International Copyright 1994 by the Hemingway Foreign Rights Trust.
Printed in the United States of America on acid-free paper
All rights reserved

21 20 19 18 17 16   6 5 4 3 2 1

First cloth printing, 2009
First paperback printing, 2016

Library of Congress Cataloging-in-Publication Data
Key West Hemingway : a reassessment / edited by Kirk Curnutt and
Gail D. Sinclair.
p. cm.
Includes bibliographical references and index.
ISBN 978-0-8130-3355-6 (cloth: alk. paper)
ISBN 978-0-8130-6236-5 (pbk.)
1. Hemingway, Ernest, 1899–1961—Homes and haunts—Florida—Key West.
2. Hemingway, Ernest, 1899–1961—Political and social views. 3. Hemingway, Ernest, 1899–1961. To have and have not. 4. Key West (Fla.)—Intellectual life—20th century. I. Curnutt, Kirk, 1964– II. Sinclair, Gail D.
PS3515.E37Z6655 2009
813.'529–dc22   2008052235

The University Press of Florida is the scholarly publishing agency for the State University System of Florida, comprising Florida A&M University, Florida Atlantic University, Florida Gulf Coast University, Florida International University, Florida State University, New College of Florida, University of Central Florida, University of Florida, University of North Florida, University of South Florida, and University of West Florida.

University Press of Florida
15 Northwest 15th Street
Gainesville, FL 32611-2079
http://www.upf.com

With deep love for their encouragement

Eugene and Marilyn Duvé

and

Beverly Curnutt

Contents

Part IV. Destination: Hemingway

Illustrations

Acknowledgments

We owe a debt of thanks to several mentors, colleagues, and friends without whom *Key West Hemingway* would not have been possible. First and foremost, we are grateful to the Ernest Hemingway Society and Foundation for providing the opportunity to work together as directors of the eleventh biennial Hemingway Conference held in Key West in June 2004. In the years before and after the conference, we learned a great deal about Key West culture and history. We were also fortunate to work with three different society presidents—Scott Donaldson, Linda Wagner-Martin, and James H. Meredith—each of whom was unfailingly encouraging about the need for expanding the scholarly understanding of Hemingway's Keys West years and career. Several members of the society board likewise assisted us in various capacities: Susan F. Beegel, Linda Patterson Miller, Rena Sanderson, J. Gerald Kennedy, Jackson R. Bryer, and Allen Josephs were among the senior leadership who supported our efforts.

In Key West, we benefited from a generous ally in Claudia Pennington of the Key West Art and Historical Society, as well as Norman Aberle, Brewster Chamberlain, and Tom Hambright, all of whom assisted us with photographs and with Erik Smith's painting of Hemingway and the regulars at Sloppy Joe's. Similarly, Susan Wrynn, James Hill, and Laurie Austin, at the John F. Kennedy Library in Boston, provided access to visual materials in the Hemingway Collection, while Adam Neal Watson assisted us at the State Archives of Florida. We are also indebted to Jim Moody for the use of Waldo Peirce's 1937 painting on the book jacket.

We wish to thank Patrick and Carol Hemingway for their strong support of *Key West Hemingway*, for their contributions to the book, and most especially for encouraging the first-time publication of Hemingway's "A Key West Girl."

We thank our home institutions—Rollins College in Winter Park, Florida, and Troy University in Montgomery, Alabama—for providing us the necessary time and financial support to bring this book to fruition.

We are grateful to have had two discerning readers, Linda Patterson Miller and Allen Josephs, recommend our manuscript to the University Press of Florida. We feel very fortunate to have worked with such an excellent staff at UPF, especially acquiring editor Amy Gorelick, project editor Marthe Walters, and our excellent copy editor, Susan Murray.

Finally, we thank our families, who have been more than tolerant in hearing our tales about Hemingway and the Keys for more than seven years. We cannot promise the stories will stop just because the book is now done.

Kirk Curnutt
Gail D. Sinclair

Abbreviations

AMF	*A Moveable Feast*
BL	*By-Line: Ernest Hemingway*
CSS	*The Complete Short Stories of Ernest Hemingway: The Finca Vingía Edition*
DIA	*Death in the Afternoon*
DT	*Dateline: Toronto*
FC	*The Fifth Column and Four Stories of the Spanish Civil War*
FTA	*A Farewell to Arms*
FWBT	*For Whom the Bell Tolls*
GHOA	*Green Hills of Africa*
GOE	*The Garden of Eden*
HOW	*Hemingway on War*
IOT	*In Our Time*
OMATS	*The Old Man and the Sea*
OTTC	*The Only Thing that Counts: The Ernest Hemingway/Maxwell Perkins Correspondence, 1935–1947*
SAR	*The Sun Also Rises*
SL	*Ernest Hemingway: Selected Letters, 1917–1961*
THHN	*To Have and Have Not*
WTN	*Winner Take Nothing*

Hemingway Chronology

The Key West Years

GAIL D. SINCLAIR

1928

March–April: In March, Ernest and second wife, Pauline (pregnant with their first child), leave Paris for Key West via Havana. Hemingway begins writing *A Farewell to Arms*. The couple arrives in Key West the first week in April, taking up residence at 314 Simonton Street, where they remain for six weeks. Hemingway's parents, Clarence and Grace, visit briefly in mid-April, as does Pauline's father, Paul Pfeiffer, by the end of the month for a more extended stay.

May–June: Hemingway friends arriving to visit by early May include John Dos Passos, Waldo Peirce, Henry "Mike" Strater, and Bill Smith. By mid-June, the Hemingways are in Kansas City to await the birth of their first child (Hemingway's second). On 28 June, Patrick Hemingway is delivered by caesarean section after a difficult labor.

July–August: Three weeks after Patrick's birth, the Hemingways travel to Pauline's family home in Piggott, Arkansas. On 23 July, Hemingway writes his editor, Maxwell Perkins, that he is on page 486 of the novel but is leaving for Wyoming, where he hopes to finish it. He travels through Kansas City (25–28 July), and by early August Hemingway is in Wyoming—moving from Folly Ranch to Sheridan Inn to Eleanor

Donnelley's Lower Branch—writing, fishing, hunting. On 18 August, Pauline joins him. Hemingway completes the first draft of *A Farewell to Arms* by 22 August.

September–December: Ernest and Pauline are back in Piggott by the end of September, remaining there until mid-October, when they travel to Oak Park, Illinois, and Massachusetts to visit the MacLeishes. In November, they see Perkins and friends Strater and Peirce in New York. On 17 October, the Hemingways join the Fitzgeralds for the Princeton-Yale game, head back to Piggott to retrieve Patrick, and then on to Key West. Lorine Thompson secures them a house at 1100 South Street for one hundred dollars per month. Hemingway meets his oldest son, John (Bumby), in New York as he arrives from Europe to spend the next few months. On the train back to Key West, Hemingway receives a telegram that his father has committed suicide on 6 December. Ernest sends Bumby on alone and travels to Oak Park to make funeral arrangements. He is back in Key West by midmonth and working on revisions of *A Farewell to Arms*.

1929

January–March: The typed draft of Hemingway's second novel, minus the ending, is completed on 22 January. Hemingway accepts Scribner's offer to serialize it for sixteen thousand dollars. He continues to revise the novel while fishing with invited friends: Mike Strater, John Dos Passos, Waldo Peirce, Maxwell Perkins, and Katy Smith, among others, including local Key Westers, all of whom he now labels the "Mob." In March, the Hemingways prepare for a return to Europe. Ernest instructs Charles Thompson to find a bigger house for the family when they return to Key West.

April–June: On 5 April, Ernest, Pauline, Bumby, Patrick, and Ernest's sister Sunny depart from Havana for Paris. Scribner's publishes the first installment of *A Farewell to Arms* in May. The June issue of *Scribner's Magazine* is banned in Boston when the novel's content is deemed too verbally and sexually explicit. Hemingway reviews the galley proofs and sends them to Perkins by the end of the month.

July–December: Hemingway and Pauline are in Spain attending the feria of San Fermin, traveling until early September. They return to Paris on 20 September, and *A Farewell to Arms* is published on 27 September. By mid-October, twenty-eight thousand copies are sold. Ernest and Pauline spend the Christmas holidays with the Fitzgeralds, John and Katy Dos Passos, Dorothy Parker, and Donald Ogden Stewart, who all keep Gerald and Sara Murphy company while attending the sick-bed of their son Patrick at a tuberculosis clinic in Switzerland.

1930

January–April: The Hemingways leave Europe on 9 January and return to Key West after a short stop in New York. They arrive the first week in February and set up residence on Pearl Street in another rented home. By now, Key West has become their home base, though they are rarely in residence more than a couple of months at a time. Hemingway complains that he has a hard time getting writing done because of visits from the so-called Mob, but by mid-March he begins work on the bullfighting treatise that will become *Death in the Afternoon*.

May–August: In June, Ernest leaves Key West to retrieve Bumby in New York. Before taking Patrick to Piggott, Pauline inspects a house on Whitehead Street (the one they later purchase) and deems it unsuitable. The family meets in Arkansas by the end of June and drives to Montana, where Ernest, Pauline, and Bumby stay at Nordquist's L-Bar-T Ranch in Wyoming for the remainder of the summer and into the fall.

September–December: Pauline leaves Montana on 14 September, accompanying Bumby to New York for his return to Europe and his mother, Hadley. On 17 September, Paramount Pictures purchases the rights for *A Farewell to Arms* for eighty thousand dollars. Hemingway's portion is twenty-four thousand dollars. Ernest breaks his right arm in a car accident on 1 November, undergoes three operations, and is hospitalized until 21 December. He and Pauline return to Piggott by Christmas Eve for the holidays.

1931

January–April: The Hemingways return to Key West. The family first rents a house on Whitehead and United streets. Ernest's mother, Grace, visits in February, meeting her grandson Patrick for the first time. Still recovering from his car accident, Ernest fishes in the Gulf and off Cuba. He writes Archibald MacLeish, "I am strong and healthy as a pig." Hemingway returns to work on *DIA* the second week of April, and on 29 April purchases the home at 907 Whitehead Street with money from Pauline's uncle Gus Pfeiffer. Pauline is two months pregnant.

May–October: The Hemingways leave Key West (Ernest first, then followed by Pauline and Patrick) for a summer in Europe, Pauline mostly in Paris, and Ernest mostly in Spain to gather research and photos for the book. By the end of September, the Hemingways, the Fitzgeralds, and the Murphys are all on board separate ships heading back to America. The friendships of the 1920s clearly have fallen on hard times. Ernest and Pauline meet Jane and Grant Mason on board the *Ile de France*.

November–December: Ernest and Pauline travel to Kansas City to await the birth of Gregory, the third Hemingway child (Pauline's second), who is born on 12 November. Pauline remains hospitalized for a month. Hemingway finishes the first draft of *Death in the Afternoon*. They return to Key West the week before Christmas. Ernest is ill with a sore throat, Pauline is recovering from the caesarean birth, and Patrick douses his newborn brother with a variety of chemicals. All recover.

1932

January: Typing is complete for *Death in the Afternoon*. Patrick swallows arsenic from ant poisoning and is violently ill. Hemingway complains in a letter to Perkins: "Since I started this book have had compound fracture of index finger—bad general smash up in that bear hunt—14 stitches in face inside and out—hole in leg—then that right arm—muscular spiral paralysis—3 fingers in right hand broken—16 stitches in left wrist and hand. Eyes went haywire in Spain. . . . Pauline's 2nd Caeserian etc. etc. etc." Serious renovations begin on the house on Whitehead Street. Gregory is baptized at the local Catholic church on 14 January.

February–April: Writing and fishing are both going well. By the end of February, Hemingway has seven stories written for a new collection (to become *Winner Take Nothing*) and is working on others. Among those completed are "Wine of Wyoming" and "The Sea Change." In March, he writes "After the Storm," a fictionalized version of a Bra Saunders story. In mid-April, Ernest leaves Key West for two months of fishing off the Cuban coast.

May–July: On 10 May, Ernest and Pauline celebrate their fifth wedding anniversary apart—Pauline in Key West, Ernest in Havana. *Cosmopolitan* publishes "After the Storm." Hemingway's passion for marlin fishing begins, and he spends sixty-five days at sea. He continues work on correcting galley proofs of *Death* and finishes writing "A Way You'll Never Be" and "Now I Lay Me." Plans for an African safari are postponed. In July, the Hemingways leave Key West for the summer, arriving in Wyoming by the end of the month.

August–December: Hemingway spends the summer writing, hunting, and fishing at Nordquist's L-Bar-T Ranch along with Pauline. He writes "The Light of the World" and offers it, along with "Homage to Switzerland" and "The Mother of a Queen," to *Scribner's Magazine*. Scribner's publishes *Death in the Afternoon* on 23 September. In mid-October, the Hemingways leave for Piggott and then Key West. *Death* is published on 15 November in England, and Hemingway begins "Fathers and Sons." He announces to Perkins that he has a new book in the works (probably *To Have and Have Not*). The family is back in Piggott from Thanksgiving through Christmas. Hemingway finishes "A Clean, Well-Lighted Place."

1933

January–April: While in New York in January, Hemingway meets Arnold Gingrich, who has just founded *Esquire*, and Thomas Wolfe. In March, *Scribner's Magazine* publishes "A Clean, Well-Lighted Place." The magazine also accepts "Homage to Switzerland" and "The Gambler, the Nun, and the Radio." In April, Arnold Gingrich signs Hemingway to write for *Esquire*.

May–August: Hemingway spends much of the summer in Cuba alternating between writing and fishing. Jane Mason has a car wreck on 24 May while transporting Bumby and Patrick Hemingway near her home in Cuba. Ernest completes the stories to be included in *Winner Take Nothing* and returns briefly to Key West on 20 July to pack for Europe. The Hemingways sail for Europe, leaving Key West on 4 August and Havana on 7 August. *Esquire's* August issue contains Hemingway's first contribution, "Marlin off the Morro: A Cuban Letter."

September–December: Scribner's publishes Hemingway's third collection of short stories, *Winner Take Nothing*, on 27 October. By late November, Hemingway finishes "One Trip Across." He and Pauline, along with Key West friend Charles Thompson, depart on 22 November for an African safari. The Hemingways and Thompson land in Africa on 8 December and enlist the famous hunter Philip Percival. The safari begins on 20 December.

1934

January–March: In mid-January, Hemingway is treated in Nairobi for amoebic dysentery. The party leaves Africa at the end of February. On 27 March, they depart France and meet the actress Marlene Dietrich aboard the *Ile de France*.

April–June: In April, *Cosmopolitan* publishes "One Trip Across." Ernest and Pauline arrive in New York ending a seven-month sojourn abroad. While in New York, Hemingway puts a down payment on a large fishing boat, the *Pilar* (his secret name for Pauline during their courtship), with a three-thousand-dollar advance from Gingrich for twelve *Esquire* articles. Hemingway is in Cuba on 1 May hours after the Batista-controlled military confrontation. He is back in Key West briefly before traveling to Miami to take delivery of the *Pilar* on 11 May. He runs it to Key West and divides time between visits from friends (the Murphys, the Dos Passoses, the Thompsons, Ada MacLeish), fishing, and drafting *Green Hills of Africa* after having written little but *Esquire* pieces in the past several months.

July–August: In the midst of the Depression, governing bodies in Key West declare a state of emergency on 2 July, claiming that half the population is on federal relief. Federal Emergency Relief Administration (FERA) funds aid the struggling Key West community, and tourism is emphasized as one means of financial relief. The house at 907 Whitehead Street is now listed in a Key West travel brochure as a tourist attraction. On 18 July, Hemingway runs the *Pilar* to Cuba. Between 20 July and 25 August, Pauline visits him there four times. Gregory spends the summer with his nanny, Ada, in Syracuse, New York. On 16 August, Ernest rescues his brother, Leicester, twelve miles at sea in a trip from Key West to Cuba that Leicester had attempted with a friend.

September–December: Ernest briefly returns to Key West the first week in September but is back in Cuba by 14 September. Hemingway writes Perkins on 3 October that he has fifty thousand words written on his safari book. He returns to Key West on 26 October and completes the first draft of *Green Hills of Africa* on 16 November. Gregory returns from New York with his nanny. The hunting trophies acquired on safari arrive from the taxidermist. Ernest, Pauline, and Patrick travel to Piggott for Christmas but leave Gregory in Key West with his nanny.

1935

January–June: *Scribner's Magazine* serializes *Green Hills of Africa* for five thousand dollars and publishes the first installment in May. Hemingway writes a letter in *Esquire* complaining about his house being on the tourist map of Key West. On a trip to Bimini with John and Katy Dos Passos and Mike Strater on 7 April, Ernest accidentally shoots himself twice in the leg. They return to Key West but make the trip again on 14 April. Pauline joins the group two weeks later, and by the end of June the family arrives as well. *Scribner's Magazine* publishes the first installment of *GHOA* in its May issue.

July–September: Hemingway returns to Key West on 16 August. He puts the *Pilar* in dry dock for engine repairs. Hemingway boxes with Key West locals. A deadly hurricane strikes Matecumbe Key on 2 September and kills several hundred veterans working for the Civilian Conservation Corps. Hemingway helps with the recovery and cleanup, triggering his political article "Panic" on 17 September, later retitled by *New Masses* editors as "Who Murdered the Vets?" On 24 September, he is in New York for the Joe Louis–Max Baer fight.

October–December: On 25 October, Scribner's publishes *Green Hills of Africa*. Hemingway works on *To Have and Have Not* in Key West. He visits New York in November and is troubled by negative reviews of *GHOA*. On 10 December, he finishes the second Harry Morgan story, "White Man, Black Man, Alphabet Man," and sends it to *Esquire* for publication. The story becomes "The Tradesman's Return" and is later incorporated in *To Have and Have Not*.

1936

January–May: Writing continues on Hemingway's third novel. In February, Hemingway and the poet Wallace Stevens get into a fistfight over Stevens's criticism of the writer. In April, Hemingway completes drafts of "The Snows of Kilimanjaro" and "The Short Happy Life of Francis Macomber." He leaves Key West on 24 April for fishing in Cuba. On 27 May, Hemingway encounters a storm at sea that nearly destroys the *Pilar*. He safely docks back in Key West.

June: Hemingway runs the repaired *Pilar* to Bimini in June to vacation with Pauline and his three sons. He meets Marjorie Kinnan Rawlings, who is vacationing there as well. In July, Hemingway writes Perkins that he has thirty thousand words of his Key West/Havana novel completed and announces that he is cutting back from twelve to six *Esquire* essays per year. He returns to Key West with plans to spend the summer in Wyoming. The Spanish Civil War begins on 18 July.

August–December: *Esquire* publishes "The Snows of Kilimanjaro" in August. Ernest and Pauline vacation at Nordquist's L-Bar-T Ranch along with Bumby and Patrick. Gregory is again in Syracuse with his nanny. The family travels through Piggott on their return to Key West in October and hires Toby Bruce to drive them. In November, North American News Alliance (NANA) hires Hemingway to report on the Spanish Civil War. By December, he writes Perkins that he has "*got* to go to Spain," but there is no immediacy. Hemingway meets Martha Gellhorn at Sloppy Joe's in Key West at the end of December.

1937

January–April: The second week of January, Gellhorn leaves Key West. She and Ernest meet in Miami on 10 January and travel to Jacksonville, where he departs for New York and she for St. Louis. Hemingway goes briefly back to Key West on 25 January, back to New York on 17 February, and sails for Europe on 27 February, arriving in March to cover the Spanish Civil War. He is joined by Martha Gellhorn and works with the film-maker Joris Ivens in April to write the script for *The Spanish Earth*. In late spring, Ernest and Martha begin an affair.

May–August: In May, Hemingway returns to New York and then Key West. On 26 May, Ernest runs the *Pilar* to Bimini, where the family joins him, and in June he completes the script for *The Spanish Earth* and *To Have and Have Not*. He is briefly in New York on 4 June and back again on 20 June. *The Spanish Earth*, narrated by Hemingway, has its premiere in New York on 5 July, and on 8 July he, Gellhorn, and Ivens attend its showing at the White House and then travel to Hollywood to promote the cause. On 10 August, Hemingway is in New York again, where he and Martha depart for Spain—Ernest on 14 August, and she two days later.

October–December: Scribner's publishes *To Have and Have Not* on 15 October. On 18 October, Waldo Peirce's portrait of Hemingway appears on *Time Magazine*'s cover. Ernest is in Madrid with Martha and working on *The Fifth Column*. In early December, Pauline leaves Key West in hopes of joining her husband in Spain for Christmas. Visa troubles prevent this, and she remains in Paris. Hemingway and Gellhorn spend Christmas together in Barcelona. Ernest meets Pauline in Paris on 28 December, and they quarrel. The couple departs for New York.

1938

January–February: Ernest and Pauline return to Key West in January, where he has spent fewer than three weeks in the last year. There is a new brick wall around their property, built by Toby Bruce, and excavations have begun for a swimming pool. In February, Hemingway tells a reporter from the *Key West Citizen*: "I am delighted to be back in Key West. It is my home and where my family is." He writes to his ex-wife, Hadley, on the same day telling her of his deep depression and suicidal thoughts.

March–August: Hemingway returns to France, where he meets Martha Gellhorn for a third time in Europe. From the end of March until the middle of May, they are together in Spain. At the end of May, Hemingway returns alone to New York and then goes on to Key West. Upon arrival there, he is involved in a minor car wreck for which he and the other driver are briefly arrested. In June, Hemingway is in New York for the Louis–Schmeling fight, and in August, the Hemingways once again return to Nordquist's ranch. Hemingway mails galleys of *The Fifth Column and the First Forty-Nine Stories* to Perkins on 20 August. He sails back to Europe on 31 August.

September–December: Hemingway is in Paris for two months, often accompanied by Gellhorn. Scribner's publishes *The Fifth Column and the First Forty-Nine Stories* on 22 October. Along with the play and stories from previously published collections, four new stories appear. On 4 November, Hemingway returns briefly for a last visit to the war effort. Pauline is in New York to meet Ernest on 24 November when he arrives from Europe. They return to Key West on 5 December to spend Christmas there. Ernest writes his mother a letter for the first time in nearly three years.

1939

January–March: Hemingway and Gellhorn meet in New York in early January, with *The Fifth Column* in production, and Ernest flies back to Key West on 24 January to receive Pauline's uncle Gus and his wife. On 8 February, Grace Hemingway visits, staying until 14 February. Ernest departs for Havana on 15 February, living in the Sevilla-Biltmore hotel for the next five weeks, though he has mail addressed to the Ambos Mundos. Hemingway works on *For Whom the Bell Tolls* and with two chapters completed returns to Key West on 14 March to spend Easter with his family, including his oldest son, Jack. The Spanish Civil War ends on 28 March.

April–October: Hemingway runs the *Pilar* back to Cuba on 5 April, where Martha joins him. In May, Martha rents the Finca Vigía, ordering and paying for its repairs herself, and she and Ernest move in together. Pauline vacations in Europe with friends in July. In August, Ernest and his three sons go to the L-Bar-T Ranch, joined by Pauline when she returns from Europe in September, but she and the children soon leave. Martha Gellhorn joins Hemingway in Billings, Montana. On 1 September, World War II begins.

November–December: Martha departs for Europe on 10 November to report for *Collier's*. Hemingway stays in Montana and works on his Spanish novel. Ernest returns to Key West to pick up the children, Pauline having left for New York, and in late November, he moves out of the Key West house. Father and sons spend Christmas in Havana, where Hemingway takes up residence.

1940

May: Pauline files for divorce, and Hemingway's second marriage and his tenure in Key West are over.

Introduction

Hemingway and Key West Literature

KIRK CURNUTT

In late 1930, shortly after an incapacitating automobile accident outside Park City, Montana, Ernest Hemingway wrote Maxwell Perkins, his editor at Charles Scribner's Sons. In the morose tone that often crept into his personal correspondence, the ailing thirty-one-year-old confessed that he was unable to complete the anatomy of Spanish bullfighting that he would shortly entitle *Death in the Afternoon*. Promising that his spirits would rise and his recuperation hasten as soon as he and his second wife, Pauline, were healthy enough to repair to Key West, Florida, Hemingway assured the worried Perkins that the winter haven the couple had enjoyed since 1928 would reinvigorate his stagnant productivity: "I'm still in bed most of the time," he admitted, "but count on Key West to fix everything up finely" (*SL* 337).

For most Hemingway aficionados, the line rings with a certain poignancy, for the then-triumphant author of *A Farewell to Arms* (1929) could not have known that within a decade his critics would come to blame the abundant diversions of America's southernmost extremity for hampering his literary development every bit as much as the sling and stitches that, for months after his car wreck, disabled his writing hand. Indeed, of all the exotic locales with which this peripatetic author is associated, Key West is the only one deemed detrimental to his art. The Michigan woods in which he spent much of his youth fishing and hunting taught him the sorrows of the *paysage moralisée* and imbued in him a reverence for natural landscapes; Italy, the site of his formative 1918 wounding as a Red Cross ambulance driver in World War I, initiated him in the metaphysical quandary of death; Paris, where he served his literary apprenticeship in the early 1920s, provided the expatriate displacement necessary to hone his craft and develop his uniquely austere voice; Spain introduced him to the bullfight, whose aesthetics provided the model for his existential credo of "grace under pressure." Key West, by contrast, is the place where marlin proved more preoccupying than manuscripts; where long, lubricious hours at Joe "Josie" Russell's Sloppy Joe's Bar were whiled away when masterpieces awaited writing; and where the duties of artistry that Hemingway had come to embody by 1930—hard work, scrupulous attention to capturing the truth of experience, the commitment not to indulge in rhetorical scrollwork or ornamentation (*AMF* 12)—gave way to the facile poses of the sportsman and adventurer.

For many observers, the belief that Key West was more of a venue for celebrity showmanship than artistic accomplishment has been reinforced by the city's posthumous treatment of its most famous resident. Throughout

2. Key West in the late 1930s, at the intersection of Whitehead and Caroline streets, around the same period that Hemingway's time on the island was ending. Courtesy of the Key West Art and Historical Society.

Paris, Pamplona, Ronda, and Venice, one can gaze reverently upon plaques and busts that unobtrusively commemorate Hemingway's connection to these sites. Key West, meanwhile, is home to vendors hocking an obnoxious array of Papa paraphernalia, including T-shirts, beer cozies, Zippo lighters, and, for a time at least, nostalgia cruises on yachts called the *Pilar* that looked nothing like the thirty-eight-foot cabin cruiser that Hemingway docked at the island's abandoned navy yard. The commercialism is so unabashed that it draws comparisons to that other favorite figurehead of Florida tourism. As one resort manager told the *New York Times* in 1994, "The mouse"—*Mickey* Mouse, obviously enough—"is to Orlando what Hemingway is to Key West." A local bookseller expressed the island ethos even more frankly: "You slap Ernie's face on anything and people will buy it. . . . We're more than happy to take their money" ("Hemingway Slept Here" 1).

Unfairly or not, that attitude has tainted perceptions of the two most prominent institutions sustaining Hemingway's Key West legacy, the Ernest Hemingway Home and Museum at 907 Whitehead Street (where Hemingway resided in the 1930s), and the Hemingway Days Festival (the island's annual celebration of Hemingway's life and writing). Unlike other Hemingway residences in Oak Park, Illinois; Ketchum, Idaho; and Havana, Cuba, the Whitehead Street abode is a privately owned, for-profit business whose mission has nothing to do with the rarified aims of scholarship and educational outreach. Whereas the Ernest Hemingway Foundation of Oak Park and the Pfeiffer-Hemingway Museum and Educational Center in Piggott, Arkansas, sponsor symposia and cultural events, the Key West house is a tourist attraction that charges ten dollars for a tour and three hundred dollars for weddings and wine-tasting rentals. There is nothing inherently wrong with such commerce, of course, other than it irks those who believe that it perpetuates simplistic and often spurious tall tales and legends. (When a *New York Times* reporter asked whether any tourists had "actually read a Hemingway book," the bookseller's optimistic reply was, "They've probably read *The Old Man and the Sea* in high school" ["Hemingway Slept Here" 1].)

Similar concerns surround the festival, which has taken place every July since 1981. Despite readings of original fiction, plays, and a popular short-story contest judged by a Hemingway granddaughter (Lorian Hemingway, herself a published author), Hemingway Days is best known for attracting legions of stout men with white beards to Sloppy Joe's Bar to compete in its notorious look-alike contest.[1] That few Key Westers decry the questionable taste of a bar appropriating the image of a writer who was undeniably hampered by alcoholism only reinforces the impression that the island values lucre above literature. As locals' comparisons to Disney World suggest, the trinketeers of Duval Street are not only untroubled about cashing in on Hemingway—they are blithely shameless about it. And that attitude has a great deal to do with why Key West has never been considered a "serious" site of Hemingway study.

The goal of this book is to change that assumption by demonstrating the complexities the island introduced to Hemingway's life and work—and, reciprocally, those that his presence have brought to it. In recent years, place has proved one of the most important prisms for understanding the author, with major essay collections such as *French Connections: Hemingway and Fitzgerald Abroad* (1998), *Hemingway and the Natural World* (1999), and *Hemingway in Italy: New Perspectives* (2006) reinterpreting the influence of Europe and the American West on his work. Yet to date our understanding of the surprisingly productive middle years Hemingway was headquartered in Key West has been limited to anecdotal biographies such as James McLendon's *Papa: Hemingway in Key West* (1972) and touristic overviews, most notably Stuart McIver's *Hemingway's Key West* (1993, rev. 2002). The fact that the two most neglected entries in the Hemingway oeuvre are both tied to the Keys and are maligned more than they are read suggests the need for a deeper analysis of South Florida's effect on him. Many of the twenty-six essays written for *Esquire* between 1933 and 1936, in addition to his experimental novel *To Have and Have Not* (1937), find Hemingway drawing from Key West's diverse multicultural history and dire economic circumstances during the Great Depression to create some of his most ethnically complex and overtly political work.[2] As imperfect as they may be, these efforts teach us much about subjects as diverse as the New Deal, veterans affairs, revolution, and the mythos of pirates. When read alongside the canonical entries in his catalogue, they likewise challenge us to reframe our perceptions of such trademark Hemingway concerns as manhood, authorship, and landscape.

Additionally, because Hemingway has proved such an important draw for Key West tourism for eight decades, the time seems ripe for assessing what the selling of his persona says about his appeal. In many ways, it is too easy to dismiss Key West's commercialization of Hemingway as an affront to literary culture, for that disdain merely reenacts rather than interrogates the modernist desire to believe that art exists outside of popular culture. It also seems rather ungenerous to a city for which tourism since the 1930s has been a survival mechanism necessary to sustain it through the boom-bust cycles of its industrial history. Moreover, the consistent appeal of an author as complicated and conflicted as Ernest Hemingway amid the noisy distractions of the city's nightclubs, beaches, and restaurants suggests that at least some of those readers who only know him from a high-school perusal of *The Old Man and the Sea* are as drawn to his gravitas as scholars who study his every tic and scribble in the hallowed groves of academe.

The Key West Literary Tradition

One preliminary benefit of a more thorough study of Hemingway's Key West years is a better appreciation of the appeal that the city has come to exert on the American literary imagination. In terms of prominence, the island may not possess the lure of New York, Hollywood, Chicago, or New Orleans. Nevertheless, there is a healthy if underappreciated genre of Key West fiction, and many of its tropes and themes evoke Hemingway. Of course, there was literature in the Keys before 1928, and Hemingway himself owes an inadvertent debt to many of these forgotten efforts. Janette C. Gardner's *An Annotated Bibliography of Florida Fiction, 1801–1980* (1983) lists roughly a dozen full-length works published before Ernest and Pauline's 1928 arrival, from Joseph Holt Ingraham's *Rafael, or the Twice Condemned, A Tale of Key West* (1846) to Mary S. Watt's *Van Cleve* (1913). Curiously, her survey does not include the most famous nineteenth-century treatment of the region—or, more accurately perhaps, the treatment by the most famous nineteenth-century writer to set a work in the Keys: James Fenimore Cooper's *Jack Tier, or the Florida Reef* (1848).

This salty dog of a yarn—-often ranked among the least discussed of Cooper's thirty-plus novels because of its reputation as a rewrite of an earlier best seller, *The Red Rover* (1827)—suggests the appeal of Key West as a literary setting. As a nautical adventure, *Jack Tier* depicts island environs as a maritime frontier where survival demands the same American resolve required to settle the northeastern wilds of *The Last of the Mohicans* (1826) and *The Deerslayer* (1841). And yet, unlike Cooper's more famous Natty Bumppo tales, the book is a relative rarity among his works in that it is not a *historical* novel. It does not, for example, tell the bizarre story of how Key West came into being. There is no mention of John Whitehead and John Simonton, the business partners who in 1821 purchased the island from a Spanish postmaster for two thousand dollars and promptly set about turning "Cayo Hueso," or "Bone Key," into an inhabitable settlement. Nor does *Tier* tell how that postmaster, Juan Pablo Salas, sold the island a second time to an unscrupulous grifter named John B. Strong, who in turn swindled the former South Carolina governor John Geddes into believing *he* owned its acres of mangroves. According to legend, Strong's double-dealing led to an armed confrontation in 1823 between opposing settlement parties, supposedly mediated by Commodore Matthew Perry, who happened to be on the island claiming it in the name of the United States. To prove who controlled the property, Perry even insisted on dubbing it "Thompson's Island" in honor of the then U.S. secretary of the navy, Smith Thompson. As historians note, the name stuck for about as long as Perry remained ashore (Browne 7–8; Ogle 5–7).

Had Cooper been interested in this history, he might have concocted a worthy successor to *The Pioneers* (1823), his fictionalization of the founding of his native Cooperstown, New York—a novel, in other words, that explored the paradoxes of nationhood, capitalism, and ecology. He might have even touched upon the democratic dynamics of Key West's early history, which included a near revolt against the overzealous, proto-Kurtzian military overseer David Porter, who succeeded Perry. Although Porter protected early citizens by policing marauding pirates, he also offended them by making no secret of his belief that the Florida Keys was an irredeemable backwater. Most egregiously, he imposed martial law so he and his underlings might profit on the salvaging industry that Simonton and Whitehead's settlers imported from Cuba and the Bahamas (Cox 55–56; Ogle 17–20). *Jack Tier* also fails to mention the Keys' rich Native American history. The island's original inhabitants are thought to have been Calusa Indians pursued southward through the Keys by rival Seminoles. According to legend, the Calusas' "last stand" was "so violent that the surviving [tribesmen] fled in their canoes to Havana," leaving behind so many skeletons that subsequent Spanish explorers dubbed the site the "Island of Bones" (Cox 5–6). By 1840, however, dispersed Seminoles fleeing the forced relocation program of Andrew Jackson's Trail of Tears attacked a small settlement at Indian Key, eighty miles north of Key West (Browne 86–89). Anxieties about an imminent invasion so aroused Key Westers that the arms trade with Havana exploded and helped create the prototype for one of the area's most enduring stock characters: the mercenary gunrunner.

For whatever reason, Cooper ignored this rich background, atypically grounding his plot instead in a contemporary conflict, the Mexican-American War of 1846–48. As such, Key West as a setting serves something of a paradoxical purpose in *Jack Tier*: while representing a last bastion of pioneer spirit in a country in which "westering" was already seen as rapidly exhausting the continental supply of available land, it also functions as a defense installation for protecting the integrity of the nation's southern borders. The novel introduces several other motifs that would become ingredients of Keys fiction: the dangerous weather (hurricanes in particular); the piratical roguery of local seamen; and, curiously, gender-bending. (In the novel's penultimate chapter, Jack Tier himself is rather improbably revealed to be the long-lost wife of the marauding captain whose monomania drives the plot to catastrophe.)

For all its rather melodramatic seafaring elements, *Jack Tier* does not acknowledge that Key West was home to a fairly conventional middle class within a short time of its founding. Even after a devastating hurricane in 1846 wiped out all but eight of its six hundred standing structures, the churches, shops, and elegant homes quickly returned. Their proliferation bespeaks the population of lawyers, doctors, and bankers who lived (though not always easily) alongside the wreckers and spongers who drove the economy. One reason that this aspect of Key West life is relatively absent from its early fiction is that most authors who employed it as a setting "never came anywhere near the place," instead happily spinning "Keys tales of pirate desperados who skulked about for treasure and preying on the innocent" purely from imagination (Ogle 38). This is true of Cooper and another notable author, Upton Sinclair. Long before *The Jungle* (1906), Sinclair cranked out young-adult dime novels under the military pseudonym of Ensign Clarke Fitch, U.S.N. The fourteenth entry in his Clif Faraday series, *Caught in a Trap: Clif Faraday's Terrible Set-Back* (1898), ostensibly takes place in Key West, but the geography is so nonspecific as to reduce the island to a generic hodgepodge of tropical imagery. It thus comes as no surprise to learn from his autobiography that Sinclair invented the adventure wholesale from New York (56).[3] To be sure, there are exceptions to this lack of familiarity. The 1841 *Knickerbocker* story "Love's Labor Lost: A Sketch of Key West," credited only to "The Author of the Drama 'Anne Boleyn,'" reveals an impressive awareness of local landscaping ("around a few of the neater dwellings, the orange, the lime, and the cocoa, have, by sedulous coaxing, been made to assume a thrifty appearance") while debunking its reputation as a pirate haven: "Many men of great intelligence are accustomed to consider this jewel imbedded in coral, as a nest of pirates, because it is the abode of 'wreckers,' not reflecting, that, although, like the lawyer and doctor, the wrecker lives by the miseries of other men, he may nevertheless be honest" (48). Yet by and large the fictional Key West existed independently of island reality. Writers found concocting a cutthroat world much easier than drawing inspiration from its real-life colorful characters.

A further consequence of this disinterest in native materials was a lack of recognition in Key West fiction of the island's multiethnic population. Thanks to its port, the city from its beginning attracted an international citizenry. As an early 1831 history noted, "The island was originally settled by persons from almost every country and speaking almost every variety of language that brought with them habits, manners, views and feelings, formed in different schools and in many instances totally dissimilar and contradictory" (qtd. in Browne 14). Drawn by the wrecking trade, Bahamian immigrants known as "Conchs" arrived in the mid-1820s, turning to sponge harvesting in the 1850s when navigational improvements decreased the frequency of shipwrecks in the Straits of Florida. Some four hundred slaves of African descent were likewise present by midcentury, their numbers growing to more than five thousand over the next two decades. Originally the chattel of wealthy merchants with Confederate sympathies, the slaves were emancipated not by Lincoln in 1863 but the preceding year by yellow fever, whose mortality rate created such a demand for labor that the Union commander Joseph S. Morgan—the island remained under Union control throughout the Civil War—offered them money and protection to abandon their masters. Eventually, many found their way into local business and government, faring "far better than blacks elsewhere in the South"

(Ogle 92). Then in 1868 came the influx of Cubans to work in the island's newfound industry, cigar-making. With many fleeing Spanish persecution during the protracted Cuba Libre movement, the immigrants at their peak accounted for nearly one in three of the city's population—a percentage that makes their relative absence from contemporaneous Keys fiction all the more striking.

Sadly, one of the few novels to depict this diversity has become one of the more obscure: Archibald Clavering Gunter's *Don Balasco of Key West* (1897). An unrepentant dime novel rife with gunplay and knockout potions, *Don Balasco* nevertheless includes as rich (and, alas, as racist) a portrait of fin-de-siècle Key West as there is in nineteenth-century fiction:[4]

> Around [Thomas Mastic, the "revenue man" hero] are the crowd that usually throng the wharf at Key West on the arrival of one of the Florida boats: sponge fishermen, long shoremen, the residents of the town, mostly Cuban; tourists, who are passing a few tropic days on the delightful island; cigar manufacturers, smoking their inevitable cigarettes; pretty, dark-eyed Spanish girls from the packing departments of the various cigar houses, and the usual blur of darkies and darky pickaninnies that go to make up the population of this town of all colored skins—white, yellow, chocolate, and black, but chiefly black. (23)

Set shortly after the 1895 death of the father of Cuban independence, José Martí, and two years before the mysterious USS *Maine* disaster in Havana, *Don Balasco* captures the frenzied buildup to the Spanish-American War. During this period, many in both Key West's new Cuban population and its older, established elite did their best to cajole the United States out of neutrality, politicking that the novel nicely conveys. Gunter even includes a reference to a contemporaneous event that deeply shocked Key West: in August 1896 Spanish forces executed a local journalist, Charles Govin, after capturing him among insurgents in the Cuban interior (Ogle 101). Gunter changes Govin's name to "Ona Milton," promotes him to publisher rather than reporter, and then adds a propagandistic twist by describing how Spanish forces snatched him off an American ship at sea (174), effectively reiterating "yellow journalism" charges that Spain was wholesale slaughtering Americans in the Gulf. Like *Jack Tier*, *Don Balasco of Key West* exploits

3. One of the more revealing pre-Hemingway novels about Key West is, unfortunately, one of the most obscure: Archibald Clavering Gunter's *Don Balasco of Key West* (1897), an espionage potboiler centered around the fight for Cuban independence that would lead to the Spanish-American War of 1898.

the island's isolation from the continental United States to depict it as a hotbed of international intrigue with dangerous ramifications for national security. This theme would last far longer than the 109 days it took the United States to win the war and expel Spain from Cuba. *To Have and Have Not* pivots on the consequences of a very different Cuban revolution, while later Key West novels such as Thomas Sanchez's *Mile Zero* (1989) explore the plight of Haitian *paysans* who unknowingly export political turmoil.

By the time of Hemingway's arrival in 1928, Key West was firmly established in the American reading public's mind as an ideal setting for espionage, smuggling, seafaring, and other themes associated with popular fiction. It should come as no surprise then that his use of its native materials was also in this vein. On the surface, his 1932 short story "After the Storm" reads like a *Jack Tier*–style adventure tale about the brutality of Keys life. As an unnamed wrecker works a newly sunken ship, he discovers a drowned woman through a porthole; before he can break the glass to retrieve the rings on her fingers, a storm intervenes; and by the time he returns Greek competitors in the salvage trade have stripped the ship of its treasures. Only when read in the context of Hemingway's fascination with death and the stoic poise necessary to survive a hostile universe does the irony of the final line ring through: "First there was the birds, then me, then the Greeks, and even the birds got more out of her than I did" (*CSS* 287). The same can be said of "One Trip Across" (1934) and "The Tradesman's Return" (1936), the two Harry Morgan stories eventually compiled into *To Have and Have Not*. Hemingway had experimented in the burgeoning "hard-boiled" mode before—most notably in "The Killers" (1927)—but Harry's tough-guy cadences are so mannered that they can sometimes seem as transparent a dime-novel invention as Thomas Mastic, the "revenue man" of *Don Balasco*. More than seventy years later, first-time readers are still shocked by the brutal moment at which Harry snaps the neck of Mr. Sing, the nefarious Chinese smuggler: "I took him by the throat with both hands, and brother, that Mr. Sing would just flop like a fish, true, his loose arm flailing, but I got him forward on his knees and had both thumbs well in behind his talk box and I bent the whole thing back until she cracked. Don't think you can't hear it crack, either" (*CSS* 405; *THHN* 53–54). This is a long way from the sensitive reflections of previous protagonists such as Nick Adams and Jake Barnes, and it left

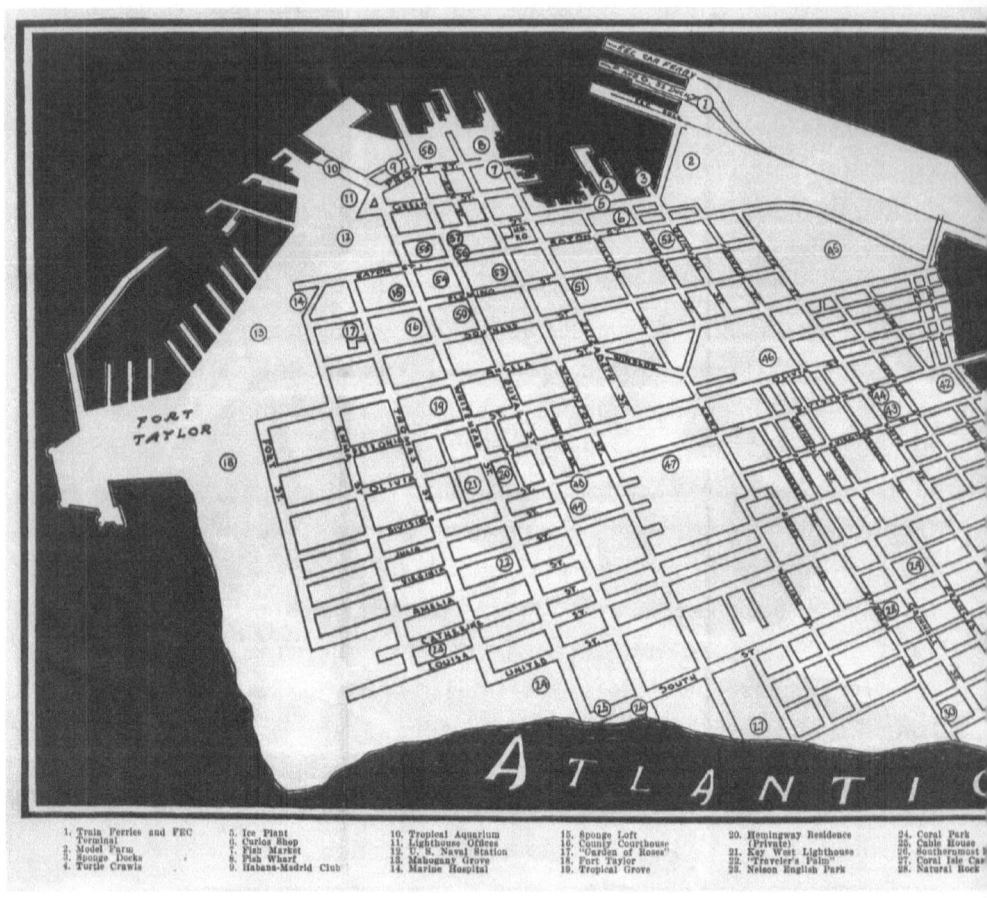

1. Train Ferries and FEC Terminal
2. Model Farm
3. Sponge Docks
4. Turtle Crawls
5. Ice Plant
6. Curios Shop
7. Fish Market
8. Fish Wharf
9. Habana-Madrid Club
10. Tropical Aquarium
11. Lighthouse Offices
12. U. S. Naval Station
13. Mahogany Grove
14. Marine Hospital
15. Sponge Loft
16. County Courthouse
17. "Garden of Roses"
18. Fort Taylor
19. Tropical Grove
20. Hemingway Residence (Private)
21. Key West Lighthouse
22. "Traveler's Palm"
23. Nelson English Park
24. Coral Park
25. Cable House
26. Southernmost Point
27. Coral Isle Cas
28. Natural Rock

4. The layout of Key West in the mid-1930s, taken from a guidebook that directed tourists to Hemingway's Whitehead Street abode. Courtesy of the Key West Art and Historical Society.

BIRD'S EYE MAP of KEY WEST for TOURISTS

many critics wondering whether the gritty world of Key West had cost Hemingway his nuance.

In reality, the novel's violence bespoke the island's fall from the glory of its cigar-making Gilded Age. Much like the wrecking and sponging industries, the tobacco factories could not sustain economic growth beyond two decades; by the early twentieth century, as the cigar bosses began relocating to Tampa to avoid hurricanes and growing labor strife with their Cuban workforce, Key West was again forced to scramble for stability. Although military construction boomed in 1917 after the American entry into World War I, the real solution was tourism. Accessibility proved full of Sisyphean obstacles, however—obstacles with which the oil baron Henry Flagler soon grew all too familiar when he embarked in 1905 upon what would prove a seven-year, $35 million struggle to link the island to the mainland with uninterrupted rail service. Hampered by monumental engineering challenges, yellow fever, and a spate of brutal hurricanes (in 1906, 1909, and 1910), Flagler's Oversea Railway lumbered into operation in 1912 only to lose upward of $400,000 a year before the most devastating Keys hurricane yet obliterated its tracks in 1935. Whereas observers had insisted that Flagler's railway would irrevocably alter Key West's character to the point that "novelists will have to move over to the West Indian islands or across the Caribbean to find homes for their smugglers, absconding cashiers, and the lone lovely daughter of the irascible, civilization-loving hermit" (qtd. in Standiford 215), the city's spiraling fortunes in the 1920s and 1930s endangered its stock characters in a wholly different way: according to Gardner's bibliography, between 1913 and 1937, only one other published novel besides *To Have and Have Not* was set in Key West (55).[5]

While economic conditions explain the presence of "smugglers" and "absconding cashiers" in *To Have and Have Not*, there nevertheless remained a great deal of "literary" technique in Hemingway's Key West fictions. Recognizing their experimental devices and strategies simply required reading these works outside of the city's affinity with "glorified pulp" (Stephens, *Critical Reception* 167). Unfortunately, only the most discerning of reviewers proved capable of this. Amid the shoot-outs and brawls, *To Have and Have Not* includes several top-notch descriptive passages every bit as arresting as the impressionistic landscapes of "Big Two-Hearted River" and *A Farewell to Arms*. Among them is the ambiguous final paragraph, a "boats against the current"–style image meant to depict the obliviousness of "winter people" to the malevolence that costs Harry Morgan his life: "A large white yacht was coming into the harbor and seven miles out on the horizon you could see a tanker, small and neat in profile against the blue sea, hugging the reef as she made to the westward to keep from wasting fuel against the stream" (*THHN* 262).

Such imagery reflects authors' awareness that Key West's abundant resources could be the stuff of high modernism as well as melodrama. Eschewing talk of pirates and pillaging, numerous poets (as opposed to novelists) arrived on the island in the same era as Hemingway to mine the symbolic potential of its coves and coral. Most famous among these was Wallace Stevens, who happened upon Key West during a 1922 business trip and subsequently began wintering at Flagler's Casa Marina Hotel the following decade (Kaufelt 31–34). One of the more curious incidents during Hemingway's Key West years was his 1936 fistfight with Stevens, who made the mistake of drunkenly disparaging the younger author at a party attended by Hemingway's sister Ursula. Despite the fisticuffs, Hemingway and Stevens shared what James R. Mellow calls an "ability to fix a scene or a moment or a revelation of character with a startling sense of urgency" (467). That urgency is palpable in Stevens's best-known Key West tribute, "The Idea of Order at Key West" (1935), which describes the "glassy lights, / The lights in the fishing boats at anchor there" as "[a]rranging, deepening, enchanting night" (*Collected Poetry and Prose* 106). This imagistic tradition would continue with the arrival of Elizabeth Bishop, who in poems like "The Fish" and "A Norther—Key West" likewise celebrated the island's power to compel the imagination to new heights of creativity. As with the pulpier fiction of Cooper and Sinclair, poets could also draw inspiration from the city without ever experiencing it firsthand. Most biographers agree that Hart Crane never actually stepped foot onto Key West. Yet his posthumously published sequence "Key West: An Island Sheaf," begun in 1926, explores the tropical juxtaposition of life and death in a way that suggests the island served the troubled writer as a fantasized realm of escape (Mariani 236).

The attention that Hemingway's presence brought to Key West between 1928 and 1940 may have garnered the island a reputation as a haven for aspiring authors, but it did little to fuse these opposing traditions of pulp and poetry into bona fide literature. Much like *Jack Tier* and *Don Balasco*, post-Hemingway fiction still tended to impose genre conventions upon the city's history and character, thereby hindering appreciation of its truly unique qualities. Thelma Strabel's historical novel *Reap the Wild Wind* (1941) won more attention for its Margaret Mitchell–style romance plot than for its informative portrait of the early days of Key West wrecking. Similarly, reviewers regarded Benedict Thielen's *The Lost Men* (1946) as James M. Cain–style noir, virtually ignoring its depiction of the 1935 hurricane that destroyed the Oversea Railway and killed hundreds of veterans working just north of Key West in a New Deal relief program (an event Hemingway angrily addressed in his essay "Who Murdered the Vets?").

Largely as a result of this inability to establish its value as literary material, Key West in the 1950s and early 1960s garnered a curious reputation as a congenial site for writing about elsewhere. James Leo Herlihy, for instance, claimed it was far easier to imagine the New York of *Midnight Cowboy* (1965) from a distance than it was to capture the very Key West streets he simultaneously prowled and depicted in his debut novel, *All Fall Down* (1962) (Kaufelt 70). When a major writer did set a work in the Keys, it was usually relegated to the same place that *To Have and Have Not* holds in the Hemingway canon: the "not his best work" category. Arriving in 1941 shortly after Hemingway's exodus to Cuba, Tennessee Williams went on to become Key West's second-most famous resident. Although he wrote triumphs such as *Summer and Smoke* (1948) and *Night of the Iguana* (1961) on the island, the one play he set on it, *The Gnadiges Fraulein*, proved one of the more dramatic failures of his career, its Broadway run closing after a single week in February 1966.

In essence, for Key West fiction to receive its due, critical values had to change so that pirates, hurricanes, and other native motifs could transcend their reputation as pulp contrivances and draw attention to deeper thematic significances. Such a change occurred in the late 1960s with the advent of postmodernism, which dismissed aesthetic distinctions between popular and literary writing, thereby making it possible for a cadre of emerging authors headed by Thomas McGuane to turn Key West into a Rosetta Stone of 1970s drift. On the surface, the island as depicted in McGuane's Keys triptych—*The Bushwhacked Piano* (1971), *Ninety-two in the Shade* (1973), and *Panama* (1978)—is not all that different from the world of over-the-top violence, sarcastic repartee, and sexual kink in *To Have and Have Not*. Indeed, when Thomas Skelton in *Shade* helplessly spies his former girlfriend, Miranda, making love to another man (16), the scene seems an overt nod to a similar moment in Hemingway when Tommy Bradley walks in on his wife, Helène, in flagrante delicto with Richard Gordon (*THHN* 190). As befits the temper of their time, McGuane's novels are more absurd than *To Have and Have Not*, with storylines about bats painted orange to entertain tourists and celebrities nailing their hands to the doors of ex-lovers. Yet this serio-comic vision was more likely to be praised for achieving exactly what Hemingway was said to have failed— namely, making a convincing case that Key West was "America in cross-section" (Stephens, *Critical Reception* 175). Such claims were made less on qualitative grounds than for the simple reason that critics in 1973 were more inclined to regard the island as "a whole culture in parable" (*Shade* 105) than they were in 1937. That is, whereas Hemingway's critics felt he treated Key West with an "excess of naturalism [that] creates an impression of unreality, the rawness exist[ing] for its own sake" (Stephens, *Critical Reception* 176), McGuane's ominously loopy world of burn-outs seemed a perfect synecdoche of America's unmoored morality in the Nixon era. As such, when one Key West literary historian describes *The Bushwhacked Piano* as "one of the few successful Key West novels" (Kaufelt 82), one senses that judgment has less to do with the aesthetic failings of other authors than McGuane's talent for extrapolating native materials to meet the zeitgeist. Claiming this by no means detracts from the formal brilliance of *Piano*, *Shade*, or *Panama*. All three are funny, challenging, and compelling in their own unique ways—not to mention at times downright beautiful. (The fishing scenes in *Shade* in particular are the lyrical equals of those in *To Have and Have Not*.) Nevertheless, there is also a very real sense in rereading period McGuane reviews that Key West's geographic identity as the "end of the [American] road" (Ogle 22) imbued island settings with a timelier salience for fiction than it had ever before enjoyed, including during Hemingway's 1930s.

As a result, what might be called the Golden Age of Key West fiction was inaugurated. Even more than his close friend McGuane, whose Keys novels are less thrillers than philosophical treatises, Jim Harrison in *A Good Day to Die* (1973) engaged the hard-boiled voice in a picaresque about saboteurs setting out from Key West to blow up a Grand Canyon dam. A decade and a half later, Alison Lurie—a Keys habitué since 1970—portrayed the city's prominent gay and lesbian community as an acerbic emulsion for exposing feminist orthodoxies in *The Truth about Lorin Jones* (1988). And in 1994, a year after John Hersey's death, his *Key West Tales* captured the more somber side of Key West with humane, empathic stories, including one that pays tribute to its long-suffering AIDS population ("Get Up, Sweet Slug-a-Bed"). Unlike other authors, Hersey channeled the inevitable influence of Hemingway in a formal as opposed to thematic way. Interspersed between the seven full-length stories of *Key West Tales* are vignettes of Key West history that, à la Hemingway's "interchapters" in *In Our Time* (1925), serve a contrapuntal function by providing epigrammatic insight into the full spectrum of the island's appeal, from entrepreneurial gold mine to tourist mecca to hideaway for those on the lam. One such vignette, "To End the American Dream," even explores Hemingway's susceptibility to the city's distractions. Central to the story is a mysterious blonde—Martha Gellhorn—whose late 1936 arrival signals the beginning of the end of both his second marriage and his residency in the Keys.

If one criticism of 1980s and 1990s Key West fiction may be had, it is that the genre generally shied away from any epic ambitions, almost as if the island's laid-back, laissez-faire attitude discouraged authors from pursuing that elusive white whale, the Great American Novel. The major exception to this rule is Sanchez's *Mile Zero*, which has garnered a reputation as "the definitive Key West novel" (G. Murphy 23) because in both sweep and style it self-consciously sets out to make a "statement" in a way that few Keys works have since *Ninety-two in the Shade*. Set in 1981 and revolving around the first space shuttle launch from Cape Canaveral, the rise of AIDS, and the murderous emergence of the cocaine trade, the novel manages to combine every imaginable Key West motif into a thriller plot with sociocultural import, a portrait of "living in a Christopher Columbus age, the beginning of one world, the end of another" (22)—an apt summation of the 1980s. Most admirably, Sanchez ties this critique of modern malevolency into Key West history, with luscious flashbacks to its wrecking and cigar-making heydays. As one reviewer at the time noted, *Mile Zero* evokes Key West's "palette, fauna and Latin Beat . . . with a superreal intensity"—so much so that "at times the background almost becomes foreground" (Abeel 7). One might revise such a statement to say that for a Key West novel to be quintessential, setting *must be* foreground.

In the twenty years now since *Mile Zero*, Key West fiction has settled into a comfortable niche as regional literature. At least two mystery writers, Tom Corcoran and Laurence Shames, have established successful detective series set in the reef regions, while longtime favorites like Lurie continue to mine the locale's symbolic status with literary titles like *The Last Resort* (1998), a pun on both Key West's isolation and its reputation as a tourist haven. Thrillers are hardly the only genre fiction to which the city lends itself: the Keys remain a choice site for historical romance (Jane Louise Newhagen's *Sand Dollar: A Tale of Old Key West* [2007]), psychological eroticism (Vicki Hendricks's *Voluntary Madness* [2002]), and even the decidedly specialized market of gay science fiction (William Eakins's *Key West 2720 A.D.* [1989]). According to George Murphy, "constants" continue to transcend differences, with authors creating a sense of place through evocations of "water . . . solitude, the exotic tropical languor (and the underlying inexorable decay), the quirkiness of the inhabitants, the natural beauty of sun and sea, [while] underlying it all is the mythic quality of 'island-ness,' as powerful here as it was for Shakespeare and his Caliban" (14). Of course, merely to contemplate depicting Key West in fiction entails confronting the specter of Hemingway, who casts a longer shadow in the city than any writer before or since. What is more often overlooked is how the supposed faults of his Key West writing tend to evaporate when read alongside the work of these other writers, from Cooper to Sanchez. His island years were not the distraction that biographers and critics have suggested. They encouraged him to explore a complex, mysterious world that, despite its cultural notoriety and commercial popularity, is only now beginning to receive its critical due.

This Book

The essays in this volume originated at the Eleventh Biennial Ernest Hemingway Society Conference. Held at the Casa Marina Hotel in Key West in June 2004, the event was attended by more than 250 Hemingway scholars and aficionados. From the 130 papers presented there, we have selected seventeen specifically designed to define the contexts in which Hemingway's Key West years are best read.

Our first section, "Hemingway in the Keys," explores how the city shaped the writer's life from 1928 on. It begins with a previously unpublished sketch from the early 1930s, "A Key West Girl," which reveals Hemingway's ambivalence toward both locals and toward the entourage that increasingly intervened between him and his art. The piece also features an introduction by Hemingway's sole surviving son, Patrick, who registers his regret for the mythologizing of his father that accelerated during his Key West years. That critique is furthered by Mr. Hemingway's wife, Carol, who depicts the dangers of literary exploitation by illuminating the gap between her husband's memories of his boyhood home and the dubious legends perpetuated in its current incarnation as a tourist attraction.

In his contribution, Lawrence R. Broer counterintuitively argues that, more than other Hemingway haunts, Key West "harmonized tensions within his complex nature," allowing him to strike a balance between the "conflicting roles with which he struggled all his adult life: those of artist as husband and father, artist as friend, and artist as man of action." By contrast, Gail D. Sinclair examines the toll of relationships lost or severed during this period. Starting with his father's death shortly after Hemingway's arrival and continuing through the 1930s, his mercurial propensities made maintaining older alliances increasingly difficult. Milton A. Cohen then expands the focus from the personal to the political by comparing Hemingway to Wallace Stevens. Despite their 1936 fistfight, the two writers suffered a similar crisis of conscience that caused them to first doubt and then defensively reassert the role of the modernist artist in an increasingly political age. Dan Monroe extends this argument by integrating Hemingway's brief and not wholly persuasive conversion to the radical Left in the mid-1930s to his disdain for Roosevelt's New Deal.

Our second section focuses on *To Have and Have Not*. The perceived flaws of Hemingway's third novel have been so elaborated upon that the elements that truly make it interesting, especially its historical and literary background, have garnered little if any attention. Noting that Sir Henry Morgan was a famous seventeenth-century pirate, for instance, Susan F. Beegel explores the rich tradition of maritime piracy it intertextually engages, including *Treasure Island*, *Peter Pan*, *The Pirates of Penzance*, and many others. Steve Paul reconstructs the background of the Cuban revolution against President Gerardo Machado in the 1930s to demonstrate how the novel's fourth, uncompleted section could have unified the fragmented narrative. Subsequently, Mark P. Ott reveals how, in 1932–33, Hemingway transformed his at-sea adventures aboard Joe "Josie" Russell's *Anita* (before he obtained his own *Pilar*) into *To Have*'s poetic fishing scenes. While Susan J. Wolfe compares the novel's depiction of sexual difference to *The Sun Also Rises* (Hemingway's most-studied assessment of androgyny and gender confusion), Mimi Reisel Gladstein examines how the 1944 film adaptation starring Humphrey Bogart and directed by Howard Hawks (from a screenplay coauthored by William Faulkner) imposed a patriotic plot upon the book's proletarian politics.

Our third section focuses on Hemingway's neglected Florida essays and short fiction. Michael J. Crowley's composition study of Hemingway's earliest Key West short story, "After the Storm" (published in *Cosmopolitan* in 1932), parses conflicting accounts of how the author first learned the legend of the sunken *Valbanera* from local fisherman Bra Saunders. John J. Fenstermaker refutes the critical commonplace that Hemingway's *Esquire* contributions suffer from an excessively macho presentation, insisting instead that the author crafted several different personae, including "teacher, insider, sportsman, celebrity, connoisseur, and artist." E. Stone Shiflet and Kirk Curnutt then offer a historical-rhetorical analysis of one specific *Esquire* contribution, "The Sights of Whitehead Street," in which Hemingway went to farcical extremes to decry his newfound status as a local tourist attraction. Next, James H. Meredith explores the sociohistorical backdrop of the federal work camp that was obliterated in the Labor Day Hurricane of 1935, killing nearly three hundred displaced World War I veterans. Contrasting the depiction of these men in Hemingway's acidic New Deal indictment "Who Murdered the Vets?" to *To Have and Have Not*, Meredith asks why, if Hemingway was as outraged by the former soldiers' deaths as his article insists, he would depict the men *farcically* in the novel. Afterward, Nicole Camastra demonstrates how Hemingway drew from South Florida history in constructing specific allusions to the state's homesteading history in his little-known story "The Strange Country."

The collection's fourth and final section, "Destination: Hemingway," includes one essay by Russ Pottle, who examines the touristic appropriation of Hemingway since 1961. Specifically, Pottle confronts the scholarly insistence that the commercialization of the writer degrades his literary status. Instead, he offers a Bakhtinian reading of both the Hemingway Home on Whitehead Street and the annual look-alike competition sponsored by Sloppy Joe's Bar. These attractions open Hemingway's image to the masses, transfiguring the official value imposed on the writer's celebrity by the literary establishment.

By addressing neglected texts and issues associated with Hemingway's South Florida tenure, *Key West Hemingway* challenges the commonplace that his 1930s writings are notable mainly for his artistic decline. Instead, these essays demonstrate how the island inspired him to grapple with politics, ethnicity, and literary experimentation as much as Petoskey, Paris, Pamplona, and others did in the more fabled era of ascendance. As the contributors here argue, Hemingway's Key West decade broadened and deepened his artistry in ways that both complicated and compelled his maturation.

Notes

1. For a history of the festival, see Davies. Two Hemingway scholars deserve credit for elevating the academic prestige of the conference: James Plath and James Nagel. It should also be noted that look-alike competitors imitate the Hemingway of the 1950s, not the Hemingway of the 1930s, when he lived in Key West.

2. See Knott's *One Man Alone: Hemingway and* To Have and Have Not.

3. Sinclair explained his research thus: "I read a book of Cuban local colour and looked up several expletives for Spanish villains to exclaim. I remember one of them, 'Caramba!' I have never learned what it means, but hope it is not too serious, for I taught it to all the newsboys and messenger boys of the eastern United States" (*Autobiography* 56). For the generic quality of *Caught in a Trap*'s locale, see the opening paragraph: "Key West [was] bathed in mellow liquid moonlight. . . . The broad harbor was alive with animation—lights were flashing, signals echoed, hails were exchanged. Tugs, cutters, gunboats—even the mightiest warships—moved here, there, everywhere to the echo of music and cheers" (Fitch 1).

4. Perhaps the only comparable work is Rockwood's sailing romance *In Biscayne Bay*, which, although only a few chapters are set in Key West, does include interesting period photographs.

5. That novel was Lydia de Bechevet's *Chantey of the Keys* (1936).

Hemingway in the Keys

A Key West Girl

Ernest Hemingway

INTRODUCTION BY PATRICK HEMINGWAY

My first acquaintance with "A Key West Girl" was at the literary conference on Ernest Hemingway held at Key West in January 1985, which I attended with my wife, Carol, and my daughter, Edwina. Scott Donaldson had run across the piece while doing research on the Hemingway manuscripts at the Kennedy Library in Boston and saw that it would be of interest if he read it at the conference and he did. As I listened to his reading, I saw at once that its inspiration was Betty Bruce, wife of T. Otto Bruce, known to his friends and taken from those initials as "Toby." Toby, who had been born and raised in Piggott, Arkansas, which has the long, hot, and humid summer of the Lower Mississippi Valley, hated that particular summer weather and, even more, the Key West version of it.

My mother, Pauline Pfeiffer, was born in St. Louis and only moved to Piggott when her father, Paul Pfeiffer, decided to purchase a 60,000-acre block of cutover bottomland in the valley of the St. Francis River and move there to develop it with draining and other capital improvements for resale as quarter-section cotton farms. If there was a single most important driving force to my mother's life, it was to get away from Piggott as soon as possible.

The young Bruces were a numerous family of redheaded kids in Piggott, and my mother remembered them as having great vitality, "like a pack of little red-furred animals, weasels perhaps." Several years later, after making her escape from Piggott by graduating with the inaugural class of the University of Missouri School of Journalism and then to France as secretary to Herbert Hoover and later, as Paris editor of *Vogue*, Pauline Pfeiffer became close friends with Hadley Richardson, my father's first wife, and the rest of the story is well told in *A Moveable Feast*.

Later, in one of her many visits to her parents in the late 1920s and 1930s, she suggested to my father that they hire Toby to come to Key West and work in the many renovation projects necessary to make the long-neglected 907 Whitehead Street into a livable home.

My father was not a do-it-yourselfer, perhaps from unhappy memories of family chores when he was a boy and teenager during his family's summer vacations at their lake cottage in northern Michigan. For the good reason that he disliked such work himself, he felt very grateful to Toby for taking it off his hands and always treated him well as an employee. The idea that he helped Toby in constructing the brick wall around 907 Whitehead is absurd as are so many of the subsequent tall tales that Toby made up about his relationship with Ernest Hemingway.

After the renovations at 907 Whitehead were completed, Toby was highly recommended by my mother to her Merner relatives in San Francisco, and Toby moved to the Palo Alto area, where the Merners had an art pottery business and where he was a great success. Palo Alto has probably one of the best all-year climates in the United States with lovely cool summers. Toby would have liked to live there forever, but Betty brought him back to Key West and so—"A Key West Girl."

A Key West Girl

When a man from up North marries a Key West girl she goes away with him all right; but later on they are always back. She brings him back and it doesn't matter what he was before or what his job was where he went. You will see him working in a filling station, or opening a beer place or a restaurant or some kind of coffee shop. She has brought him back and she won't ever leave again.

He can't make any money in Key West unless he is working for the government because he is a stranger if he lives there thirty years. No stranger's place can do much business. So if he starts to drink or anything she has a good excuse to leave him and it's over. If she is back in Key West and with her people she is happy.

The tragic part is when she leaves him up north or out west or anywhere and he doesn't come back and she ships her stuff home by express instead of freight and her folks have to pay the charges on a sewing machine expressed from San Diego, California. That sometimes makes a wound that all the time she is home until she dies will never heal.

If the husband was in the navy; she will bring him back or lose him. If he was in the army; she will bring him back or lose him. But if he was a Key West boy, a ball player say, she will bring him back. She will not lose him because once she puts pressure on him to come back he comes because the same thing pulls him back that pulls her. It is not only by the accident of time that the world was never conquered by Key Westers.

907 Whitehead Street

CAROL HEMINGWAY

> He looked back to where the fort was well astern, the red-brick build-
> ing of the old Postoffice starting to show up above the Navy yard
> buildings and the yellow hotel building now dominating the short
> skyline of the town. There was the cove at the Fort, and the lighthouse
> showed above the houses that strung out toward the big winter hotel.
> (*THHN* 155)

In this passage describing Key West, as seen by the character of Harry
Morgan from a boat on the water, Hemingway gives prominence to the
landmark of the lighthouse, across the street from his own home at 907
Whitehead Street.[1] The Key West lighthouse dominates its area on the
island and is famous today, lately featured in a PBS series on American
lighthouses.

My first visit to Key West was in January 1985, when the winter writer's conference in that town was devoted to papers and panels on Ernest
Hemingway. Walking down Whitehead Street from our hotel, my husband, Patrick, Ernest Hemingway's second son, was taken aback to see
a large banner stretched across the house, "Welcome Home, Patrick!"
As we started on the tour of the Hemingway Museum without revealing
our identity, Pat became more and more uncomfortable. Patrick's home?
The tour guide's talk and the furnishings of the house little resembled
clear memories of his boyhood home. We did not complete the tour, but
slipped away and mounted the stairs from the second-floor hall, exiting
through the door of a small wooden enclosure to the roof. Here every-

5. The Key West lighthouse, as seen from across the street at the Hemingway home—
a very different vantage point from the one Hemingway's proletarian hero, Harry Morgan,
would have enjoyed. Ernest Hemingway Collection/John F. Kennedy Presidential
Library and Museum, Boston.

thing remained unchanged for Patrick, and he gazed with delight at the full view of the lighthouse.

Pat told me of his affection for the roof where he had spent many childhood hours, especially at night, when the stars were bright and he taught himself the constellations from a book. In the 1930s (the Hemingways purchased the house in 1931), there was no light pollution in the Key West sky, excepting the lighthouse, whose beam swung from east to west across the Whitehead Street house, lighting up the roof as well as the boys' room on the second floor. During the day, on the roof Pat could see boats on the water and ships disappearing below the horizon, the visual proof to a young boy that the earth is round.

Standing on the roof, Pat and I had a good view of the grounds of the house with the well-defined boundary of the brick wall, built in the mid-1930s by chauffeur-handyman T. Otto Bruce, known as "Toby," with bricks left over from the elimination of the streetcar tracks. Pat pointed out a hole in the six-foot wall on the northeast side; a hole that came about because of the complaints of a neighbor who felt she "couldn't breathe." The Hemingways were quick to agree to her request for an opening that provided ventilation and also a good view of the yard and later, more entertainingly, of the swimming pool.

Prior to World War II, when the government built a water pipeline down the Keys from the mainland to Key West, the island was dependent on the collection of rainwater in cisterns. From the roof, the architectural details of the house having to do with the collection of rainwater were clear: gutters and a roof sloping to a central drain, culminating in the wooden-roofed concrete cistern on the ground behind the house, a universal feature of prewar Key West buildings. There was a well on the property providing brackish water, the only private well on the island. This unique well later provided the water for the swimming pool, making it an especially attractive feature in the Key West of the 1930s.

Pat noted the lush, tropical vegetation of the grounds, which didn't exist during his childhood because of the shortage of water. Then there were two date palms flanking the front entrance; later one died and was cut down. The vista from the roof then was an open, grassy yard with some trees selected by Pauline Hemingway and planted by the gardener, Jimmie Smith. Pauline Hemingway tried royal palms, which didn't take, although a fig tree on the Olivia Street side flourished, probably because it grew over the drain field for the cesspool. The yard was dotted with Spanish bayonets.

In back of the house stood the coach house. The upper floor became Hemingway's study, connected to the second floor of the main house by a walkway resembling a covered bridge with the walk on top. The walkway was torn down in the late 1930s. After the divorce in 1940, Pauline Hemingway rented out the big house and converted the coach house into an apartment that she used as a base when she was traveling.

The Whitehead Street house was built in the 1850s by Asa Tift, a northerner turned Key West shipbuilder turned Confederate sympathizer. The house is in the French/Spanish colonial style common to New Orleans, a major influence on Key West. Its two-story verandas with wooden floors, and its French door/windows, kept open, give an insight into what was needed in the tropics in the years before air-conditioning, i.e., cross-ventilation. The ground plan of the house is Federal, based on a center hall upstairs and downstairs, with large rooms opening off the hall on both

6. *The Taft-Hemingway House*, a preservationist's rendering dating from 1967, shortly after 907 Whitehead Street was first opened to the public. Ernest Hemingway Collection/ John F. Kennedy Presidential Library and Museum, Boston.

sides.[2] A square addition at the back housed the kitchen on the ground floor and an additional bathroom on the second floor, off the bedroom of Ada Stearns, the children's nanny. On the lower veranda at the back of the house, Ernest Hemingway practiced boxing on a punching bag anchored to the floor. Rattan furniture similar to designs featured today in Martha Stewart summer catalogues provided seating and side tables on the other verandas.

Having lived some years in Europe and worked as an editor for Paris *Vogue*, Pauline Hemingway had definite ideas for the furnishing of the house, such as the simple lines of hand-blown chandeliers brought from New Orleans. While living in the Paris apartment at 6 Rue Ferou near the Luxembourg Garden, Pauline had purchased Spanish eighteenth-century antiques that she later, in December 1931, had shipped to Key West. Pauline was sick with a bad cold in January 1932 when the furniture arrived, so her sister, Jinny Pfeiffer, took charge of unpacking and placing items, hanging a Waldo Peirce painting of a brace of partridges and shotgun over the original fireplace in the dining room. The Hemingways burned charcoal from the Keys in the fireplace, the only heat in the house with the exception of the electric cooking stove and the round electric heaters in the bathrooms.

> "He left his bicycle on the front porch and went in the hallway closing the front door the termites had tunneled and riddled." (*THHN* 176)

A termite called woodworm thrives in the Key West climate, where little by little it destroys woodwork and furniture. This was the unhappy fate of the eighteenth-century antiques so exactly chosen by Pauline Hemingway and finding the perfect architectural setting in the house at 907 Whitehead Street. At the time of the sale of the house in the early 1960s by the then owners Patrick, Gregory, and Mary Hemingway, many pieces of the furniture were brittle shells. Patrick Hemingway took what was left to his house in the Oakland hills above Berkeley, California. The house and all its contents burned in 1967.

Unfortunately, little remains of a visual record. Pat Hemingway remembers the Johnson Wax Company of Racine, Wisconsin, coming to Key West in the 1930s and photographing all the interiors of the house for an ad.[3] In the photo chosen for the advertisement, the Spanish side table with wrought iron below is flanked by two French bergère-style chairs, one actually a chaise lounge. There is also a partial view of a Spanish walnut chest. One of the three André Masson forest paintings, perhaps *Ville d'Avray*, hangs over the table between two sets of doors. The fine print of the ad reads, "High French doors allow the Florida sunlight to stream across richly polished floors of virgin pine in Mrs. Hemingway's Spanish Colonial house—built 85 years ago." The photograph also shows Moroccan throw rugs resting on those highly waxed pine floors.

The living room ran the length of the house, pierced by long, arched French door/windows. The wall space between the graceful doors was filled either with floor-to-ceiling bookcases—the Hemingways owned a large library—or Hemingway's paintings, such as the other Masson paintings. In *Green Hills of Africa*, Pauline Hemingway as P.O.M. comments on the Masson paintings:

"JOHNSON'S WAX GIVES
permanent BEAUTY
TO FLOORS AND FURNITURE"

says MRS. ERNEST HEMINGWAY

● High French doors allow the Florida sunlight to stream across richly polished floors of virgin pine in Mrs. Hemingway's Spanish Colonial house — built 85 years ago.

● Mrs. Ernest Hemingway, charming wife of the famous novelist, is a successful writer in her own name.

● There are no disfiguring signs of wear to mar the beauty of floors or furniture in Mrs. Hemingway's interesting Key West home. She says, "All my things are protected with genuine wax. It gives a rich, satiny polish that lasts indefinitely, resists dirt and requires very little upkeep."

Johnson's Wax is very economical to use. It cleans as it polishes and gives lasting beauty to floors, linoleum, furniture and woodwork.

For sale (paste or liquid) at grocery, hardware, paint, drug and department stores. Send the coupon.

Rent the Johnson Electric Polisher from your dealer at small cost.

JOHNSON'S WAX
for floors and furniture

● S. C. Johnson & Son, Inc., Dept. NG-10, Racine, Wis. Enclosed is 10c. Please send me a trial can of Johnson's Wax and interesting booklet.

Name_____

Address_____

City_____State_____

7. Pauline Hemingway's testimonial for Johnson's Wax offers one of the few remaining visual records of the interior of 907 Whitehead Street during the Hemingways' tenure. Courtesy of S. E. Johnson and Sons.

"By God, isn't it good looking country?" I said.

"Splendid," Pop said. "Who would have imagined it?"

"The trees are like Andre's pictures," P.O.M. said.

"It's simply beautiful. Look at that green. It's Masson." (96)

She was equally proud of the Juan Gris paintings. In a letter to her husband on 6 May 1932, Pauline Hemingway wrote about the visit of a struggling young painter. "He was so crazy about *The Guitar Player* [the Juan Gris painting Pauline and Ernest Hemingway bought in Paris in 1931] that he won me. He asked if it was Picasso and I was pleased he'd heard of him." Gris's *The Bullfighter* and, later, Paul Klee's *Monument under Construction* also hung in the living room. After the divorce, when Ernest Hemingway took his paintings to Cuba, Pauline Hemingway purchased in New York a small Klee painting of a pear, which she hung in the living room.

In a letter to Waldo Peirce on 15 April 1932 from Key West, Hemingway wrote: "Have your two partridges with shotgun, a damn fine picture, over the fireplace in the dining room. Everybody in Paris, that is Miro [*sic*] and Masson and those birds, were crazy about your two pike, pickerel rather, on the platter and the trout" (*SL* 358). Across the hall in the dining room a long Spanish dining table, also with ironwork below, was flanked by benches on both sides and a chair at each end. There was a high chest of dark walnut with glass doors. Miró's *The Farm* hung on one wall and an unusual taxidermy creation—a ruffed grouse in a natural setting with a curved glass front like a picture—filled another, as well as the Peirce still-life of fish.

> "I've tried to take care of you and humor you and look after you and cook for you and keep quiet when you wanted and cheerful when you wanted."
> (*THHN* 186)

In the Johnson Wax ad, Pauline Hemingway endorses the wax product—either liquid or paste—"All my things are protected with genuine wax. It gives a rich, satiny polish that lasts indefinitely, resists dirt and requires very little upkeep." In restoring the house after the initial purchase, Pauline was directly involved with the workmen and undertook many chores to enhance the beauty of the house. Just as Pauline's taste dictated the furnishings of the house, her management governed the operation of the staff consisting of a gardener, handyman/chauffeur, laundress, cook, and nanny.

The yard man was Jimmie Smith. His duties in the yard always included weeding, picking off insects such as beetles on the plants, burying dead barracuda around the bases of trees for fertilizer, and mowing with a hand mower. There was a lot of grass. Patrick remembers hearing the continual whirr of the lawn mower. (Another familiar sound was the ice house whistle, which sounded at 9 a.m., noon, and 5 p.m. Few people had clocks.) In a 1931 letter to her husband, when she was readying the house for occupancy, Pauline Hemingway speaks of repairing the roof and also notes that half of the yard had been weeded. Pauline became intensely interested in gardening, supervising Jimmie Smith in his work. She consulted with Key West botanical experts in searching out appropriate vegetation for the northern tropics. After her death in 1951, when Patrick and his first wife, Henrietta, lived in the Whitehead Street house, Dennis Martin, a well-known photographer for the *National Geographic* and botanist, told Pat that the yard contained many unusual plants not found elsewhere and reflecting Pauline's originality.

When Patrick was a little boy, Ina Hepburn, an African American woman who lived several blocks away, came each week to do the laundry. She washed the clothes and linens in a large galvanized tub over a wood fire behind the coach house. Ina rubbed the wash by hand with big yellow bars of soap and stirred the tub with a wooden stick. She set up her ironing board and charcoal iron in the yard behind the kitchen. When finished, Ina carried the folded linens to a large armoire chest at the top of the stairs on the second floor. A thrifty, hard worker, Ina sent all of her children to college from her earnings as a laundress.

Miriam Williams was the accomplished cook, trained by Pauline Hemingway. Pat remembers that most dinners featured fish, which was indeed plentiful in the Keys: kingfish, grouper, snapper, shrimp, as well as the famous conch used in salads. Turtle meat was also plentiful. Pauline interspersed the local fish caught by her husband and friends with orders of barnacles (*percebes*) from Spain and kippers that came in a wooden box from Scotland. When they were small, Patrick and his younger brother Gregory ate at the children's table in a small pantry room off the kitchen. Most of their food was prepared by Ada Stearns, the nanny, who was not an inspiring cook. Birthday dinners regularly included hamburgers, mashed potatoes, and peas.

Pauline could also vary the diet with game birds. In a letter written 5–6

January 1932 to Maxwell Perkins, Hemingway refers to killing fourteen snipe with Charles Thompson. When John Dos Passos was expected for a visit, Patrick would accompany his father out to shoot shorebirds—black-bellied plover and yellowlegs—which young Pat would retrieve as they fell on the beach or in the water. Dos had the reputation of possessing a large appetite. Patrick remembers his father saying that "Mr. Dos Passos could eat the pants off a brass monkey."

Dos Passos had first recommended Key West to the Hemingways as a place to live. When they took up permanent residence there, more and more of the crowd of couples from New York and Paris visited with great frequency. In addition to Dos Passos and his wife, Katy Smith, Sara and Gerald Murphy, Ada and Archibald MacLeish, Dawn Powell, Dorothy Parker, Waldo and Alzira Peirce all gathered at Whitehead Street for dinner. Esther and Canby Chambers moved from New York to Key West, too, after Canby's bout with polio. This group of couples formed a lively social circle of witty, intelligent people who all interacted on the same level. These strong personalities reveal themselves and their camaraderie in the exchange of letters wonderfully assembled by Linda Miller in *Letters from the Lost Generation*.

The men and some of the women were a heavy-drinking and -smoking crowd typical of the period. Scotch was popular; rum drinks and Spanish wines were easily available. Cocktails such as martinis were served most often on the veranda or in the living room/library, where on a table sat a novel sage grouse mount, a male in the full display of fanned tail and enlarged throat sacs, attached to a silver arched stand with holes in which to place cigarettes. Other cigarette boxes and ashtrays were in abundance.

Ernest Hemingway's ambition was to own a Capehart record player. However, his brother-in-law, Carl Pfeiffer in Piggott, Arkansas, was the manufacturer's representative for a different company and sent the Hemingways a less desirable player. Nevertheless, they set it up in the living room and played the records sent to them as gifts or special orders. While involved with a play adaptation of Hemingway short stories entitled *It Just Catches*, I asked Pat if he remembered his father's choice of Cole Porter songs. The director of the play and I had decided to use Cole Porter as incidental music, knowing that Porter had known Hemingway. Pat listed "You're the Top," "Tomorrow," and "Experiment" as favorites. Pat remem-

8. As Mrs. Ernest Hemingway, the former Pauline Pfeiffer cut a glamorous figure in Key West. Ernest Hemingway Collection/John F. Kennedy Presidential Library and Museum, Boston.

bers his father humming the last named. (The song "It's Bad for Me" occupies a prominent position in the story "The Snows of Kilimanjaro.") In a letter to Gerald Murphy dated 7 November 1934, Hemingway asked Gerald to send him a recording of "Experiment" to replace one that was broken. He also enclosed a check.

Pauline Hemingway had collected recipes from her travels and worked with Miriam to reproduce sophisticated menus for the dinner parties. The influence was largely French and English from the cheese soufflés, curried rice rings, popovers (Yorkshire pudding), to the salads with vinaigrette dressing served on French plates decorated with humorous drawings and epigrams. Chocolate mousse chilled in small silver cups was a favorite dessert. Pauline Hemingway wisely refused to give out recipes as she said she never wanted to be served her own food in someone else's house.

and a thousand breakfasts come up on trays in the thousand fine mornings of the next three years; or the ninety of the next three months. (*FC* 82)

French, too, for the Hemingways, was the custom of having breakfast in the master bedroom, usually on the large bed. Patrick Hemingway has noted that his father was fond of eating and reading in bed, authenticated by George Leavens's later photograph of Hemingway reading the *New York Times* in bed at the Finca Vigía in Cuba. The bedroom gained elegance from Pauline's accessories. Her dressing table sported a complete French dresser set in tortoiseshell and gold. The bedspread was French as well in white chenille with a large fanned-tail peacock in full color at the center. In the bedroom, too, were the couple's portraits—one of Pauline holding a cigarette by Waldo Peirce and the other, very showy, a full-length portrait of Hemingway by Luis Quintanilla. The latter burned up in Patrick Hemingway's California house.

Lorine Thompson, wife of Charles Thompson, kept Pauline's portrait, and a Waldo Peirce painting of infant Patrick sitting on his nurse's lap, in her Key West house. The Thompsons early on became close friends of the Hemingways in Key West. Lorine told Doris Hemingway, Leicester Hemingway's wife, that she was holding the paintings to give to Patrick. (Hilary Hemingway corroborates what her mother related to Patrick and me.) By the 1980s, Lorine Thompson was very old and failed to communicate her intentions in her will. When she died in 1985, her house and all its contents went to her elderly brother in Georgia, T. F. Carter. Mr. Carter wrote Patrick and me that he had no knowledge of the ownership of the paintings and sold the house with its contents to Robert Crane of Key West. Though apprised by the lawyer George Bobrinskoy of the provenance of the paintings, Robert Crane has never returned the paintings to the Patrick Hemingway family.

> he passed the frame houses with their narrow yards, light coming from the shuttered windows; the unpaved alleys, with their double rows of houses; Conch town, where all was starched, well-shuttered, virtue, failure, grits and boiled grunts, under-nourishment, prejudice, righteousness, inter-breeding, and the comforts of religion. (*THHN* 193)

Toby Bruce's family were sharecroppers in Piggott, Arkansas, where they knew the Paul Pfeiffer family. Pauline Hemingway described them to Patrick as "bright-eyed little animals." Talented with his hands, Toby did carpentry work in Piggott, and when invited to come to Key West he continued woodworking for the Hemingways by constructing some of the upstairs furniture in Ada Stearns's bedroom. He also acted as chauffeur, helping out on the long drives from Key West to Piggott and to the L-Bar-T Ranch in Wyoming. Budd Schulberg, the screenwriter, wintering in Key West, cast Toby Bruce in a movie about the Everglades, which perhaps stimulated his imagination for fiction. Toby yearned to range out of Key West and for a time worked at pottery in an arts and crafts operation owned by Pfeiffer relatives, the Merners, in Palo Alto, California. Toby loved the Bay area and dreamed of staying there but instead was drawn back to Key West by his wife, Betty Merino Bruce.

The Merinos owned an appliance repair business in Key West that grew through the years with the importance of electric appliances such as washing machines and refrigeration. As small-town storeowners, the Merinos were important townspeople and native Conchs. Betty Bruce cut a figure in Key West that could not be duplicated on the West Coast. Hemingway wrote a fictionalized piece about Betty entitled "A Key West Girl" that describes a marriage between a Key West native and a man from "up North," Arkansas being considered the North in Key West.[4] There is not any way to make money in Key West except by odd jobs such as working in a filling station or coffee shop. This is indeed the fate of a "stranger" who even after thirty years of residence cannot become a Conch. Should the couple try another part of the country, the woman will always go back, shipping her sewing machine home from, say, San Diego, at great expense, which is never forgiven by her Conch family. She pulls her husband back with her. "It is not only by the accident of time that the world has never been conquered by Key Westers."

Toby Bruce lived on in Key West past the deaths of Pauline and Ernest Hemingway. When Bernice Daniels bought the Whitehead Street house in 1961 from Patrick, Gregory, and Mary Hemingway, she lived in it a few years before deciding to sell tickets and open it to the public. Knowing nothing about the history of the house, she turned to Toby Bruce (and probably Betty), who were quick to make up stories that to their minds were colorful and corny, such as the fabrication about the "last penny" spent on the swimming pool and the tasteless "urinal" adapted for the cats drinking nearby. In September 1934, Hemingway wrote to Gerald and Sara

9. The backyard of 907 Whitehead Street, featuring the pool that would later inspire an erroneous legend that is still told today to tourists in Key West. Ernest Hemingway Collection/John F. Kennedy Presidential Library and Museum, Boston.

Murphy cheerfully describing his decision to build a swimming pool where he could have daily exercise following work. Thus the pool was hardly a subject of acrimony between the Hemingways.

Bernice Daniels was serious about restoring the Key West house in the manner of its original state. She evidently purchased Spanish-style furniture, which was readily available in Miami and stemmed from the Spanish revival of the 1930s. The Country Club Plaza district in Kansas City, Missouri, and even some buildings in Bozeman, Montana, give evidence in the stucco walls, wrought-iron work, and tile roofs of the popularity of the style in that period. The overall attempt is legitimate, yet it is simply not truthful when passed off as the original furnishings.

Some winter people rode by the house on bicycles. They were laughing. In the big yard of the house across the street a peacock squawked. (*THHN* 262)

In the 1930s, William Demeritt was the superintendent of the Seventh Lighthouse District. In addition to his lighthouse duties, he developed an aviary on the lighthouse property. It was from this source that the Hemingways obtained the peacocks that roamed the grounds of 907 Whitehead Street. They roosted in the trees near the house at night and were very noisy, sometimes to the neighbors' distress. To this day, Patrick Hemingway has a fondness for the peacock's loud *Cawwwww*.

In 1985, Patrick and I searched in vain for any songbirds in the yard of the Key West house. None of the redstarts, ovenbirds, or yellow-throated warblers, ever plentiful in Pat's childhood, were to be seen. The enthusiastic spraying for mosquitoes in Key West may account for the decline of the bird life in the place Audubon so valued.

Pat also tells of the pet raccoons kept in a large cage in the yard. Esther Chambers painted a tropical scene with flamingos and palm trees on the back of the cage. Beginning with four raccoons, the number dwindled to a loving couple—Roger Herbert and Miriam Hopkins. The two were fastidi-

10. Peacocks obtained from the lighthouse supervisor William Demeritt added a touch of tropical exoticism to the Hemingway yard. Ernest Hemingway Collection/John F. Kennedy Presidential Library and Museum, Boston.

ous in their habits, carefully picking up and devouring the canned dog food they were fed. One morning Hemingway discovered Roger Herbert munching on his partner, Miriam Hopkins, despite having had a full meal of the dog food. Infuriated by this scene of connubial cannibalism, Hemingway grabbed his shotgun and killed Roger.

In 1985, to journalists from the Palm Beach television station WPTV, assembled at Key West, and again in a feature article by the author Mark Burrell in the *Miami Herald* of 21 August 1994, Patrick Hemingway made clear that there were no cats on the property at 907 Whitehead Street. True, Ernest Hemingway was fond of cats, as seen in the proliferation of cats at his home in Cuba. But during the Key West years he did not possess a single cat. The current owners of the house and operators of the house tours make false statements when they insist that the current crop of six-toed cats is descended from cats the Hemingways owned.

Patrick tells the story that on one occasion a neighbor's cat wandered into the yard: "It had been in an accident, just run over by a car, and it had a terrible back injury and wasn't going to live. So my dad, who was very kind-hearted to animals, decided to put it out of its misery and shot it and gave it to the yard man, Jimmie, to bury." Mysteriously, the cat revived and was soon seen dragging itself around but with only one eye. After publication of the Burrell article, the *Miami Herald* received a letter to the editor that corroborated Patrick Hemingway's account:

September 8, 1994, "Tropics"

It did my heart good to read Mark Burrell's August 21 article on Ernest Hemingway. I lived and grew up at 919 Whitehead Street until my marriage in 1944. My sisters and I were the neighborhood children who owned the cat Hemingway shot in the eye. He had not been run over, but was crippled from birth, and walked with an erratic gait. We doubt seriously that Hemingway shot him for any humanitarian reason. He was just practicing for his big game hunts to Africa! We always knew Hemingway had shot him, but when we try to tell people the real story they don't believe it.

The six-toed cats were ours; the first a gift to my mother from a lady who also loved cats like we do. I still have a six-toed cat. Thanks to Mr. Burrell and Patrick Hemingway for setting the record straight.

O. K. Jaycocks, Key West

Unlike the tense, quarrelsome atmosphere depicted by the tour guides under the current 907 Whitehead Street management, Ernest Hemingway spent many productive writing years surrounded by family life, bountiful hunting and fishing, and visited by a circle of like-minded friends. Welcome home, Patrick? The house today bears little resemblance to Patrick Hemingway's memory of what he called, in a *Playboy* article written in December 1968, "a magical childhood." Yet there are telling details. Like the cement sidewalk with its imprint of a young girl's foot in Willa Cather's *Lucy Gayheart*, the house holds tight to small features of the past. Pat showed me the bathroom floor tile where the outline of an iron burned an image. He pulled aside the leaves of a Spanish bayonet in the yard to expose a tiny green frog living within.

"This is a grand house. Do you remember it across from the light house? One that looked like a pretty good Utrillo, somewhere between that and Miro's Farm."

Ernest Hemingway to Waldo Peirce, Key West, 15 April 1932 (*SL* 358)

Notes

1. Small and large details concerning the house at 907 Whitehead Street and the life within were told to me by Patrick Hemingway.

2. The *Hemingway Review* editor Susan Beegel informed me of the Web site for the architecture as well as the name of the Key West librarian/historian Mr. Thomas L. Hambright, who provided information about the lighthouse keeper.

3. In 1997, following up on Pat's memory of the Johnson Wax ad with the photographers capturing shots of the interior of the house in the 1930s, I called the S. C. Johnson & Sons headquarters, still in Racine, Wisconsin, and spoke to Mr. James P. May, director of corporate public relations. He and his successor, Ms. Therese Van Ryne, plus Ms. Clara Norred were tremendously helpful in locating the one advertisement.

4. From the 1985 visit to the Key West conference, I remembered Scott Donaldson reading aloud the manuscript piece "A Key West Girl." Scott Donaldson very kindly shared his remembrance of where he had found the manuscript page at the Kennedy Library, and James Roth, curator of the Hemingway Collection, tracked it down.

Only in Key West

Hemingway's Fortunate Isle

LAWRENCE R. BROER

To be true to Ernest Hemingway's Key West experience, one has several obligations. The first is to discover as Hemingway did in that first week of April 1928 that the town he later dubbed the "St. Tropez of the Poor" was a great place to play (Hotchner 154). The second is more demanding. It requires comprehending the significance of Hemingway's literary achievement in the place where he can be understood best.

As evidence of that achievement, consider that in these crucial, transformative years of Hemingway's career, which he referred to as his "belle époque" (*SL* 443), he wrote all or parts of some of his most important works, including *A Farewell to Arms* (1929), *Death in the Afternoon* (1932), *Winner Take Nothing* (1933), *Green Hills of Africa* (1935), "The Short Happy Life of Francis Macomber" (1936), "The Snows of Kilimanjaro" (1936), *The Spanish Earth* (1937), *To Have and Have Not* (1937), *The Fifth Column* (1938), and the initial portion of *For Whom the Bell Tolls* (1940).

Several aspects of Hemingway's development stand out in these works—specifically, tremendous confidence in his talent, concern with literary theory, and self-conscious literary experimentation. Hemingway's artistic integrity, which demanded that he never repeat himself, led to new forms no one else had attempted before. He said about *Green Hills of Africa*, which he compared to landscape painting, that it contained not only the best writing he had ever done, but that "extra dimensional quality" that he was always working for (qtd. in Baker, *A Life Story* 275). He explained, "I am trying, always, to convey to the reader a full and complete feeling of the thing I am dealing with; to make the person reading feel it has happened to them" (*SL* 380). In *To Have and Have Not*, he said he had learned how to make a narrative move so that it seemed short when it was long. About the stories in *Winner Take Nothing*, Hemingway insisted that he was trying to make, before he was through, "a picture of the whole world—or as much of it as I have seen. Boiling it down always, rather than spreading it out thin" (*SL* 397). About the metaphysical dimensions in "Homage to Switzerland," he said he had invented a new form of story, "three stories in one. . . . Anybody will have been there when they read the Homage" (*SL* 367). He was similarly gratified by *Death in the Afternoon*, and by such stories as "The Sea Change," "After the Storm," and "The Snows of Kilimanjaro."

Such accomplishments make a revisionary case for arguing that Hemingway's Island in the Sun turned the years 1928–40 into one of, if not *the*, happiest and most creatively adventurous times of Hemingway's life. Admittedly, Michael Reynolds's description of Key West's boiling sun that first week, with Hemingway fresh from his Paris apprenticeship via the Havana ferry, seems less than idyllic:

> Each morning the sun came up like bullfire, turning the island on its spit. If he rose early enough to walk down Simonton to South Beach, he could squint at the red-orange cusp rising out of the dark ocean, and in the late afternoon from the La Concha Hotel, he and his wife could watch it settle down, inch by inch, and then quite suddenly disappear below the blue-black horizon. Between the sun's rise and fall, Key West warmed itself, the tropic humidity rising until sweat ran down the bridge of his nose as he hunched over the pages of his novel begun in Paris. In the eighties by day and seventies by night, the weather was mild by local standards, but to the couple fresh from Paris and without clothes for the climate, it was uncomfortably warm and humid. (*Homecoming* 168)

Such passages remind us just how remote Key West was. Except for the Havana ferry and the twice-daily trains, visitors had a tendency to stay simply because the city had no way to get them in or out in enough numbers to support a good-sized hot dog stand. Reynolds describes the island as a

11. Hemingway overlooking the then-dilapidated streets of Key West, shortly before a fishing excursion, late 1920s. Ernest Hemingway Collection/John F. Kennedy Presidential Library and Museum, Boston.

time zone unto itself, where the only real clock was the rise and fall of tides, made still more isolated by the disappearance in these hard Depression years of half the island's population (*Homecoming* 69). The town was nearly bankrupt. Rum-running was among the top cottage industries, and peeling paint was everywhere. As Hemingway wrote Maxwell Perkins: "There was a pencilled inscription derogatory to our fair city in the toilet at the station and somebody had written under it—'if you don't like this town get out and stay out.' Somebody else had written under that 'Everybody has'" (*SL* 277). While Key West, as old-time Conchs said, had never been "closer to the bone" (McLendon 115), Pauline remarked to her new friend Lorine Thompson that she had never seen Ernest so content.[1]

Pauline herself would have preferred the salons of Paris, worrying that Ernest would use the sleepy, laid-back village as his personal fishing dock, and signing her letters "from your old friend in the backwater" (L. Miller, *Letters* 86). Hemingway's enthusiasm for Key West spilled over in letters to all his friends; to Waldo Peirce he declared that, "By God that's a fine place" (*SL* 282). "Paris . . . was a fine place to be quite young in," he explained, "a necessary part of a man's education. . . . But me, I now love something else" (*BL* 158). Hemingway's idea of heaven had metamorphosed from a big bullring with "me holding two barrera seats" (*SL* 165) to the azure waters of the Gulf Stream, with Papa in the *Pilar* battling a giant billfish.

Among priorities Hemingway established in this period, foremost was "to know where I can find what I want," and what he wanted most Key West provided in awesome abundance: in Carlos Baker's view, "a total immersion in the sensuous experience of living" (*A Life Story* 261). Smelling of the Gulf Stream, it was in the air he breathed, it was in the town's delirium of vegetation, and it was in the street music of rich dialects—English, Cuban Spanish, and lilting Caribbean. Food being one of Hemingway's foremost pleasures, especially Cuban cuisine, it was in that first Key West dinner he may have had at Delmonicos on Duval Street for fifty cents: aroz con pollo, green turtle steak, fish a la minuta, and Spanish garbanzos (McLendon 40). The island's elemental rhythms facilitated everything he now loved to do: "Being on the sea; the work in catching a very big fish; fighting, fornication, the elation of drinking; a storm; and enjoyment of danger can all make you feel so good physically and give you such a physical enjoyment of life that you can be ashamed of being so happy when most people have no enjoyment" (*SL* 431). Boxing, perhaps Hemingway's favorite connection to the locals, was among the author's main Key West pleasures. He coached and refereed many matches on Thomas Street, at the property now occupied by the Blue Heaven restaurant, and sparred with local fighters at fifty cents a round (Burke 29).

Clearly Hemingway's greatest delight in these years was fishing the Gulf

Stream—the great blue river, as he called it—for marlin, which he called "monstering" (*SL* 282). This allowed him to exercise his intensely competitive nature in personal tests of strength, courage, and endurance, all essential components of his work, and it provided spectacular trophies. "Marlin are strange and wild things," he wrote in "On the Blue Water"

> of unbelievable speed and power and a beauty, in the water and leaping, that is indescribable. . . . There is always a thrill that needs no danger to make it real. It may be a marlin that will jump high and clear off to the right and then go off in a series of leaps. . . . Or it may be some fish that you will never see at all that will head straight out to the northwest like a submerged submarine and never show and at the end of five hours the angler has a straightened-hook. There is always a feeling of excitement when a fish takes hold when you are drifting deep. . . . In hunting you know what you are after and the top you can get is an elephant. But who can say what you will hook sometime when drifting in a hundred and fifty fathoms in the Gulf Stream? There are probably marlin and swordfish to which the fish we have seen caught are pygmies; and every time a fish takes the bait drifting you have a feeling perhaps you are hooked to one of these. (*BL* 240, 238–39) [2]

One of Hemingway's finest stories, "After the Storm," immortalizes a real-life adventure on the Gulf Stream told to Hemingway by Captain Bra Saunders, the sun-creased Conch who was Hemingway's close fishing buddy and the most respected of Key West's charter boat captains (*SL* 323). *The Old Man and the Sea* (1952) and *Islands in the Stream* (1970) attest that the sea and its spiritually regenerative qualities dominated Hemingway's literary imagination from 1928 until the last years of his life. Many critics contend that Hemingway's experience on the Gulf Stream resulted in a wiser, more integrated vision of men and nature. According to Susan F. Beegel, Hemingway saw the sea as a living being, the "Eternal Feminine" ("Santiago" 132–34). Certainly its beauty and power increased Hemingway's capacity for portraying elementary experience, those sensory-heightened moments he evokes so vividly.

There are other, deeper reasons why Hemingway was so happy living and working in Key West. The island harmonized tensions within his complex

12. Fishing the Gulf Stream provided Hemingway a physical outlet that balanced the intellectual demands of his art. Ernest Hemingway Collection/John F. Kennedy Presidential Library and Museum, Boston.

nature, allowing him to resolve (albeit tentatively) conflicting roles with which he struggled all his adult life: those of artist as husband and father, artist as friend, artist as public figure, and artist as man of action. As to the first of these, he wrote to Pauline's mother in 1936 that Key West was as close to living a regular normal life as he had known (*SL* 434–36). The house on Whitehead Street, an outright gift from Pauline's uncle Gus, along with the new Ford roadster, was his first permanent house in the United States, and became a wonderful place to work, even in hot weather.[3]

No matter where he might roam—Wyoming, Montana, Cuba, Africa, Spain—Key West was always a place that seemed to fix him up when

Hemingway came back, a place that seemed to release his creative energies. He told Waldo Peirce that away from Key West he felt as if "in a state of suspended something or other" (*SL* 283). In a typical instance he described returning from the boredom of Pauline's family home in Piggott to write three stories for *Scribner's Magazine*, "A Clean, Well-Lighted Place," "Homage to Switzerland," and "The Gambler, the Nun, and the Radio." Other places, like Billings, Montana, or Sheridan, Wyoming, were often good to him because they were like Key West (Baker, *A Life Story* 238). He wrote Janet Flanner: "We have a fine house here. . . . I could stay here damned near all the time and have a fine time watching the things grow and be happier than I understand" (*SL* 387).

Those "growing things" included not only a variety of animals and trees and the gin tree he wished he could plant, but also his sons, John ("Bumby"), Patrick, and Gregory. Though he scolded Peirce for being too bloody domestic for preferring parenting to fishing, and, worse, complained to Dos Passos that Peirce had exchanged *cojones* for nursing bottles (*SL* 445), Hemingway was not only a good provider but a close friend to the boys, seeing constantly to their welfare. "These kids are really good companions," he told Pauline's mother, "and are very funny, and I think . . . very smart" (*SL* 434). He later added: "You ought to see what a big boy Gregory is and I go to Church every Sunday and am a good father to my family or as good as I can be. I happen to be in a very tough business where there are no alibis" (*SL* 350).

Of course, the Key West years are the time in which the Papa of legend emerges, announcing himself now to friends and editors as "Poor ole Papa," "Papa is broke," "old Pappy fishing alone" (McLendon 61).[4] His patriarchal jurisdiction encompassed diverse groups whose differences represent contraries within Hemingway himself, those of the writer who needed the intellectual stimulation of fellow artists but who preferred the company of more simple men: fishermen, hunters, and outdoorsmen such as Bra Saunders, Charles Thompson, Joe "Josie" Russell, and Toby Bruce.[5] For Marjorie Kinnan Rawlings, this paradox was a key to Hemingway's character—some sort of "inner conflict between the sporting life and the literary life; between sporting people and the artist" (qtd. in Baker, *A Life Story* 288). She saw her own sporting friends as delightful companions, but as a literary person she was worlds away from them. In the relaxed atmosphere of Key West's bars and fishing holes, under his sometimes cheerful (sometimes not) tutelage, such distinctions for Hemingway dissolved into the compatible mass he dubbed "The Mob." He took pride that his nonliterary friends welcomed him as one of their own, relishing the fact that because of the scar on his forehead (left by a falling Paris skylight in March 1928) locals mistook him for a big northern bootlegger or dope peddler. Nobody, he bragged, believed he wrote books (SL 277).[6]

Many Key West locals played storied roles in Hemingway's fishing and literary life between 1928 and 1940: Bra Saunders's half brother, Burge, Hemingway's sometimes guide and navigator; Hamilton Adams, an apprentice writer who helped aboard the *Pilar*; charter-boat captain Jackie Key; Edward Adams, a local newspaperman; and J. B. Sullivan, a machinist. Sullivan, a former construction worker on the Key West extension of Henry Flagler's Florida East Coast Railway in 1906, said that Hemingway might have been a skid-row character except for his quick intelligence and warmth that showed itself at once among nonliterary people (Baker, *A Life Story* 192). It was typical of Hemingway's sympathy for common men and women that as the shades closed down on numerous literary friends and rivals at decade's end—notably, Sherwood Anderson, Virginia Woolf, Ford Madox Ford, Thomas Wolfe, and F. Scott Fitzgerald—he was more affected by the death of Josie Russell, who passed suddenly after an emergency operation in Havana in 1941.

If one were to single out those Key West natives to become Hemingway's most steady companions, they would be Charles Thompson, Josie Russell, Bra Saunders, and Toby Bruce. It was not uncommon to see these four together, yet each plays his distinctive part in Hemingway's Key West drama. Charles Thompson, whose family admittedly was not exactly indigent, owned a fish house, a cigar factory, a ship's chandlery, an icehouse, and a hardware store and tackle shop. Thompson's competitive nature and love of hunting and fishing equaled Hemingway's own. Baker cites a hunting trip to Cody, whose goal was to see who could bring down the biggest elk (*A Life Story* 208). A little older than Ernest, Charles had, by the time of their 1928 acquaintance, spent the majority of his twenty-nine years in Key West. Hemingway wrote Peirce that, "We are going to run Charles for president to end the depression on the platform of give every man enough rope to hang himself" (SL 358). Thompson joined Hemingway gladly on the African safari in the fall of 1933, whereas Archibald MacLeish and Mike Strater declined because neither relished the prospect of spending two months on safari with a friend so competitive that he would make a death-struggle contest of each day's hunting. Thompson was more than up to the challenge. He functioned for Hemingway as Ed Ricketts did for Steinbeck, as an alter ego, their adventures on the Gulf Stream the equivalent of those of Ricketts and Steinbeck on the Sea of Cortez.

Probably the most infamous of Hemingway's Key West gang was trusted friend and favorite drinking companion Joe "Josie" Russell, best known as the owner of the now-famous bar Sloppy Joe's.[7] It was Josie's boat—a fast, thirty-two-foot cabin cruiser, the *Anita*—as well as Josie's free-flowing booze and beloved bar that drew Hemingway inevitably to him. Hemingway's interest in Josie, whom he nicknamed "Joe Grunts," was both personal and literary. Hemingway said that on an extended trip aboard the *Anita* they had been rammed so often by aggressive swordfish that the boat was beginning to leak (Baker, *A Life Story* 243). This was also the boat in which Russell had made more than 150 rum-running trips from Cuba to the American mainland, inspiring the character of Harry Morgan in *To Have and Have Not* (Baker, *A Life Story* 239). Hemingway complained that Josie was the only one of his friends who seemed completely willing to go anywhere without his wife. "Of course," said Hemingway, "he has had his wife longer than any of my other friends, too." He added that Mrs. Jane Mason, about to join them fishing, "is almost as apt going places without her husband as Mr. Josie is without his wife. But then Mrs. Mason has also had her husband for a long time, too, although Mr. Josie I believe there is no doubt has had his much much oftener as well as longer than Mr. Mason" (*SL* 446). Thinking of Josie as the older brother he never had, Hemingway told Pauline after Russell died that he felt he "should have protected him better and truly" (*SL* 524).

Bra Saunders, too, must be numbered high among Hemingway's drinking and fishing companions. A white Bahamian from Green Turtle Key, he was an experienced Gulf Stream fisherman familiar with all the waters from Cuba to the Rebecca Shoals off the Tortugas. It was with Captain Bra that Hemingway landed his first sailfish, a feat that marked the onset of Hemingway's lifelong passion for big-game fishing, particularly billfish. In their first trip to the Dry Tortugas, Hemingway spent every spare minute pumping Bra for all sorts of fishing information, from catching to cooking (Lawrence 117). Facetiously or not, Hemingway suggested to Bra on a jaunt to the Bahamas that their trip be known as the "great Saunders Pidgen and Wild Og Scientific Expedition." If any of the men were mauled by a hippopotamus, they would be "martyrs to Science" (SL 323–24). On a trip in 1934, going out on the Pilar every day for a month, Hemingway invited Charles Cadwalader, the director of the Academy of Natural Science of Philadelphia, and Henry W. Fowler, his chief ichthyologist, to join him and study the habits of marlin and identify the different species. Fowler said that the knowledge that he gained was enough to permit him to revise marlin classification for the entire North Atlantic. It was the first of Hemingway's serious contributions to the scientific community and the International Game Fish Association (Lawrence 166).

It was with Toby Bruce, or "Tobes," originally from Piggott, that Hemingway had his most enduring Key West friendship. A mechanic, expert craftsman and more, "Tobes" was infinitely sympathetic and adaptable to Hemingway's needs throughout the Key West years and beyond. Handyman, secretary, nurse, chauffeur, banker, drinking and hunting companion, Bruce earned a reputation as the author's "fix-anything" man that belies his closeness to Hemingway. Despite Pauline's aloofness toward him, Bruce related to Hemingway as a protector both practically and emotionally. It was Toby who built the brick wall around the house on Whitehead Street to keep tourists out. And it was Toby who remained Hemingway's intimate through three marriages and who worked with Mary after his 1961 death, sorting out literary materials rescued from Sloppy Joe's. As if to protect his friend a final time, Toby is said to have remarked to Mary after the author's suicide that Papa was only "on a long trip" (McLendon 209).

Members of Papa's flock of artists included Mike Strater and Waldo Peirce, John Dos Passos and Archibald MacLeish and their wives Katy and Ada, and Gerald and Sara Murphy. Peirce was "a huge bearded man who reminded Dos [Passos] of Neptune on a baroque Roman fountain" (Baker, A Life Story 193). Mike Strater, president of the Marine Tuna Club, and an avid fisherman and good mechanic and sailor, was known simply as "The President." "The Mob" also occasionally included family members, sister Carol and brother Leicester, and old boyhood friend Bill Smith (L. Miller, Letters 220).

Papa summoned the literati to Key West, including an exuberant Maxwell Perkins, and gathered them aboard the *Pilar* as often as possible for extended fishing trips to the Marquesas, the Tortugas, Bimini, and Cuba. Nothing better explains Hemingway's love of Key West than the Marquesas and the Dry Tortugas, his favorite fishing spots. The Marquesas are a necklace of keys consisting of one large island and five small ones. Thirty miles beyond the Marquesas are the Dry Tortugas, another cluster of small islands. Maxwell Perkins came to regard fishing these Key West waters as an annual institution, describing his times there as the best he had ever had in his life. James McLendon notes that Hemingway's friendship with Charles Thompson never ended with a quarrel, whereas we know certain of his artist friends were not so lucky (27). Most notable of these quarrels was that which broke out with Archibald MacLeish after an abortive trip to the Tortugas. Hemingway wrote Peirce that MacLeish had become righteous, fussy, and a bloody bore. MacLeish countered that Hemingway was fed up with the world and "I was fed up with him. We never could have gone on as close friends" (*SL* 406). While the literati accused Hemingway of he-mannish posturing and petulant jibes at fellow writers, the prevailing feeling among fishing pals and cronies alike was that Hemingway was a man who enhanced life for his friends. Things became more enjoyable when done with him or looked at through his eyes.

Perhaps the most critical balancing act Hemingway achieved on his island paradise was that of the artist and the man of action, a conflict Rawlings had worried would ruin him had he less love and discipline. What fostered Hemingway's relationship with Charles Thompson was that the responsibility of running a store meant Thompson could fish only in the late afternoons, and this worked perfectly with Hemingway's schedule of work and play. Proceeding on the manuscript of *A Farewell to Arms* in the spring mornings of 1928, Hemingway would later join Thompson in his eighteen-foot motorboat to fish the local waters. Hemingway wrote to Perkins what becomes a major refrain in the decade to follow: that because of this salubrious schedule of writing and fishing he never felt better or more confident that he is writing as well as anyone and will only get better: "I would like to stay right here until it [*Arms*] is done as I have been going well here and it is such a fine healthy life and the fishing keeps my head from worrying in the afternoons when I don't work" (*SL* 277). Ten years later the Key West magic persisted. Beginning work on *For Whom the Bell Tolls*, he wrote Perkins, "[I] am down to 198 pounds . . . working the way I do now I feel as happy and as good as when I was going good on *A Farewell to Arms*" (*SL* 482–83).

Examples of fishing and writing as intertwined and mutually fortifying experiences abound. Hemingway told Ivan Kashkeen that "writing isn't silly and neither is the Gulf Stream . . . going to fish tomorrow and write the next day" (*SL* 432). Complaining that he had lost a 700- and a 1,000-pound marlin, he said, "Well, what the hell I really have another trade beside marlin fishing and am very anxious to get back to work at it" (*SL* 448). And elsewhere: "Been working like a horse and the day finished out in the aft at 3pm with Patrick and caught two big sailfish" (*SL* 444). Hemingway's exuberance about progress on *To Have and Have Not* paralleled that of recent fishing triumphs. Excited about the 514- and 610-pound tunas he had caught, he informed Perkins that he was ready to give the New York critics both barrels in the spring and fall (*SL* 448).

The force most likely to strain Hemingway's deliberate balance of work and play was the acquisition of the *Pilar* in May 1934. The *Pilar*'s long-range capabilities increased Hemingway's desire to seek out more distant fishing areas. His exhilaration took him away for weeks or even months at a time, leaving any land-spawned annoyances or interruptions behind (Lawrence 131). Hemingway explained that "[g]oing out and driving myself in the boat for a while in any kind of weather am o.k. now" (*SL* 436). Pauline wrote Sara Murphy that "Mr. H is like a wild thing with his boat. I see him at ten minute intervals hours apart and from notes on doors saying why he can't get home until 3 instead of 12:30" (L. Miller, *Letters* 85–86). Yet despite such distractions, Hemingway's commitment to his art remained steady. Lawrence reminds us that while Hemingway went out on the *Pilar* every day for a month, he worked continuously on *Green Hills of Africa* (166). Hemingway answered Rawlings that his twin trades, as he called them, writing or the pursuit of a giant marlin, were not in conflict, but mutually fortifying. He received as much pleasure from one as the other. There was no reward like writing well, but fishing made him absolutely animally happy and kept him from going crazy when his soul-searing, indoor trade became difficult or impossible to do (*SL* 449–50).

For the man Hadley had described as having so many sides to him one could hardly make a sketch of him in a geometry book, the natural beauty of Key West's sun and sea was the sovereign remedy. "No doctor's prescription," Dos Passos said, "was ever pleasanter to take" (qtd. in G. Murphy 86). Maxwell Perkins had admonished Hemingway, "For God's sake don't get to be too much of a naturalist or you won't have time to write" (qtd. in Reynolds, *The 1930s*). But for those who feel that if Hemingway had played less in these halcyon years, he might have written more or better, one could respond, "or maybe not at all," certainly not with the celebratory joy at the heart of his life and work. If there is an essence of Ernest Hemingway that explains the man happily at work in the house on Whitehead Street and the man at play in the photos at Sloppy Joe's, Tennessee Williams—that other famous Key West scion—captures it perfectly in his final tribute to Hemingway:

> Hemingway never retired from his life into his workshop. He knew that an artist's work, the heart of it, is finally himself and his life, and he accomplished as few artists that have lived in our time, or any, the almost impossibly difficult achievement of becoming, as a man, in the sight of the world and time he lived in, the embodiment of what his work meant, on its highest and most honest level, and it would seem that he continued this achievement until his moment of death, which he would undoubtedly call his "moment of truth," in all truth. (6)

Hemingway's halcyon island life ended gradually rather than precipitously. The great hurricane of 1935 played its part. The destruction of the Florida East Coast Railway and creation of the new Overseas Highway marked the end of the isolation he cherished: "The road brings in every son of a bitch I ever knew or who ever read a line I wrote" (*SL* 484). The appearance of a beautiful blonde in a black dress at Sloppy Joe's in December 1936 was a second coup de grâce to Hemingway's tranquil island life (Lawrence 139). His first meeting with Martha Gellhorn began a liaison that sent the author's domestic life into a tailspin from which it never recovered. Yet, as Baker says, Hemingway's Key West legacy had been solidly established—twelve years during which he had produced seven books, acquired the *Pilar* and the house on Whitehead Street, and enjoyed an African safari, frequent visits to Europe, many sporting vacations in Montana and Wyoming, and the freedom to spend two years in warring Spain (*A Life Story* 345). By 1940, he had completed numerous essays and short stories on his Spanish Civil War experience and was 100,000 words into his new novel, *For Whom the Bell Tolls*. In Cuba, he would continue both fishing the blue waters of the Gulf Stream that he loved and the fruitful balance of work and play established during the Key West years.[8]

Notes

1. Pauline immediately took to Lorine, a graduate of Agnes Scott College and the head of the Social Science Department at Key West High School. They formed a friendship as close as the one their husbands were forming. They would later go into business together, operating a drapery and upholstery store on Caroline Street (McLendon 14).

2. It should be noted that through improved technique and publicity, Hemingway helped turn a curious pastime into a competitive sport. His letters abound with exuberant reports of billfish caught, as in his letter to Perkins in 1936: "We hooked and landed another triple header on sailfish—caught 7 in 4 days" (*SL* 438). His frequent fishing expeditions became standard topics at local bars and in international news. But marlin fishing became the sport most closely associated with Hemingway's name, the fish that offered him a variety of challenges and aroused his fierce competitive spirit.

3. Hemingway frequently comments that because of cooling breezes it was never too hot in Key West (Reynolds, *Homecoming* 36). The Hemingways actually stayed in several residences before moving to the house on Whitehead Street: first, a home at 1100 South Street, where the author finished *A Farewell to Arms*; next, a larger house on Pearl Street; then, a third house on the corner of Whitehead and United streets.

4. Although the "Papa" legend begins in the Paris years while Hemingway was still in his twenties, it was nurtured into full bloom in Key West. It probably first appeared in a letter to Charles Thompson after Hemingway's 1930 car wreck in Montana in which he broke his right arm. He signed his letter with his left hand, "Poor old Papa." Key West old-timers said that the sobriquet came into common usage after the author, still under forty, returned from the Spanish Civil War in 1937, no doubt with his encouragement.

5. This list should include Carlos Gutiérrez and Gregorio Fuentes, both of whom played enormously important roles in Hemingway's fishing and literary life. From Gutiérrez, sea guide and fishing advisor, Hemingway learned about the bonanza of huge marlin to be had out of Havana's harbor (Lawrence 162). Hemingway told Perkins in 1939 that to prepare to write "about the old commercial fisherman who fought the swordfish alone in his skiff for 4 days and four nights"—i.e., *The Old Man and the Sea*—he was taking Carlos out in his skiff so as to "get it all right" (*SL* 479). Both Carlos and Gregorio took turns as first mate of the *Pilar*. Gregorio Fuentes, the lean and laconic Canary Islander, had followed the sea since boyhood, accompanying Hemingway on his second trip to the Tortugas. In the Finca years, as mate and cook aboard the *Pilar*, Gregorio became an extended member of the Hemingway family. It was Gregorio who first told Hemingway the story of the old fisherman and the giant marlin in 1935.

6. Hemingway quipped: "They haven't even heard of Scott. Several of the boys I know

have just been moved by first reading of Kipling. A man introducing Robert Service's work would earn money if there was any money to earn—but there isn't" (*SL* 277).

7. Sloppy Joe's was a small bar at the foot of Duval Street when Hemingway first patronized it in 1928. Shortly after Prohibition ended, it was moved to 428 Greene Street. Then, in 1937, it moved to its present location on Duval Street (Lawrence 112). Even though Hemingway frequented all the Sloppy Joe's locations over the years, it is the present one with which he is most closely associated.

8. In a sense, Hemingway's Key West literary legacy continues long after Hemingway left for Cuba. Stuart McIver, to whom I am indebted for my title, "Only in Key West," reminds us that while Hemingway remains Key West's "Patron Saint," the fabled island continued to pull novelists, playwrights, poets, biographers, historians, editors, and publishers into Hemingway's magnetic field. The list of major American writers to thrive in Key West, including eight Pulitzer Prize winners, reads like a "Who's Who" of major American writers—to name only a few, Truman Capote, Hunter Thompson, Tom McGuane, and Jim Harrison. Still, as McIver says: "It was Hemingway's town when he lived there. It's still his town" (*Hemingway's Key West* 85).

The End of Some Things

Hemingway's Decade of Loss

GAIL D. SINCLAIR

Ernest Hemingway achieved a level of fame of which few literary men can boast. While he garnered initial critical distinction with *In Our Time* (1925) and *The Sun Also Rises* (1926)—works that helped define the modernist movement—his popular renown was largely a product of his Key West years. As Michael Reynolds notes, 1928–40 was the period in which the author became more important to his audience than his oeuvre: "Where once his fiction drew attention to his active life, now that life drew attention to his writing" (*The 1930s* 171). That attention was hardly accidental: whether or not he could admit it, Hemingway cultivated his reputation as a celebrity whose life was worthy of envy and adoration. As James McLendon argues, "When Hemingway arrived in Key West in 1928, a slightly-published twenty-eight-year-old author, he came searching for his myth, if not consciously then subconsciously." He grounded that myth, furthermore, in "machismo"—a quality that was abundant in the gritty streets of Key West and a quality that, to Hemingway's detriment, has been inextricably attached to his name ever since.

At the heart of Hemingway's self-consciously crafted macho persona is a pugnacious confidence and seemingly testosterone-driven combativeness that often erupts when challenged. Thus, the 1930s are marked by famous public feuds with a host of literary notables, from Gertrude Stein to Max Eastman and many lesser names. However much the media delighted in

13. Despite the balmy domesticity of Key West, Hemingway's marriage to Pauline
Pfeiffer—his second—would end much as his first to Hadley Richardson had
a decade earlier: in adultery. Ernest Hemingway Collection/John F. Kennedy
Presidential Library and Museum, Boston.

reporting these fracases, Hemingway's surliness exacted a personal cost as
he began to demand ever-increasing and unconditional loyalty from family
and friends as if to shield himself from outside criticism. Unable to tolerate
any dissent on the home front, Papa began a pattern of breaking off relationships with members of his inner circle that left him emotionally alienated and unable to connect without resorting to poses that struck those
around him as belligerent and one-dimensional.

Studying this pattern is crucial to recognizing why the Key West years were a decade of unrest for Hemingway—something critics have not always appreciated. McLendon labels this time "the best ten years of his life" (181), even while recording the personal fallings-away that came with ever-increasing rapidity as the 1930s progressed. In the preceding essay, Lawrence Broer argues that the decade was "one of, if not *the*, happiest and most creatively adventurous times of Hemingway's life," a happiness that accounts for the literary experimentation and theorizing that characterize his years on "the fortunate isle." From one standpoint, these assessments are certainly true. And yet we cannot ignore the growing sense of a man at war on many fronts.

The first important losses in Hemingway's personal life occurred prior to his taking up residence in Key West, but they set the stage for others that followed. His 1927 divorce from Hadley Richardson—forced by his affair with Pauline Pfeiffer—and the resulting feelings of guilt and personal failure clouded the beginning of Hemingway's new stage. Then, on 6 December 1928, his father, Dr. Clarence Hemingway, committed suicide. Hemingway's ambivalence toward his parents had surfaced in his early fiction, especially in such Nick Adams stories as "The Doctor and the Doctor's Wife" (1924) and "Now I Lay Me" (1927), and the suicide only strengthened the son's psychological conflict. In letters immediately following his father's death, Hemingway's tone seems matter-of-fact, although one can sense the deep emotions held in check. He writes to F. Scott Fitzgerald: "My Father shot himself as I suppose you may have read in the papers. Will send you the $100 as soon as I reach Key West. . . . I was fond as hell of my father and feel too punk—also sick etc.—to write a letter but wanted to thank you" (*SL* 291).[1] With Maxwell Perkins he is a bit less terse:

> Hope to be back at Key West Tuesday morning and at work on the book again. My Father shot himself—Don't know whether it was in the N.Y. papers. I didn't see any of the papers. I was very fond of him and feel like hell about it. Got to Oak Park in plenty of time to handle things—Funeral was Sat. aft. Have everything fixed up except they will have damned little money—went over all that too. Realize of course that thing for me to do is not worry but get to work—finish my book properly so I can help them out with the proceeds. What makes me feel the worst is my father is the one I cared about. (*SL* 291)

14. Ernest and Pauline with Hemingway's parents, Clarence and Grace, during the latter's surprise visit to Key West in 1928. In December of that year, Clarence would commit suicide. Ernest Hemingway Collection/John F. Kennedy Presidential Library and Museum, Boston.

Two months later, in February 1929, Hemingway wrote to John Dos Passos projecting a façade of having put the suicide behind him. He confides: "My old man shot himself but it was no help financially—on the contrary! . . . Come on down kid [to Key West]" (*SL* 295). By September, he was joking about his father's death: "Old Hem ruined by his father shooting himself—Keep guns away from Katherine's [Katy Smith Dos Passos] old man—" (*SL* 304).

In the wake of his father's death, Hemingway assumed the position of guardian for his extended family, which included not only his mother but also his youngest sister, Carol (born 1911), and brother Leicester (born 1915). As with later relational roles, Hemingway's need to call the shots did not set particularly well with those whom he expected to obey his directives. Consequently, in the early Key West years, family frictions caused another important loss: an irrevocable break between Ernest and his sister Carol, twelve years his junior. Despite the difference in their ages, Ernest and Carol had always been close—protective older brother and worshipful younger sister. Besides providing financial support, Ernest encouraged

Carol's visits during breaks from Rollins College, located several hours north of Key West in Winter Park, Florida, where she was a student. But in 1933, Carol married her college sweetheart, John "Jack" Gardner, against her brother's objections. In a 24 January 1933 letter to a friend, Carol wrote that Hemingway would be "madder than any irate father," and that she would incur his "everlasting wrath" (letter). She was right. Hemingway never spoke to her again.

Biographers also like to cite Hemingway's equally difficult relationship with his mother, Grace Hall Hemingway. Beginning around 1916 and throughout the 1920s, childhood resentments sometimes gave way to open hostility. Grace's famous "bankruptcy" letter after her son's return from the war (Reynolds, *Young Hemingway* 136–38), as well as her open disapproval of *In Our Time* and *The Sun Also Rises* (Reynolds, *Paris Years* 198–99; *Homecoming* 92), clearly did not sit easily with Hemingway. After Dr. Hemingway's death, Grace and Ernest kept the reciprocal disapproval generally in check, although it lingered beneath the surface and occasionally erupted. Some of what has been assigned to Grace as malicious treatment seems unfounded. Sending Dr. Hemingway's suicide weapon to Ernest, for instance, was done at his request and was not an overtly malicious act. The accompanying chocolate cake, one of her paintings, and a gift for Bumby were an odd accompaniment to the gun, to be sure, but the package contents did not signal traceable ill intent. Perhaps because she was dependent upon her son's financial largesse, Grace seems to have been careful not to incur his anger, thanking him on many occasions for his generosity. In return, Ernest usually kept his responses cordial. He also could be kind, assuring Grace: "Never worry because I will always fix things up—can always borrow money if I haven't it—So don't ever worry" (*SL* 295). A postscript to this letter, while further striving to diminish her concerns, also interjects caution: "You have been *fine* about everything. Remember not to worry and not to hold things back from me but don't bother me with general run of stuff—The more I'm let alone and not worried the better I can function" (*SL* 296).

Mrs. Hemingway visited Ernest just twice during the Key West years, once in February 1931 and not again until February 1939, when she saw her seven-year-old grandson Gregory for the first time. Grace stayed at the Casa Marina Hotel, nearly a mile away, rather than with the family. For whatever

15. Hemingway's sons in the mid-1930s (*left to right*):
Patrick (b. 1928), John (b. 1923), and Gregory (b. 1931).

reasons real or perceived, Hemingway's public and private condemnation of his mother seemed to heighten through the 1930s. Two years before Grace's death in 1951, he would confide to Charles Scribner: "I hate her guts and she hates mine. She forced my father to suicide. . . . I will not see her and she knows that she can never come here" (*SL* 670). He did not attend her funeral, although, as he had been doing with her living expenses, he paid for it.

Hemingway's patriarchal sphere broadened in the Key West years as he began developing and corresponding with a far-ranging surrogate family. There, too, he assumed the fatherly voice that would deepen to a sometimes ridiculous level in the coming years. Writing to Archibald MacLeish, he usually signed himself "Pappy" or "Papa," the trademark moniker his young son, Bumby, first used in the 1920s. To Maxwell Perkins, he wrote that Thornton Wilder was "a nice boy [aged thirty-one]" (*SL* 278). F. Scott Fitzgerald, Henry "Mike" Strater, and others similar in age and often slightly older than Hemingway also found themselves called "kid" in letters where "old Hem" provided worldly opinions about writing, marriage, parenting, sports, travel, and a plethora of topics about which he had strong convictions.

Hemingway seems to have taken special interest in offering literary counsel to Fitzgerald in these years, even though Fitzgerald was nearly three years older, had achieved success earlier, and had been responsible for bringing the younger author to Charles Scribner's Sons in 1925. Hemingway's tongue-in-cheek tone signals recognition that his advice is a bit pompous, as when he cajoles, "You're not burned out and you know plenty to use—if you think your [*sic*] running out of dope, count on old Hem—I'll tell you all I know—whom slept with who and whom before or after whom was married—Anything you need to know—" (*SL* 306).

Following the 1931 death of Fitzgerald's father, Hemingway wrote in a tone more didactic than sympathetic: "I'm sorry you had a trip to U.S. on such sad business. Hope to read your acct. of it between board covers rather than in Post. Remember us writers have only one father and one mother to die. But don't poop away such fine material" (*SL* 340). Hemingway's advice only becomes harsher as the decade progresses and Fitzgerald sinks into greater need for emotional and professional support.

Hemingway's own need for approval also grew throughout the decade. If the critical response was mixed, his negative reactions to it became highly predictable and ever more pronounced. Already naturally defensive, Hemingway grew increasingly antagonistic as the accolades declined and the barbed assaults increased. Neither the general public nor the critics were as satisfied as he was with his literary progression, and that friction took its toll. Hemingway began using the pen almost as much for retort against detractors as for creative output. His combative spirit was increasingly manifested in fistfights, verbal confrontations, severed relationships, and defensive prose as Hemingway alienated family members, close friends, literary mentors, peers, and critical detractors alike.

Hemingway sprinkled criticism of his peers, like that of his family, widely and with seeming reckless abandon. In the late 1920s he had turned against mentors like Gertrude Stein and Sherwood Anderson. He now would continue to cast off additional literary cohorts one after another. And these rejections were not subtle. In a remarkable failure to acknowledge his own modus operandi for dealing with discarded friends, Hemingway wrote to Arnold Gingrich, editor of *Esquire,* in the fall of 1934: "It goes against my digestion to take shots at anyone who's ever been a friend no matter how lousey [*sic*] they get to be finally. Besides, I've got the gun and it's loaded and I know where the vital spots are and friendship aside there's a certain damned fine feeling of superiority in knowing you can finish anybody off whenever you want to and still not doing it" (*SL* 411).[2] Unfortunately, for a growing number of one-time friends, his self-proclaimed restraint becomes less and less enforced as the man and the myth become more entwined.

The biographer Kenneth Lynn has commented that by 1932, with the publication of *Death in the Afternoon,* Hemingway had become "an overbearing know-it-all" whose work now "testifie[d] to the invasion of Hemingway's serious writing by his myth" (396). Katy Smith, who had known Hemingway since childhood and had married his friend John Dos Passos, bears out Lynn's assessment of the writer's growing self-importance. During a 1934 visit to Havana, she wrote Sara and Gerald Murphy that their mutual friend was not "irascible and truculent" as she had believed him to be before, but "had a tendency to be an Oracle I thought and needs some best pal and severe critic to tear off those long white whiskers which he is wearing" (L. Miller, *Letters* 100). Hemingway's charm, which had held them all in its spell during the Riviera years of the mid-1920s, was being supplanted by an off-putting bravado increasingly wearing on his companions' patience.

Hemingway's tolerance was thinning as well. In 1934, he confided to painter and regular guest Waldo Peirce that Archibald MacLeish, a poet and friend who had been so often and so cheerfully invited to Key West in the early years, had gotten, "Righteous, fussy, and a bloody bore. . . . I shouldn't write this. So forget it. But he kept asking for it and asking for it. I only like the people I like. Not the bastards that like me." Baker footnotes this letter with MacLeish's statement about Hemingway: "He was fed up with the world and I was fed up with him. . . . It was my fault as much as his. But . . . it was inevitable: we never could have gone on as close friends" (*SL*

406). Although the relationship continued in the form of friendly letters through the mid-1930s, as the Key West decade and its frustrations wore on, tensions mounted. Michael Reynolds reports: "Hemingway's behavior with old friends was erratic, combative, sometimes intolerable. Before he returned to the Spanish War in mid-August [1937], his relationship with Archie MacLeish was once again strained, this time over the production of the Joris film" *The Spanish Earth*, for which Ernest was to write the narration (*The 1930s* 273).

Hemingway's involvement in the Spanish conflict seems to have been an important catalyst for several other shifts along his personal fault line. Reynolds reports that the close friendship with John Dos Passos was "ruined beyond repair" in this period (*The 1930s* 273). Of most significance was the execution of Dos Passos's friend and literary translator, José Robles, accused by Communists of being a spy and fascist sympathizer—charges that proved patently false. Hemingway chose to break the news to Dos Passos at a public luncheon where, in the words of Lynn, "[Hemingway] let Dos Passos know by the manner in which he spoke that in his politically sophisticated judgment Robles had got what he deserved" (448–49). Not surprisingly, "Dos Passos for his part was deeply offended by the callous way in which Hemingway had given him the bad news and by his condescending treatment of him as though he were a shrinking violet and a simpleton" (449). By March 1938, Hemingway sealed the split with a venomous letter whose apologetic opening lines—"I'm sorry I sent you that cable from the boat. It seemed funny when I sent it. Afterwards it seemed only snotty" (*SL* 463)—quickly shifted to accusations and ended with unforgivable insult. He writes:

So long, Dos. Hope you're always happy. . . . Always happy with the good old friends. Got them that will knife you in the back for a dime. . . . Honest Jack Passos'll knife you three times in the back for fifteen cents and sing Giovanezza free. Thanks pal. Gee that feel's good. Any more old friends? Take him away, Doc he's all cut. (*SL* 464)[3]

Hemingway's impatience with Fitzgerald, one of his oldest literary friends, also grew as Scott often unwisely exposed weaknesses to the younger but increasingly more successful writer. Whenever this happened, or conversely when Fitzgerald was critical of Hemingway's work, merciless attacks almost inevitably followed. After what Ernest considered Fitzgerald's negative response to *Green Hills of Africa*, Hemingway rejoined in two ostensibly friendly letters written only five days apart. In the first, dated 16 December 1935 from Key West, he sarcastically writes: "Was delighted from the letter to see you don't know any more about when a book is a good book or what makes a book bad than ever. That means, anyhow, that you're not haveing [*sic*] any sudden flashes of insight or intelligence that would mean The End" (*SL* 424). In the second letter, written on 21 December—five years to the day from when Fitzgerald would drop dead of a heart attack—Hemingway lands a much more vicious blow, inviting a melancholic Fitzgerald to Key West where he will help him end it all if Scott wishes. He chides:

> I'll write you a fine obituary that Malcolm Cowley will cut the best part out of for the new republic and we can take your liver out and give it to the Princeton Museum, your heart to the Plaza Hotel, one lung to Max Perkins and the other to George Horace Lorimer. If we can still find your balls I will take them via the Ile de France to Paris and down to Antibes and have them cast into the sea off Eden Roc and we will get MacLeish to write a Mystic Poem to be read at that Catholic School (Newman?) you went to. (*SL* 428)

Not satisfied to leave it there, Hemingway encloses his own poem graced with mocking lines like "Fling flang them flung his own his two finally his one . . . no ripple make as sinking sanking sonking sunk." He signs off: "So long Scott—Let me hear from you. Merry Christmas! Pauline sends her love. Yours always affectionately, Ernest" (*SL* 429). From a man so keenly focused on the precise use of words, Hemingway astounds with his willingness to disregard the wounding power of this dramatic prose.

That Hemingway's friends suffered barbed insults is undeniable. That his wives paid a high price for loving him was inescapable. Hadley had already done so. Pauline, a participant in that marriage's demise, would later recognize the signs of her own dissolving union, although, like Hadley, she could not keep the danger at bay.[4] Lynn reports that "Nineteen thirty-two, the year of *Death in the Afternoon*, also marked the beginning of the end of Hemingway's second marriage" (403). The year before, Pauline had been pregnant for a second time, which was not something she wanted, and the child was not destined to be the daughter Ernest hoped she would deliver. (Gregory, Hemingway's third son and their second, was born in 1931.) On board the *Ile de France* for their return from Europe, the Hemingways met the gregarious young Jane Mason and her husband, Grant, head of Pan American Airways's Cuban operations. An instant friendship began, and the two couples enjoyed many social outings over the next two years, especially after Hemingway acquired the *Pilar* in 1934. Jane was a well-known blonde beauty who would have made any wife nervous about her husband's fidelity. No account can say with certainty that an actual affair ensued, though Hemingway later bragged it had, but Havana's famous Floridita bar boasted many evenings graced by an increasingly famous writer and his beautiful drinking companion.

Kenneth Lynn has labeled Jane Mason a manic-depressive and believes that Hemingway "conceivably" found in the socialite "his very own Zelda, except that he proposed to make her well by giving her lessons in marlin fishing and by telling her over and over that she wasn't crazy" (404). It seems unlikely Hemingway sought a woman with psychiatric issues, having made clear his belief that Fitzgerald's wife was a hindrance to her husband's literary career. Bernice Kert more aptly speculates that Jane's instability had the opposite effect: "Ernest resisted falling in love with women who had emotional problems. He liked to describe his various wives as 'happy, healthy, hard as a rock'" (250). What is generally agreed is that Hemingway wrote "A Way You'll Never Be" to cheer up "a hell of a nice girl going crazy from day to day" (Baker, *A Life Story* 228).[5]

The events that pushed Jane Mason over the brink and sealed the end of any long-term relationship began on 27 May 1933, when she was involved in a car accident while driving Hemingway's two oldest sons, Bumby and Patrick, back to her Cuban home, Las Jaimanitas. Her Packard was forced off the road and rolled over a number of times before landing upside-down at the bottom of a ravine. No one was seriously injured, but Jane was clearly traumatized and a few days later fell—or jumped, according to literary legend—from her home's second-story balcony, breaking her back. Her husband, who had dealt with previous suicide attempts, sent his wife with strict supervision to New York, where she remained hospitalized for many months and in a body cast for the next year. Hemingway would again spend time with Mason during her recuperation in the summer months of

16a-b. Although it is unclear whether their relationship was sexual, Jane Mason pursued Hemingway with an ardency that would inspire a vicious portrait of her as the adulteress "have" Helène Bradley in *To Have and Have Not. Left*: Mason with Carlos Gutiérrez on the *Anita*, 1933. *Right*: Aboard the *Pilar*, mid-1930s. Ernest Hemingway Collection/John F. Kennedy Presidential Library and Museum, Boston.

1934, although her back brace probably prohibited any physical relationship. Additionally, they were most often accompanied by others on the *Pilar* as Ernest enjoyed fishing off the Cuban shore and working on the manuscript that became *Green Hills of Africa*.

Ultimately, Jane Mason was not a threat to Pauline. Yet the relationship prefigures more serious events to unfold as the decade and the Hemingway marriage wore on. The African safari beginning in December 1933 had temporarily buffered the second Mrs. Hemingway from other women interfering in her marriage as she and Ernest set off for several months of travel. Hemingway wrote of these adventures in *Green Hills of Africa*, labeling his wife P.O.M. (Poor Old Mama). While the nickname has an affectionate ring, it does not possess the intimacy of "Pilar," his secret name for Pauline during their 1926 affair, nor does it suggest passionate engagement. Pauline's own account of the African adventure "hints rather than dwells on her changing moods" and seems all too keenly aware that one marital threat safely avoided did not ensure immunity from another, possibly fatal attack (Kert 255).

Martha Gellhorn arrived in Key West on a post-holiday trip not long after Christmas 1936. Wearing an eye-catching black dress, the attractive young blonde, along with her mother and brother, decided to stop at Sloppy Joe's for a drink. As was often his custom, Hemingway occupied a space at the bar. Although Gellhorn later remembered him as "a large dirty man in untidy somewhat soiled white shorts and shirt" (qtd. in Moorehead 101), she was obviously intrigued by the famous writer. Martha was herself a published author whose first novel, *What Mad Pursuit* (1934), borrowed Hemingway's phrase "nothing ever happens to the brave" as its epigraph. In September, just before meeting Hemingway, she had published a collection of short stories under the title *The Troubles I've Seen*. The critic Lewis Gannett likened her prose style to Hemingway's: "Her writing burns. . . . Hemingway does not write more authentic American speech. Nor can Ernest Hemingway teach Martha Gellhorn anything about economy of language" (qtd. in Kert 289).[6] Such praise, we might anticipate, initially led to an attraction but no doubt also fueled intense competition later in the relationship. The battles between Martha and Ernest were for the future, however, and the fight at hand was the losing one in which Pauline was unwittingly about to engage.

Martha Gellhorn's attraction to Hemingway at first seemed worship from afar, calling him a "glorious idol." From Ernest's point of view, a potential new conquest had walked into his watering hole, and the pursuit was on. She was astute enough to recognize his interest, perhaps not very thinly veiled, and stayed in Key West after her mother and brother left. Hemingway did not hide from Pauline Gellhorn's extended presence, as noted by Martha's post-visit thank-you letter remarking, "[I]t was good of you not minding my becoming a fixture, like a kudu head, in your home"

(Gellhorn, *Selected Letters* 47). "For five years Ernest's extramarital energy had been absorbed in Jane Mason," Kert writes, "but Jane was married and Martha was not. Jane's friendship with Pauline, according to her own recollections, inhibited her intimacy with Ernest. Martha was a stranger to the scene" (291). She quickly moved to a position of familiarity with Hemingway's urging and her own complicity.

Hemingway kept his family at bay in the spring of 1937, refusing Pauline's wish to accompany him to Spain. He wrote to her family explaining his dictum: "I would sort of worry about her and I have to work fairly hard and wouldn't let her go into Spain in any event." Correspondence from Martha revealed perhaps the more pertinent reason for his desire to go without his wife. A 15 February 1937 letter from St. Louis reached Ernest just before his departure: "This is very private. We are conspirators . . . and I have personally already gotten myself a beard and a pair of dark glasses." She closes with "write if you can. Please don't disappear. Are we or are we not members of the same union? Hemingstein, I am very very fond of you. Marty" (qtd. in Kert 294). From Pauline, he receives a terse, "Would love to be with you instead of being here with nobody and the sea. . . . So goodbye big-shot-in-the-pants, good luck and why not start keeping me informed?" (qtd. in Lynn 468). Needless to say, Hemingway did not honor her request, at least not in respect to his maneuvers toward the woman eventually to become Pauline's replacement.

As planned, Hemingway and Gellhorn met in Madrid during late March 1937. While the exact nature of his relations with Jane Mason at Cuba's Hotel Floridita are uncertain, his tryst with Martha at Spain's Hotel Florida would soon become obvious. Baker reports that she arrived in the besieged city after much difficulty via a complicated and circuitous route. Not many days after Gellhorn's arrival, the hotel was bombed, forcing occupants out of their rooms and into the hallways. When Ernest and Martha emerged from his room, their affair became common knowledge.

Back in Key West, however, Pauline was still in the dark, or at least pretended not to know. She had safely weathered Jane Mason and hoped to ride out this new storm in similar fashion. But evidence of her husband's infidelity piled up over the next two years. Under the pretext of promoting Joris Iven's war documentary *The Spanish Earth*, Ernest and Martha met at the Second American Writers' Congress in New York in June 1937 and again at the Roosevelt White House on July 8. They traveled together in Spain during the autumn and through Christmas Day of 1937, a trip that ended with Pauline's meeting Ernest in Paris on 28 December, accusing him of infidelity, and threatening a Jane Mason–inspired jump from the balcony. In the spring of 1938, Ernest and Martha made a third trip to Spain, with brief meetings in Paris both before and afterward. As evidence mounted, Pauline's growing desperation worked against her, and the marriage unraveled over the remaining months of 1938. On 15 February 1939, Hemingway moved from Key West to Cuba, and by May he was living there with Martha in a rented home outside Havana, the Finca Vigía, that they would later purchase.

Whether Pauline was not aware of Hemingway's three-year extramarital affair or chose to ignore it, she could not have avoided its manifestations in the fiction during this time. A subplot in Hemingway's Key West novel *To Have and Have Not*, published in October 1937, depicts an unhappy wife who rejects her straying husband. Helen Gordon tells him, "I've tried to be a good wife, but you're as selfish and conceited as a barnyard rooster" (*THHN* 183). She continues: "I was your partner and your little black flower. Slop. Love is just another dirty lie" (*THHN* 185). The following year, Hemingway published his play *The Fifth Column*, featuring a thinly disguised Martha Gellhorn (Dorothy) and himself (Philip) as lovers. One female protagonist, Anita, attempts to talk Philip out of impulsively entering a relationship "with that big blonde." His response: "I *want* to make an absolutely colossal mistake" (*FC* 42, emphasis mine). The final scene depicts Philip and Dorothy's breakup, but Bernice Kert notes:

> All the memories evoked here, with a certain mournful finality, belong to his ten years with Pauline—the Crillon and the Ritz, Nairobi, the long white beach at Lamu, Sans Souci on a Saturday night in Havana. "I've been to all those places," says Philip contemptuously, "and I've left them all behind. And where I go now I go alone, or with others who go there for the same reason I go." If he was not quite ready to leave Pauline, Ernest seemed to be using the forum he liked best—his own fiction—to prepare her for trouble ahead. (309)

Hemingway and Pauline would not officially divorce for another two years, but a death knell had sounded, and the slow but steady decline in their relationship continued. By 1940, the author's tenure in Key West, the marriage, and the decade were officially over.

Characterizing Hemingway's life during this decade is not easy, and clearly the angle of one's vision determines the perspective. The 1930s began for Ernest Hemingway with a new hometown, a new wife, a growing family, and a rising career. He had chosen America/Key West/Pauline for this decade sandwiched between his European/Lost Generation/Hadley period and his Cuban/Finca Vigía/Martha retreat. In his writing, he experimented with book-length nonfiction, drama, and magazine serialization as well as continuing his work with the short story and novel genres of his first professional phase. Hemingway's stature as a literary and popular figure was assured, and to some extent the decade had been a "belle époque," but the downward spiral from personal and professional happiness to greater uncertainty in both arenas gained momentum. Michael Reynolds notes that although he became an icon during the Key West decade, Hemingway's remaining history was to become "an old American story of promise fulfilled through fortitude and good fortune, a tale of rewards beyond all expectation, a cautionary tale of the Dream and its dark side" (*The 1930s* xx). Hemingway would confess to Hadley in July 1939: "Life is quite complicated. And you don't always have luck. . . . Important thing for me to do is not get discouraged and take easy way out like your and my noted ancestors" (*SL* 493). He would not resort to such a measure for more than two decades, but the dark seed was already deeply imbedded.

Notes

1. In this letter, dated 9 December 1928, Hemingway thanks Fitzgerald for help at the time of his father's suicide. Hemingway learned of his father's death when traveling by train from New York to Key West with his young son Bumby. Caught short of funds, he asked Fitzgerald to wire money so that he could travel immediately to Chicago and send Bumby on to Key West (*SL* 291).

2. In this letter to Gingrich, Hemingway specifically has Gertrude Stein in his sights, but his hostile metaphor could easily be read as targeting any one of the friends and mentors he turned on during the decade. There is unintended irony and psychological complexity here as well, considering the writer's eventual death by his own hand.

3. For a book-length study of these relationships, see Stephen Koch's *The Breaking Point: Hemingway, Dos Passos, and the Murder of José Robles.*

4. Bernice Kert's *The Hemingway Women* is a comprehensive and useful study of the author's romantic relationships, marriages, and infidelities.

5. Carlos Baker cites a 26 November 1933 letter Hemingway wrote to Clifton Fadiman as the source of this information (*A Life Story* 604).

6. *New York Herald Tribune*, 25 September 1936.

Beleaguered Modernists

Hemingway, Stevens, and the Left

MILTON A. COHEN

Ernest Hemingway and Wallace Stevens had more in common than resid-
ing in Key West at the same time and being on the giving and receiving
ends of a 1936 black eye.[1] Highly regarded as modernist innovators of the
1920s, both writers were made painfully aware that their status had slipped
by the mid-1930s, and that their writing was indifferent to contemporary
problems of the Depression. Both perhaps also sensed that their comfortable lives—Stevens as an insurance executive, Hemingway with his large
home and cabin cruiser in Key West—sharply contrasted with the widespread destitution of the times.[2] All around them, their contemporaries—
writers and critics—were becoming politicized, moving left (many em-
bracing communism) and calling for a politically engaged literature. Both
Hemingway and Stevens responded to this leftist pressure in complex,
sometimes contradictory ways that mingled defensiveness and repudiation
with self-examination and gradual recognition of political and economic issues. Although apolitical by temperament, each writer gradually developed
a kind of political consciousness under the pressure of the times and his own
conscience, while rejecting the Marxist path of that leftward movement.
To be sure, they expressed this new consciousness in quite different ways,
reflecting their contrasting personalities. Hemingway at first concealed his
leftward movement beneath blustering hostility, then positioned it so as
not to appear as merely following the crowd. Stevens candidly expressed in

his letters and poems his sense that he was "headed left," but also revealed a deeply conflicted and somewhat confused sensibility. Just as they reflected the pull of leftist politics on even apolitical writers in the 1930s, so these two writers also typified the political disaffiliation that set in by the end of the decade. For once the ideological ferment of the 1930s had simplified into the war politics of the 1940s, both writers easily and permanently shed their political personas.

To read Hemingway's vituperative comments on leftist writers and critics in 1934 and 1935, one might assume that he was smarting from political attacks on his previous books, *Death in the Afternoon* (1932) and *Winner Take Nothing* (1933). In a December 1934 article for *Esquire*, "Old Newsman Writes," he heaps scorn on "the literary revolution boys." Any writer, he declares, "is cheating who takes politics as a way out. It is too easy." And he advises the novice writer: "[D]on't let them suck you in to start writing about the proletariat if you don't come from the proletariat, just to please the recently politically enlightened critics" (*BL* 183–84). The following year, he is even blunter in *Green Hills of Africa*: the leftist New York writers are "[a]ll angleworms in a bottle . . . afraid to be alone in their beliefs"; the leftist critics whose praise they seek are the "lice who crawl on literature" (21–22, 109). Repeatedly, he declares in print that writers must work alone, free of political allegiance and fashionable causes.

Surprisingly, however, ideological attacks on his writing before *Green Hills of Africa* were relatively sparse. True, in 1928 Mike Gold called him "heartless" and "too bourgeois to accept the labor world" (qtd. in Solow 62).[3] And Isidor Schneider, writing in *The Nation* in 1931, criticized the simplifications of the so-called "Hemingway school," noting that Lenin was opposed to "baby talk" in writing (184, 186). But overall, liberal and leftist critics did not directly attack *Death in the Afternoon* and *Winner Take Nothing* on ideological grounds. At most, Granville Hicks and Malcolm Cowley faulted Hemingway's concerns in *Death* for being parochial and not living up to its concluding advice to see the world clearly and as a whole if one wants to save it (Meyers, *Critical Heritage* 163–64, 164–70). Not until the reviews of *Green Hills of Africa* in late 1935—that is, *after* many of Hemingway's attacks against the Left—do leftist critics such as Hicks and Edmund Wilson fault Hemingway's subjects as "detached from the great social issues of the day" (in Wilson's words) and urge him, as Hicks did, to write about contemporary social conflict: strikes and such (Meyers, *Critical Heritage* 217, 215).

Why, then, was Hemingway so defensive against the leftist writers and critics in 1934 and 1935? Several reasons suggest themselves. First, and most generally, he was always thin-skinned—one might even say paranoid—about criticism (despite his boasts to the contrary); and the higher he rose in critical and popular esteem—this was especially true after the huge success of *A Farewell to Arms* in 1929—the more certain he was that the critics wanted to knock him down. A passage from "Old Newsman Writes" is revealing:

Of course the boys are all wishing you luck and that helps a lot. (Watch how they wish you luck after the first one). . . . All the critics who could not make their reputations by discovering you are hoping to make them by predicting hopefully your approaching impotence, failure and general drying up of natural juices. (*BL* 184, 185)

Beyond paranoia, however, Hemingway may well have sensed just how out of touch his writing was in the early 1930s, how far removed his subjects were from the overriding economic problems of his readers. The bullring, the Gulf Stream, and the Serengeti Plain were a long way from the breadlines, failed banks, and Hoovervilles one could see in any American city or town at the time. While writers and critics in increasing numbers felt obliged to document and respond to these problems, Hemingway's interests moved in the opposite direction: toward the leisure pursuits available only to the rich, including Spanish bullfights, African safaris, and Florida deep-sea fishing. Hicks hit it exactly in his review of *Green Hills of Africa*: "He is very bitter about the critics and very bold in asserting his independence of them, so bitter and so bold that one detects a sign of a bad conscience" (Meyers, *Critical Heritage* 215).

To these motives a third could be added. Hemingway's belligerence against leftist critics in 1934–35 was a kind of reaction-formation: it belied his desire to be lionized again, as he had been in the 1920s, by the New York critical establishment, and it concealed his quiet overtures to the very leftist critics he publicly reviled. At virtually the same time that *Green Hills* slams the leftists, Hemingway published "Who Murdered the Vets?," his scathing diatribe against the government, in the very magazine that epitomized "the literary revolution boys": *New Masses* (17 September 1935; see Trogdon 168–71). True, the journal had solicited his article, but he could have easily sent it to *Esquire*, which published everything he submitted, or to some other magazine. Why *New Masses*? The article itself was not leftist, but its antigovernment intensity—and radical venue—prompted Hicks to write: "[It] had a quality that had been disastrously absent from his previous work. . . . [It] suggested that Hemingway was going somewhere" (Meyers, *Critical Heritage* 213). In addition to the article, why did Hemingway send *New Masses* a telegram—"best luck [and] congratulations"—on the magazine's twenty-fifth anniversary in late 1936? Finally, and most strangely of all, why did he write to the leftist critic John Weaver in early 1936 that he hoped to write a "study of the mechanics of revolution" (qtd. in Reynolds, *The 1930s* 225)? Critics generally credit the Spanish Civil War with Hemingway's political reawakening and wary movement to the left. But it really began earlier, more quietly, and more locally beneath a smokescreen of declarations to the contrary, such as this one in a letter to Maxwell Perkins, written only a week after the letter to Weaver and stating that he would never again "notice [the New York bunch], mention them, pay any attention to them, nor read them. Nor will I kiss their asses . . . make friends with them, nor truckle to them" (*OTTC* 243).

Hemingway's political dilemma in the mid-1930s thus functioned on two levels. Publicly (and in rather noble terms), once the Spanish Civil War broke out, it was how to reconcile his belief in authorial independence (seeing for yourself, "writing truly") with the need to join forces with other writers and intellectuals against fascism. Privately, and rather less flatteringly, it was how to regain his standing with leftist critics and writers while not appearing to jump on the political bandwagon and thus betraying his declarations of authorial independence. The outbreak of the Spanish Civil War neatly resolved his private dilemma by providing a bona fide cause and a culture with which he had long been associated. And his persona as journalist allowed him to play both sides of the fence: to appear faithful to his ethic of "writing truly," while obviously garnering support for the antifascist Loyalists, especially through the 1937 film he helped produce, *The Spanish Earth*.

But what about domestic politics, where there was no single, shining cause to rally writers? *To Have and Have Not* demonstrates the strategy

Hemingway arrived at: it empathizes with the common people—Harry Morgan and the Conchs—while lambasting "professional" revolutionaries (the Cubans) and revolutionary writers, represented by Richard Gordon. The Conchs show a genuine proletarian unity, helping each other out and sometimes even referring to each other as "brother" (*THHN* 83). Harry Morgan's dying words indirectly affirm this camaraderie in declaring that a man alone has no chance. The Cuban revolutionaries, on the other hand, are murderers, killing a fellow proletarian, Albert, for no good reason, and providing Harry a perfect justification for thinking: "What the hell do I care about his revolution. F— his revolution. To help the working man he robs a bank and kills a fellow works with him and then kills that poor damned Albert that never did any harm. That's a working man he kills" (*THHN* 168). Moreover, the novel strains itself to make a fool of Richard Gordon in every possible way (shades of *The Sun Also Rises*' Robert Cohn): as a writer, husband, lover, understander of people, and friend of the proletariat. Hemingway thus presents himself as having strong proletarian sympathies while maintaining his iconoclastic individualism by having nothing to do with programmatic leftists.

It may well be argued that, in fact, these *were* Hemingway's sympathies, not merely a strategy. Michael Reynolds, for example, writes: "Neither right nor left, but opposed to government of any sort, he trusted working-class people, but not those who would lead them to the barricades and not the masses en masse" (*The 1930s* 211). But why then does the novel take such pains to ridicule Richard Gordon? (Or was it John Dos Passos? Or was it a projection of Hemingway himself—a self-warning against becoming a Richard Gordon—just as in Paris he had ridiculed aesthetes while, beneath his shadow-boxing facade, he was one himself.) The excessiveness of this satire has more to do with Hemingway's projected self-image than with the demands of his plot.

The strategy paid off handsomely. By 1937, with his pro-Loyalist involvement in Spain, Hemingway had become the darling of the Left. While virtually all reviewers pointed out the many shortcomings of *To Have and Have Not*, leftist critics praised its proletarian sympathies. Alfred Kazin and Malcolm Cowley both spoke of Hemingway as beginning "a new career" (Cowley), of having "worked his way out of a cult of tiresome defeatism" (Kazin). Phillip Rahv, writing in *Partisan Review*, went even further, referring to his "conversion" and "surrender" to "the social muse" (Meyers, *Critical Heritage* 235, 232, 240). When Hemingway addressed the Second American Writers' Congress on 4 June 1937, he was greeted with "thunderous applause from the 3,500 who jammed the hall for this, his first public political statement" (Reynolds, *The 1930s* 270). Little wonder. The speech—and Hemingway's activism regarding Spain generally—positioned him squarely in the mainstream of Popular Front ideology: i.e., despite our differences on communism, we can—and must—unite to fight fascism. By 1938, Herbert Solow, a critic for *Partisan Review*, identified a significant change in literary politics; he titled his article "Substitution at Left Tackle: Hemingway for Dos Passos." The article contrasts Dos Passos's fall from favor with the *New Masses* editor and critic Mike Gold (in Gold's review of the combined *U.S.A.*) with Hemingway's rise to "beatified" heights for critics like Gold, Hicks, and Cowley (62–64).

Perhaps his newly elevated critical status fortified Hemingway to treat political themes in *For Whom the Bell Tolls* with more complexity and ambiguity than he had in *To Have and Have Not*. Once again, the protagonist is fundamentally apolitical, but now actively fights for the common people and against fascism. When asked if he is a communist, Robert Jordan pointedly says, "No. I am an anti-fascist" (*FWBT* 66). But Hemingway's sympathetic portrayal of the Partizans nonetheless recognizes their sometimes ugly motives and gruesome actions, particularly in the Loyalist massacre that Pablo organizes. Robert Jordan must work with Pablo in blowing the bridge, knowing that he is a murderer and will surely kill the men that he recruited for their horses. Distrust of professional revolutionaries, now Russian, carries over from *To Have and Have Not*, but rather than simply contrast these two groups (the people and the professionals), as that novel does, *For Whom the Bell Tolls* intertwines their contradictions in Robert Jordan's ambivalent political attitudes. He recognizes the Russians' brutal power politics, but enjoys being an "insider" at Gaylord's Hotel (Russian headquarters) and admires the cynical wisdom in the Russian journalist, Kozlov. Although he fights with the Partizans, he enjoys the privileges of the party insiders, realizes that he "corrupted very easily" (*FWBT* 245). Perhaps most remarkable of all, he admits that, unlike the saintly Anselmo, his own feelings about killing have a darker side: enjoyment. But while the novel candidly depicts Robert Jordan's ambivalence, it cannot resolve its own: it equivocates on—or rather abstains from judging—a major is-sue that it boldly recognizes: the Communists' political murders. Robert Jordan claims they no longer bother him, but he refuses to pass judgment: "My mind is in suspension until we win the war" (*FWBT* 261). Like Scarlett O'Hara, he tells himself that he will think about the unpleasant facts some later day—when he, like his creator, writes "truly" about them (*FWBT* 264). But since this *is* Hemingway's supposedly "true" book about the war, the author ducks the issue. And as in fiction so in fact: three years earlier, when Dos Passos wanted to uncover and publicize the Communists' mur-der of his friend and translator José Robles, Hemingway warned him that doing so would harm the Loyalist cause, condescending advice that led to permanent estrangement between these two writers.

In *For Whom the Bell Tolls*, Hemingway's politics scored a rather remark-able coup: applauded by leftists (except the CPUSA, or the Communist Party of the United States, which, after the Russo-German pact, no longer occupied the moral high ground);[4] applauded by the general public, itself now awakening to the threat of fascism with the fall of France. Yet, this coup also marked the end of Hemingway's brief romance with the Left, once again very much in keeping with the many American writers who dis-affiliated from Communism by the end of the decade. As Edmund Wilson accurately observed in 1939, Hemingway—in the latter half of the 1930s as he had been in the 1920s—was "a gauge of morale" for writers and intel-lectuals (Meyers, *Critical Heritage* 207–13).

Wallace Stevens's entanglement with the Left shows some striking simi-larities to Hemingway's, but also differences. Throughout the 1920s, Stevens's critical appeal was more rarified, less widespread than was Hemingway's. Gorham Munson's 1925 depiction of Stevens as a dandy tended to stick, and some reviewers of his revised *Harmonium* in 1931 continued to use the term, complaining of his "overly fastidious verse."[5] None of the reviews of the 1931 *Harmonium*, however, was explicitly political. At most, Horace Gregory found its "highly polished surfaces . . . still unbroken" and "static" (28).

Thus, when Stevens's next book of poems—the 1935 *Ideas of Order*—responded pointedly to the prevailing climate of leftist ideology, Stevens was, like Hemingway, not reacting to critical attacks so much as to the ever-intensifying calls from the Left for writers to address contemporary problems. And like Hemingway, Stevens's responses to this pressure were complex. At times, he seems bitter: "Marx has ruined Nature / For the moment," he complains in "Botanist on Alp (No. 1)" (*Collected Poetry and Prose* 109). And ruined art, too, at least its more aristocratic forms: the divertimento in "Mozart, 1935" and the waltz in "Sad Strains of a Gay Waltz." These lighthearted pleasures, he laments in "Sad Strains," are no longer viable when "The epic of disbelief / Blares oftener and soon, will soon be constant" (*Collected Poetry and Prose* 101). In the book's opening poem, "Farewell to Florida," the speaker grimly anticipates returning to "My North"—to "wintry slime" and "a slime of men in crowds"—and he senses there is no escaping from "the violent mind / That is their mind, these men, and that will bind / Me round" (*Collected Poetry and Prose* 98).

In "Mozart, 1935," the menacing, constricting crowd is also present, but here Stevens expresses a more intricate ambivalence to these difficult times and the demands they place on the poet. The tone pervading this poem mingles regret, nostalgia, bitterness, and acceptance. Mozart's music represents for Stevens—as earlier listeners so often misconstrued it—the untroubled art of an aristocratic age: the "unclouded concerto," "that lucid souvenir of the past, the divertimento." It is caviar for the elite—much as Stevens's critics saw his own poetry as being. But now the times are grim:

> If they throw stones upon the roof
> While you practice arpeggios,
> It is because they carry down the stairs
> A body in rags.

The speaker therefore urges the poet seated at the piano—Stevens himself, of course—to "Play the present" with all its cheapness and vulgarity, and, in response to "the body in rags" to "strike the piercing chord," to be "the voice of angry fear, / the voice of this besieging pain." Running all through this grudging recognition of the deteriorating present is regret for the lost Mozartian past: "We may return to Mozart. / He was young, and we, we are old." But the poem ends in a clear assertion that the poet must somehow respond to the times, must indeed become its voice: "The snow is falling and the streets are full of cries. / Be seated, thou" (*Collected Poetry and Prose* 107–8).

"Mozart, 1935" expresses Stevens's recognition that art can never be "pure," detached from ephemeral reality, that poetry—his poetry—must change with and in some sense respond to its time, even when those times are hateful and ugly. He expressed the same sentiments in a series of remarkable letters to Ronald Lane Latimer, the first publisher of *Ideas of Order*.[6] On 31 October 1935, Stevens writes that "when *Harmonium* was in the making . . . I then believed in *pure poetry*, as it was called. I still have a distinct liking for that sort of thing. But we live in a different time, and life means a good deal more to us now-a-days than literature does" (*Letters* 288). He continues in another letter dated 5 November 1935:

> The only possible order of life is one in which all order is incessantly changing. Marxism may or may not destroy the existing sentiment of the marvelous; if it does, it will create another. . . . I do not believe in Communism; I do believe in up-to-date capitalism. It is an extraordinary experience for myself to deal with a thing like Communism. . . . Nevertheless, one has to live and think in the actual world, and no other will do. (*Letters* 291–92)

When Stevens penned this letter, *Ideas of Order* had already appeared and received a provocative review from Stanley Burnshaw in the *New Masses*. Writes Burnshaw about *Harmonium*:

> It is the kind of verse that people concerned with the murderous world collapse can hardly swallow today except in tiny doses.
>
> And it is verse that Stevens can no longer write. His harmonious cosmos is suddenly screeching with confusion. *Ideas of Order* is the record of a man who, having lost his footing, now scrambles to stand up and keep his balance. . . . Acutely conscious members of a class menaced by the clashes between capital and labor, these writers [Stevens and Haniel Long] are in the throes of struggle for philosophical adjustment. And their words have intense value and meaning to the sectors within the class whose confusions they articulate. (41–42)

Stevens's response to this review, like Hemingway's response to leftist criticism, was many-sided and contradictory. He writes to Latimer on 9 October 1935:

> The review in the Masses was a most interesting review, because it placed me in a new setting. *I hope I am headed left*, but there are lefts

and lefts, and certainly I am not headed for the ghastly left of [*New*] Masses. . . . These professionals lament in a way that would have given Job a fever. . . . [T]he whole left now-a-days is a mob of wailers. I do very much believe in leftism in every direction, even in wailing.

Then he adds: "They have the most magnificent cause in the world" (*Letters* 286–87, emphasis mine). Although this letter is a tangle of contradictions, it is clear that Stevens had as little sympathy with "professional" leftists as Hemingway did. But, like Hemingway, he was enticed by the prospect of appearing in the premier magazine of the Far Left: "it placed me in a new setting." A few weeks later, on 21 November 1935, he confided to Latimer: "Merely finding myself in that milieu was an extraordinarily stimulating thing" (*Letters* 296). More puzzling, what did he mean when he wrote "I hope I am headed left" and "I do very much believe in leftism in every direction"? This from an insurance executive who claimed to admire Mussolini![7]

Stevens seems quite open-minded in this letter about Burnshaw's review, but it must have gnawed at him, for he immediately wrote a long poem in response entitled "Mr. Burnshaw and the Statue." He describes his purpose in a 31 October 1935 letter to Latimer: "You will remember that Mr. Burnshaw applied the point of view of the practical Communist to *Ideas of Order*; in 'Mr. Burnshaw and the Statue' I have tried to reverse the process: that is to say, apply the point of view of a poet to Communism" (*Letters* 289).

One might have expected the poem to be contentious—a rebuttal—and it is often described that way. But Stevens called it "a general and rather vaguely poetic justification of leftism" (*Letters* 295). Again, that word. The poem gave Stevens much difficulty—just as Hemingway struggled with his first expression of "leftism" in *To Have and Have Not*. It also poses the reader difficulty in interpreting its rather opaque symbols, but with the help of Stevens's explicit glosses in letters, an argument emerges that can be condensed as follows.[8] The marble statue of horses is, Stevens writes, a symbol of civilization (*Letters* 366). The speaker, assuming perhaps the perspective of the Communist critic Burnshaw, declares that that the statue is dead, "a thing of the dank imagination" (*Collected Poetry and Prose* 570). He then invokes celestial paramours to sing "requiems for this effigy" (571). In place of the statue comes a new, grimier symbol, the "trash can at the end of the

Chapter 5

world" where "buzzards . . . eat the bellies of the rich" (572). This repugnant image represents a future controlled by "the mass" (571). But out of this trash and waste emerges

faint, portentous lustres, shades and shapes
Of rose, or what will once more rise to rose
and
For a little time, again, rose-breasted birds
Sing rose-beliefs.

(Collected Poetry and Prose 573)

Social change is thus cyclical and inevitable. What the masses trash today may arise, phoenixlike, into something beautiful tomorrow, even if it is politically pink and idealistic ("rose-beliefs"). "It is not enough to be reconciled / Before the strange," the speaker tells his celestial muses. "It is only enough / To live incessantly in change":

So great a change
Is constant. The time you call serene descends
Through a moving chaos that never ends.
. . . .
But change composes, too, and chaos comes
To a momentary calm. . . .
Shall you,
Then, fear a drastic community evolved
From the whirling, slowly and by trial; or fear
Men gathering for a mighty flight of men,
An abysmal migration into a possible blue?

(Collected Poetry and Prose 573–74)

Stevens's "leftism," then, is an uneasy acceptance of this constant whirling, this incessant change, and a hope that even "abysmal migrations" may become flights into "a possible blue."

And where does Mr. Burnshaw come in? He does not (beyond one oblique reference and the initial voice noted above). "Forget about Mr. Burnshaw," Stevens advises one inquiring critic in 1940 (*Letters* 367). He had followed his own advice by then, deleting all references to Burnshaw—

and whole sections of the poem—in its second book appearance in *The Man with the Blue Guitar* in 1937. By the time Stevens's *Collected Poems* appeared in 1954, the poem—and indeed the book originally containing it, *Owl's Clover*—had disappeared from the collection altogether. That omission reflects Stevens's final thoughts on the matter of the poet's political responsibility, which he expressed succinctly in a lecture-essay, "The Noble Rider and the Sound of Words," in 1941, just six years after the "Burnshaw" poem: "I might be expected to speak of the social, that is to say sociological or political obligation of the poet. He has none. That he must be contemporaneous is as old as Longinus and I dare say older. But that he *is* contemporaneous is almost inevitable" (*Collected Poetry and Prose* 659). Stevens goes on to lump political obligation with other "pressures of reality," such as the turbulent times—pressures that "individuals of extraordinary imagination" must resist or evade (*Collected Poetry and Prose* 650, 656). Like Hemingway, he happily put the matter behind him when World War II began.

The political odysseys of Hemingway and Stevens in the 1930s were by no means unusual; although belated, they largely replicated the pattern among 1930s writers and intellectuals of attraction to the Left, uneasy residence within its gravitational pull, as cramped independence chafed against political idealism or expedience, and relieved or bitter disaffiliation in the war years. But Hemingway and Stevens also represent a notable subset of this pattern: that of the essentially apolitical modernist who, having established his reputation before 1929, now finds his professional aloofness challenged by leftist critics and proletarian aesthetics. Both writers at first reacted defensively to the new movement, not so much from being attacked by leftist critics as from feeling bypassed and artistically obsolete.[9] But at almost the same time (1935–36), both were quietly finding ways of accommodating or even joining that leftward swing. Stevens's "heading left" meant recognizing that the idea of "pure" poetry was no longer viable, that the poet must live in and respond to his own tumultuous, unpoetic times.[10] Hemingway's more dramatic swing to the left fell squarely within the antifascist ideology of the Popular Front, ostensibly prompted by the Spanish Civil War, but also concealing his desire to bask once again in critical approbation. Nor were these two modernists alone: one sees political defensiveness in E. E. Cummings, Robert Frost, Archibald MacLeish, and even William Carlos

Williams, all having established their reputations between 1910 and 1929, all attacked by leftist critics in the early or mid-1930s.

That Stevens and Hemingway righted their leftward tilt at the end of the 1930s also typified the larger disaffiliation of writers and intellectuals. As Daniel Aaron observes, the cumulative impact of several events in the late 1930s (e.g., the Moscow trials and Russia's brutality in the Spanish Civil War), culminating in the Russo-German pact of August 1939, prompted a large number of disaffiliations and renunciations of membership in the CPUSA (327, 376).[11] But that these two writers shed their political skins so easily and thoroughly speaks to how fundamentally apolitical they really were, how much they were responding to the pressure of the times. In the imagery of "Mozart, 1935," once the mob outside was no longer throwing stones on the roof, they could go back to practicing arpeggios, to composing concertos, to doing what they did best.

Notes

1. When Stevens dared to disparage Hemingway in front of his sister Ursula at a Key West cocktail party sometime around 19 February 1936, Hemingway "raged out into the rain to settle the matter," confronting Stevens, "a large man, a little drunk, a little belligerent, twenty years Hemingway's senior." Stevens managed to land a few blows, but Hemingway decked him. The poet appeared at Whitehead Street the following day to apologize and to beg Hemingway to keep the incident a secret—which Hemingway did not do (Reynolds, *The 1930s* 221–22).

2. This twinge of guilt was definite for Stevens: his letters in the early 1930s, for example, describe the increase of burglaries in his neighborhood (*Letters* 266–67) and feeling reticent about mentioning the purchase of artwork as "not permissible subjects now-a-days" (unpublished letter; qtd. in Filreis 16).

3. I have not been able to find the original quotation in the *New Masses*.

4. On 23 August 1939, the Soviet Union signed a nonaggression pact with Nazi Germany, enabling Germany to invade Poland with impunity and Russia to occupy the eastern half of Poland. This pact betrayed the antifascist stand Russia had assumed for several years (the "Popular Front") and thus disillusioned many leftists who were attracted to communism for its antifascist stand. On orders from Moscow, the CPUSA defended the pact.

5. See Munson, "The Dandyism of Wallace Stevens"; and Larsson, "The Beau as Poet."

6. Filreis reveals in *Modernism from Left to Right* that Latimer's questions to Stevens about his views of politics and poetry were really ghostwritten by Willard Maas, a communist writer and critic (121). Although Stevens somewhat distrusted the evasive and shifty Latimer (who went under several aliases), Stevens's answers to Latimer-Maas's questions were sincere.

7. In his 31 October 1935 letter to Latimer, Stevens wrote, "I am pro-Mussolini, person-

ally" (*Letters* 289). His views on Mussolini, however, were as confused and contradictory as his views on the Left in the letter quoted above. He expressed sympathy for Ethiopia after Mussolini invaded it, but felt that he "is right, practically" (*Letters* 295).

8. See letters to Latimer, 5 November 1935 (*Letters* 290–91), and to Hi Simons, 27 August 1940 (*Letters* 366–68).

9. See, for example, Stevens's antiproletarian "The Drum-Majors in the Labor Day Parade" and "Polo Ponies Practicing" (*Collected Poetry and Prose* 562–63), both written in 1934.

10. Although this recognition seems rather far removed from social advocacy, Stevens's reputation in the latter half of the 1930s changed enough to prompt a fellow poet, William Carlos Williams, to begin a review of *The Man with the Blue Guitar and Other Poems*: "The story is that Stevens has turned of late definitely to the left." But Williams was rightly skeptical: "I should say not from anything in this book" (50).

11. Pells describes the "sense of political and personal betrayal [that] instantly swept through the entire intellectual community" with the announcement of the Russo-German pact (347). For an example of a published disaffiliation, see Hicks's 1939 letter to the *New Republic* (244).

Hemingway, the Left, and Key West

DAN MONROE

Ernest Hemingway probably first heard of Key West from his friend and fellow writer John Dos Passos, after the latter's peripatetic travels took him to the island in 1924. "It's a vacation paradise, like no other in Florida. You ought to try it," Dos Passos wrote (qtd. in Carr 231). When Hemingway returned to the United States in 1928 so his pregnant second wife, Pauline, could be attended by an American doctor, the young couple visited Key West in April. Hemingway immediately fell in love with the sleepy island's unique combination of natural beauty, superb fishing, and relative isolation from the American mainland. His working proclivities suited life in the Keys. He rose at dawn, writing in the salty coolness of early-morning sea breezes, and then knocked off in the afternoon for fishing, or "monstering," as Hemingway called saltwater angling because of the size of the ocean fish (*SL* 282). Key West, Hemingway informed Maxwell Perkins, his editor at Scribner's, was the perfect vista for laboring on the manuscript of a novel: "I would like to stay right here until it is done as I have been going so very well here and it is such a fine healthy life and the fishing keeps my head from worrying in the afternoon when I don't work" (*SL* 277). When he completed the manuscript of *A Farewell to Arms*, Hemingway insisted that Perkins retrieve it personally in Key West so he could treat the workaholic editor to a week of fishing (Baker, *A Life Story* 199).

Almost simultaneously with the book's publication, the United States was rocked by a cataclysmic economic collapse. In October 1929, the stock market crash augured a seminal event of American history, the Great Depression. It is difficult for those living seven decades later to realize the pervasive effects of the economic catastrophe on the United States. By 1933, an estimated 12.8 million people were unemployed, nearly 25 percent of the workforce. The prices of farm products, wages, bank reserves and deposits, per capita income—every indicator of economic health—fell precipitously. The human cost that these statistics reflect was immense and unprecedented. Suicide rates climbed, birth rates fell. Legions of men wandered town and country searching for work if only for a meal in payment. Throughout the nation were startling scenes of poverty and desperation: people searching garbage dumps for food; men sleeping on park benches, on iron gratings, and under bridges; shanty towns cobbled together from scrap tin and wood (Watkins 43–44, 55).

Key West had missed the economic expansion that had typified the 1920s in much of the United States. A tariff on pineapples had largely ruined a canning business that had employed hundreds of local residents. The sponging trade vanished under competitive pressure from synthetic versions and more cost-efficient operations elsewhere in Florida. The cigar industry, once a staple of Key West's economy, had moved to more favorable environs in the Tampa area. These misfortunes cost the community some fourteen thousand jobs in the decade preceding the Great Depression, and the ensuing dramatic downturn reduced the remaining islanders to stark penury. By July 1934, an estimated 80 percent of island residents subsisted on government relief payments; city and county governments were bankrupt from lack of tax revenue. Because the municipal government was unable to pay the salaries of sanitation workers, garbage sat heaped in the streets, rotting and festering in the summer's stifling heat. That month, one of the alphabet agencies that the Roosevelt administration created to cope with the devastation, the Federal Emergency Relief Administration, or FERA, took over the governing of Key West. The regional FERA administrator, Julius F. Stone Jr., effectively ruled the community. As he declared to the *New York Times*, Stone refused to evacuate the populace to the mainland but was determined instead to clean up the garbage, beautify the island, and market it as a tourist haven (1–3; see also Bouland).

Literary radicals, already alienated by the conspicuous consumption and unequal prosperity of the 1920s, viewed the Depression that gripped Key West and the rest of the United States as the death knell of the capitalist system. Odd though it may seem, they saw this collapse as the precursor to a new and more promising future, a collectivized one of shared burdens. Those already on the Left felt strengthened convictions; others moved decisively to the Left in attitude and literary approach. As with all reform movements, a certain amount of intolerance flourished against dissent from the new orthodoxy. "Every poem, every novel and drama, must have a social theme or it is merely confectionary," insisted Mike Gold, editor of the Communist *New Masses* (qtd. in Ellis 105; see also Aaron 33–34).

In the early 1930s, ensconced in his tropical idyll when not traveling, Hemingway published books on bullfighting, hunting in Africa, and another short-story collection, as well as essays on marlin fishing. Against the backdrop of the Depression and literary radicalism, his interests seemed somehow frivolous and, in the view of many critics, unforgivably divorced from the national crisis. In a review of *Death in the Afternoon*, Max Eastman accused Hemingway of being too sentimental about bullfighting, of glorifying a blood sport in an effort to prove his masculinity (Meyers, *Critical Heritage* 176). Malcolm Cowley suggested that the Great War had taught writers like Hemingway to become detached, to harken back to better times, to write about simple themes such as the brief life and death struggle in the bullring. This habit of Hemingway's was, wrote Cowley, "now becoming a vice" (Meyers, *Critical Heritage* 169). It was time for Hemingway to address the present and future, new themes, such as the fact that Spain, as a "revolutionary society," might find bullfighting anachronistic. Granville Hicks chose to ridicule Hemingway's tongue-in-cheek suggestion in *Death* that one ought to contemplate the condition of the world with a bottle in hand, so it could be thrown or the contents consumed as the situation demanded. Hicks's rejoinder was: "If, in other words, you are troubled by the world, resort to personal violence; and if personal violence proves, as it usually does, to be dangerous, ineffective, or undignified, console yourself with drink—or skiing, or sexual intercourse, or watching bull fights" (Meyers, *Critical Heritage* 164). In his review of *Green Hills of Africa*, Hicks suggested that hunting made for a boring read, and he openly asked Hemingway to address the "contemporary American scene": "I should like to have Hemingway write a novel about a strike . . . because it would do something to Hemingway" (Meyers, *Critical Heritage* 215). Only by writing about labor strife and other socially relevant topics could Hemingway grow as an artist, according to Hicks. He had to recognize that hunting, fishing, and bullfighting were trivialities, and the author should take up grand issues. Hicks denied the implication that he was suggesting that Hemingway become a Communist, but then conceded it would be good for Hemingway and the communist movement if he did.

Hemingway's reaction to the critical onslaught was as one might expect of him, volcanic and defiant. He told Maxwell Perkins that the critics "have to attack me to believe in themselves," and he vowed to "survive this unpopularity" (*SL* 423). He famously promised to beat up Max Eastman for questioning his virility and did engage in brief fisticuffs with him when the two chanced to meet in Perkins's office (Reynolds, *The 1930s* 275–76). In other correspondence, Hemingway hinted that literary critic Edmund Wilson was senile (*SL* 446), and he called the *New York Times* reviewer John Chamberlain "that unfortunate convert to Economics religion" (*SL* 400). He blamed critics for F. Scott Fitzgerald's writer's block and suggested that reading their vituperative commentary could destroy a writer (*SL* 408; *GHOA* 23).

He was dismissive of the current literary enthusiasm for communism, regarding it as a fad. "Everyone tries to frighten you now by saying or writing that if one does not become a communist or have a Marxian viewpoint one will have no friends and be alone," Hemingway wrote to Soviet critic Ivan Kashkin in 1935. "I cannot be a communist now because I believe in only one thing: liberty. . . . But the state I care nothing for" (*SL* 418–19). In Hemingway's opinion, only talentless writers showcased their class consciousness or wrote only on the proletariat. His libertarian instincts and the very nature of his creative process made it seemingly impossible for Hemingway to join the craze for collectivism.

Hemingway's attitude toward the event that helped trigger the critical onslaught against his work, the Great Depression, was in many respects conventionally conservative. Although he had abandoned the religion, middle-class morality, and genteel tradition of Oak Park and his parents, there was still much of Oak Park in Hemingway. After his father's death, he quickly assumed the role of family patriarch, doling out money for his mother's support. He expected his sister Carol to seek approval for marrying John Gardner and cut them out of his life when they married without it. He rebuked Waldo Peirce for sending his current lover, pregnant with Peirce's child, to Key West because doing so might offend local sensibilities and embarrass Hemingway and his friends. Certainly, his comments on Jews and ethnic minorities reflected the views of the white, Protestant social classes of the time. In response to the economic chaos, Hemingway acted as a prudent bourgeois family man of means. In 1931, he placed a substantial sum of cash in a safety deposit box as insurance in the event of bank failures. After the Roosevelt administration took the national currency off the gold standard, Hemingway worried about the prospect of an inflationary run that would render money worthless as had been the case in postwar Germany. Michael Reynolds has noted that Hemingway also saw the Depression as a great buying opportunity in the stock market (*The 1930s* 85). While thousands tried desperately to liquidate equity accounts, Hemingway bought blue-chip stocks at bargain basement prices. The wealth from royalties, payments for articles, and money from the Pfeiffer family largely insulated Hemingway from the effects of the social catastrophe going on around him, but he had eyes and ears. He told George Albee in 1932 that hard times were instructive for a writer and that the experience of standing in a breadline might inspire. He lived in a community, Key West, that had escaped the prosperity of the 1920s and slipped further into economic despair in the first years of the Depression (*SL* 332–35, 357–59; Reynolds, *The 1930s* 38–39, 78–79, 82, 119; Ogle 144–45).

Hemingway expressed considerable contempt for the New Deal and Franklin D. Roosevelt. In Key West, Julius F. Stone used federal funds to refurbish nightclubs and local homes for the tourist trade, while promoting the wearing of shorts and the riding of bicycles. Stone had a passion for publicity, and he hired artists to create colorful brochures touting Key West as a vacation spot. Hemingway regarded all of these activities with disdain. He condemned the New Deal as "[s]ome sort of Y.M.C.A. show. Starry eyed bastards spending money that somebody will have to pay. Everybody in our town quit work to go on relief. Fishermen all turned carpenters. Reverse of the Bible" (*GHOA* 191). In *To Have and Have Not*, a federal bureaucrat and his fawning assistant try to bully their charter-boat captain with self-important talk and turn in the hero, Harry Morgan, for rum-running. As a result of the actions of Roosevelt's alphabet men, Morgan's boat is confiscated, leading to his desperate gambit to pilot Cuban revolutionaries after they rob a Key West bank. Morgan is killed in the attempt (76–84). In his correspondence, Hemingway criticized Roosevelt for attempting to weaken

17. Mayor and Mrs. William H. Malone join in volunteer efforts to beautify
Key West to entice the tourist trade in the wake of the city's 1934 bankruptcy.
Courtesy of the Monroe County Library, Key West.

the currency, in his opinion, a kind of dishonesty. He also condemned him
for failing to evacuate war veterans in the face of a hurricane in 1935. "Harry
Hopkins and Roosevelt who sent those poor bonus march guys down there
to get rid of them got rid of them all right," he wrote bitterly to Perkins (*SL*
422, see also 391–92, 429–32; Reynolds, *The 1930s* 148, 196–97, 200).

In part because of the New Deal's arrival on the island, Key West's al-
lure began to fade for Hemingway. Stone's colorful brochures actually featured the Hemingway house as a site for gaping tourists, number eighteen on a list of forty-eight "things to do" in Key West (Trogdon 149), an
act that incensed Hemingway. Katy Dos Passos decried the "New Dealers"
and the changes that had been wrought to the island. According to Katy,
federal programs paid "old art trash" and "phony uplifters" to paint bad
murals on café walls, peddle cork candlesticks, hang fishnets everywhere,
and weave baskets, while bureaucrats organized tours to "observe the poor

Hemingways" (L. Miller, *Letters* 109–10). In a piece for *Esquire* lamenting his high-profile status on the island, Hemingway claimed that he paid an elderly black man afflicted with a disease similar to leprosy to stand at the entrance to this house and announce himself as Hemingway to startle un-invited guests (*BL* 192–97).[1] To Katy Dos Passos, Key West had become "a paradise of incompetents, all floating around in a rich culture of humani-tarian graft, a kind of hierarchy of the Dole" (L. Miller, *Letters* 110).

Once Hemingway had peppered his friends with plaintive telegrams and letters begging them to join him in the Keys for the wonderful fishing, refreshingly warm temperatures and breezes during winter, and good food, drink, and frivolity. Now, his letters increasingly complained about winter visitors distracting him and preventing him from writing. He complained to Sara Murphy in February 1936: "If we could only keep the visooters away. . . . I *have* to do my work in the winter and here there is only two months of winter left and the last twelve days have been solid with the brain sucking time eating bastards thick as grunts" (L. Miller, *Letters* 155). After Pauline built a large pool, he would gloomily troop across to his work house in the morning, only to find his concentration broken as the inevitable winter visitors splashed and sloshed through a swim. The once sleepy and forgotten oasis had awakened under the prodding of federal bureaucrats as tourism increased after Stone's promotional efforts and an overseas highway opened in 1938, and with it, Hemingway's once placid residence had turned into a vacation nook for various friends. The disintegration of his marriage to Pauline also played a role in Hemingway's disenchantment. Island resi-dents were sympathetic to Pauline in the marital battle that commenced with the appearance of Martha Gellhorn in Hemingway's life; other Key West locals were annoyed at the portrayal of the island and its people in *To Have and Have Not*. After he moved to Cuba, Hemingway attributed his exodus from Key West to a desire to avoid the tourist crowds on the island (Baker, *A Life Story* 358).

Though Hemingway's reaction to the Depression, the New Deal, and Franklin D. Roosevelt reflected his conservative midwestern background, he was never an indifferent observer of the world around him. Certainly, the suggestion that he abandon bullfighting, hunting, and fishing as top-ics and focus instead on the ongoing social catastrophe was a bit unfair. Hemingway had written on socially conscious topics since the beginning of his writing career, though perhaps less as an advocate than as a fact-reporting journalist. Filing stories for the *Toronto Star* in 1922–23, Hemingway had criticized the Versailles Treaty as "an unjust, conqueror's peace" imposed by reactionary French politicians intent on bleeding Germany in revenge without regard for future consequences (*DT* 90). He had covered the aftermath of the Greco-Turkish War, movingly portraying the desperate flight of Christian refugees from Thrace, and he had contrasted the incompetent and corrupt Greek leadership with the stolid professionalism of Greek troops. While in Germany, Hemingway reported the effects of galloping inflation on a schoolteacher and his family who were reduced to two meals a day because a single egg cost 4,000 marks (*DT* 232, 244–45, 284).

He defended himself from critics by noting his long interest in the problems of the world and suggested that many of his detractors were new to the realization of humanity's flaws, which he had been chronicling for years. As Hemingway told John Dos Passos:

> It's damned funny when I used to get the horrors about the way things were going those guys never took the slightest interest nor even followed it. . . . [T]hen when you've gotten as hot about something or as burned up and finally completely disillusioned on the *working* of anything but intelligent political assassination then they start out and say, "Don't you see the injustice, the Big Things that are happening. Why don't you write about them etc." (*SL* 374)

Robert O. Stephens has noted that as a reporter, Hemingway wrote unflattering word portraits of various politicians at international conferences that clearly conveyed his critical attitude to the reader (*Hemingway's Nonfiction* 186–89). He lampooned the Soviet diplomat Georgi Tchitcherin as a man inordinately fond of military uniforms because he had been dressed as a girl until age twelve. He ridiculed the fascist strongman Benito Mussolini for perpetually scowling to conceal a weak mouth and for having the bad taste to wear a black shirt and white spats. The Turkish military leader Ismet Pasha looked to Hemingway more like an "Armenian lace seller" than a general, bereft of charisma and physically indistinct (*DT* 253–56; 257–59).

Further, his willingness to engage in political commentary, if infrequently, was not limited to his 1920s journalism. Hemingway's short story

"Wine of Wyoming" is a perceptive, though modest, critique of the United States in 1928 and the limitations of the American dream offered to immigrants. A French Catholic couple, the Fontans, ruefully reflect upon their move to Wyoming in pursuit of a better life. Instead of prosperity, they were persecuted for making beer and wine, the consumption of which was integral to their culture. As Catholics surrounded by a Protestant majority, they hope for victory for Al Smith in the 1928 presidential election, but have little real prospect for change (*CSS* 342–54). As "Wine" suggests, Hemingway's choice of topics in his short fiction amounted to a form of social commentary (Johnston 159–67; Martin, "Crazy in Sheridan" 13–25). In the stories published as *Winner Take Nothing*, Hemingway wrote about a down-on-his-luck salvage diver, prostitutes, war dead, homosexuals, and immigrants—i.e., the downtrodden and social outcasts. It was in itself a socially conscious act, if one that he did not openly acknowledge. For him, he was simply writing of the world as it actually was and taking the reader there so he or she could experience it as well. As he told his mother-in-law: "I am trying to make, before I get through, a picture of the whole world—or as much of it as I have seen. Boiling it down always, rather than spreading it out thin. These stories are mostly about things and people that people won't care about—or will actively dislike. All right. Sooner or later as the wheel keeps turning I will have ones that they *will* like" (*SL* 397). He battled for the inclusion of banned words in his fiction and fought genteel tradition; as Michael Reynolds has noted, Hemingway's focus on social outcasts expanded the accepted boundaries for American writing (*The 1930s* 88).

So while Hemingway had already written a fair amount of unrecognized social commentary, it is probably true that, despite his denials to the contrary, he indulged his critics and wrote a bit in the proletarian vein, though perhaps without much enthusiasm at times. Jeffrey Meyers has suggested that *To Have and Have Not* was Hemingway's answer to those who charged him with not caring about the social crisis of the Depression; in the novel, Hemingway depicts the life of Harry Morgan, the heroic fisherman and charter-boat captain who is battered in a corrupt society and finally dies under tragic circumstances (*A Life* 296). It has also been suggested that the massive hurricane disaster of 1935 that killed war veterans employed by the federal government to build bridges in the Florida Keys outraged

Hemingway and stimulated his social conscience. He wrote and published an essay expressing his anger in a Communist journal, the *New Masses*, which he had once derided as "the most puerile and shitty house organ I've ever seen" (*SL* 216). His decision to publish "Who Murdered the Vets?" was perhaps proof of his desire to placate the Left with a bit of outrage directed at the government's obvious neglect of forgotten citizens.[2]

Hemingway also echoed an argument, typical of the Left and then being advanced in the Senate Munitions Committee, an investigating body of Congress, that arms manufacturers, bankers, and Wall Street interests had maneuvered the United States into the Great War (Wiltz 13–17, 19–21). An influential article, "Arms and the Men," had appeared in *Fortune* magazine in spring 1934, just as the Hemingways were returning from Africa. The article, and others like it, claimed that arms manufacturers stoked war fears and sabotaged peace initiatives to drive up the international demand for the weapons trade (53–57, 113–26). The world situation was deteriorating, Japan had invaded Manchuria in 1931, Germany and Italy were rearming in defiance of the impotent League of Nations, and Italy invaded Ethiopia in 1935. Isolationist sentiment became widespread in the United States. The desire to curb the arms trade, the Munitions Committee investigation, and the subsequent neutrality acts were a reflection of American desire to avoid involvement in another world war.[3]

Hemingway initially shared the isolationism of the majority of Americans. In an essay published in *Esquire* in 1934, describing a visit to Paris, Hemingway lamented that it had become commonplace to speak of the inevitability of war. Most Parisians took it as a given with equanimity. Hemingway strongly urged an American isolationist policy. "Europe," he wrote, "has always had wars. But we can keep out of this next one. And the only way to keep out of it is not to go in it; not for any reason. There will be plenty of good reasons. *But we must keep out of it*" (*BL* 158). He told his mother-in-law in 1937 that his desire to keep the United States out of a European war prompted him to go to Spain: "This is the dress rehearsal for the inevitable European war, and I would like to try to write anti-war war correspondence that would help to keep us out of it when it comes" (*SL* 458).

The tragedy of the Spanish Civil War challenged Hemingway's isolationism. He became a passionate advocate for the beleaguered Spanish Republic.

If he found the American scene uninspiring, as he had once told Arnold Gingrich, Spain excited his emotions. As he wrote in *For Whom the Bell Tolls*, the cause of Republican Spain was "something that you could believe in wholly and completely and in which you felt an absolute brotherhood with the others who were engaged in it" (*FWBT* 235). Taking a page from the communists, Hemingway even expressed a willingness to discipline himself to avoid harming the war effort, by which he meant that he was willing to suppress bad news if revealing it would harm the Republic and aid Franco (*SL* 463–65). "War is a hateful and dirty business," wrote Hemingway, "but when one has become involved in a war there is only one thing to do: win it" ("Treachery in Aragon" 26). With that attitude, Hemingway's dispatches from the front in Spain put the best possible light on the military situation for the Loyalists while downplaying the rising superiority of Francisco Franco's fascist armies (Meyers, *Life into Art* 34). During the war, he brooked no doubt or reservations in support for the Spanish Republic, despite the bloody internecine purges the Communists conducted among the Spanish political factions loosely allied against Franco. He sundered a friendship of long standing with John Dos Passos because of the latter's outrage at the execution of a close friend, José Robles, in Spain. Hemingway accused Dos Passos of being naïve—perhaps his friend was a traitor (*SL* 463–65). He was willing to tolerate Soviet-inspired political killings because to draw attention to such atrocities might undermine support for the Republic.

With his passion aroused by his experiences in Spain, Hemingway began touting the virtues of American munitions trade with Republican Spain. In a series of articles in the pages of *Ken* magazine, Hemingway made the case for an end to isolationism. He argued that Hitler clearly intended war, but his drive for conquest could be disrupted if one of the Axis powers was defeated and discredited in Spain. The Italian fascist conscript army fought poorly; the Spanish could defeat them if properly supplied. He directly challenged American complacency:

> Right now there is a lot of talk about oceans. It seems we are protected by the oceans so we do not need to care what happens. But, brother, when a war starts we will be put in it. And you'll hate those oceans, both the Atlantic and the Pacific, when you ride over them in the good old vomit-stink of transports. There is only one way to avoid,

or to postpone, that ride. That is to beat Italy, always beatable, and to beat her in Spain, and beat her now. Otherwise you will have to fight tougher people than the Italians, and don't let anybody ever tell you that you won't. ("The Time Now, The Place Spain" 36–37)

The American refusal to arm Spain was "criminal stupidity," for which Hemingway faulted an Anglophile U.S. State Department (*HOW* 293). He considered Neville Chamberlain a dupe for the wealthy stockholding class that grew rich during war, at least a faint echo of the argument that special interests provoke war. His pieces included gruesome photographs to drive home his points. With photos of savagely mangled Italian war dead as a backdrop, Hemingway wrote that the men of the International Brigades were fighting, at fifty cents a day, for every American; unless the brigades stopped the fascists, other Americans would have to fight them. Amidst the blood and bombs of the Spanish Civil War, hoping to save from fascist tyranny a nation and a people he had grown to love, Hemingway abandoned his isolationism and embraced international interventionism ("H. M.'s Loyal State Department" 36; "Call for Greatness" 23; "False News to the President" 17–18).

Once the war in Spain had been lost with Franco and the fascists victorious, Hemingway felt released from the wartime discipline that had curbed his criticism of the defunct Republic. In his famed novel of that war, *For Whom the Bell Tolls*, Hemingway lashed out at the Left for undermining the fight against fascism (*FWBT* 228–34; Meyers, *Life into Art* 34–53). The Communists had engaged in bitter factional warfare and bloody purges behind the lines, destroying the unity necessary for successful military operations. As the Communists tightened their control, political commissars had trumped military commanders in the field with predictably disastrous results. Soviet and other foreign Communists had disproportionate influence in the war, conducting it to serve the latest Stalinist directive rather than the people of Spain. Hemingway alludes to these leftist mistakes in an unflattering manner in the novel, at times a blunt retrospective on the reasons for the failure of a seemingly noble cause. As he had in his journalism of the 1920s, Hemingway in the novel also drew unflattering word portraits of political figures he found detestable, such as the French Communist André Marty, whom Hemingway described as kill-crazy and having a face the color of waste from beneath an old lion's claws (*FWBT* 416–17). He even dared to criticize the Spanish Communist Dolores Ibárruri, the fabled La Pasionaria, the heroine of Republican Spain (*FWBT* 309). Clearly, Hemingway's alliance with the Left to defeat Franco had not blunted his critical faculties or his innate skepticism of politicians and political movements.[4]

During the Depression decade, critics, particularly those on the Left, savaged Hemingway for his alleged indifference to the social catastrophe proceeding around him. Yet Hemingway's work reflects an artist who, though primarily concerned with perfecting his craft and following his own vision, was not indifferent to events or necessarily reluctant to comment on them. His own traditional background and libertarian instincts prompted him to condemn the social welfare schemes of the New Deal, examples of which he witnessed in Key West. Hemingway assimilated the antimunitions trade argument and repeated it in a piece for a leftist magazine, and he published a strong isolationist statement in *Esquire*. His opinion changed in the face of the fascist threat in Europe. Hemingway's experience in Spain and devotion to the Republic prompted him to reconsider the merits of interventionism, at least to allow the Loyalists to purchase American arms. Once the war ended, Hemingway used his political novel *For Whom the Bell Tolls* as a vehicle to criticize elements of the Left in the Spanish conflict. His emotional engagement in Spain and willingness to jettison previous conclusions defies the then conventional wisdom that he was a kind of literary roué who simply drank, fished, and made love. If Hemingway's politics are difficult to categorize, his artistic commitment to present the world as he found it to his readers is clear. "A true work of art endures forever," he wrote, "no matter what its politics" (*SL* 419).

Notes

1. See E. Stone Shiflet and Kirk Curnutt's essay in this collection.

2. In the August 1935 letter to *Esquire* titled "He Who Gets Slap Happy," Hemingway had lampooned the same veterans whose ranks would be decimated by the hurricane in September.

3. Two books echoed the *Fortune* magazine article: Seldes's *Iron, Blood, and Profits* and Engelbrecht and Hanighen's *Merchants of Death*.

4. For archival evidence of Soviet duplicity in Spain, see Radosh, Habeck, and Sevostianov's *Spain Betrayed*.

II

Revisionary Readings
of *To Have and Have Not*

Harry and the Pirates

The Romance and Reality of Piracy in Hemingway's *To Have and Have Not*

SUSAN F. BEEGEL

> Oh, better far to live and die
> Under the brave black flag I fly
> Than play a sanctimonious part
> With a pirate head and a pirate heart
>
> W. S. Gilbert, *The Pirates of Penzance*

In *To Have and Have Not*, Professor MacWalsey calls Key West "The Gibraltar of America" after the port that guards the narrow entrance to the Mediterranean, once haunted by Barbary pirates (135). Key West and its sister port of Havana guard opposite sides of the Straits of Florida—a strategic entrance to and exit from both the Gulf of Mexico and the Caribbean Sea. The island belongs to the historic marinescape of piracy, that part of the ocean world once known as the Spanish Main. The Florida Keys with their 220-mile-long protective coral barrier, their surrounding maze of more than 1,600 uninhabited mangrove islands, and their proximity to Cuba, Mexico, South and Central America, as well as the busy international shipping lanes of the Straits and the Yucatan Channel, have been a den for pirates almost since Ponce de León discovered them in 1530. The tradition of oceangoing crime is unbroken from the sixteenth century, when fierce Elizabethan sea dogs, epitomized by Sir Francis Drake, marauded these waters, "seeking in one deft move both to singe the Spaniard's beard and to line their . . . pockets with gold and silver" (Rediker 57), to our own time with its thriving trade in "cocaine, refugees, and revolution" (G. Murphy 54).

Key West's piratical history helped inspire Ernest Hemingway's *To Have and Have Not*, a gritty Depression-era novel of smuggling illegal aliens, rum, guns, and revolutionaries across the Florida Straits. The novel belongs to a literary tradition that began not long after Spain sold Florida to the young United States in 1819 and Key West was settled in 1820. The first mentions of the Keys in American literature involve piracy (see Voyer), beginning in 1822, when *The Narrative of the Capture, Sufferings, and Escape of Captain Barnabas Lincoln and His Crew* was published, recounting the trials of men taken by Mexican pirates off Key Largo. In 1825, we have *Narrative of the Shipwreck of the Brig Betsy and the Murder of Five of her Crew by Pirates* by Daniel Collins. The *Betsy's* crew, shipwrecked on an uninhabited mangrove island, was captured by fishermen and sold to pirates. The 1830s bring the first mention of Key West in literature, "Death of a Pirate," from John James Audubon's *Ornithological Biography* (G. Murphy 27–31). The pirates in these nineteenth-century narratives of maritime misdeeds have since become real estate developers, environmental rapists, anti-Castro militants, and drug dealers, but the literary tradition they began continues today in the vibrant crime fiction characterizing not only the Florida Keys, but also South Florida. Contemporary writers such as John D. MacDonald, Carl Hiaasen, Thomas McGuane, John Leslie, and James Hall were alike hardboiled in the steaming waters of the Gulf of Mexico. They are also the descendants of Ernest Hemingway, himself the principal literary scion of Key West's piratical heritage.

In *To Have and Have Not*, with a style that would powerfully influence his successors, Hemingway combined the tough-guy hero and wisecracking dialogue of Dashiell Hammett's *The Maltese Falcon* (1930) with the literary naturalism of Jack London's *The Sea Wolf* (1904) for a graphic look at Depression-era piracy in the Keys. As we begin to explore Hemingway's indebtedness to the pirate tradition, it is important to establish that first and foremost his crime writing is harshly realistic. Hemingway, like the maritime historian David Cordingly, understood that actual piracy was not a subject for romance:

Pirates were not maritime versions of Robin Hood and his Merry Men. Piracy, like rape, depended on the use of force or the threat of force, and pirate attacks were frequently accompanied by extreme violence, torture, and death. . . . Seamen who resisted a pirate attack were hacked to death and thrown over the side. The typical plunder was not chests full of doubloons and pieces of eight, but a few bales of silk and cotton, some barrels of tobacco, an anchor cable, some spare sails, the carpenter's tools, and half a dozen black slaves. (Cordingly xiv)

Extreme violence, torture, and death are fundamental in *To Have and Have Not*. Consider: "It was a close-up picture of the head and chest of a nigger with his throat cut clear across from ear to ear and then stitched up neat and a card on his chest saying in Spanish: 'This is what we do to Lenguas largas'" (39). Or "I took him by the throat with both hands and that Mr. Sing would flop just like a fish, true. . . . But I got him forward onto his knees and had both thumbs well in behind his talk-box, and I bent the whole thing back until she cracked. Don't think you can't hear it crack, either" (53–54). Or "[T]hey leaned over and slid the body up and over the stern. . . . Albert turned over twice in the white, churned, bubbling back-suction of the propeller wash before sinking" (*THHN* 161). The potential rewards of this mayhem are as low as the risks are high—not galleons of Spanish treasure, but bare survival for the out-of-work fishermen of Key West and their wives and children. When the wounded Wesley moans, "Ain't a man's life worth more than a load of liquor?" (69), Harry Morgan's unspoken answer is "No."

Less obvious than the novel's realism, however, is its simultaneous in-debtedness to the romantic tradition of piracy. The immortal children's books *Treasure Island* and *Peter Pan*;[1] the swashbuckling films of Errol Flynn and Douglas Fairbanks Sr.; the illustrations of Howard Pyle and his disciple N. C. Wyeth; and even Gilbert and Sullivan's comic opera *The Pirates of Penzance* (1879) are also present in *To Have and Have Not*, along with the myths that have grown up around historic pirates including Captain William Kidd (ca. 1645–1701), Blackbeard (Edward Teach, d. 1718), and of course Sir Henry Morgan (ca. 1635–1688). Hemingway well understood the appeal of the popular genre booksellers call "men's blue-sky adventure."

In *To Have and Have Not*, a battered World War I veteran asks Richard Gordon: "Did you ever write for *Western Stories*, or *War Aces*? I could read that *War Aces* every day" (210). In spite—or perhaps because of—his experience with the cruel realities of war and its aftermath, the vet prefers escapist literature to Gordon's contrived and politically slanted brand of social realism, and we sympathize. Part of Hemingway's genius, and the source of his universality, is to craft high literature that nevertheless reaches out to the common reader with exotic locations and fast-paced storytelling. For his Key West novel, set in the historic marinescape of the Spanish Main, Hemingway chose to interweave both the reality and the romance of the pirate tradition.

Harry Morgan, the protagonist of Hemingway's *To Have and Have Not*, is the namesake of the great seventeenth-century English pirate Sir Henry Morgan. Morgan is the protagonist of histories beginning with Alexander Exquemelin's *De Americaensche Zee-Roovers*, translated into English as *The Buccaneers of America* (1684), and Captain Charles Johnson's *A General History of the Robberies and Murders of the Most Notorious Pyrates* (1724). Many romantic stories descended from these classic works feature Morgan; for example, *Howard Pyle's Book of Pirates* (1921), read by the narrator to his young son in Hemingway's "A Day's Wait" (1933). Nor was Hemingway the only twentieth-century American realist attracted to the Morgan legend. John Steinbeck's first novel was *Cup of Gold: A Life of Sir Henry Morgan, Buccaneer, with Occasional Reference to History* (1929).

Purportedly a gentlemen's son from Wales, the historic Henry Morgan made his way to the New World to join an expeditionary force against the Spanish in Hispaniola. Eventually basing himself in Port Royal, Jamaica, after England seized the island from Spain in 1655, Morgan created a small fleet manned by soldiers and sailors, deserters and runaway slaves, cutthroats and criminals (Cordingly 41). Over the course of sixteen years, he managed "to sack eighteen cities, four towns, and thirty-five villages in New Spain . . . rak[ing] in the booty" (Rediker 58). He was a brilliant seaman and tactician; his capture of Portobello against heavy odds was perhaps the most successful amphibious assault of his century (Cordingly 48), and his sacking of Panama the most notorious. Ashore, Morgan's pirates were known for rape, loot, pillage, and for torturing victims to learn where their valuables were hidden. They used friars and nuns as hostages and civilian shields, and held entire towns to ransom, threatening to burn them down if the gold and silver coin was not forthcoming.

Morgan and his men were hunted by the Spanish authorities—Morgan assumed his position as "Admiral of the Brethren of the Coast" when the preceding pirate "Admiral" was executed in Havana. When England was at war with Spain, Morgan sailed as a privateer with a letter of marque from the king legalizing his harassment of the enemy and taking of fat Spanish prizes for division among respectable investors. When England was not at war with Spain, he continued his piracy unsanctioned by the state. His career depended on England's mood with respect to Spain—at one point he was arrested and carried to London for trial as a pirate; later he was released, knighted, and made lieutenant-governor of Jamaica. There he died of the combined effects of tropical fevers, dropsy, and alcoholism in 1688, leaving behind thousands of acres of sugar plantations, and his "very well and entirely beloved wife" of twenty years, Dame Mary Elizabeth Morgan (from Morgan's will, cited in Cordingly 43). Sir Henry Morgan is arguably the most famous pirate in English history, and one aspect or another of his legend echoes in virtually every pirate story penned, filmed, or painted since his time, including *To Have and Have Not*. When Hemingway chose to name his protagonist Harry Morgan, the allusion to the pirate tradition was less than subtle.

In addition to a piratical name, Harry bears a piratical appearance. He is an amputee; only a stump of his right arm remains, the memento of a rum-running foray and a gun battle with Cuban officials of the port of Mariel. When working, he wears a hook strapped to his stump (*THHN* 115). Amputeeism is a common element in pirate literature, and has a firm basis in grim historical reality. Cordingly writes: "Wooden legs . . . were not fictional devices. . . . Pirates, like the wounded seamen who ended their days in Greenwich Hospital, were always vulnerable to serious injury when working a ship in a storm or when attacking another vessel" (8). His *Under the Black Flag* lists example after example of pirates losing arms and legs in historic skirmishes. In the seventeenth and early eighteenth centuries, the golden age of piracy, the treatment of such wounds "was often rough and ready . . . [with] the ship's carpenter the most suitable man to tackle the job" (Cordingly 8). Hemingway evokes these shipboard operations of an era before antisepsis and anesthesia when Harry says of his arm, "Me and a doctor cut it off. . . . I held still and he cut it off" (92). Because doctors are obligated by law to report gunshot wounds to the police, Harry's operation may have been clandestine and therefore primitive.

Amputeeism also belongs to the romantic tradition of piracy. We think first of J. M. Barrie's Captain Hook, whose arm Peter Pan has cut off in a duel and fed to a passing crocodile. Instead of a right hand, the captain wears an iron hook, which he uses to rip and tear his victims (68). Hook is a storybook villain, with long black curls, a dandified outfit from the era of Charles II, eyes that gleam red in anger, a holder that allows him to smoke two cigars at once, and an implacable, Ahab-like resentment against Peter Pan. "[U]ndoubtedly," writes Barrie, "the grimmest part of him was his iron claw" (69). Long John Silver, of Stevenson's *Treasure Island*, is also an amputee, an old sailor who has lost a leg in his country's service and has no pension (55):

> His left leg was cut off close by the hip, and under the left shoulder he carried a crutch, which he managed with wonderful dexterity, hopping about upon it like a bird. He was very tall and strong, with a face as big as a ham²—plain and pale, but intelligent and smiling. Indeed, he seemed in the most cheerful spirits, whistling as he moved about. (59–60)

Whereas Captain Hook's iron claw creates fear, Long John Silver's crippled state inspires pity and disarms suspicion. "I thought I knew what a buccaneer was like," Jim Hawkins recalls, "a very different creature, according to me" (60), and that is how the treacherous Silver wins a berth as cook on the *Hispaniola*. Today, however, Long John Silver, with his crutch and his parrot on his shoulder, as illustrated by N. C. Wyeth, and as played by Wallace Beery in the 1934 movie, is the epitome of what we think a buccaneer was like.

Hemingway uses this tradition to great effect in *To Have and Have Not*. Harry Morgan's missing arm, like Long John Silver's missing leg, humanizes him. Marie's sexual acceptance of her husband, in spite of his wound; her affectionate gazing at him as he lies asleep with his stump propped on a pillow; and her cutting up his meat "as for a small boy" (126) all add tenderness and vulnerability to Hemingway's pirate. Like Silver, Harry continues to be self-reliant, adapting with dignity to a physical loss that ought to be devastating to a working fisherman. We see him using his hook and his good arm to shift and lift heavy demi-johns of gasoline for the boat. Hemingway tells us that Harry performs this task "handily" (115). Harry can wisecrack about his loss. When Bee-lips pressures him to tell what happened to his arm, Harry retorts, "I didn't like the look of it so I cut it off" (92). His missing arm is the badge of his life of crime and in part responsible for Harry's fatal last voyage—"I've got no boat, no cash, I got no education. What can a one-armed man work at? All I've got is my cojones to peddle" (147). Like Long John Silver, who knocks a sailor down with his crutch and then hurls himself on the prone victim and stabs him to death (108), Harry remains a lethal opponent despite his handicap, confidently taking on four Cuban bank robbers, holding the forward grip of his Thompson gun in his hook (172). In his characterization of Silver, Stevenson claimed to be seeking "maimed strength and masterfulness . . . the idea of the maimed man ruling" (qtd. in Cordingly 6). The same terms apply to Harry Morgan.

Yet as with Captain Hook, Harry's iron claw is the grimmest part of him. We are left with this image of Harry executing a wounded Cuban bank robber: "Harry felt around on the cockpit floor until he could find the big-faced man, who lay face down, felt for his head with the hook on his bad arm, hooked it around, then put the muzzle of the gun against the head and touched the trigger. Touching the head, the gun made a noise like hitting a pumpkin with a club" (172–73). The hook, that fearsome prosthetic, dehumanizes both killer and victim in this scene, as Harry grips a man's head in his claw and executes him at point-blank range. This is no longer the stuff of pirate yarns and children's storybooks. But it is a compelling example of Hemingway's gift for simultaneously exploiting the adventure tradition and its appeal to the common reader while exposing the fundamental obscenity of actual violence.

The hook aside, it is difficult to visualize Hemingway's Harry Morgan without Humphrey Bogart getting in the way. Short, slight, and dark, the actor played a memorable Morgan in Howard Hawks's 1944 film adaptation of *To Have and Have Not*. In the actual novel, however, Harry Morgan is tall, broad-shouldered, and fair, and if he resembles an actor it would be Errol Flynn in the 1935 swashbuckler *Captain Blood*, taking box offices by storm between the publications of the first two Harry Morgan short stories ("One Trip Across" in *Cosmopolitan* [April 1934] and "The Tradesman's

Return" in *Esquire* [February 1936]).[3] As we see Harry from Marie's point of view, he exudes sexual magnetism, as a pirate hero should:

> She watched him go out of the house, tall, wide-shouldered, flat-backed, his hips narrow, moving, still, she thought, like some kind of an animal . . . and when he got in the car, she saw him blonde, with the sun-burned hair, his face with the broad Mongol cheek bones, and the narrow eyes, the nose broken at the bridge, the wide mouth and the round jaw, and getting in the car he grinned at her and she began to cry. "His goddamn face," she thought. "Every time I see his face it makes me want to cry." (128)

Marie is not the only woman excited by Harry's barbaric male beauty. Mrs. Laughton, the drunken wife of a rich tourist, exclaims: "Gee, he had a beautiful face. . . . Like a Tartar or something. . . . He looked kind of like Genghis Khan or something." "He only had one arm," her husband says, and she replies, "I didn't notice." Freddy tries to persuade her that Harry actually has a face "like a ham with a broken nose on it," and she can only say, "My, men are stupid. He's my dream man" (136–37). Harry is "in like Flynn."

Whether or not Hemingway had Errol Flynn in mind when he wrote his description of Harry Morgan, the character shares Flynn's strapping blond good looks, broken nose, and roguish sex appeal, and the novel contains a moment that evokes one of the best-known (and sexiest) scenes in *Captain Blood*—a scene possibly based on Exquemelin's oft-quoted but dubious assertion that the historic pirate Henry Morgan began his career as an indentured servant in the West Indies (Cordingly 53). The film's protagonist, the English physician Peter Blood, has been wrongfully convicted of treason for treating a wounded rebel. Blood is shipped to Port Royal, Jamaica, to serve a ten-year sentence as an indentured slave, and put up for sale in the public market where the island's rich men come to purchase labor for their plantations. The slaves undergo a humiliating physical inspection, but Blood is defiant and refuses to cooperate. This captures the sympathetic attention of a beautiful planter's daughter, Arabella Bishop, played by a radiant young Olivia de Havilland. She asks her rich uncle to buy Blood for her, stamping her feet like a spoiled child and loudly exclaiming, "But I want you to!" when her uncle refuses. She then makes a spectacle of herself by enthusiastically and publicly bidding for Blood, and finally acquires him for ten pounds. Blood, however, proudly dismisses Arabella, refusing to show gratitude for having been purchased as chattel. Insulted, she consigns him to hard labor with her uncle's other slaves.

Captain Blood echoes in *To Have and Have Not* when, just after Marie's reflection on Harry's animal magnetism, he walks into Freddy's bar. Mrs. Laughton, seeing him for the first time, might be Arabella at the slave market. "Isn't he wonderful?" the rich tourist's wife calls out. "That's what I want. Buy me that, Papa" (130). Harry ignores her entirely, asking Freddy, "Can I speak to you?" But when Mrs. Laughton, with an air of benevolent proprietorship, answers that question herself—"Certainly. Go right ahead and say anything you like"—his own proud dismissal is abrupt and vicious, "Shut up, you whore" (130). We cannot say of Harry, as Barrie wrote of Captain Hook, that "the elegance of his diction, even when he was swearing . . . showed him one of a different cast from his crew" (69). When Freddy chides Harry—"You can't call a lady a whore in a decent place like this"—he is unmoved: "A whore. Hear what she said to me?" (130). Of course, Harry has things reversed. In Mrs. Laughton's perception, he is the whore—a "have not" whose sexual favors can be purchased. He simply reverses the insult upon her, accusing her of soliciting when she is the one who expects to pay.

Both prostitution and sexual slavery have a prominent place in the reality and the romance of piracy. In the time of the historic Henry Morgan, Port Royal, Jamaica, and the island of Tortuga were notorious for "spectacular orgies of drinking, gambling, and womanizing as the buccaneers blew their money in the taverns and whorehouses" (Cordingly 48). And so, from *Captain Blood* to the recent Johnny Depp/Disney film franchise *Pirates of the Caribbean* (2003–7), there is scarcely a pirate movie without at least one spectacular pirate orgy. Historically, women on vessels captured by pirates were subject to rape or enslavement, or held for ransom. Very few actual pirate captains had wives and families, with the monogamous Sir Henry Morgan and his much-beloved wife, Mary Elizabeth, being a notable exception. Blackbeard, for example, was "married" fourteen times and is reputed to have prostituted one sixteen-year-old "wife" to his crew (Cordingly 71).

And so in the romantic tradition no pirate story is complete without a captive beauty sexually menaced by drunken louts. A late eighteenth-century melodrama, *Blackbeard, or The Captive Princess*, may have begun the theme so eagerly taken up by the pirate movies of Hemingway's time. In *The Black Pirate*, for instance, the crew draws lots for a kidnapped princess, played by Billie Dove, just as they have previously drawn lots for a pet monkey. In *Captain Blood*, Arabella Bishop is captured by French pirates, and when their captain refuses to sell her to Blood for pearls worth twenty thousand pieces of eight, the men duel for her on the beach in one of the swordfights that made Errol Flynn famous. "Now I own you as once you owned me," the victorious Blood proclaims.

To Have and Have Not spins these sexual themes not into romance, but into grim naturalism. Harry is no Captain Blood—he's a "bad-dream man" (*THHN* 137), as Freddy warns. And Mrs. Laughton is not the young Olivia de Havilland; she has "a bad complexion" and "the face and build of a lady wrestler" (129). The novel's sympathies instead lie with actual prostitutes—girls from Big Lucie's place who come into Freddy's for sandwiches and Coca-Cola, poor women being driven out of business by a government curfew and by exclusion from Key West's bars (93). They are the "have nots," fundamentally decent women (Albert tells us that "two or three of the hardest working married women in town used to be sporting women") driven to prostitution in order to survive (99). There is even the suggestion that Harry's wife, Marie, was once a prostitute—as he lies dying, he worries about how she will support herself and their daughters—"She's too old to peddle her hips *now*" (175, emphasis added). This is the feminine form of Harry's "peddling his cojones" (147), a type of courageous and necessary female outlawry. The novel reserves its contempt for several rich and beautiful princesses who are not "hard-working" but who instead prostitute themselves in marriage and in adultery for lives of moneyed ease and pleasure. Dorothy Hollis, on the yacht *Irydia IV*, could be a cruel parody of the lovely shipboard captive. "Extraordinarily pretty, with a small, very fine figure"—she is the wife of a rich and alcoholic Hollywood director, and the lover of a succession of gold-digging and alcoholic young men. While her drunken lover Eddie lies "on his back snoring," she takes luminol and masturbates (241–43).

But romantic pirate stories need a love interest, whether it is between Captain Blood and Arabella Bishop, or the Black Pirate and his princess.

And always, the pirate hero rescues the heroine. In *To Have and Have Not*, the once beautiful but now aging and coarsened former prostitute Marie Morgan is the unlikely romantic heroine, apparently rescued by Harry, who unlike the many impotent and cuckolded rich men in the novel, has the "cojones" both to protect his wife and make an honest woman of her. One of Marie's fondest memories is of Harry "smacking" a man who "[said] something" to her when they were walking in a park in Havana (258). Hemingway, however, is the realist who wrote, "if two people love one another, there can be no happy end to it" (*DIA* 122), and the "romance" of *To Have and Have Not* ends not with a young couple being joined in wedlock, but with a long-married couple being separated by death. Marie is left to express her heroism by confronting her widow's lot with courage, dignity, and the work ethic of the "have nots": "And if I live now twenty years what am I going to do? Nobody's going to tell me that and there ain't nothing now but take it every day the way it comes and just get started doing something right away" (261).

Together with the historic Captain Kidd, popularly believed to have been the son of a Presbyterian minister (Ritchie 27), the historic Sir Henry Morgan gave us the image of the pirate as a gentleman who turned to the dark side. This tradition became such a cliché of the fictional genre that by 1880 W. S. Gilbert could rely on it for the humorous conclusion of *The Pirates of Penzance*. The pirates are captured and their true identity revealed: "They are no members of the common throng. They are all noblemen who have gone wrong" (232). And so they "resume their ranks and legislative duties," taking their hereditary seats in the House of Peers (232). The Morgan story certainly exemplifies the pirate tradition's moral ambiguity. The gentleman's son turned scourge of the Caribbean, Sir Henry Morgan was a highly successful pirate and plunderer, and a highly successful planter and businessman. He was a cruel and unscrupulous murderer nearly hanged for his crimes; and a bold and audacious privateer rewarded with a knighthood and a government sinecure. Government officials and wealthy aristocrats deplored his crimes; government officials and wealthy aristocrats invested in his privateering voyages. Morgan's story begs us to ask, as so many pirate stories do, exactly who the pirates are in our society—desperate men who "live by the sword and laugh at the gallows," as pirate movie trailers would have it—or businessmen and politicians?

"Away to the cheating world go you," Gilbert's Pirate King sings to Frederic, "Where pirates all are well-to-do" (26). The cheating world of Hemingway's *To Have and Have Not* is the Key West yacht basin, a gated community of well-to-do pirates. One pirate vessel is the yacht *New Exuma II*, named for a Bahamian island that was a notorious pirate haunt in the eighteenth century (Cordingly 153). The wealthy and unmarried owner, Wallace Johnston, has "rather special" sexual pleasures, pleasures that have gotten him arrested (he is *interdit de sejour* in Paris), and that seem to involve raping boys, since he is "bored" by compliant men his own age (233). Johnston is "well known from Algiers to Biskra" (232). This is not only a zone where the wealthy sexual tourist can travel to slake any vice, but historically was the famous Barbary Coast, the cruising ground of mid-seventeenth-century Turkish pirates who terrorized the shores of the Mediterranean in oared galleys rowed by slaves. Indeed, slavery was the most lucrative aspect of this piracy, with more than forty thousand Christians captured and sold in the markets of Tunis and Algiers during this period (Kemp 58). Johnston, with his unearned fortune and Harvard master's degree, also keeps a slave masquerading as a companion—Henry Carpenter, whose trust fund has been mismanaged, and who willingly prostitutes himself to Johnston in order to continue to live a life of luxury.

Near the *New Exuma II* is an unnamed vessel, a "black, barkentine-rigged three-master" (233). She shares her black-painted hull, camouflaged to avoid easy detection at night, with a succession of pirate ships in works of fiction (Cordingly 170).[4] Her owner, a grain broker and speculator, is also an outlaw. Wanted by the Internal Revenue Bureau for tax evasion, he has been warned not to leave United States coastal waters, something that any vessel moored in Key West is ideally poised to do without detection (234). A man with "an incapacity for either remorse or pity," this well-to-do pirate tries not to worry about "the men he broke" or the exits they made, despite the novel's catalogue of their suicides by leaping from buildings, stepping in front of trains, taking it in the garage with the motor running, or using "the native tradition of the Colt or Smith and Wesson" (236, 238). Rather, he thinks of his victims as suckers, "the by-products of successful speculation" (238).

This yachtsman also has something in common with Billy Bones, the *Treasure Island* pirate who gave us that "eternal song":

Fifteen men on the dead man's chest—
Yo-ho-ho, and a bottle of rum!
Drink and the devil have done for the rest—
Yo-ho-ho, and a bottle of rum! (Stevenson 8)

As Bones has been warned by Dr. Livesey that he will die if he does not stop drinking—"The name of rum for you is death" (18)—so Hemingway's yachtsman has been warned that alcohol will kill him in a year if he does not stop drinking for at least three months (233). But the speculator calls for a Scotch and soda to hold his conscience at bay and to allay his worry about the Internal Revenue Bureau. Like the many "rummies" in this book, he is a sucker for death (238). His fortune is a dead man's chest; drink and the devil have done for him.

On board the neighboring *Alzira III*, we have "a pleasant, dull and upright family" (238).[5] The father is "a man of civic pride and many good works," but more importantly, his daughter's fiancé is "a Skull and Bones man, voted most likely to succeed, voted most popular, who still thinks more of others than of himself" (239). A secret society at Yale University for the sons of the wealthy and powerful, the still-extant Order of Skull and Bones was formed in 1832 by William Huntingdon Russell, whose family fortune came from acquiring opium in Turkey and smuggling it into China. Each year senior members "tap" fifteen juniors for initiation into the group. The roster of Skull and Bones graduates includes many famous American politicians and captains of industry—Whitney, Taft, Harriman, Weyerhauser, Rockefeller, Goodyear, Pillsbury, Kellogg, Vanderbilt, Heinz, Bush, and Kerry are among the names to be found there (see Robbins).

The allusion to piracy—Hemingway mentions Skull and Bones three times in two paragraphs—is forceful. "For more than two centuries," writes David Cordingly, "a black flag with a skull and crossbones emblazoned on it has been the symbol for pirates throughout the Western world":

[I]t appears in all the pirate stories from Walter Scott to Robert Louis Stevenson. . . . The masterful pictures in Howard Pyle's *Book of Pirates* and N. C. Wyeth's illustrations to . . . *Treasure Island* . . . helped to fix the image in people's minds. . . . W. S. Gilbert's stage directions in *The Pirates of Penzance* instruct the pirate king to unfold a black flag with a skull and crossbones. . . . The 1926 silent film *The Black Pirate* with

Douglas Fairbanks, Sr., begins and ends with a shot of the traditional pirate flag billowing in the wind. (115)

The "pleasant, dull and upright family," then, with their ties to Skull and Bones, are among the wealthy social elite who, as Gilbert's Pirate King knows, "play a sanctimonious part" (25). Hemingway asks us to do the math to discover that their piracy consists of profiteering—their wealth comes from "selling something everybody uses by the millions of bottles, which costs three cents a quart to make, for a dollar a bottle in the large (pint) size. . . . [I]t's more economical to buy the large, and if you make ten dollars a week the cost is just the same to you as if you were a millionaire" (240). This is a type of piracy Harry feels when he is forced to pay twenty-eight cents a gallon to fuel his boat at the Standard Oil dock (37).[6]

The pirates of the yacht basin are the power elite of the society that has made Harry Morgan an outlaw, and they require us to reevaluate his own piracy and the nature of his heroism. Historically, seventeenth- and early eighteenth-century pirates were seamen who had revolted against the low wages and brutal discipline of the British navy and merchant marine. Marcus Rediker writes:

> [P]iracy was deeply imbued with the collectivistic tendencies produced by life and labor at sea. Against the omnipotent authority of the merchant ship master stood the limited authority of the pirate captain and other officers, who were elected by the crew. In contrast to the hierarchical pay system of the merchant service, pirates distributed their plunder in markedly egalitarian fashion. . . . These outlaws maintained the maritime division of labor but strictly limited its tendency to function as a hierarchy of status and privilege. . . . [E]ven more revealing, pirates abolished the wage. They considered themselves risk-sharing partners rather than a collection of "hands" who sold their labor on the open market. (107)

These realities underlie the romantic tradition of the pirate as an outlaw-hero, a Robin Hood figure redistributing the ill-gotten gains of the rich. It is no coincidence that both Douglas Fairbanks and Errol Flynn played Robin Hood in addition to pirate heroes. *Captain Blood*, not surprisingly for a movie produced in the middle of the Depression, places the strongest emphasis on piracy as a form of collectivist labor and social redress. Blood's pirate crew is comprised of wrongfully deported indentured slaves who mutiny against a brutal plantation owner and seize a ship. By the end of the film, the men are restored to their full rights as British subjects, and Blood, like the original Morgan, is made governor of Jamaica.

The boundaries of the law are permeable in the pirate tradition, and both historic and fictional characters cross back and forth. Historically, pirates created their own sets of laws, sailing under articles or pirate "codes," which also feature in pirate romances such as *Captain Blood* or today's *Pirates of the Caribbean*. These codes described pirate duties such as keeping pistols and cutlasses clean, specified how plunder was to be shared among the crew, listed compensations for the loss of a limb or crippling injuries, and spelled out punishments such as death or marooning for offenses including bringing women or boys on board, and for desertion during battle (Cordingly 99–100). Pirate codes underlie the romantic pirate tradition of honor among thieves, law-abiding outlaws, and Robin Hood heroes. Hemingway's outlaw Harry Morgan fits the traditional mold. While we often think of him as a down-on-his-luck fisherman trying to feed his family, the novel tells us that he was once a member of the Miami police force. The Smith and Wesson police special Harry once used to uphold the law he now uses in the commission of his crimes (44).

At the beginning of the novel, Harry appears as a relatively law-abiding citizen. While not above smuggling liquor, he steadfastly refuses to carry "anything that can talk," even when offered the breathtaking sum of three thousand dollars to land three revolutionaries anywhere on the Keys (4). Instead, he is trying to make an honest living by chartering his boat to rich sportfishermen. His client, Mr. Johnson, a presumably wealthy man who might be one of the yacht basin pirates, is the villain of the piece, stiffing Harry for three weeks' charter and the loss of his fishing rod and tackle, for a total of $825 (27). Harry, a working man with a family to feed, is left without enough money even to buy gas for the trip home, let alone purchase a load of liquor to smuggle.

A rich man's dishonesty forces Harry to meet with Mr. Sing, another "have" who has made a fortune exploiting "have nots." Mr. Sing talks "like an Englishman" and is "dressed in a white suit with a silk shirt and black tie and one of those one-hundred-and-twenty-five-dollar Panama hats" (30).

A broker who takes money from impoverished Chinese immigrants to arrange their illegal passage to the United States, Mr. Sing clearly subscribes to the pirate dictum that "dead men tell no tales." He expects Harry to murder or maroon the immigrants and pays extra for what Harry "is supposed to do." "Big business," says Frankie, "Ship Chinamen never come back. Other Chinamen write letters say everything fine" (35). Harry murders Mr. Sing "to keep from killing twelve other chinks" (55), and although he keeps their money, he sets the immigrants back on shore in Cuba where they can indeed tell tales. Harry also decides not to kill his alcoholic friend Eddy, who has stowed away on board and witnessed the murder. Despite the risk that Eddy will talk when he's drunk and the tempting opportunity to kill Eddy while he is sleeping, Harry's decision seems basically sentimental: "[W]hen everything had come out so nice I didn't have the heart. . . . [T]here's no point in spoiling it by doing something you'd be sorry for afterwards" (65). Harry even pays Eddy the four dollars a day owed to him for his work on Mr. Johnson's fishing charter. Squarely in the romantic tradition of piracy, Harry in this episode appears as the compassionate outlaw-hero, robbing from the rich to give to the poor.

In Harry's next adventure, both he and his black accomplice, Wesley, badly wounded, are endeavoring to return to Key West with a load of smuggled liquor and a boat shot up by Cuban customs. The novel mitigates their crime, which seems trivial given that Prohibition is over and the purchase and sale of liquor is legal in the United States (70). The purpose of the bootlegging, no longer especially lucrative, is simply to avoid paying import duties and federal taxes. Harry has returned to smuggling only because "the depression had put charter fishing on the bum" (85). As with Eddy, Harry cares for Wesley, bandaging the black man's wound (Wesley does the same for him), keeping him warm, promising to get him to a doctor, and ignoring Wesley's babbling despite the urge to hit him.

But the story pits lawbreaker against lawmaker when Harry is spotted dumping liquor in the mangroves by wealthy sportfishermen aboard Captain Willie's charter boat, the *South Florida*. White-flannelled and cloth-hatted men of "civic pride and good works" (239), they are federal officials: the arrogant Frederick Harrison, who proclaims himself "one of the three most important men in the United States today," and his secretary, Willis (80). The Skull and Bones type of pirate, they are the men responsible for low government wages, rigging food prices, and planning to beautify the "stinking jerkwater little town" of Key West into a tourist spot (81, 84, 80). They want to take Harry into custody, and Harry ultimately will lose the boat that is his livelihood and independence when they report its number to the authorities. Once again *To Have and Have Not* asks us to question who the real pirates are in our society—certainly not the working fishermen of Key West, who keep solidarity with one another. "Most everybody goes in boats calls each other brother," Captain Willie tells his rich passengers, even as he warns Harry and takes Harrison and his secretary back out to sea. Like the historic Morgan's men, the island's fishermen consider themselves "Brethren of the Coast."

"Through the ages," Rediker writes, "sailors have built an extraordinary tradition of labor militancy" (205), a tradition that underlies the coming-together of mutineers and deserters to sail for themselves as pirates. "Let's stand by one another and take care of ourselves," a pirate captain might proclaim in recruiting a crew from the wage slavery, debt peonage, and brutal physical discipline of the early eighteenth-century merchant marine and navy (244). To a degree, labor militancy underlies Harry's piracy: "But let me tell you, my kids ain't going to have their bellies hurt and I ain't going to dig sewers for the government for less money than will feed them. . . . I don't know who made the laws but I know there ain't no law that you got to go hungry" (96).

"You talk like a radical," says Albert, and indeed this speech is part of Harry's attempt to recruit him to the pirate life. The system of labor has betrayed men like Albert, and ended their obligation to the law, or so Harry argues. "You got three kids in school that are hungry at noon," he reminds Albert. "You got a family that their bellies hurt and I give you a chance to make a little money" (95). "You always worked, didn't you?" Harry asks persuasively, "You never asked anybody for charity" (96). When Albert asks Harry why "there ain't any work at living wages anywhere," Harry targets corrupt government officials working a real estate scheme on the backs of the poor:

> "What they're trying to do is starve you Conchs out of here so they can burn down the shacks and put up apartments and make this a tourist town. . . . I hear they're buying up lots, and then after the poor people

are starved out and gone somewhere else to starve some more they're going to come in and make it into a beauty spot for tourists." (96)

But although the pirates of the golden age have their historic origins in the cauldron of labor unrest, it's important to realize that they were not oceangoing versions of Joe Hill or Tom Joad. Bold and decisive professional seafarers, pirates of the seventeenth and eighteenth centuries were tough and ruthless men seeking not social reform, but plunder and an independent life, free from the brutal authority of the navy or the crushing exploitation of the merchant marine (Cordingly 12). Harry's equally piratical goal is simply to feed his family without becoming a wage slave to the malignant systems of government and big business that have driven him to crime. If Harry is truly piratical, then we must ask whether *To Have and Have Not* actually is, as so many critics have argued, botched "Left-Wing propaganda" (Cyril Connolly); an unconvincing "free translation of Marx and Engel's 'Workers of the world unite'" (Malcolm Cowley); a failure to grasp "the social theme as involving the class structure of society" (Delmore Schwartz) (Meyers, *Critical Heritage* 228, 235, 255). These interpretations hinge on misreading Harry's dying words—"No matter how a man alone ain't got no bloody fucking chance" (225)—as a "stutter of faith in the collective idea," as Philip Rahv put it (Meyers, *Critical Heritage* 242).

To Have and Have Not, with its yacht basin pirates, Skull and Bones men, and corrupt government officials, is undoubtedly a ringing indictment of capitalism and its excesses. But, as Harry's final, fatal voyage attests, the novel is also a ringing indictment of communism's revolutionary zeal and pious brutality. Harry encounters four left-wing avatars of class struggle and the collective idea when he agrees to provide a getaway for Cuban revolutionaries robbing a bank in Key West.[7] The novel's previous villains—Mr. Sing, Frederick Harrison, Wallace Johnston—pale by comparison. Gilbert's Pirate King sings of how those who seek to acquire and hold political power "manage somehow to get through / More dirty work than ever I do" (29), and so it is with Harry and the bank-robbing revolutionaries. Like so many characters in *To Have and Have Not* before them, Hemingway's revolutionaries continue the romantic tradition of exposing other elements of society as more black-hearted and bloodthirsty than the pirate himself. But there is nothing romantic about what happens next.

To Have and Have Not unmasks the soulless violence that can exist at the heart of social conflict. Needing an extra hand for the trip, Harry tricks his naïve friend Albert into joining him by saying that he has a fishing charter (145). Things go wrong from the start when one of the Cubans, a cold-blooded killer named Roberto, murders Albert at point-blank range with a submachine-gun burst. Albert's only crime has been to hesitate in casting off the lines. If Harry, himself a more discriminating killer, subscribes to the morality Hemingway espouses in *Death in the Afternoon*—"So far, about morals, I only know that . . . what is immoral is what you feel bad after" (*DIA* 4)—then this time he is squarely in the wrong: "Standing, he looked down at Albert and he felt sick inside. The poor hungry bastard, he thought" (160). And, when they heave the body overboard, he thinks, "It made me feel bad to dump him like that" (164). Another robber, an idealistic and but dangerously zealous boy named Emilio, tries to apologize for the killing. "You see," he says to Harry, "This man Roberto is bad. He is a good revolutionary but a bad man. He kills so much in the time of Machado he gets to like it. He thinks it is funny to kill. He kills in a good cause, of course. The best cause" (157–58). Emilio naively believes that after the revolution, things will be different—"We just raise money now for the fight" (166).

Given the violent labor unrest and growing socialist and communist movements in the United States during the 1930s, the Cuban example in *To Have and Have Not* is more threatening than exotic, something for Americans to ponder, especially given the presence of potentially violent groups like the disaffected World War I veterans in this text—"We are the desperate ones. The ones with nothing to lose. We are the completely brutalized ones" (206).[8] While sick about Albert and planning how to retake the boat from the armed bank robbers, Harry listens to Emilio with manufactured and treacherous sympathy—"I guess you've got a good program if you're out to help the working man," he says. "I was out on strike plenty times in the old days when we had the cigar factories in Key West" (166). The boy describes the goals of the revolution in a series of clichés: "We want to do away with all the old politicians, with all the American imperialism that strangles us, and with the tyranny of the army. We want to start clean and give every man a chance. We want to end the slavery of the *guajiros*, you know, the peasants, and divide the big sugar estates among the people that work them" (166). Emilio regrets the necessity for the "present phase" of the revolution very much. He hates "terrorism," and feels very bad about "the methods for raising the necessary money" (167).

Emilio's cause, opposing a "murderous tyranny" that "suck[s] the blood from the nation" (167) is just—but Harry understands and *To Have and Have Not* underscores the lethal hypocrisy of revolutionary violence that only perpetuates "murderous tyranny" in a new guise. Unlike the idealistic "little boy," the cynical and world-weary Harry does not believe that the end will be "worth the means" (169, 166). Harry, like his creator, Ernest Hemingway, is too familiar with the real consequences of violence to believe that a revolution will benefit the "workers of the world." "F— his revolution," Harry thinks:

> To help the working man he robs a bank and kills a fellow works with him and then kills that poor damned Albert that never did any harm. That's a working man he kills. He never thinks of that. With a family. . . . The hell with their revolutions. All I got to do is make a living for my family and I can't do that. Then he tells me about his revolution. To hell with his revolution. (168)

This does not sound like a political conversion in the making, convincing or otherwise.

To Have and Have Not ends in brutal and graphically described violence, as Harry, in an effort to thwart his own murder and the hijacking of Freddy's boat, guns down the four revolutionaries and is himself fatally gut-shot in the process.[9] As he lies dying, Harry does not think about politics or collectivist organization; he thinks about how his widow will support herself, and about where he went wrong, in the practical rather than moral sense. Piracy, to Harry, is simply a dangerous business, "like trying to pass cars on the top[s] of hills," okay for a while with luck, but certain to end in disaster eventually (225). "I guess I should have got a job in a filling station or something," he thinks. "I should have quit trying to go in boats. There's no honest money going in boats anymore" (174). In his own eyes, his mistake was wanting to continue the proud tradition of independence and self-reliance inherent in owning his own boat and in making a living on the sea with the strength of his body and the quickness of his mind. "I guess what a man like me ought to do is run a filling station," Harry thinks, and then, realistically,

"Hell, I couldn't run no filling station" (174–75). He is not cut out for a life spent serving customers and tending a cash register. So when Harry says, "No matter how a man alone ain't got no bloody fucking chance," his final statement is not a call for organized labor or collectivism, but rather a comment on the predicament of the individual—and even manhood itself—in a modern world that crushes independence, self-reliance, and productive labor in favor of incorporation, service, and speculation. "Better far to live and die / Under the brave black flag I fly," sings Gilbert's Pirate King, "Than to play a sanctimonious part, / With a pirate head and a pirate heart." Despite the efforts of so many critics to make out a sanctimonious part for Harry in his dying words, he is true to the song he sings, and lives and dies a Pirate King.

Notes

1. Other possible literary influences, not explored here, are Lord Byron's "The Corsair," Sir Walter Scott's *The Pirate*, and Captain Marryat's novel of the same name.

2. Harry, too, has "a face like a ham with a broken nose on it," at least according to Freddy (*THHN* 137).

3. According to Michael Reynolds's *Hemingway's Reading*, the author's Key West library included a novel by Rafael Sabatini, *St. Martin's Summer*, but did not include *Captain Blood* (item 1826, 178). Michael Curtiz, who directed the film adaptation of *Captain Blood*, would also direct *The Breaking Point*, a 1950 adaptation of *To Have and Have Not* (G. Phillips, *Hemingway and Film* 59). Errol Flynn was nominated for an Academy Award for his performance as Mike Campbell in the 1957 film version of *The Sun Also Rises*, and Hemingway wisecracked, "Any picture in which Flynn is the best actor is its own worst enemy" (qtd. in G. Phillips, *Hemingway and Film* 131).

4. In addition to her black hull, the yacht's barkentine rig—a combination of square sails and fore-and-aft rigged sails—is also piratical, designed for fast sailing both before and along the wind with a minimal crew. The barkentine rig was favored by American slave-runners as well.

5. *Alzira III* is named for Alzira Boehm, third wife of Hemingway's good friend, the artist Waldo Peirce. The couple visited Hemingway in Key West. My thanks to Dr. William Gallagher for pointing out this inside joke. See his excellent article on the Peirce-Hemingway friendship.

6. Harry's unhappy confrontation with Standard Oil prices would be pregnant with meaning for contemporary readers. The founder of the Standard Oil Company, John D. Rockefeller (1839–1937), was one of the great robber barons of American history. From the 1870s onward, Standard Oil used every conceivable type of monopolistic practice (including sending in gangs of thugs to intimidate competitors) to control prices and gouge customers. At the time of his death in 1937, the year *To Have and Have Not* was published, Rockefeller

was perhaps the most loathed man in America, with personal assets worth $1 billion at the height of the Great Depression. One of Rockefeller's fellow robber barons, the Standard Oil partner Henry M. Flagler (1830–1913), would use his personal fortune to develop the entire east coast of Florida as well as the Keys by building railroads and tourist hotels. His actions created a real estate bubble that claimed the life savings of many Americans—including Hemingway's own father—when it burst (Reynolds, *Homecoming* 199–201). The Flagler railroad to Key West was destroyed during the 1935 hurricane, further deepening the Depression for islanders. For the Flagler story, see Standiford and Wilkinson.

7. The revolutionaries are certainly piratical—they strike from the sea, rob and pillage on shore, and escape across the water and its international boundaries. But they are more accurately described as terrorists; their violence is for a cause, a political end that in their minds justifies any means. This type of politicized piracy is a growing twenty-first-century problem, with stateless terrorists using the sea to deliver weapons, launch attacks, and sell both legitimate and stolen cargo for funding. For instance, analysts believe that Osama bin Laden controls as many as twenty aging freighters (Langewische 39).

8. "What's the next move? They've got to get rid of us. You can see that, can't you?" asks a tall vet (*THHN* 205). The novel is clearly set before the 1935 Labor Day Hurricane, when nearly three hundred vets living in a labor camp would die due to government negligence—or deliberate policy—delaying their evacuation from a low-lying key in the track of the storm. Hemingway wrote about the hurricane in "Who Murdered the Vets?" (see Trogdon 168–71).

9. John James Audubon's "Death of a Pirate" is surprisingly similar. The story was told to Audubon by a seaman and bird-hunter who, when hunting in the mangrove keys, once came across a dying pirate and the mangled corpses of two of his victims, members of a rival gang. "His dress plainly disclosed his occupation," Audubon's narrator recalls, "a large pistol he had thrust into his bosom, a naked cutlass lay near him on the ground, a red silk handkerchief was bound over his projecting brows, and over a pair of loose trousers he wore fishermen's boots" (G. Murphy 29). Like the Coast Guard men who nurse Harry Morgan, wiping his face with water and dabbing his bloody lips, Audubon's narrator also nurses the pirate, bathing his wounds, and listening to his dying words, "as his breath struggled through the mass of blood that seemed to fill his throat" (Murphy 29). "Friend," the pirate says, "I am an outlaw. I have been for many years a Pirate. . . . The instructions of my parents were of no avail to me, for I have always believed that I was born to be a most cruel man. . . . I have no objection to die—I am glad that the villains who wounded me were not my conquerors—I want no pardon from *any one*—Give me some water, and let me die alone" (Murphy 29). Harry, too, is unconquered by the villains who wounded him. He, too, neither repents nor confesses; he, too, seeks no pardon, and asks for nothing but water. And he, too, emphasizes his aloneness.

Tropical Iceberg

Cuban Turmoil in the 1930s and
Hemingway's *To Have and Have Not*

STEVE PAUL

To Have and Have Not is the only novel Ernest Hemingway published in his lifetime that he set on American soil. Significantly, however, he explores the state of his native land through an extended contrast to a much different life on the island of Cuba. There Hemingway's characters are buffeted by violent political upheaval, while at home they are ravaged by bleak economic change. The novel is a dark work, informed by a dark world, and it provides clues to Hemingway's thinking about the revolutionary impulses that spread around the globe in the 1920s and 1930s. Hemingway clearly was wrestling with the value of rebellion and the geopolitical influence of the United States, and in doing so he seems to be coming to terms with revolution and repression. His success is debatable, but Hemingway's struggle is there, both directly and indirectly.

To fully understand its content and context, a reader needs to know more than Hemingway delivers in the novel. Biographers and commentators have reliably painted the general backdrop for *To Have and Have Not* as, in part, a picture of a "lost dream, the death of the Cuban revolution that began so idealistically, and the rise of oppressing army control" (Reynolds, *The 1930s* 233). Not surprisingly then, several details of the Cuban political chaos of the early 1930s relate to the storylines and themes of *To Have and Have Not*. While bits of evidence can be unearthed easily from the novel as published, much of it also exists in manuscript versions. Those include a projected part 4 and other sections omitted from the final work. For a full sense of Cuban rebellion as a relevant impetus for *To Have and Have Not*, we must examine some of those unpublished manuscript pages, which are located at the Hemingway Collection in the John F. Kennedy Library and Museum in Boston.

In May 1933, Hemingway spent three weeks in Cuba with the photographer Walker Evans. Years later, Hemingway wrote, "We were both working against Machado at the time" (qtd. in Mellow 180). Yet the statement presents a problem. Written in 1952, nearly twenty years after the Hemingway-Evans experience in Cuba, Hemingway's comment came at a time when many people might well have believed that the famous writer had been involved in something so apparently political, so brave and overtly aggressive. This was, after all, the Hemingway who had campaigned for the Republican side during the Spanish Civil War in the documentary film *The Spanish Earth* (1937) and who lamented Franco's inevitable fascist victory in *For Whom the Bell Tolls* (1940). It was the Hemingway who armed and outfitted his boat, the *Pilar*, to hunt German submarines in the waters off Cuba during World War II. Yet it was a rare admission by Hemingway about his political activities in Cuba, and it has never been made clear what he meant. What was Hemingway's work against the Cuban dictator? Had he run guns, rum, and refugees in his friend Josie Russell's boat? People prone to biographical readings of Hemingway's novels might take away that notion from *To Have and Have Not*, but, as with the other writings, it would not be wise.

Perhaps the more relevant question might be whether Hemingway's work against Cuban president Gerardo Machado was done in the literary trenches. It is also difficult to make that case. For one thing, Hemingway wrote his first short story about Cuban chaos in the early fall of 1933, some five months after his sojourn with Evans and two months after Machado toppled from power and fled the island. Published in *Cosmopolitan* as "One Trip Across," the short story later became part 1 of *To Have and Have Not*. Mellow agrees that Hemingway's characterization "was something of an exaggeration; both may have been sympathetic to the rebels who were opposing the entrenched Machadistas, but there is no evidence that Hemingway and certainly none that Evans, were actively engaged in toppling the regime, other than artistically" (180–81). More likely Hemingway meant that he and Evans were working *despite* rather than *against* Machado. Despite the dangers in a time of rebellion and revenge, each gathered material that he turned into art. Hemingway could very well have argued that by exposing Cuba's violent upheaval in "One Trip Across," he shone a light on the Machado species and tyranny everywhere. In the tradition of great literature, of course, he could have seen himself tapping a universal theme good for all time. "A thousand years makes economics silly," he wrote, "and a work of art endures forever" (*GHOA* 109). All revolutions are suspect anyway. Hemingway "disliked political systems at least as much as their practitioners," Scott Donaldson asserts (*By Force of Will* 94). Whatever the country, whatever the turmoil, Hemingway invented his own political stance, which more often than not was antipolitical.

Hemingway's relationship with Cuba began in 1928, when he first set foot in Havana. He and his new wife, Pauline, were returning from Paris to the United States, and their brief stop at the crescent island on the way to Key West made an impression. Only ninety miles from the Keys, Cuba soon became a frequent destination as Hemingway pursued the sport of deep-sea fishing.

Spring fishing trips and long stays in Havana in 1932 and 1933 gave Hemingway an opportunity to witness the effects of rebel bombing campaigns and Machado's ruthless repression. Contemporary news accounts painted the picture: "The secret police and *porra*, or strong-arm squads, have orders to break up any open meeting or seize anyone acting suspiciously. Homes and offices are invaded, suspects are sent to prison by military courts or held incommunicado in military fortresses without trial" ("Cuba's 'New Deal'"). The Spanish *ley de fuga* (law of flight) had been revived, according to most contemporary reports. That meant countless students and political prisoners were being "found in the streets shot to death after being beaten and tortured" ("Cuba's 'New Deal'").

Against this backdrop of violence, Hemingway had asked his editor, Maxwell Perkins, to provide an official letter stating that he was working on a book about fishing the Gulf Stream. "In case of getting into a jam in Cuba (know a few too many people there). . . . In a time of revolution it might keep me from getting shot and it would most certainly help me with the book. I wish you could get something from the State

Department stating the same thing" (*OTTC* 184–85). As Hemingway understood, Cuba may have been liberated from Spain, but its overriding dependence on the United States, codified in the Platt Amendment, was painfully clear:

> During the first thirty years or so of independence from Spain, Cuba, led by ex-soldiers of the war of 1895–8, had failed to create a credible political system. Partly the fault lay in old Spanish habits of corruption and desire for personal gain. But blame lay also with the United States, which with a dominant economic position did not see the evils of an ambiguous political one. Thus several times American action or threat of action prevented the seizure or the legitimate capture of power by the Liberal Party, which, for all its evident faults, under Jose Miguel Gomez was a genuine popular movement; finally, when the Liberals gained power in 1925, Jose Miguel was dead, and his successor Gerardo Machado was unable to resist the blandishments of autocracy and, ultimately, tyranny. This tyranny was underwritten by the United States in the 1920s in the interests of a quiet life and business confidence, but the attraction of American power was too great for Cubans, so that by 1933 it was Washington rather than Havana which, again as in the 1890s, held the key to Cuba. (Thomas 364–65)

In 1933, Cuba's economy was reeling. The United States had been the island's largest customer for sugar. Now the States imported more sugar from Hawaii and the Philippines. Cuban exports had fallen by 90 percent ("Cuba's 'New Deal'"). Prices fell, and Cuban growers were losing money. Unemployment was rampant. Machado's grip on the island had tightened since 1928. Elected president to one term, he seized a second and refused to let go. A revolt led by former president Menocal failed in 1931. The next year, Machado reneged on a reform agreement and imposed martial law. Terrorism against his reign increased.

In May 1933, as Evans and Hemingway walked the simmering streets of Havana, Franklin D. Roosevelt sent Sumner Welles, an assistant secretary of state, to Cuba to broker a resolution. Welles's mission, at least briefly, seemed to be an ingenious balancing act: "To Machado, Welles promised a new commercial treaty to relieve economic distress if he reached a political settlement with the opposition. To opposition leaders, Welles promised a change of government and participation in the subsequent administration if they joined the mediations and supported an orderly transfer of power" (Perez 260). Welles's negotiations with Machado grew increasingly rancorous over the next several weeks, and the Cuban president warned he would repel any American military intervention. A bus drivers' strike snowballed into a paralyzing general work stoppage in August, and violence erupted in the streets (Perez 262).

The potential for American intervention in Cuba remained as much of a fuse for political unhappiness as Machado's iron hand. After Machado fell on 12 August 1933, debate over the United States' role continued in both countries. Cuban students and intellectuals increasingly focused on the overwhelming influence of American economic interests. "Eighty per cent of the sugar industry belongs to citizens of the United States; the remainder is controlled chiefly by American creditors," one journalist reported. This was equally true for tobacco, and American capital also controlled the "banks, railroads, street car lines, electric plants, telephone systems and other public utilities" ("Sugar, the Great White Specter"). The United States may very well have entered an economic depression, but its corporate leaders still knew how to make money. And the Cubans were well aware of what that meant to them. The student uprising, according to a reporter on the scene, was "bent upon re-conquering the independence of Cuba in the spirit of the Cuban poet-martyr, Jose Martí, who prophesied that after independence the war for liberty would be fought." And for some, America was not the only problem. Opposition leaders proposed an economic plan designed to "protect the people from future Machados" (Porter, "Cuba Libre" 2).

The opposition was not single-minded or united. The factions that sprang up amid whispered meetings and public rallies are dizzying: radicalism meant communism to some, fascism to others, Spanish-style socialism to yet others. Moderates believed in peaceful revolution. Racism simmered below the surface. The student-led organization known as ABC counted some four thousand to five thousand members ("Cuba's 'New Deal'"), alternately identified as middle-class reformists and right-leaning fascists. The propulsion toward reform became more complicated after Machado, as military and civil influences sought a viable equilibrium. "Under the impact of all these conflicting ideas Cuba no doubt is in for a long period of confusion and unsettled political conditions," the journalist Russell Porter wrote ("Cuba Libre" 16).

Hemingway did not try to represent the variety of political opinions in Cuba, certainly not the moderates. He gave voice to at least one slice of radical leftist opposition in part 3 of *To Have and Have Not*:

> "We are the only true revolutionary party," the boy said. "We want to do away with all the old politicians, with all the American imperialism that strangles us, with the tyranny of the army. We want to start clean and give every man a chance. We want to end the slavery of *guajiros*, you know, the peasants, and divide the big sugar estates among the people that work them. But we are not Communists." (166)

The revolutionary's desire to give "every man a chance" anticipates, of course, the thematic lament of protagonist Harry Morgan that "a man alone ain't got no bloody fucking chance" (225). It was an echo that allowed some leftist critics of the 1930s to sense a collectivist leaning in Hemingway, even as he rejected the idea and stood up for his own independence.

Hemingway divided *To Have and Have Not* into three parts. Each has a chapter title of "Harry Morgan" and a seasonal subheading: Spring, Fall, Winter. Hemingway wrote each part at three different times, spanning more than three years of the Cuban upheaval from 1933 to late 1936. Hemingway generally obscures the historical background, and thus a detailed chronology of Cuban politics has always been difficult to discern in the fabric of the novel. It is possible, however, to lay *To Have and Have Not* against the template of history and see how Hemingway molded the news of the day to his own uses. Unpublished sections of the book, including an exploratory part 4, also reveal some clues that help to ground the novel in its Cuban context.

As Hemingway began to put the pieces together and to finish writing in the summer of 1936, he described to Maxwell Perkins his plan for knitting a narrative involving Key West and Cuba: "The book contrasts the two places—and shows their inter-relation—also contains what I know about the mechanics of revolution and what it does to the people engaged in it" (*SL* 448). Chronologically, *To Have and Have Not* begins under the shadow of Machado in 1933 and continues past his reign, especially in part 3. In that time of coup and chaos, Cubans witnessed a leadership succession of no fewer than seven presidents. Pulling the strings was military strong-man Fulgencio Batista, a mixed-race Cuban whose parents worked on a sugar plantation. Batista emerged from the so-called "Sergeant's Revolt" of September 1933, which followed Machado's departure. Although at first aligned with factions of the ABC, Batista consolidated his power by ousting Machado-era officers and building a new military order. In January 1934, Batista ended the short-lived provisional presidency of Ramon Grau y San Martín and built a new government around Carlos Mendieta, which the United States quickly recognized (Perez 275).

Those who favored a civil society saw Batista's military control as a be-trayal of the true revolution and contrary to the ideals of a democratic government. Perez writes: "As the civilians continued to advance on their 'march to create a new Cuba,' the army became an increasingly reluctant escort" (273). Just as Machado's dictatorship looms over part 1 of *To Have and Have Not*, Batista is the unspoken heavy of part 3. One might specu-late whether Hemingway imagined himself "working against" Batista as he wrote the book in 1936 and early 1937. Though perhaps Hemingway felt constrained to say so when he made his remark about "working against Machado," perhaps he really intended to say "Batista" but did not. After all, at the time he wrote that letter, in 1952, Batista was on the verge of seiz-ing control again in a coup that ended Cuba's constitutional government. According to Walter Houk, who was on the staff of the American embassy at the time, Hemingway knew better than to commit his political opinions of Cuba to paper, or to voice them in public (interview).

To Have and Have Not begins with intrigue and gunfire as Harry Morgan unwillingly becomes exposed to the Cuban violence of 1933. Morgan re-buffs a revolutionary's plea to transport three men to the States—not even for $1,000 each. Such action involves too much risk if he is caught, Harry concludes. "I don't care who is President here," he tells the man named Pancho. "But I don't carry anything to the States that can talk" (4). And Harry asserts a fearless disregard for the cause: "I'm sure you've cut plenty people's throats. I haven't even had my coffee yet" (5). (Throat-cutting was well known, having been documented in photographs circulated in Havana, which suggested how the ABC dealt with informers.) Soon the three men leave the café and are gunned down in a burst of violence. Harry witnesses the scene in close detail even as he hops over the bar for safety. The revolution and the countervailing oppression thus touch Harry, and, whether he knows it or not, those forces implant their cruel dynamics, which play out during the course of the novel.

Harry is then betrayed by his bumbling American fishing customer, Mr. Johnson. Johnson can be seen as the ugly American, symbolic of the arrogant capitalists whose shadow looms uncertainly in the background of the Cuban violence and whom Hemingway returns to skewer in the yachts of a Key West marina in the last section of the novel. Johnson fishes and flees, leaving town and owing Harry hundreds of dollars. Yet Harry deflects his revenge. He agrees to carry a group of Chinese aliens away from Cuba, but instead he pockets the cash and concocts a fiendish betrayal as he kills the leader of the Chinese group and deposits the rest on a Cuban beach. In Hemingway's vision, men become desperate during times of revolution, and their desperation is compounded by the kind of economic imbalance that marked the world of the 1930s. "I ain't no radical," Harry says. "I'm sore. I been sore a long time" (97). His soreness is in large part economic, caused by the growing poverty around Key West. "Everybody in our town quit work to go on relief," Hemingway writes of the period in his African travelogue (*GHOA* 191). And the Key West of *To Have and Have Not* provides a constant collision of rich and poor, of those who have and those who have not, as the title implies. Thematically, Harry pays for his crime against the Chinese when, in the rum-running part 2 of *To Have and Have Not*, he loses an arm. In addition to the desperation of the Key West economy, Harry suggests he has been a victim of Cuban corruption: "Somebody didn't pay somebody so we got the shooting," Harry says. "That's Cubans all right" (86). One might profitably dwell on the symbolism that it was Harry's right arm that dangled useless after the shooting while his left arm remained intact. What is clear is that Harry identifies with the working man, despises the capitalist swells who are ruining Key West, but he also fears the excess of leftist revolution.

In an unpublished section of *To Have and Have Not*, Hemingway depicts the writer Richard Gordon and his wife at breakfast discussing recent events, including the death of the lawyer Simmons. Simmons, also called Bee-lips (a character loosely based upon Hemingway's Key West compatriot George Brooks) is shot by Cuban revolutionaries after they rob a Key West bank. Gordon identifies the perpetrators as "the Joven Cuba crowd," a cell of left-wing extremists of the *auténticos* faction, who were loyal to the ousted president, the intellectual Ramon Grau y San Martín. Gordon explains that the same group held up Havana's city hall and were responsible for a string of kidnappings intended to finance the revolution. "It's a wonderful story if anybody could write it," he says (item 204, folder 5, 132). Perhaps Hemingway recognized that he was indeed in the midst of writing the story and did not need Gordon's comment. Perhaps also Gordon's casual regard for the revolutionaries and their crimes—what exactly, one might ask, is wonderful about the story?—would have only confused Hemingway's depiction of him as a shallow, ineffective writer. In any event, Hemingway omitted such specific identifiers of the revolutionaries, and portrayed them mainly by their actions and their words.

But who were they, and where do they fit in the storyline of the novel? Joven Cuba (Young Cuba) formed as a clandestine organization in January 1934 expressly to fight the Batista-Mendieta government. The group was led by Antonio Guiteras, a minister under Grau (Perez 276). Joven Cuba is not mentioned by name in the published version of *To Have and Have Not*, but the bank robbery and its aftermath occur in part 3. At least one of the bank robbers who confront Harry Morgan is clearly a teenager, a boy, which suggests his revolutionary affiliation as Joven Cuba.

The city hall robbery Richard Gordon refers to occurred in Havana on 18 October 1934. Four Cubans toting machine guns held up a cashier and made off with $157,000 in American currency, bundled in a flour sack. "It is believed the robbers may have been radicals," the dispatch reported, "intent on getting funds for the purchase of arms, ammunition and explosives for the terrorist campaign they have been waging for several months" ("Havana City Hall Robbed"). The news of the crime echoes Gordon's assessment and suggests that Hemingway was keeping track. Hemingway was known to read the *Times* and other New York newspapers regularly (McIver, *Hemingway's Key West* 13), and Toni D. Knott reports that his Cuban typist supplied him with Cuban newspaper stories (*One Man Alone* 228). In fact, Hemingway was in Havana at the time of the holdup, breaking in his new boat, the *Pilar*, and working on *Green Hills of Africa*, so his knowledge of the holdup likely was gained with some immediacy. By December 1934, while Hemingway was back in Key West, rumors of an all-out revolt were rampant in Cuba, and Batista warned against it. In another unpublished section of *To Have and Have Not*, a character prepares for a revolution expected in March (item 204, folder 7, 210). On 9 March 1935, the Batista-backed President Carlos Mendieta declared a state of siege in the midst of a bombing campaign by rebels and a looming general strike. At least one Joven Cuba leader was arrested during the weekend violence (J. Phillips, "Havana Swept by Gun Fire"). Batista's power over the island tightened, and he quickly quashed the strike. From his exile in Miami, Grau, the first post-Machado president and acknowledged leader of the *auténticos*, declared that revolution against the military regime was inevitable ("Grau Says Revolt in Cuba Is Certain"). In May, Batista's army killed Grau's surrogate in Cuba, Antonio Guiteras (Perez 276).

As for kidnappings, Joven Cuba members were suspected in the abduction in June 1935 of Antonio San Miguel, president of the Guantanamo & Western Railway. The kidnappers released the seventy-eight-year-old man three days later after failing to secure their ransom demand of $286,000 (J. Phillips, "Kidnappers Free Wealthy Cuban"). Seven Joven Cuban members eventually were sentenced to death in the case ("Cuba Dooms Kidnapper").

In January 1936, Hemingway, reading the newspapers in Key West, surely would have noticed that the Cuban army gunned down suspected kidnappers of Paulino Gorostiza Jr., son of a manufacturer. Batista himself reportedly headed the manhunt that led to the fatal gun battle and arrests of eight other suspected abductors ("Cuban Force Slays 3 in Kidnap Chase"). As late as November 1936, while Hemingway was well into the writing of *To Have and Have Not*, the Cuban military was hunting down members of Joven Cuba after learning of a plot to assassinate the chief of the National Police ("5 More Cubans Held in an Alleged Plot").

It is likely that Hemingway saw the action of part 3 as unfolding in 1935, rather than in 1936 as he was writing it. Richard Gordon, in the unpublished breakfast conversation, says the kidnapping had occurred "all this last year," and we would understand that as some period after October 1934, the time of the city hall heist. An omitted chapter clearly is set before the failed revolution of March 1935. Close readers of the novel also know that Hemingway's timeline for part 3 precedes the devastating Matecumbe hurricane of Labor Day 1935 because a bar scene includes reveling veterans who likely would have perished in the storm—or, at least if they survived the hurricane, would have mentioned it in passing (*THHN* 200).

Despite the continued cycle of armed struggle and repression, by December 1936, when Hemingway was completing the novel, a "Pax Batistiana" (Perez 277) had settled over Cuba. The sugar economy was rebounding. Daily life in Havana was calmer, and tourists were returning in greater numbers (Porter, "Batista's Army" 6). Hemingway wrote to Maxwell Perkins from Key West that a recent trip to Cuba had yielded what he needed "and am back here now to not move until the book is done" (*SL* 455).

By that point, Harry Morgan's feelings about the revolution had evolved from disinterest in part 1, written three years earlier, to something more like disgust in part 3. Harry's emotions emerge violently on the boat with the bank-robbing Joven Cuba leftists. They have forced him, after the holdup and shooting, to pilot them home from Key West. As the boat makes its way across the water, one of the Cubans fatally shoots Harry's mate, Albert. Harry's anger rises toward revenge: "They all double cross each other," he says of the Cubans. "They get what they deserve. The hell with their revolutions" (168). Harry is particularly offended that these supposed forces of the people would kill a working man like Albert. Yet Hemingway gives a sympathetic voice to one of the revolutionaries. In conversation with Harry, the Cuban boy argues that their backs are to the wall: "I hate terrorism. I also feel very badly about the methods for raising the necessary money. . . . But there is no choice. There is an absolutely murderous tyranny that extends over every little village in the country." Under Machado, the boy tells him, "we were ruled by clubs." Now, under Batista's military regime, with the army having grown to a force of twenty-five thousand, "we are ruled by rifles, pistols, machine guns, and bayonets" (167). In other words, the boy says, the ends justify the means. Harry Morgan must have felt that, too, as he gripped his Thompson gun with his good left hand and let loose.

Hemingway had told Perkins the novel would include "the story of a shipment of dynamite and all of the consequences" (*SL* 448). As it turned out, that storyline remains only on the cutting-room floor in the unpublished part 4. In this section, radicals seek the aid of a well-to-do American in Key West, asking him to take a boatload of explosives to Cuba for the March revolution. The rebel eggs the man on by suggesting that hunting tyrants—"Gómez in Venezuela, Pedroza in Cuba, Hitler, Mussolini" (item 204, folder 7, 200)—is more important, a more useful activity, than hunting and killing animals. ("Pedroza" probably was meant as a reference to Eleuterio Pedraza, who, like Batista, participated in the sergeant's revolt of 1933. Spelled correctly or not, perhaps in Hemingway's mind he was a fictional stand-in for Batista himself.)

In an encounter with the Key West sheriff, an attempt to ascertain how dangerous the mission would be, the American asks what he knows about the Cuban rebels. But in the end, as the unpublished storyline plays out, he decides against carrying the dynamite. Instead, he recommends Richard Gordon for the task.

Later in the manuscript, a narrator, an unidentified Cuban, delivers a soliloquy on the calculus of dynamite, tyranny, and revolution. It is a rambling speech and sometimes contradictory, spanning a dozen handwritten pages. Yet it is often reminiscent of the familiar narrative voice of Hemingway. In it a reader can hear Hemingway wrestling with revolution and its consequences. The narrator explains how the dynamite would be used to blow up certain bridges over the Almendares River. That would delay troops on their way to the city from Camp Columbia, Batista's lavish headquarters outside Havana. Just as the young rebel who confronts Harry "hates terrorism" and regrets the violence he and his compadres employ (167), the narrator here hates dynamite as a tool of protest. Yet, he suggests that "noise" must be made if one is trying to oust a regime, and it helps to make noise so that important Americans will know that the people are unhappy with the American-supported tyrant. Tyranny suppresses noise, he says, so dynamite becomes useful. Resorting to dynamite also means you are already defeated. "But," he continues, "if you are right you are never beaten for long. The victory grows in the soil of defeat. The bloodier the defeat the richer the soil for it to grow in." The character clearly despises the brutality under Machado, but says Batista is less interested in killing than in making money and being popular. Terrorism, he says, is hopeless, but dynamite, and the thought of taking down bridges when the revolution raises its head again, "is all I live for now" (item 204, folder 11, 416–27). Hemingway, of course, returned to the subject of dynamite and bridges in his next novel, *For Whom the Bell Tolls*. And he likely omitted this strand of the manuscript to allow the arc of *To Have and Have Not* to come to a natural resting point with the death of Harry Morgan and its more intimate echoes within Marie Morgan's debilitating grief.

Crafting a novel always involves making choices, and some of the choices Hemingway made between manuscript and published work reveal the writer's struggle to keep his persona and political identity in check. This manuscript version, for example, includes a bar scene in which characters make "Hemingway," the writer and Key West resident, a brief subject of conversation. Richard Gordon calls him a "big slob" and, in an internal monologue, reveals his envy of the more successful author. Someone asks whether Hemingway is a radical, and the bartender says he does not know. Hemingway wisely omitted all of that from the finished product. Readers of *To Have and Have Not* were left to debate Hemingway's radicalism for themselves. In chapter 24, as Harry Morgan lay dying, Hemingway takes readers on a tour of the yacht slips of Key West and satirizes the moral bankruptcy of capitalism and the arrogance of the ruling class. Yet Hemingway's portrait of revolution is also something less than admiring. In a way, despite their own nation's history, it reflects modern Americans' frequent ambivalence about the messy consequences of violent political upheaval.

Before completing *To Have and Have Not*, Hemingway expressed that ambivalence in *Green Hills of Africa* through the voice of his wife, Pauline: "All we see or hear is revolutions," she says. "I'm sick of them" (*GHOA* 192). The breakfast scene that opens the deleted part 4 in Richard Gordon's Key West kitchen includes a similar weary refrain from Gordon's wife. She says she is bored by revolution and Machado was not that bad for the Cubans anyway. She tells Richard she would rather hear about the bank robbery. "Anything but revolution," she says (item 204, folder 6, 133).

In the end, Hemingway believed, politics diminished fiction and his own political stance was beside the point. Readers are invited to sympathize more with Harry Morgan's stark and desperate independence than with the revolutionaries, whose killings and other crimes seem something less than admirable. Despite his public insistence at the Second American Writers' Congress on 4 June 1937 that living under fascism was particularly bad for writers, Hemingway never really lost his "cynical distaste for all politicians," as Donaldson writes.[1] In the years after *To Have and Have Not*, he "re-emphasized his abiding lack of faith in governmental solutions to social problems, and reaffirmed his personal and artistic independence from all political parties and ideologies" (*By Force of Will* 121). Hemingway was adamant about that; it became his public image, and Harry Morgan symbolizes the struggle of self-determination. "If anyone thinks that I am worried about anyone reading political implications in my stories, he is wrong," he told a reporter two decades after *To Have and Have Not* appeared as his most politically oriented novel. "My only concern is that my stories are straight and good" (qtd. in O'Leary 26). Yet, as we know, little in Hemingway's stories is ever so simple.

Note

1. The speech appeared in the leftist broadside *New Masses* two weeks after the Congress under the title "Fascism Is a Lie" (*Conversations* 193–95).

The *Anita* Logs and *To Have and Have Not*

The Gulf Stream as Transcribed Experience

MARK P. OTT

Upon moving to Key West in 1928, Ernest Hemingway became increasingly enthralled with deep-sea fishing and the Gulf Stream. He had fished since he was a small boy, of course: photos exist of a three-year-old Ernest, cane pole in hand, trying his luck off the dock near Petoskey, Michigan. But while his fishing for trout in his teens and twenties could be seen as a natural extension of this boyhood hobby, Hemingway's interest in saltwater fishing was completely different. More scientific than experiential, more ichthyologist than Huck Finn, the change is evident in his post–*Death in the Afternoon* work in a large part thanks to the consecutive marlin seasons that he spent on the Gulf Stream each late April to August from 1932 to 1937.[1] A careful record-keeper his whole life, Hemingway scrupulously maintained logs of these trips, the earliest of which served a literary purpose by functioning as a raw reference resource as he composed "One Trip Across," the first section of *To Have and Have Not*.

More than any other documents, the fishing logs reveal the daily minutiae of Hemingway's life in the 1930s. Dense in observed detail, they give convincing evidence of Hemingway's education as an aspiring marine scientist while showing his progression from a novice saltwater fisherman to an acknowledged expert who contributed to several authoritative texts such as *American Big Game Fishing* (1935), *Atlantic Game Fishing* (1937), and *Game Fishing of the World* (1949). The logs include many mundane details, such as menus and libations, but they also find Hemingway crafting short, precise, representational descriptions of what he observed on the Gulf Stream. The exact observations in these logs generated the stylistic transformation that occurred in Hemingway's work between the publication of *A Farewell to Arms* (1929) and *The Old Man and the Sea* (1952), a period in which Hemingway's strategy for writing transformed from "learning something from the painting of Cézanne that made writing simple true sentences far from enough to make the stories have the dimensions that I was trying to put in them" (*AMF* 13) to ultimately desiring that his books about the sea contain illustrations by Winslow Homer (C. Murphy, 76).

The gist of this transformation can be found in a description of the Gulf Stream in *The Old Man and the Sea*:

> The old man knew he was going far out and he left the smell of land behind and rowed out into the clean early morning smell of the ocean. He saw the phosphorescence of the Gulf weed in the water as he rowed over the part of the ocean that the fisherman called the great well because there was a sudden deep of seven hundred fathoms where all sorts of fish congregated because of the swirl the current made against the steep walls of the floor of the ocean. Here there were concentrations of shrimp and bait fish and sometimes schools of squid in the deepest holds and these rose close to the surface at night where all the wandering fish fed on them. (28–29)

Hemingway's precise language identifies the observed world of the stream, directly classifying the marine life. Like Winslow Homer's brushstrokes, each word is representational, establishing order within the natural world equal to the compositional order of the canvas. In *The Old Man and the Sea*, Santiago is aware of what is beneath the surface of the ocean. He has studied the Gulf Stream, and he understands the organic unity that exists within nature. These observations—the result of having spent hundreds of days on the Gulf Stream from 1932 to 1952—seemed to initiate a subtle shift in Hemingway's writing: while still short and representational, his descriptions of fishing no longer convey the disorder and instability of modernity suggested in "Big Two-Hearted River." Instead, his prose implies a quest for the system of integration behind the chaotic surface. It is a quest that began in the 1930s and whose preliminary stages can be traced in "One Trip Across."

Hemingway's initiation into big-game fishing occurred in 1932 when he first stepped aboard Joe Russell's boat, the *Anita*, for a ten-day trip to Cuba that stretched into two months (Reynolds, *The 1930s*). Hemingway chartered Russell's *Anita* for a second time in April 1933 for two more months of marlin fishing. During this second trip, he logged his daily experiences into a copy of *Warner's Calendar of Medical History*. The basic form of entries in the fishing logs begins with a notation about the fuel status, the weather (sky, clouds, wind, temperature), a description of the Gulf Stream, a list of passengers, and the time of departure. The logs are written in English, but Hemingway uses Spanish names for the marine life. This Cuban vocabulary would have been new to Hemingway. He later noted the struggle to identify different species of marlin: "White marlin are called *aguja blanca*,

18. Before obtaining the *Pilar* in 1934, Hemingway (*left*) fished aboard the *Anita*, owned by the original Sloppy Joe's proprietor, Joe "Josie" Russell (*second from right*). Logs from their excursions would inspire *To Have and Have Not*. Ernest Hemingway Collection/ John F. Kennedy Presidential Library and Museum, Boston.

striped marlin are called *casteros* or *aguja de casta*; black marlin are called *pez grande*, or *aguja negra*. Blue marlin are confounded with the black called, sometimes *azules* or *aguja bobos*" ("Marlin Off Cuba" 81).

Just as he had learned modernism at the knee of Gertrude Stein, Hemingway learned about fishing from trip captain Carlos Gutiérrez, whose schooner *Paco* had briefly rendezvoused with the *Anita* during its 1932 expedition. A Cuban commercial fisherman, Gutiérrez had been trolling the Gulf Stream since 1884, when he was six years old (Baker, *A Life Story* 228). Since 1912, the fifty-four-year-old Gutiérrez had been keeping a record of all his catches, with dates and weights. Hemingway, ever the keen observer and good student, would follow his example. On 14 July 1933, he transcribed his first conversation with Gutiérrez onto the cover of a "Standard School Series" marble notebook, his first makeshift log. Writing in fragmented sentences, Hemingway took down Gutiérrez's responses to his questions:

> Males always looking for females pair when find them male rush boat and refuse to leave when female hooked. . . . Carlos had one could not get into boat and sharks bit off all except head and (shoulders) which weighed 12 arrobas. . . . Carlos has had an aguja jump over the boat— hooked four at once—landed three. (*Anita* Fishing Log, 1933)

Through examples from the extremes of his own experience, Gutiérrez educates Hemingway about the basic parameters of the marlin season, explaining breeding habits and how to hook them. What Hemingway writes down indicates what he did not know and provides the index for his subsequent education. The image of an *aguja negra* (black marlin) getting so large that it looked like a whale would have stimulated Hemingway's Melville-fed imagination. (Significantly, the Melville revival would be just past its peak in the early 1930s.) Hemingway's transcription of Gutiérrez's lecture also set the pattern of his own entries; if possible, everything should be quantified: the swiftness of the wind, the depth of the water, the gas in the tank, and the barometric pressure.

At some point during his adventures aboard the *Anita*, Hemingway conceived "One Trip Across," the first section of *To Have and Have Not*. Available evidence does not allow us to pinpoint the exact date. On 23 February 1933, he wrote Maxwell Perkins: "Am on Chapter 4 of the novel—

going well. See my way all the way to the end. Don't know whether we ever talked about this one" (*OTTC* 183). In a 13 March letter, Hemingway asked Perkins for a letter to get him out of any possible "jams" in Cuba, dictating to him the exact words he wanted: "This will certify that Ernest Hemingway is at work on a book dealing with the migratory fish of the Gulf Stream, their habits and capture with special reference to the fishing in Cuban Waters from a sporting standpoint" (*OTTC* 184). A chronology of resulting locations is straightforward: from 13 April to 20 July, Hemingway was in Havana fishing for marlin on the *Anita* (Baker, *A Life Story* 244). He then spent 21 July to 3 August in Key West, preparing for his departure to Europe and Africa. He returned to Havana on 4 August, and on 7 August, he left Havana for Spain, where he would remain through October. Carlos Baker asserts that Hemingway began the story sometime that April (*A Life Story* 607), but Michael Reynolds dates it to that September in Madrid (*The 1930s* 146). From Madrid on 16 October, Hemingway wrote his mother-in-law a long report on his new fiction, which he had hoped to include in his upcoming story collection, the patchy *Winner Take Nothing* (published eleven days later on 27 October):

> It is a third as long as the average novel. It may be a very good story. Is almost entirely action and takes place in Cuba and on the sea. Plenty of action. It is exactly the story that this present book needs i.e. Winner Take Nothing. But it will be as well or better in another book. . . . *I am trying to make, before I get through, a picture of the whole world—or as much of it as I have seen. Boiling it down always, rather than spreading it out thin.* (*SL* 397; emphasis added)

Especially noteworthy is the language that he uses to describe his method at this point: making a "picture of the whole world," "boiling it down always." More directly than anywhere else in his writing, this is Hemingway's declaration of a writing method that was his approximation of literary naturalism. There is the documentary impulse to picture the environment in whole, yet also the imperative that he "boil" down that picture to its most primitive, essential elements. Clearly, the story Hemingway refers to here is "One Trip Across," which would be published in *Cosmopolitan* in April 1934. And although two questions can never fully be resolved—on what day did Hemingway begin "One Trip Across," and did he have his fishing log from the *Anita* beside him to spur his imagination?—what is certain is that Hemingway almost instantly began fictionalizing his personal experience from fishing the Gulf Stream.

In the first pages of *To Have and Have Not*, it becomes clear that Hemingway's main character, Harry Morgan, must conquer his environment if he is to survive. Opening with a frontier-style shoot-out in a Havana café, Hemingway establishes three distinct geographic stages for his proletarian protagonist. Havana is a wide-open town, devoid of law and order; shoot-outs are common, and retribution is swift. Key West is a despoiled Eden, a microcosm of America in the Depression, where distasteful tourism is a desperate palliative for deeper economic and moral troubles. Once Key West is contaminated, Morgan is forced out into the Gulf Stream. The Gulf Stream between Key West and Havana thus becomes a no-man's land, a contested space where violence settles disputes in the midst of an indifferent natural world.

Hemingway's first description of the Gulf Stream appears as Morgan is taking a tourist, Mr. Johnson, out fishing for marlin:

> The stream was in almost to soundings and as we came toward the edge you could see her running nearly purple with regular whirlpools. There was a slight east breeze coming up and we put up plenty of flying fish, those big ones with the black wings that look like the picture of Lindbergh crossing the Atlantic when they sail off.
>
> Those big flying fish are the best sign there is. As far as you could see, there was that faded yellow gulfweed in small patches that means the stream is well in and there were birds ahead working over a school of little tuna. You could see them jumping; just little ones weighing a couple of pounds apiece. (11–12)

The passage is indicative of the influence of the fishing logs. Locations, wind direction, tide color, and animal life are all worth commenting on, and the most descriptive moment—the picture of Lindbergh crossing the Atlantic—seems an appropriate popular culture reference from the mind of a narrator nurtured on the mass media. Even in noting the weight of the tuna, Harry Morgan makes a practical, rather than lyrical observation; the tuna exist as an economic resource for him, and these small ones are not worth harvesting.

The description of this first fishing sequence thus evinces the narrative technique of the fishing logs, thereby allowing Hemingway to establish Morgan's expertise as a fisherman. Hemingway's descriptions are direct, rich in color imagery, and active, as when Johnson, Morgan's customer, fishes for marlin:

> I opened the bottle and was reaching it toward him when I saw this big brown buggar with a spear on him longer than your arm burst head and shoulders out of the water and smash that mackerel. He looked as big around as a saw log. . . . You could see his fins out wide like purple wings and the purple stripes across the brown. He came on like a submarine and his top fin came out and you could see it slice the water. . . . He hit him pretty hard a couple times more, and then the rod bent double and the reel commenced to screech and out he came, boom, in a long straight jump, shining silver in the sun and making a splash like throwing a horse off a cliff. . . . He was a fine fish bright silver now, barred with purple, and as big around as a log. (15–16)

The colors of the fish ("shining silver," "bright silver"), the dynamism of the movements, the excitement of the battle: Hemingway is letting the reader know that he is an expert fisherman. Deep-sea fishing, like herding cattle or hunting big game, is an endeavor that needs to be trusted to seasoned experts who know the Gulf Stream. Most importantly, the key words underpinning the sequence—"log," "submarine," "purple," "wagging," even the image of the horse—are all introduced and repeated in the fishing logs of April 1933.[2]

Several May 1933 entries are also reshaped into this scene. In the novel, Morgan narrates: "I was at the wheel and was working the edge of the stream opposite that old cement factory where it makes deep so close in to shore and where it makes a sort of eddy where there is always lots of bait. Then I saw a splash like a depth bomb, and the sword and eye, and open lower-jaw and huge purple-black head of a black marlin" (20). In the log entry for 13 May, Hemingway writes:

Out at 110 trolled to Cojimar
close to shore—saw one marlin
opposite **cement factory** and

a huge **covey of flying fish**—
made turn and Josie saw
another marlin with (illegible)
tail out—too far already
to catch—opposite target
range a (black) marlin cut
across (illegible) from shorewards
like a dolphin chasing
fish—bit EH's bait—
slacked and hooked in second
slack—at 229 jumped about
8 times—gaffed at 234. (*Anita* Fishing Log, 1933, emphasis original)

The location of the two moments is the same. The cement factory would become a regular feature of the log and a place where Hemingway caught many of his larger marlin. According to Gregorio Fuentes, the first mate aboard the *Pilar*, Hemingway tried to fish the same edge of the Gulf Stream, where the green water met the blue, along a stretch of coastline now called the "Hemingway mile": "Hemingway's mile which is somewhat longer than the orthodox mile was measured from the shooting range in Las Cabañas fortress at the mouth of Havana Bay to the House of the Priest (or the Pink House)" (Fuentes 117).[3] Hemingway's entry captures both the thrill of sighting a large marlin and the satisfaction of catching one. Hemingway is particularly interested in the dynamics of the marlin's motion—"like a dolphin chasing fish"—and also what technique was required to hook him. By recording the number of jumps and the precise time it took to land the marlin, Hemingway is recording for his own satisfaction evidence of his improved skill as a fisherman.

The cement factory would be the site of another notable catch on 17 May. Again, the language of the log would later appear in *To Have and Have Not*. The log reads:

1255 opposite Cojimar and
cement factory big striped marlin
struck EH kingfish bait
in a smash and surge—
slacked him long and hooked

him solid—swung shoreward
and jumped high—came
toward us and jumped again—
out and high toward shore—
fought deep from then on—
came in close to shore—
opposite **cement factory**—
line caught on rock—
broke at 150—line chafed
through along a six inch
stretch nearly through in
two other places—lost about
100 years of line—some evidently
caught on spire of rock when
fish swang [*sic*] it against
current—EH felt it but [rods?]
but couldn't believe it—seems
impossible to lose a marlin
like that—while broken line
came in we did not know
what had happened—EH fighting
weight of boat swinging in
current which was really like
a mill race—we would
go toward fish—gain line
then [illegible] fish stayed down
and long we throw out
the current would carry
boat away—didn't know
this at the time that it
was strength of fish—
most punishment I ever took—
was a beautiful striped
marlin to weigh 150 lbs
gutted and head off
Carlos said (*Anita* Fishing Log, 1933, emphasis original)

More directly than other log entries, this incident appears in *To Have and Have Not*. Re-creating the moment, Hemingway transformed his own loss of a striped marlin into Mr. Johnson's loss of a black marlin. Using the flying fish from the entry of 13 May, Hemingway writes: "The nigger was still taking her out and I looked and saw he had seen a patch of flying fish burst out ahead and up the stream a little. Looking back, I could see Havana looking fine in the sun and a ship just coming out of the harbor past the Morro" (13). When Johnson loses the fish, it is for the same reason that Hemingway did. As Harry Morgan explains:

> "Listen," I told him. "If you don't give them line when they hook up like that they break it. There isn't any line will hold them. When they want it you've got to give it to them. You have to keep a light drag. The market fisherman can't hold them tight when they do that even with a harpoon line. What we have to do is use the boat to chase them so they don't take it all when they make their run. After they make their run they'll sound and you can tighten up the drag and get it back." (18)

Although Hemingway, the relative novice, would lose the actual fish in 1933, in the novel he uses the voice of Morgan, the expert, to chastise and educate Johnson, the urban outsider and fishing amateur.

A few pages later, Hemingway recycled the simile of the "mill race": "About four o'clock when we're coming back close in to shore against the Stream; it going like a mill race, us with the sun at our backs; the biggest black marlin I ever saw in my life hit Johnson's bait" (19).[4] The "mill race" is meant to illustrate the motion of the Gulf Stream current; in the middle of the stream it flows eastward, and along the edges it flows westward. A fishing boat leaving Havana benefits from the current as it heads out for the day, and again when it returns to harbor. For the thirty-three-year-old Hemingway, this battle with a striped marlin was "the most punishment he ever took" (*Anita* Fishing Log, 1933), and it is one of the few places in the log in which he used underlining for emphasis.

The Morro lighthouse has a recurring presence in all of Hemingway's writing about the Gulf Stream. It represents the safety of Havana harbor, providing a reference point for all the boats at sea. When Hemingway departed Key West for Cuba on 12 April, he recorded the details of his passage and his relief at sighting the lighthouse:

Left Key West 1250PM
Sand Key 140PM
Morro 130AM
good stream about 2 hours out
[illegible]
extraordinary action of porpoises in
front of tankers off sand key
saw glare of Havana 8PM little
current until approaching Cuban coast (*Anita* Fishing Log, 1933)

Harry Morgan, too, refers to the Morro when he makes the reverse journey, departing Havana for Key West: "I went out the harbor and past the Morro and put her on the course for Key West; due north" (41). The precise tracking of the passage of time also would make its way into the novel, as well as the Sand Key lighthouse (63).

Again and again in the log there is evidence of the intense responsibility Hemingway felt to maintain a precise document. He was acutely aware of the passage of time. On 21 April, he felt compelled to make entries at 7:45 a.m., 8:40, 8:45, 10:15, 10:25, 12:45 p.m., 1:00, 1:25, 1:30, finally noting, "in @ 6:00."[5] The long gap between 1:30 and 6:00 p.m. is explained in an incident that underscores the "brotherhood" of the Gulf Stream. As the crew of the *Anita* aided another boat, the *Celia*, Hemingway records:

PM saw two boats together
and ran over to investigate. *Celia*
of Cojimar and another boat with
small marlin landed and a
Black Marlin of 26 *arrobas*
took pictures gave them
water and beer. (*Anita* Fishing Log, 1933)

A black marlin of twenty-six *arrobas* would weigh over six hundred pounds and would be celebrated by the whole community of fishermen. Hemingway was always quick to use a camera for documentation, and the ritual of the photograph was the culmination of the celebration. The reader has no idea here whether Hemingway himself enjoyed a moment of camaraderie, or if he felt burdened by the obligation he felt to assist the *Celia*. The log is only about what Hemingway observes, not what he feels.

Despite the detached quality of the log, Hemingway would later mine imagery from the month of April for both *To Have and Have Not* and *The Old Man and the Sea*. Noting each species of marine life he encountered, on 21 April, Hemingway writes:

> 1015 saw two loggerhead turtles
> hooked up
> 1025 small marlin on surface turning
> in circles in search of bait—circled
> him 6 or 8 times—he turning
> smaller all the time—then went
> down—a few minutes later saw large
> hammer head fin (*Anita* Fishing Log, 1933)

This image reoccurs in part 3 (Winter) of *To Have and Have Not*. Hemingway creates a conversation between Harry Morgan and his wife, Marie, prior to their lovemaking. Morgan has already lost his arm in a gunfight:

> "Listen, do you mind the arm? Don't it make you feel funny?"
> "You're silly. I like it. Any that's you I like. Put it across there. Put it along there. Go on. I like it, true."
> "It's like a flipper on a loggerhead."
> "You ain't no loggerhead. Do they really do it three days? Coot for three days?"
> "Sure. Listen, be quiet. We'll wake the girls." (113)

The loggerhead turtle was listed as a "threatened species" in 1970, which makes it a prescient metaphor for Morgan. Although there is no evidence that Hemingway knew of the decline in the loggerhead population, he certainly must have been aware that they frequently ate the marine debris found floating in harbors. At this point, Morgan, barely scavenging a living off the Gulf Stream, has taken on the qualities of a loggerhead, fulfilling Hemingway's deterministic design for the novel. In *The Old Man and the Sea*, Hemingway would again use the image of the loggerheads making love, writing: "[Santiago] had a friendly contempt for the huge, stupid log-gerheads, yellow in their armour-plating, strange in their love-making, and happily eating the Portuguese men-of-war with their eyes shut" (36–37). Significantly, Hemingway feels liberated here to express his "contempt" for loggerheads in a way from which his naturalist design for *To Have and Have Not* restricted him. In the universe of the Gulf Stream, Harry and Marie Morgan are the Darwinian equivalent of scavengers, eating the Portuguese men-of-war, "the falsest thing in the sea" (*OMATS* 36).

By part 3 of *To Have and Have Not*, in which Harry is found lying on the deck of his boat, shot in the stomach by Cuban revolutionaries, Hemingway employs the Gulf Stream symbolically in a manner that foreshadows *The Old Man and the Sea*:

> There was no sign of life on her although the body of a man showed, rather inflated looking, above the gunwale, lying on a bench over the port gasoline tank and from the long seat alongside the starboard gun-wale, a man seemed to be leaning over to dip his hand into the sea. His head and arms were in the sun and at the point where his fingers almost touched the water there was a school of small fish, about two inches long, oval-shaped, golden-colored, with faint purple stripes, that had deserted the gulf weed to take shelter in the shade the bottom of the drifting launch made in the water, and each time anything dripped down into the sea, these fish rushed at the drop and pushed and milled until it was gone. . . .
>
> They were reluctant now to leave a place where they had fed so well and unexpectedly. (179–80)

Having the human blood mix with the waters of the Gulf Stream, Hemingway strives to achieve a unity of what Ray West calls a "double im-plication," where the emotional force of the idea is intensified by the shock the image supplies (150). The enduring world of the Gulf Stream is juxta-posed here with the image of a life wasting away. The fish, unable to com-prehend the regularity of the drip, parallel the uncomprehending Morgan, who is unaware of the natural laws that control his fate. Combining with the image of the suckerfish, Morgan's "inflated" body becomes an ironic image of Harry's ultimate insignificance in the scheme of nature. Forty pages later, Harry finally utters his last words:

"A man," Harry Morgan said, looking at them both. "One man alone ain't got. No man alone now." He stopped. "No matter how a man alone ain't got no bloody fucking chance."

He shut his eyes. It had taken him a long time to get it out and it had taken him all of his life to learn it. (225)

Morgan's words are "not heard" by those around him, underscoring the futility of the knowledge he has acquired; his death is determined by his position in a class-oriented society, driven by laws of nature.[6] Indeed the Darwinian echoes are accentuated in the final pages of the novel, as the tycoon Henry Carpenter tries to go to sleep by reading: "He lay, now in his pyjamas [sic], on his wide bed, two pillows under his head, the reading light on, but he could not keep his mind on the book, which was an account of a trip to the Galapagos" (234).

Writing the final pages of the novel in 1937, Hemingway returned again to the imagery of the Gulf Stream in an attempt to create some structural unity within a work that he had begun in 1933. Concluding the novel through the eyes of Harry Morgan's working-class widow, Marie, Hemingway writes:

Through the window you could see the sea looking hard and new and blue in the winter light.

A large white yacht was coming into the harbor and seven miles out on the horizon you could see a tanker, small and neat in profile against the blue sea, hugging the reef as she made to the westward to keep from wasting fuel against the stream. (262)

In the pared-down description of the sea as "hard and new and blue," Hemingway is moving toward the style he would employ in *The Old Man and the Sea*. The Gulf Stream again represents an unforgiving and time-less natural force that should not be resisted, and Hemingway offers little hope to the struggling working class. The seascape and the fertility and abundance that characterized the Gulf Stream in part 1 are absent. By the conclusion of the novel, only a grim lesson is harvested: the marlin of part 1 has gotten away, and nature remains indomitable.

The prolonged composition of *To Have and Have Not* reveals Hemingway at an aesthetic crossroads. He explored different literary forms throughout the 1930s, expanding his repertoire of techniques through experimentation that culminated in the creation of *For Whom the Bell Tolls* (1940). Yet in

1933, in the first pages of *To Have and Have Not*, Hemingway is composing through the lens of literary naturalism, creating "realistic" descriptions in an attempt to accurately portray Harry Morgan's world. The fishing logs of the *Anita* were clearly a compositional aid, a source book he could open to stimulate his imagination as he re-created scenes that he had lived. At first, largely unaware of what exists beneath the Gulf Stream—his metaphorical "iceberg"—Hemingway sought to transcribe his experience, learning the science of the world above and within the water so that by 1952 he could accurately unify Santiago's world—from the constellations of Orion to the great depths in the wells of the Stream—in *The Old Man and the Sea*.

Notes

1. In the Hemingway Collection at the John F. Kennedy Library in Boston, fishing logs exist from 1932, 1933, 1934–35, 1937, 1939, 1941, and 1945. Several articles have been written examining these records, though none have noted the connection between the fishing logs and the published text of *To Have and Have Not*. See Byrne, "New Acquisitions"; L. Miller, "Matrix"; and Watson, "Hemingway in Bimini."

2. Hemingway's verbs in the fishing log are always notable, as on 17 May, the "big striped marlin" struck the bait in a "smash and surge." On 30 June, Hemingway would write: "Huge broadbill—come high high out—turn in the air and come straight down—like a jackknife dive."

3. Fuentes's *Hemingway in Cuba* is more anecdotal than scholarly, and it is filled with inaccuracies. This description of "Hemingway's mile" should be taken as a rough approximation.

4. According to *Merriam-Webster's Collegiate Dictionary* (11th ed.), a "mill race" is a "canal in which water flows to and from a mill wheel" (755).

5. Hemingway's shorthand notations for time are impossible to duplicate in print. For 12:45 p.m. he would write "12" and then add the 45 in superscript, underlined twice. Rather than misrepresent an element of punctuation that did not exist, I have decided to type the numbers consecutively.

6. Bender argues that Darwin's ideas were not important to Hemingway: "It is important to remember that during the years when Hemingway became a writer, Darwin's ideas were passé. . . . But in the early stages of Hemingway's career, the disillusionment caused by World War I, the possibility of a Marxist solution to social injustice, the Waste Land view of modern life, the intensifying interest in Freud and Jung (both were heavily influenced by Darwinian thought), and the beginnings of New Critical thought in the aesthetics of Ezra Pound and T. S. Eliot: these were the prevailing currents of American literary thought" (170). Evidence countering Bender's assertion of Darwin's unimportance to Hemingway exists in that the Finca Vigía library included *Charles Darwin and the Voyage of the* Beagle*: Unpublished Letters and Notebooks* (1946) and *The Darwin Reader* (1956).

"The Poor Are Different from You and Me"

Masculinity and Class in *To Have and Have Not*

SUSAN J. WOLFE

According to Matthew J. Bruccoli, Hemingway's notorious remark about F. Scott Fitzgerald in the original *Esquire* version of "The Snows of Kilimanjaro" (1936) is "the defining anecdote about the two writers" (2). Distorting the views expressed by Fitzgerald's narrator in his 1926 short story "The Rich Boy," Hemingway disparages his literary rival for romanticizing the rich:

> He remembered poor Scott Fitzgerald and his romantic awe of them [the rich] and how he started a story once about them that began "The very rich are different from you and me." And how someone had said to Scott, "Yes they have more money." But that was not humorous to Scott. He thought they were a special glamorous race and when he found they weren't it wrecked him just as much as any other thing wrecked him. (qtd. in Bruccoli 2)[1]

Ironically, Hemingway essentializes the rich every bit as much as Fitzgerald does—but not by glamorizing them. Instead, his tendency is to denigrate them, most often by impugning the masculinity of men of means. As Ira Elliott has asserted vis-à-vis *The Sun Also Rises*, Jake Barnes's "'anxieties about homosexuality [are] conjoined with class antagonism'—his antipathy for the rich, 'the mincing gentry,'" allowing Hemingway to attack the latter by conflating the possession of wealth with effeminacy (88).[2] As Elliott points out, the homosexuals in Hemingway's lost-generation classic use ar-chaic upper-class speech forms and otherwise affect "an aristocratic pose" (82). Unlike their performance of femininity, however, their performance of class is offensive, in part because they are mimicking the behavior of the upper class (to which they do not belong) but also because this upper-class behavior is (in Hemingway's world) offensive in and of itself.[3] The phrase "the mincing gentry" thus reveals how upper-class behavior is equated with femininity, since the term "mincing," according to the *American Heritage Dictionary*, means not only "affectedly refined" but also "dainty." The adjec-tive derives from the verb "to mince," which may be used to describe speech that is affected or excessively formal, or in reference to a gait characterized by "very short steps or excessive primness" (798). The word "prim," when applied to men, suggests effeminacy, as does "dainty." Such adjectives thus call attention to the overlapping of categories of gender and class in *The Sun Also Rises*. The overlap also occurs in *To Have and Have Not*, although in a far more stringent and deterministic way: one of the striking themes of this 1937 novel is how being "Haves" perforce precludes males from being "real men."

In *To Have and Have Not* then, the gentry may not all be effeminate, but none exude the natural traits of masculinity associated with protagonist Harry Morgan. Richard Gordon, Tommy Bradley, and John MacWalsey lack Harry's strength, courage, bravery, and fortitude. Morgan tries might-ily to support his family against insurmountable odds (the Depression, big government, the penurious wealthy, and the physical handicap of his lost arm), and is perfectly capable of satisfying his wife, Marie (even when he fears his amputation renders him an imperfect lover). Although Harry is vi-olent and crude, his masculine resolve makes him heroic, even if he (and the class he represents) are doomed to be exploited at the hands of the "Haves." In *The Sun Also Rises*, Count Mippipopolous, despite his wealth, can be considered "quite one of us" (as Brett Ashley terms him [40]) because, like Jake and Brett, he copes with his war wounds and exudes stoic endurance. There are no comparable figures in *To Have and Have Not*. Rather, its rich men are invariably contemptible. They are physically and sexually inept, morally bereft, and undisciplined. They rarely care for the strangers whose lives they ruin, or, for that matter, for their own families.

Harry Morgan's declining fortunes are, in fact, the fault of such men, not the Great Depression crippling the Key West economy. From the novel's opening, his luck begins to sour as the wealthy Mr. Johnson cheats him. Johnson, who charters Harry's boat for three weeks of fishing, not only leaves without paying but also manages to lose Harry's rod and reel in the bargain. Tired of holding the spool of the reel, Johnson removes the harness and screws the drag down so that when the fish hits, all the tackle goes overboard. Because he reneges on his agreement to pay for both the lost tackle and the charter, Johnson is shown to lack honor as well as skill and physical strength: "All right. There it was," Harry says after Johnson flees Cuba owing him $825. "I had forty cents, and, anyhow, the plane was in Miami by now." It is a mark of Harry's heroic self-sufficiency that he blames himself for trusting the deceitful tourist: "I should have known better" (27). Since this is the novel's opening chapter, Johnson's duplicity and penuriousness are largely responsible for inaugurating Harry's economic decline.

Another poor specimen of manhood is Mr. Sing, the wealthy Asian whose income derives at least in part from "shipping Chinamen"—that is, smuggling them illegally into the United States. At the outset Hemingway presents Sing as smooth and slick, his aura of sophistication obscuring his underlying barbarism: "Mr. Sing was about the smoothest-looking thing I'd ever seen. He was a Chink all right, but he talked like an Englishman and he was dressed in a white suit with a silk shirt and black tie and one of those hundred-and-twenty-five-dollar Panama hats" (30). Although Sing implies that Harry can simply get rid of his cargo—i.e., murder the Chinese immigrants—if he is caught smuggling them, he is not, unlike Harry, overtly violent. He-man fisticuffs and gunslinging are not for him; rather, he pays others to dirty their hands committing his violent acts and thus eludes responsibility for his crimes. He directs Harry to embark for the Tortugas, but agrees that it would be foolish to land there, and allows Harry to select his destination for delivering the twelve Chinese men into America (32).

Since Sing does not stipulate a destination, he implies that the twelve men may be murdered because he already has their money; he does not take the risk of voicing the suggestion, however. The Cuban helpmate Frankie, who introduces Sing to Harry, observes that other Chinese men who have been shipped simply "disappeared": "Big business. . . . Ship Chinamen never come back. Other Chinamen [not the ones who have been shipped] write letters say everything fine" (35). To avoid "killing twelve other Chinks" (55),

Harry breaks Sing's neck and drops his body in the Gulf. However brutal, this hands-on murder is depicted as the necessary moral counterpart to the smuggler's monied perfidy. Harry ironically impugns Sing's civilized exterior while treating the bite to the shoulder that the dying profiteer gave him: "Hell, no, that bite wasn't poisonous. A man like that probably scrubbed his teeth two or three times a day. Some Mr. Sing." At the end of the day, Harry decides that Sing's upper-class pretensions spelled his doom, for "[h]e certainly wasn't much of a business man" (60).

In part 2, the equation between upper-class manhood and immorality is applied to bureaucrats instead of cheats and killers. Frederick Harrison, who claims to be "one of the three most important men in the United States today" (80), stands for the indifference of the rich and powerful toward the struggling poor, and he demonstrates the means by which government bureaucracy exerts control over poor people by enforcing the laws it establishes. (Harrison is Hemingway's derogatory portrait of Julius F. Stone Jr., the director of Florida's Federal Emergency Relief Agency [FERA] charged with saving the Key West economy. Hemingway was particularly irate at Stone for turning 907 Whitehead Street into a tourist attraction.) Spotting Harry's boat while it is on a rum-running expedition, Roosevelt-appointee Harrison plans to report him as a "lawbreaker" and a "bootlegger." His guide on his fishing expedition, Captain Willie, understands and sympathizes with the simple fact that to feed his family Harry must resort to what Harrison deems criminal activity. As the captain angrily says to Harrison, "Who the hell do you eat off of with people working here in Key West for the government for six dollars and a half a week?" (81). By part 3, Harry's boat has been impounded by the government, presumably at Harrison's order. Yet despite his governmental position, Harrison is shown to be personally ineffectual. When he demands that Captain Willie draw alongside Harry's boat so that they can take him into custody, Willie instead warns Harry and sails away, ignoring the red-faced bureaucrat's demands while ironically assuring him he will receive his full money's worth on his fishing charter: "I thought you'd be interested in these things as a government man," Willie says when Harrison tells him to "*shut* up" about the schools of sailfish he will show him. "Ain't you mixed up in the prices of things that we eat or something? Ain't that it? Making them more costly or something. Making the grits cost more and the grunts less?" (84). When he cannot draw upon the official power of the government, Harrison is powerless: he lacks both the ability to steer the boat and the courage and physical prowess to seize control from Captain Willie. Like the very rich Hemingway describes later in the novel, Harrison stands in contrast to Harry. Despite his authentic masculinity, however, Harry is finally no match for the forces aligned against him: as Harrison fulminates about the respect he is due for being "one of the biggest men in the [Roosevelt] administration" (80), a wounded Harry is valiantly struggling to dump his bootleg cargo. Eventually, the wound is revealed to have cost him both his boat and his right arm.

In part 3, Harry, by then an amputee without other options, must agree to carry four Cubans on another boat, the *Queen Conch*, which he has to borrow from bar owner Freddy Wallace (based on Joe "Josie" Russell of Sloppy Joe's Bar fame). Since Harry refused to transport Cuban revolutionaries in the first chapter of the novel, his willingness to do so at this late stage marks his desperate need for money. Fellow fisherman Albert Tracy, who has been trying to provide for his family by doing manual labor through a federally supported work plan, asks to be carried as a member of Harry's crew. Because FERA has cut workers like Albert to three days of subsistence employment, he, too, must also make his living through smuggling (96). Albert's desperation thus illustrates the futility of a working-class man's attempt to support his family by legal means. When Albert realizes that his and Harry's cargo is composed of Cuban revolutionaries who rob banks to finance their terrorism, he objects and is promptly shot to death by Roberto, the most violent Cuban. Looking down at Albert's body, Harry thinks, "The poor hungry bastard," and he realizes he must again kill if he is going to survive—this time three men instead of the single smuggler Sing (160). He manages to do so, but not without being shot in the stomach, a wound that ultimately proves fatal.

After a dying Harry delivers the novel's moral in chapter 23—"No matter how a man alone ain't got no bloody fucking chance" (225)—Hemingway controversially switches his method of presentation to itemize the immoralities of the rich anchoring their yachts in the old Key West navy basin. What *To Have and Have Not* loses in aesthetic cohesion it gains in thematic clarity, for the juxtaposition of Harry and the Haves makes it obvious that what the wealthy most lack is authentic masculinity. For Hemingway— who, as he had in *The Sun Also Rises*, caricatures gay men as effeminate

19. Hemingway strikes a pose with the submachine gun he sometimes employed to kill marauding sharks. His proletarian alter ego in *To Have and Have Not*, Harry Morgan, dies on the receiving end of a similar weapon—one man alone. Ernest Hemingway Collection/John F. Kennedy Presidential Library and Museum, Boston.

if not outright shrewish—homosexuality is one obvious sign of this deficiency. Henry Carpenter, for example, is currently earning his keep by servicing Wallace Johnston "with his rather special pleasures" (232), thus ensuring that Johnston will not have to pay "blackmail to the bus boys and sailors" (229). Johnston, both a rich man and a homosexual, is a member of the "mincing gentry" twice over, but Carpenter, an heir who has learned to supplement the two hundred dollars per month from his mother's trust fund by "land[ing] safely with his knees under some rich man's table" (232), is even more despicable. As Hemingway informs us, he will commit suicide in a matter of weeks when Johnston's "hospitality" runs out because he lacks the manly resolve to establish his economic autonomy. Lest we miss the point, the narrator clarifies the contrast between rich and poor: "The money on which it was not worth while for [Carpenter] to live was one hundred and seventy dollars more a month than the fisherman Albert Tracy had been supporting his family on at the time of his death three days before" (233). Carpenter is, in short, not only a parasite but a coward, another rich man who cannot face the grim challenges of getting by as Harry and Albert do.

Aboard another yacht, the ineffectual manhood of a sixty-year-old alcoholic speculator is measured by intemperance. Although his doctor has told the man that continuing to drink will ensure his death in a year, he yearns to seek escape from the woes of an Internal Review Bureau investigation into his business tactics through "all that chemical courage that had soothed his mind and warmed his heart for so many years" (234). As a corrupt capitalist, he neither loves his wife nor respects his sons, so he lies there alone, "in a pair of striped silk pyjamas that covered his shrunken old man's chest, his bloated little belly, his now useless and disproportionately large equipment that had once been his pride, and his small flabby legs," feeling remorse only because he has finally ruined himself (236). He desires a drink so he will not have to admit that his financial manipulations have harmed others:

> He would not need to worry about what he had done to other people . . . who'd moved from houses on the Lake Shore drive to taking boarders out in Austin, whose debutante daughters now were dentist's assistants when they had a job; who ended up a night watchman at sixty-three after that last corner; who shot himself early one morning before breakfast and which one of his children found him, and what the mess looked like; who now rode the L to work, when there was work . . . trying to sell, first, bonds; then motor cars; then house-to-house novelties and specialties . . . until he varied the leaning drop his father made from forty-two floors up . . . to step forward onto the third rail in front of the Aurora-Elgin train, his overcoat pocket full of unsaleable combination eggbeaters and fruit juice extractors. (237)

Unlike Harry, whose suffering allows him to show compassion for both Eddy and Albert (despite his referring to them as "niggers"), the speculator has long justified his market manipulations by dismissing the very notion of human solidarity. The people that he ruined may have committed suicide in a variety of ways, "but that never worried him. Somebody had to lose and only suckers worried" (238). Without the comforts of alcohol, however, the man cannot maintain such callousness, and he quickly orders a whiskey from his steward to assuage his guilt.

Not all of the Haves' lack of masculinity is so overtly odious. The yacht moored next to the speculator's is occupied by the family of Jon Jacobsen, whose wealth, social standing, and health seem secure relative to those who occupy other slips in the basin. The Jacobsens are a happy, well-adjusted family, all of whose members love one another. Jon Jacobsen himself has done many good works and is open-minded, generous, sympathetic, and understanding. He even treats his crew, all of whom like him, very well. He has earned his money by bottling something that costs three cents a quart to make and marketing it for a dollar a pint. (Bernice Kert makes the interesting suggestion that this is Hemingway's subtle attack on the family of his then wife, Pauline Pfeiffer, who derived a portion of their wealth through pharmaceutical interests [281].) The narrator notes ironically that such capitalist ventures do not result in suicides, and everyone aboard this yacht sleeps soundly—that is, they are not kept awake by worry or guilt. Profiting by overcharging for a decent product may not be heinous in this culture, but, while the Jacobsen family has a yacht with a fourteen-member crew, Harry Morgan is forced to resort to smuggling to support his family.

However, Jacobsen, like the other rich men described in this chapter, does not escape his share of misery, for he has sexual problems. He cannot satisfy his wife, and has never been able to do so; unlike the speculator, Jacobsen has never been a sexual athlete. He is fortunate, however, that his wife is an understanding woman: "[W]ith a lovely girl like Frances intention counts as much as performance." Jacobsen's lack of sexual prowess is expressly linked to his social class; the narrator states that "[t]he type of man who is tapped for Bones is rarely also tapped for bed" (239). The Order of the Skull and Bones is, of course, an elite society at Yale University; the family names of those initiated into the group have included Vanderbilt, Rockefeller, Whitney, Taft, Pillsbury, Kellogg, and Bush.[4] We are thus meant to view Jacobsen as among the very wealthiest men in the United States, and to conclude that all of them are inept lovers.

Sexual inadequacies are rampant on other yachts as well. Occupying the *Irydia IV* are Eddie, a "professional son-in-law of the very rich, and his mistress, named Dorothy, the wife of that highly paid Hollywood director, John Hollis," who, like the speculator, is drinking himself to death, his brain "in the process of outlasting his liver" (241). Eddie, who also drinks too much, has passed out, and Dorothy Hollis's internal monologue pities her husband briefly while admiring herself in the mirror. In *Hemingway's Genders: Rereading the Hemingway Text*, Nancy R. Comley and Robert Scholes identify Dorothy Hollis as one of Hemingway's sexually insatiable women, but they also observe that both Dorothy's husband and her lover, because they drink too much, are too incapacitated to perform sexually. Hollis's cirrhosis prevents him from engaging in sexual intercourse, and while her lover lies comatose, "Poor Dorothy is left to masturbate her evening away" (41). Unlike Comley and Scholes, however, I emphasize here the impotence of her husband and her lover rather than Dorothy's own insatiability, because these men, like the other rich men described in chapter 24, are unable to satisfy a woman sexually. Nothing in Dorothy's monologue identifies her as insatiable; in fact, she is concerned that she may "end up a bitch" because, now that John has "drunk so much he isn't any good," she has turned to Eddie and "now he's tight" (244). In fact, more than half of her monologue, nearly two pages, is devoted to her speculations on the reasons for men's marital infidelities, and much of the remainder to the fact that John and Eddie do not qualify as real men: "Damn Eddie, really. He shouldn't have really gotten so tight. It isn't fair, really. No one can help the way they're built but getting tight has nothing to do with that" (245).

Although minor characters, Eddie and the Hollises are present in order to demonstrate the sexual problems of the rich. They strongly resemble two other characters in the novel's truncated subplot, Tommy and Helène Bradley, with one exception: the impotent Tommy Bradley does not simply tolerate Helène's infidelity—he condones it. (The Bradleys are a brutal caricature of Grant and Jane Mason, whose marriage of convenience made it convenient for Jane and Hemingway to indulge their mutual attraction to each other. By the time of *To Have and Have Not*, of course, Hemingway had already parodied the Masons in "The Short Happy Life of Francis Macomber.") The author Richard Gordon (yet another caricature, this time of John Dos Passos) is merely the latest among the writers whom Helène "collects." Their affair ends when Tommy Bradley observes them in flagrante delicto and exits quietly, smiling (189). Significantly, Gordon cannot finish making love after the intrusion, leading Helène to impugn his manhood: *"So that's the kind of man you are. . . . I thought you were a man of the world. Get out of here"* (190). Gordon's masculinity is diminished even more when he returns home to discover that his wife, Helen, fed up with his philandering, has decided to leave him for Professor John MacWalsey. Why? "He's a man," Helen insists. "He's kind and he's charitable and he makes you feel comfortable and we come from the same thing and we have values that you'll never have" (187).

It may seem odd for Hemingway, even through one of his female characters, to attribute manhood to a professor like MacWalsey—to an intellectual rather than a man of action, that is, or to one without obvious physical prowess (although he also attributes manhood to a professor in *For Whom the Bell Tolls*—i.e., Robert Jordan). Yet when Richard insists that MacWalsey is a drunk, Helen immediately compares him to her working-class father, whose values are that "same thing" that she and MacWalsey "come from":

> He drinks. But so did my father. And my father wore wool socks and put his feet in them up on a chair and read the paper in the evening. And when we had croup he took care of us. He was a boiler maker and his hands were all broken and he liked to fight when he drank, and he could fight when he was sober. He went to mass because my mother wanted him to and he did his Easter duty for her and for Our Lord, but mostly for her, and he was a good union man and if he ever went with another woman she never knew it. . . . and if he did it was because he couldn't help it and he was sorry and repented of it. He didn't do it . . . from barnyard pride. . . . He was a man. (187)

Helen's father, in short, was strikingly like Harry Morgan: a strong man who worked with his hands and fought with his fists. Secure in his manhood, he had no need for extramarital affairs to bolster his ego; if he did have affairs, "He didn't do it . . . from barnyard pride" (187). He was also a loyal and gentle family man who attended church largely to satisfy his wife and tended his children when they were ill. Exactly how MacWalsey upholds these values is unclear, but in defending him through a comparison to her father, Helen also implicitly praises Harry, the rough working man who possesses great physical and emotional strength. Although Helen never meets Hemingway's hero, her attraction to the authentic masculinity he stands for is underscored by a female "Have" who does: Mrs. Laughton, who, like Helen, is the wife of an ineffectual writer. In chapter 14, Harry denounces Mrs. Laughton as a "whore" when she tells her husband to "buy me that, Papa," referring to Harry (130). She sees in Harry's willingness to stand up for himself a regal pride that arouses her enervated eroticism: "Oh, he had a beautiful face. . . . Like a Tartar or something. I wish he hadn't been insulting. He looked kind of like Ghengis Khan in the face. Gee, he was big. . . . He's my dream man" (136–37).

Throughout *To Have and Have Not*, then, Hemingway attributes upper-class iniquities to a lack of masculine strength and resolve, whether embodied by dishonesty, cupidity, alcoholism, or, most blatantly, sexual dysfunction. All of these deficiencies stand in marked contrast to Harry's innate manhood, which is first and foremost demonstrated throughout the novel by his physical strength. As previously noted, he kills Sing with his bare hands. More subtly, after he has been shot in the arm during the rum run in part 2, he manages to steer, weigh anchor, and dump forty-pound sacks of liquor overboard by himself (67–75, 85–87). In these scenes, Harry's masculinity is racially coded as a *white* working-class trait. Wesley, the black man whom Harry carries as a crew member, has also been shot; although his wound is far less severe, he lies moaning and complaining, even "blubber[ing]" with his face in a sack (75), thus forcing Harry to do everything (literally) single-handedly. Another sign of Harry's inherent strength, Hemingway insists, is his acceptance of Wesley's apology for not helping dump the illegal rum: "Hell. . . . [A]in't no nigger any good when he's shot. You're a all right nigger, Wesley" (87). Wesley's weakness is indicative of the novel's unwillingness to attribute authentic masculinity to any of its African American characters, from the "nigger" who baits tackle during Johnson's charter to Albert Tracy, whose lack of composure during the bank robbery occasions his death. Obviously, what contemporary readers will regard as Harry's racism obscures his heroism for us. Yet in Hemingway's moral scheme, Harry's ability to comfort Wesley while forgiving him for his crying is yet one more sign of his manhood: it shows him taking responsibility for someone who needs protection.

By the time Harry contemplates the danger involved in helping the Cuban bank robbers escape Key West, he realizes he has only his masculinity to rely on for his survival, for the only trait or skill he has left to sell is his *cojones*: "The hell with my arm," he tells Albert in chapter 9. "You lose an arm you lose an arm. There's worse things to lose than an arm. You've got two arms and you've got two of something else. And a man's still a man with one arm or with one of those. To hell with it. . . . I got those other two still" (97). Despite the cartoonish insistence on testicular fortitude, Harry's purpose is not simply to exert his manhood out of pride; it is, rather, to keep his family. The dangerous trip is the only option left to him, and in that sense it is a reassertion of his masculine self-reliance. By depriving him of his arm and his boat, big government, as he sarcastically notes, has deprived him of his ability to earn his own way through honest work: "I could sell the house and we could rent until I got some kind of work," he thinks. "What kind of work? No kind of work. I could go down to the bank and squeal now and what would I get? Thanks. Sure. Thanks. One bunch of Cuban government bastards cost me my arm shooting at me with a load when they had no need to and another bunch of U.S. ones took my boat. Now I can give up my home and get thanks. No thanks. The hell with it, he thought. I got no choice in it" (148).

Unlike Albert Tracy, he cannot dig sewers for the government for less money than it takes to feed his family, for a one-armed man cannot wield a shovel. But even if he could, he would not choose subsistence work—the very thought offends his pride in self-reliance: "[M]y kids ain't going to have their bellies hurt and I ain't going to dig sewers for the government for less money than will feed them. I can't dig now anyway. I don't know who made the laws but I know there ain't no law that you got to go hungry" (96). Harry further underlines his masculine individuality by disassociating himself from any ideological affiliation. Having heard rumors that some unidentified "they"—whether government men like Harrison or rich entrepreneurs—are trying to starve out the Conchs so they can tear down their shacks in order to renovate the place for rich tourists, he is quick to insist he is not a radical; he is just "sore" (97).

Equally important, unlike the wealthy, Harry is a good and devoted sexual partner. He and his wife, Marie, are completely compatible; each still finds the other attractive despite the fact that, by their mid-forties, their struggles have aged them. Richard Gordon, passing a weeping Marie as she rushes by to tend to her mortally wounded husband, only views her as a blowsy, overweight, bleached blonde. Because she is not conventionally beautiful like either Helène or Helen, he can only imagine her as a wife, meaning she must be repulsed by sex. He pictures her husband, too, convinced that Harry (whom he does not know) must hate her for her appearance (177). Superficial and easily seduced by wealthy femme fatales like Hélène, Gordon has completely missed the point.

Unfortunately, many Hemingway critics do as well. Comley and Scholes describe Marie as another of Hemingway's "insatiable" women (41), rather than seeing her as Harry's feminine counterpart, a woman whose sexuality both appreciates and mirrors his. In chapter 12, Marie is content with Harry's sexual prowess, and the thought that she "could do that all night if a man was built that way" (115), should be read in the context of her closing interior monologue in chapter 26, in which she laments Harry's death because "I know there wasn't any men like him. I know it too damned well and now he's dead." In her sudden widowhood, Marie reminisces about his desire for her and his steadfastness: "He said he never had anything like me and I know there wasn't any men like him. . . . And he was so goddamned good to me and reliable too, and he always made money some way and I never had to worry about money, only about him, and now that's all gone" (260). During their marriage, Marie takes sexual pleasure only in intercourse with Harry, and he only with her. A real woman, she appreciates a real man; she simply enjoys this physical act with someone she loves. Sex is no more about power for her than it is for her husband. She is not, in short, one of Hemingway's "bitches," unlike Hélène Bradley, Helen Gordon, or Mrs. Laughton.

Critics have argued repeatedly that manhood and heroism are synonymous in Hemingway's fiction, and that the real mark of both is courage and stoicism in the face of death. John J. Seydow, for instance, claims that for Hemingway "heroism and its generic synonym, manhood, occurs when an individual, aware that he is face to face with apparent death, conducts himself with 'grace' at 'the moment of truth'" (40). Harry Morgan displays that courage and stoicism when he dumps sacks of liquor, ignoring the pain in an arm so badly wounded it is later amputated. He displays it again, when, lying with a wound coiling coldly in his belly, he lies back quietly and "takes it" (175), enduring both pain and cold. But most of all he displays it in his marriage and commitment to his family. That devotion, as well as his desire to live, his endurance, and his bravery, make him a man—as opposed to the rich, who spend the novel desperately trying to avoid admitting that they are not, apropos of Fitzgerald, a "special glamorous race."

Notes

1. Only in the original version of Hemingway's story from which this quote is drawn, published in the August 1936 issue of *Esquire*, did the anecdote reference Scott Fitzgerald. Following its publication, a wounded Fitzgerald wrote to Hemingway, asking him to "Please lay off me in print" and to remove his name from subsequent publications of the story (qtd. in Bruccoli 191). Hemingway did so, and when the story was republished in book form two years later in *The Fifth Column and the First Forty-nine Stories*, he attributed the remark to "poor Julian," the version that persists today (*CSS* 53). Of particular interest here is the fact that Fitzgerald seems to deny in his 16 July 1936 letter to Hemingway that he holds the wealthy in awe: "Riches have *never* fascinated me, unless combined with the greatest charm or distinction" (qtd. in Bruccoli 191). In his fine treatment of the Hemingway-Fitzgerald friendship, Bruccoli quotes from the letters exchanged among Hemingway, Fitzgerald, and Maxwell Perkins regarding Hemingway's use of Fitzgerald's name (190–94).

2. Elliott here is citing Dollimore (69).

3. My use of the concept of gender performance is drawn from Judith Butler's *Gender Trouble: Feminism and the Subversion of Identity* and later works. In *Gender Trouble*, Butler argues that gender is a construction that must be constantly performed in order to exist: "Gender ought not to be construed as a stable identity or locus of agency from which various acts follow; rather, gender is an identity tenuously constituted in time, instituted in an exterior space through a *stylized repetition of acts*" (140). She also argues, as does Michel Foucault in *The History of Sexuality, Volume I*, that sexual binarism serves a regulatory purpose, including the repression of homosexuality. Nonetheless, although I use this term, I do not claim that Hemingway regards Harry Morgan as constructing gender through performance; rather, I simply argue that Harry's performance of gender is equated with his social class: in this novel, only working-class men are seen to perform masculinity adequately. Though Hemingway appears to play with the connections between heterosexual desire, heterosexual acts, stereotyped masculinity, and maleness in other works (such as the posthumously published *The Garden of Eden*), he appears to conflate these categories in *To Have and Have Not*. In this novel, Harry Morgan is figured as a "natural man," uncorrupted by wealth, and thus performs masculinity well, while wealthy men do not.

4. Susan F. Beegel also notes this in her essay in this collection.

Hemingway, Faulkner, and Hawks

The Nexus of Creativity that Generated
the Film *To Have and Have Not*

MIMI REISEL GLADSTEIN

Paradoxes and ironies are the stuff of the modern and postmodern ethos. In that context, it is instructive to explore how the seemingly incompatible creative powers of Ernest Hemingway and William Faulkner were yoked in the service of Howard Hawks's directorial genius to create a classic of its genre, the 1944 film version of *To Have and Have Not*. With Jules Furthman as the initiating "yeast," Hawks achieved the presumably paradoxical distinction of taking what he claims he described to Hemingway as "the worst story he had ever written"—what in his mind "was a bunch of junk" (qtd. in G. Phillips, *Hemingway and Film* 50)—and turned it into film magic.[1] As an admirer of both Hemingway's and Faulkner's work, Hawks was in a unique position to facilitate this unusual artistic mix. Although some have maintained that the result was far from the work of either writer (Hemingway's in particular), a revisionist reading argues otherwise. In terms of theme, character, political morality, and even dialogue, Hawks's film is far more faithful to the novel than the superficial differences in time frame and setting have led most critics to appreciate. Analyzing how Hollywood adapted the ethos of Hemingway's most noirish novel into a cinematic triumph teaches us much about the meaning of adaptation itself—specifically, how fidelity ought to be measured according to the spirit rather than letter of the source material.

One of the early ironies is how *To Have and Have Not* was sold—in particular how Hemingway was invoked to attract an audience. The trailer begins with the image of a typewriter superimposed on a spinning globe. The juxtaposition of these images evokes the writer and his worldwide fame and writing scope. The names of countries are flashed one by one: Spain, Italy, Africa, France. These places are the locations for the most popular settings of Hemingway's novels and short stories. Once the image of the adventuresome writer has been established, the narrator reminds the audience of Hemingway's public persona, the soldier of fortune and guide to an invigorating world of excitement. The frame reads: "Ernest Hemingway takes you to the danger zone of the mid-Atlantic."

To cement the connection between Hemingway's work and the film, the book cover is then shown. The narrator proclaims: "Adventure and romance as only Hemingway can write it." But Hemingway did not write the screenplay; thus, irony number one. The film would not be adventure and romance as only Hemingway could write it, but an amalgam in which some lines came directly from the original novel, with a dash of Furthman, more than a little Faulkner, and some lines provided by Hawks as scenes were shot. In other words, *To Have and Have Not* was, in all senses, a collaboration.

Yet this was a fact that the trailer made only indirectly, almost as an afterthought. After Hemingway's touting, Hawks's name appears onscreen to give him a plug: "Another triumph from Howard Hawks who directed *Sergeant York*." Gary Cooper, the star of *Sergeant York*, had won an Academy Award for his portrayal of the World War I hero in that 1941 film, and so the public was familiar with the excellence attached to Hawks's name. Of course, there was a Cooper-Hemingway connection as well: the actor had portrayed Robert Jordan in Sam Wood's 1943 film version of *For Whom the Bell Tolls*.

Interestingly, Faulkner's contribution was *not* trumpeted in the coming attraction. Nor would it have had much impact as a draw for the average moviegoer in the mid-1940s. His importance, however, is signaled by that fact that he and coauthor Jules Furthman were given an entire frame in the titles to acknowledge their screenplay. This is significant in that sometimes the authors of a screenplay were buried in the credits among set designers, costumers, assistant directors, and many other unheralded individuals.

One of the small paradoxes here is how Faulkner, noted for a reticulated style almost diametrically opposite to Hemingway's spare prose, should so effectively assume the Hemingway voice. Thrown into the mix is the added small irony that, while critics generally concede that Faulkner did not have much respect for the "art" of motion pictures, he did some fine screenwriting. Indeed, Bruce Kawin claims that Faulkner did his best work for Hawks: "The story of Faulkner the screenwriter is fundamentally that of his relationship with Howard Hawks" ("Faulkner's Film Career" 165). This may be due to the fact that Hawks sought him out because he respected Faulkner's writing, especially *Soldier's Pay* (1926). In his regard for writers, Hawks was unlike fellow Hollywood luminaries such as Jack Warner, who characterized them as "schmucks with typewriters."[2]

Despite the collaborative nature of the project, the trailer makes clear that Hemingway was the main selling point for the film. How ironic then that what was originally sold as all Hemingway should, in the majority of the critical commentary for more than a half century since its first screening, be described as a film in which very little of Hemingway made its way into the final product. From the film's initial reviews such as Bosley Crowther's complaint that "what Mr. Hawks and his scriptwriters have done to Mr. Hemingway's tale is to shape it out of all recognition" (24) to Susan F. Beegel's assessment that "Hemingway's novel is virtually unrecognizable in the film" ("Conclusion" 288), there has been a general disparagement of Hawks's film as an adaptation of Hemingway's novel.

A strong argument can be made against this assessment. A close reading of both novel and film demonstrates quite a different interpretation of the adaptation's efficacy. Perhaps the overriding paradox lies in the fact that although there may not be literal conformity between the novel and the movie, the film adaptation does maintain fidelity to Hemingway in matters of characterization, style, and theme. There is general consensus among contemporary adaptation theorists that, because of the demands of the film medium, a successful adaptation will necessarily make changes. The important factor is that those changes communicate the spirit and themes of the original text.[3] Hawks's movie can thus be characterized as authentic in that the impetus and objective of its changes are consistent with Hemingway's characters, theme, and tone.

What has led to the common perception that Hemingway's novel is virtually unrecognizable in the film? At the heart of the issue lies the question of plot and characters. Half of the characters in the novel are left out of the film, and only part of the storyline is retained. According to Hawks, he and Hemingway decided that for purposes of translating the book to film, the first and last parts of the plot, basically the "action," would make the most coherent movie. The Richard Gordon/John MacWalsey adultery storyline is left out, as is the derogatory portrait of the sexually insatiable Helène Bradley. In Hawks's opinion, the "haves" subplot would distract from the story of Harry Morgan and his wife, Marie. Additionally, Hawks had the idea that he wanted to flesh out the tale by presenting events preceding the book's beginning. He claims that he and Hemingway roughed out a plan for the film script.[4] In Hemingway's story, Harry Morgan and his wife are middle-aged, the parents of three daughters. The Morgans' situation is a rarity in Hemingway's works; they have a long-standing, mutually loving, and sexually satisfying marriage. Hawks thought it would be interesting to explore this love-match by focusing on how the Morgans meet and fall in love.

A small problem pointed out by some bothered by the alteration is that if Hawks is trying to tell how the couple in Hemingway's novel met, he has made some awkward adjustments in their age differential. In the novel, the Morgans are both in their mid-forties. The film version, however, creates an age disparity with Bogart approximating Harry's age in the novel, not what he might have looked like when he and Marie first met. In keeping with telling the story of how they met, Bacall plays a much younger version of Marie, whose maiden name is Browning. This change in time period also allows for a different ending, a happier one, since Harry obviously cannot die in this version, which happens years before the events of the novel. The shift also requires additional changes, such as the collapsing of the roles of Harry's two interchangeable African American employees, Eddy Marshall and Albert Tracy, and the deletion of several minor colorful characters (the shady lawyer Bee-lips, for example).

Another major change is in the setting. Yet this came about not as a result of a creative decision but from a warning from the Office of Inter-American Affairs, which threatened to deny the film an export license because of the sensitivities to issues of Cuban-American relations in the 1940s.

Hawks credits Faulkner with the idea of moving the action from Key West and Cuba to Martinique, thereby involving Harry in the battle against the Vichy French instead of Hemingway's anti-Machado revolutionaries. Gene D. Phillips explains that Faulkner had, the year before, written a screenplay about General Charles de Gaulle that was not produced (*Hemingway and Film* 52). He was, therefore, more conversant with the battle against the Nazi collaborators than Cuba's political upheavals. Other alterations necessarily follow from the change of time and place.

Despite these major changes, there remain many correspondences between the novel and film *To Have and Have Not*. Initially these correlations are strong, starting with imagery. The novel begins: "You know how it is there early in the morning in Havana with the bums still asleep against the walls of the buildings" (3). A similar ambiance is set early in the film when Harry finds not an anonymous bum but his mate, Eddy, passed out on the dock. Whether the reader has to imagine the bums asleep against the walls of buildings or the viewer comes upon Eddy in a drunken stupor sprawled out on the dock, the slightly sordid atmosphere is established. In the text, when Eddy makes his first appearance, Harry comments: "Eddy looked pretty bad. He never looked too good early in the morning; but he looked pretty bad now" (9). The film's Eddy looks none too good either when Harry throws water on him to wake him out of his drunken stupor (Kawin, *To Have and Have Not* 72). Walter Brennan's interpretation of the "rummy" Eddy further confirms Hemingway's influence on the style of the film. Brennan develops a kind of bouncy, edgy, and quirky walk for the character, thus actualizing Hemingway's description: "He walked with his joints all slung wrong" (9).

Both the action of the novel and the film follow from Harry's initial refusal to carry illicit cargo and the events that lead him to change his mind. He is a foreigner, and he does not want to get involved in local island politics. In the novel he argues with the Cuban revolutionaries who want him to smuggle them into the United States. He refuses, telling them, "Listen, I don't care who is president here" (4). Harry explains that he makes his living with the boat and if he loses her, he loses his living.

A variation on this scene initiates the movie's plot. This time, however, it is the free French who try to hire Harry at a much less lucrative rate. His response in the movie mirrors the one in the novel: "I don't care who runs

France or Martinique" (Kawin, *To Have and Have Not* 96). Trying to convince the novel's reluctant Harry to smuggle them into the United States, one of the Cubans says, "Afterwards, when things are changed, it would mean a good deal to you" (*THHN* 4). This exact line is uttered by one of the Frenchmen in the movie. In the novel, the discussion takes place in the Pearl of San Francisco Café, while in the film it happens in the hotel office above the bar. This probably results because the hotel and its owner, Frenchy, are key to the film's plot, and Frenchy is the one who makes the connection between Harry and the free French. The hotel serves as a setting for many scenes in the film.

In Hemingway's text, a gun battle erupts when the Cubans leave the Pearl, killing some of them. Similarly, in the film, gunfire erupts when the Frenchmen leave the Marquee Hotel, where Harry is at the bar with Johnson and Frenchy. Some are killed in this scene also, and some get away. Both scenes are important in establishing the lawlessness of the setting, the cheapness of life, and the precariousness of Harry's situation.

The Mr. Johnson episode is another area of close correspondence between novel and film. Johnson is Harry's fishing client, and his failure to pay his bill leaves Harry in the unenviable position of having to risk himself and his boat. In both versions, Johnson, one of the "haves," shows his lack of character. In fact, much of the dialogue between Johnson and Harry is duplicated exactly from the book, even to the most inane detail. Johnson approaches the boat and asks, "Well are we going out?" Harry responds, "That's up to you." Johnson then asks, "What sort of a day will it be?" Harry says: "Just about like yesterday. Maybe better." Johnson decides, "Let's go then" (*THHN* 9). Since Johnson has been running a tab, Harry has to ask him for money for gas. Again, the dialogue is identical:

"I'll need some money for that."
"How much?"
"It's twenty eight cents a gallon. I ought to put in forty gallons anyway. That's eleven dollars and twenty cents." (*THHN* 10; Kawin *To Have and Have Not* 74–75)

Johnson gives him fifteen dollars and tells him to apply the change to his bill. By using the same clipped dialogue, the same rhythms and tones of speech, Hawks creates strong parallels between text and screen. For the readers of the novel, the film's dialogue is recognizably Hemingwayesque—brief, declarative sentences.

Also in keeping with the fidelity to Hemingway's text, there is the same dialogue about why "Horatio," identified only as "the nigger" in the novel, should be on board. Harry explains that he is there to bait the hooks, and Johnson resents paying him a measly dollar a day for that labor. Harry assures Johnson of Horatio's ability to "bait" rapidly (Kawin, *To Have and Have Not* 78). Many lines about Johnson's inept fishing skills and the carelessness with which he loses the equipment also move directly from page to screen. Johnson balks at having to pay for the loss. The screenplay follows the novel's dialogue as Harry explains that if he rented a car and drove it over a cliff he would have to pay for it. The only difference is that Eddy is given Johnson's rejoinder, "Not if he was in it" (Kawin, *To Have and Have Not* 188). Many other lines—even the sum Johnson owes ($825 for the days of charter and losing the rod and reel and line)—are transposed unchanged from the text to the screen. In both works, Johnson offers to settle up in the morning, and he and Harry have a drink together. And in both works Johnson, a cheat and four-flusher, has no intention to pay as he plans to catch an early plane off the island. In the film, however, the double-dealer is killed, whereas in the novel he gets away (Kawin, *To Have and Have Not* 102). Nonetheless, the result is the same: Harry has lost his rod, reel, line, and eighteen days of charter work. This leaves him vulnerable to the enticement of an illegal venture. The literal accuracy, actions, and dialogue taken straight from the page to the screen are a main component in establishing the adaptation's faithfulness to its source.

In keeping with this fidelity, there is also a more abstract parallelism, a kind of resonance between Hemingway's text and Hawks's and Faulkner's. As stated earlier, Hawks wanted to tell the story of how Harry and Marie met and fell in love. In this, he succeeds admirably because the Harry and Marie of the film are believable antecedents to Hemingway's original characters. The book depicts them as an independent duo, living on the margins of society, a pair that are very much in love. But, whether in their younger or older incarnations, they are essentially the same characters; their traits and personalities have not changed. Hemingway's Marie is tough and resilient. She is a survivor. At the end of the novel, she stoically accepts Harry's death at the hands of the Cubans: "I guess you find out everything in this goddamned life. . . . Well, I've got a good start" (*THHN* 261). As a young woman, Hawks's Marie shows those same tough and resilient traits. The "good start" that the older Marie refers to in the book is demonstrated by how her younger version handles adversity in the film.

For example, Marie's poise and buoyancy are evident in the film's stolen wallet scene. In it, Marie takes Johnson's wallet, and Harry calls her on it. It is early in their relationship. Harry leads her into his room and locks the door. Rather than getting agitated or frightened, Marie remains cool and collected. When Harry looks in the wallet, he finds that Johnson did have sufficient traveler's checks to pay him, although Johnson had claimed he had to go to the bank in the morning. Harry also discovers the early-morning plane reservation, before the time set for their meeting. He suggests that he and Marie should share the spoils of the wallet and asks her what she thinks would be fair (Kawin, *To Have and Have Not* 88–92). Later, Marie accompanies Harry downstairs to confront Johnson. She evidences no nervousness or hesitation in this scene.

Not only is Marie cool when caught as a thief; she is likewise reliable in an emergency situation. When Paul de Bursac, a leader of the Free French movement, is shot, Harry is called upon to remove the bullet from his wound. During the makeshift operation, de Bursac's wife, Helene, faints. Without missing a beat, Marie quickly steps in (Kawin, *To Have and Have Not* 150–51). The sight of blood does not faze her. When the Vichy police question Marie, she flippantly tells them that she got off in Martinique to buy a new hat. The inspector slaps her when she repeats the claim, and yet she coolly continues, finishing her sentence (Kawin, *To Have and Have Not* 108). A key example of her reliability in an emergency is in the final part of the film. The Vichy French, under the leadership of Captain M. Renard, detain Eddy and are about to take Marie and Harry in. Knowing that she will pick up on his clues—they are already like an old married couple in that respect—Harry requests a cigarette. He tells her, "You'll find some in that drawer, Slim." She tosses him the cigarettes and leaves the drawer open. Harry then requests matches and maneuvers his way to the drawer, which contains a gun. Firing from the drawer, Harry kills one of Renard's men and intimidates the others (Kawin, *To Have and Have Not* 175).

Hawks's proto-Marie is thus cool under fire and plays her part without flinching. In this climactic action scene Harry and Marie work as a team, thus prefiguring their marriage. The behavior of the film Marie provides exposition for the mutual love and respect exhibited by the couple in the novel. Both in the novel and the film, Marie is portrayed as a woman who has been around, who has had many men. She is independent and hard-drinking like other Hemingway heroines. In a tense bar scene with Cricket (played by Hoagy Carmichael), she tells him she needs a drink and orders a "Scotch and soda" (Kawin, *To Have and Have Not* 114). In the world of drink symbolism, that is more of a man's drink, not very ladylike. But then, Hemingway does not characterize Marie as a "lady." Though she may have known many men, Hemingway's Marie is convinced of Harry's unique-ness: "There ain't no other men like that. People ain't never tried them don't know. I've had plenty of them" (*THHN* 114). The Hawks-Faulkner-Furthman Marie is experienced with men, and like Hemingway's character, gives them all up for Harry. In a key scene, when she and Harry want a drink, she demonstrates her savvy and ability to manipulate men as the couple repairs to the Zombie bar. They realize they are broke, and Marie offers to do something about their impoverished state. She picks out a likely mark, approaches him for a light, and Harry leaves her dancing with him. The scene fades, and the next scene begins with her knocking on Harry's door with a bottle for them to share. She describes it as "like shooting fish in a barrel . . . men like that" (Kawin, *To Have and Have Not* 113). It is a convincing antecedent to Hemingway's more mature Marie, who recalls, "I've had plenty of them" (*THHN* 115).

If the Bacall character in the movie is a convincing younger version for the novel's Marie, then Humphrey Bogart's Harry seems to have walked straight from Hemingway's pages. The consistency of characterization has been noted even by those who complain about the lack of correspondence between film and novel. Gene D. Phillips identifies Harry as the "typical Hawksian hero: a man who achieves self-respect by stoically maintaining his personal integrity" (*Hemingway and Film* 54). Both Harrys value cour-age, competence, and loyalty to comrades. The film persona of Humphrey Bogart—competent, reserved, and cool under pressure—fits nicely into the Hemingway code-hero mold. The character of Harry Morgan in Hemingway's novel is an ideal fulcrum for joining the film persona of Bogart, the Hawks Hero, and Hemingway. In a telling side note, Jeffrey Meyers makes the point that there not only are resemblances between the film character Bogart created and the character Hemingway created in the novel, but that the "similarities between Humphrey Bogart and Ernest Hemingway are quite striking" ("Bogart and Hemingway" 446).[5] After pointing out a number of biographical parallels, he concludes that both created, one in fiction and one on film, "tough heroes, torn between ironic fatalism and despairing courage, who sought authenticity and adhered to a strict code of honor" (449).

In terms of the love story, the main differences are external and superficial and can easily be attributed to the time differential between the two texts. In the film, Marie is literally and figuratively "Slim," as her nickname designates; in the novel, she is fat. In the film, she is young; in the novel she is older and has three children. In the one, she is a girlfriend; in the other a wife and mother. But the chemistry that would lead to the loving relationship in the novel is apparent in the film and is probably most evident in the famous whistle scene, the "come-on" that ignites the love affair. That exchange is preceded by several scenes of give-and-take, the one and then the other getting angry and leaving each other's respective rooms. Finally, they kiss, and as Marie gets ready to leave, she expresses herself in a manner that could be called Hemingwayesque—that is, what is not said is as important as what is. She tells him: "You don't have to say anything and you don't have to do anything. Not a thing. Oh, maybe just whistle. You know how to whistle, don't you, Steve? [Harry's nickname]. You just put your lips together and blow" (Kawin, *To Have and Have Not* 120). Harry is left speechless, emitting only a wolf whistle. Everything is innuendo and double entendre, the kind of hard-boiled dialogue in which Hemingway excelled and which by 1944—thanks in no small part to the noir of "The Killers" and the book version of *To Have and Have Not*—had infiltrated the culture. Guillermo Cabrera Infante, writing of Hemingway's influence on Hollywood, claims that in the 1930s and 1940s, movie actors spoke like Hemingway characters, and behaved like them, drinking and carrying on in a convivial manner even as they were basically unhappy (6–9).[6]

A minor Hemingway flavor that makes its way, via Hawks, into the film script is in the matter of nicknames. In the movie, as already noted, Harry calls Marie "Slim." She counters that she does not like his doing so because she is, in fact, quite slender. In turn, for no apparent reason except in response to his having nicknamed her, she calls him "Steve" throughout much of the film. Film buffs are aware that "Slim" is the nickname Hawks had for his wife and "Steve" is what she called him. And while this may be Hawks putting his personal stamp on the story, it is also very much in keeping with the Hemingway persona. Hemingway was called by a variety of pet names throughout his life, from the early "Hemingstein," "Tatie," and "Wemedge" to the most universally well-known "Papa." He also had nicknames for many of the people in his life, calling his first son "Bumby," Marlene Dietrich "The Kraut," and Martha Gellhorn "Marty"—to name a few. Having the two main characters use nicknames for each other in the film thus reinforces the Hemingway tone.

Hawks's narrative ends in Marie's union with Harry; Hemingway's begins in the union and concludes with separation. But love moves both plots. In the novel, Harry risks his life to get money for Marie and his family. This is consistent with the film's younger version, "Steve," who does a similar thing for "Slim." The Bogart character uses the money he earns from his dangerous venture with the free French to get a ticket back to the United States for Marie. She, however, does not go, but shows her faithfulness by staying on the island to wait for him. Again, there is coherence between Marie in the novel and Marie in the film: both wait loyally while the man they love navigates dangerous waters.

Stylistically, Hawks's *To Have and Have Not* also resonates with Hemingway-like technique. Even Gerald Mast, who finds "little resemblance" between the movie and the novel, acknowledges "an unmistakable Hemingway aroma and flavor" about the film (245). Like Hemingway, Hawks was the master of detail and economy, getting the maximum of meaning in the minimum of verbiage. Hawks called this a "three-cushion style," an allusion to pool or billiards when the ball ricochets or cushions itself against the sides of the table before going in the pocket, and he claims to have learned it from Hemingway, who spoke of his "three-cushion shot." Another word Hawks used to describe his film technique is "oblique." One telling example is the scene where Harry first encounters Marie. Harry comes up to his room with Frenchy. Marie is just coming out of hers, which is opposite his. He goes into his room, and she rests herself against his door frame and asks, "Have you got a match?" He tosses the matches across the room to her, and she catches them easily, lights her cigarette while he is eyeing her and Frenchy is eyeing the two of them. She says, "Thanks," tosses the matches back and leaves. It is all there, the attraction and her coolness of character, but Marie has only two lines: "Have you got a match?" and "Thanks." No one else speaks (Kawin, *To Have and Have Not* 85–86). Just as the Hemingway reader must read between the lines, supplying the seven-eighths of the iceberg that is not visible, so too, in this scene, meaning is carried in looks, pacing, and style—and not in verbal exchange.

Later in the film, when it is apparent that Marie and Harry will be a couple, again little is said directly. Marie thinks Harry is leaving with Eddy. In one of the most understated proposals in the history of American film, he says: "We're leaving here for good. The three of us." Harry warns Marie that they will probably be broke, and it might be a rough time for a while. Rather than specifically address the question of what direction their relationship will take, she tells him that it might be forever, inquiring if that frightens him. Rather than answer her question, he responds, "How long will it take you to pack?" (Kawin, *To Have and Have Not* 218). Thus, the screenplay dialogue, in what it does not say, evidences an oblique, Hemingwayesque style, in which the audience can fill in, answering the questions that are not asked, banking or ricocheting off the context of the situation to arrive at the proper conclusion to the "shot." Harry does not have to propose marriage; Marie gets the message of what is not said.

One constant in much of the criticism about the film *To Have and Have Not* (1944) is that it is really just a reworking of *Casablanca* (1942), which had been such a popular film for Warner Brothers. The argument ran that here again was Humphrey Bogart in an exotic locale, neutral and independent at first, but eventually taking a stand against a Nazi government. Notwithstanding such superficial similarities, that facile comparison does not take into account major character and plot differences. *Casablanca's* Rick Blaine is a "have"—he is the owner of his own club, a figure of glamour. He has funds and status within his community. The film ends with his noble renunciation as he sends the woman he loves off to do her duty by her freedom-fighter husband. In the last frame, Rick walks off into the mist with Captain Louis Renault as he utters that famous exit line: "Louis, I think this is the beginning of a beautiful friendship." *To Have and Have Not's* protagonist is quite different. Harry is definitely a "have not." The clubs he sits in are not his, and in fact, he is behind in his payments to the owner, Frenchy. Harry gets involved with the cause initially because he needs money. Unlike Rick, who is in love with the wife of the French freedom-fighter, Harry tells Mrs. de Bursac that she made a fool of herself. Eventually, when Harry decides to help, he claims that he does so for personal reasons, that he likes Frenchy and the de Bursacs, and he does not like Renard and his cronies with their strong-arm tactics. Instead of a romantically sad but noble ending, in the last scene of Hawks's movie Harry, Marie, and Eddy dance off into the credits.

Still another thematic parallel between novel and film is the issue of comradeship. Hemingway's Harry, as he lies dying, articulates it: "[A] man alone ain't got no bloody fucking chance" (*THHN* 225). Hemingway would return to the theme in the title allusion of *For Whom the Bell Tolls*, drawn from John Donne: "No man is an *Iland*, intire of it selfe."[7] In the Hawks film, Harry's commitment to his friends is substantiated through a "strings" metaphor. In one scene, before their relationship is cemented, Marie is trying to do something for Harry such as untie his shoes, get him something to eat, or run him a hot bath. He refuses each offer and then asks her to walk around him. She does and then he asks her if she runs into anything, obviously implying that there are no strings attached to him (Kawin, *To Have and Have Not* 157). Though he presents an independent bravado, his actions belie his inferences. When Frenchy shows up to let him know that the Gestapo has Eddy, he bolts down the steps. Marie calls after him, "Look out for those strings, Steve. You're liable to trip on them and break your neck." Frenchy is confused and proclaims that he does not see any strings. Marie responds that they are there but they just don't show (Kawin *To Have and Have Not* 211). Earlier in the story, Eddy ironically expresses the theme of mutual dependence. Harry is going on a dangerous mission and tells his deckhand he cannot go. Eddy stows away and when he is found says, "You and me's got to stick together when we're in trouble." He begins to realize that the reason Harry had not wanted him along was: "You was afraid I'd get hurt! You was thinkin' o' me" (Kawin, *To Have and Have Not* 201–2).

Hence the theme of the film and the novel are essentially similar. For one motive or the other—be it money, love, friendship, or political conscience—one will be forced to enter the fray and if one is alone one has "no bloody fucking chance." Still, whether Harry kills as in the movie or is killed as in the novel, he remains, à la Santiago in *The Old Man and the Sea*, destroyed but not defeated. And to this major Hemingway theme Hawks remains true. In the film, the ending is positive, in no small part because Harry is not alone; Marie and Eddy are with him. The possibilities for him on Martinique are destroyed, but he is undefeated.

In conclusion, let me reiterate the theoretical basis for my thesis that *To Have and Have Not* is an acceptable adaptation of Hemingway's novel. A cinematic adaptation does not necessarily have to be a point-by-point graphic illustration of a literary text. It can be a variation on the narrative framework, an artistic re-creation—and here we have a number of artists involved—of the characters and some circumstances of the original. Without attempting literal, page-by-page fidelity to its source, a satisfactory adaptation can be something very much like the multiple versions of Greek and Roman myths that the ancient bards produced in their telling, retelling, and elaborating on the stories. When Euripides wrote *The Trojan Women*, he chose to tell the story of what happens after Homer's *Iliad* ends. In this case, Hawks reverses the procedure; since Hemingway has told us the end of the Harry Morgan story, Hawks, with Faulkner's assistance, decides to tell us how it all began.

Notes

1. Lozano-Moreno expresses doubts about Hawks's version of the story. Since Hawks was the buyer, perhaps he was trying to depreciate a valuable property in order to get it at a lower price. Obviously, he thought the material rich or he would not have paid so much for it. Hemingway had sold it to Howard Hughes for $10,000 and Warner Brothers then paid Hughes $92,000 for it. Also, the result, if he made a good picture out of "junk," would present him as a genius that could turn dross into gold (195–96). My interpretation owes a great deal to Lozano-Moreno's comprehensive study.

2. See Kawin, "Faulkner's Film Career." Jack Warner's gaucherie was a Hollywood commonplace, and this particular quotation has been repeated often.

3. See Stam's *Literature through Film* (4), and Griffith's *Adaptations as Imitations: Film from Novels* (41).

4. In *Howard Hawks, Storyteller*, Mast quotes Hawks as saying: "So we sat around for two weeks and evolved the story that we did which was the meeting of the two people in his story and it had very much the same background" (243).

5. Among the similarities Meyers describes are dates of birth (1899), love of weak fathers, and dislike for their stronger mothers. He also notes that both Hemingway and Bogart were heavy drinkers, each had four wives, and both had a passion for boats. He maintains that "they acted out in real life the public personae—Bogie and Papa—they had established in their work" ("Bogart and Hemingway" 449).

6. Mine is a loose translation of Cabrera's text, which reads: "La mayor parte de los

guiones de entonces eran comedias de Broadway, pero un poco más tarde cada personaje de cada película de Hollywood no solo hablaban como los personajes de Hemingway sino que bebian y eran alegres pero infelices, igual que los personajes de Hemingway." He maintains that soon it was impossible to tell whether Hemingway characters spoke like Hollywood actors or whether Hollywood characters spoke like Hemingway wrote.

7. "No man is an *Iland*, intire of it selfe; every man is a peece of the *Continent*, a part of the *maine*; if a *Clod* bee washed away by the *Sea, Europe* is the lesse, as well as if a *Promontorie* were, as well as if a *Manner* of thy *friends* or of *thine owne* were; any mans *death* diminishes *me*, because I am involved in *Mankinde*; And therefore never send to know for whom the *bell* tolls; It tolls for *thee*."

Tourism, Celebrity, Natural Disaster

Hemingway's Neglected Florida Fiction and Essays

Reexamining the Origins of "After the Storm"

MICHAEL J. CROWLEY

Ernest Hemingway's "After the Storm" (1932) recounts the powerful and memorable story of one man's struggle against the elements in an attempt to loot a sunken ship. The narrator's actions are only one step removed from grave-robbing, and his matter-of-fact descriptions of these actions are uncomfortably cold-blooded. Unaffected by the deaths of 450 passengers and crew, the narrator estimates the treasure in the grave he is attempting to loot at "five million dollars worth" and explains, "It made me shaky to think how much she must have in her" (*CSS* 284, 285). But the story is the first in a collection entitled *Winner Take Nothing*, and the narrator is doomed to failure. Unable to break the closest porthole and reach the drowned woman with rings on her fingers that he sees within, he is forced to return to Sou'west Key empty-handed. Greeks with more men and better equipment find the ship and take the safe and all of the valuables before the narrator can make his way back. Juxtaposed with the narrator's description of his fruitless attempts to loot the ship are his speculations about what must have happened on board the ship as the captain attempted—skillfully but ultimately in vain—to make it through the storm.

"After the Storm" is an important if relatively neglected story in Hemingway's oeuvre in part because it marks his first use of material from his Key West years. The characters he met and the waters he fished in Key West play instrumental roles in it, while the story itself plays a defining thematic role as the first piece in *Winner Take Nothing*. (The preliminary title of the collection had, in fact, been *After the Storm, and Other Stories* before Hemingway came up with a more evocative alternative.)[1] The story is additionally important because it offers insight into Hemingway's literary method and the various approaches by which critics gauge it, whether source studies, composition histories, or biographical analysis. No sooner had "After the Storm" appeared in *Cosmopolitan* than Hemingway boasted to friends and family that he had taken it verbatim from a story told to him by Bra Saunders, the Conch fisherman who served as Hemingway's Gulf Stream guide in the late 1920s and early 1930s.[2] As Hemingway insisted to Maxwell Perkins a few weeks after the publication of *Winner Take Nothing*, the story was written "word for word as it happened to Bra" (*SL* 400). Since the appearance of Carlos Baker's *Ernest Hemingway: A Life Story* (1969), Saunders has widely been credited as the source of the story, with only a smattering of critics—Susan F. Beegel, most notably—examining its various drafts to question the ways in which Hemingway transformed the original anecdote. For a writer whose stylistic simplicity often suggests that he merely transcribed experiences around him with little imaginative transformation, this is a dangerous oversight, for it obscures the inevitable role that invention played in his writing.[3] Whatever Hemingway's reasons for denying any creative contribution to "After the Storm"—and he made similar claims for "Out of Season" (1923) and "Hills Like White Elephants" (1927)—his account of the story's genesis was itself such a convincing, well-told tale that he effectively obscured his role in its writing, the thematic import it held for him, and even the circumstances under which he first heard the *donnée*.

According to James McLendon's *Papa: Hemingway in Key West* (1972), Ernest and Pauline arrived in Key West on the last day of the first week of April 1928 (22). Hemingway adjusted quickly to the new environment, making friends easily and acquainting himself with the town. He soon found a hospitable bar in Sloppy Joe's, a fellow fisherman in Charles Thompson, and "a professional fishing guide who knew every shoal and key and mangrove swamp from Homestead to the Dry Tortugas" in the aforementioned Bra Saunders (Baker, *A Life Story* 192). In this period, Hemingway spent his mornings working on *A Farewell to Arms* and his afternoons and evenings fishing with Thompson. Pauline, in the meantime, "with her pregnancy and fragile size was having considerable difficulty adjusting to the island's heat" (McLendon 29–30). To escape the climate, Pauline took a train to her parents' home in Piggott, Arkansas, while Hemingway remained in Key West, inviting several friends to join him for fishing and good times in what he called "The St. Tropez of the Poor" (McLendon 34).

Exactly who he invited and when those guests arrived is somewhat unclear. Carlos Baker lists Henry "Mike" Strater, John Dos Passos, Waldo Peirce, and Bill Smith (*A Life Story* 193), all of whom formed a group that, according to McLendon, Hemingway dubbed the "Mob" (35). [4] During their stay in Key West, the Mob went to the Dry Tortugas, hiring Bra Saunders to take them. It was on this trip, according to Baker, that Saunders told the group of his discovery of the sunken *Valbanera* and his attempts to break a porthole so he could loot the ship, the story that eventually became "After the Storm" (*A Life Story* 193–94). [5]

Baker's account of the 1928 fishing trip has influenced nearly all of the biographies and most of the criticism on "After the Storm" published in the past forty years. Baker is unambiguous about when Saunders told Hemingway the story, and he emphasizes Hemingway's debt to Saunders, calling "After the Storm" "Bra Saunders's tale of the sunken liner" (*A Life Story* 241). Baker does not address Hemingway's fidelity to the original tale, nor does he question the veracity of Saunders's story: "Bra was the first to find her, and nearly killed himself in successive vain attempts to crack open her portholes to get at the loot inside" (*A Life Story* 194). For Baker, "After the Storm" owes its artistic success to Saunders: "This was a yarn direct from life, piratical in flavor, with its own intrinsic form. It was the kind of story he [Hemingway] liked to know and tell—one man alone against the elements, strong and self-reliant, pitting his courage and endurance against great odds" (*A Life Story* 194).

In *Hemingway's Craft of Omission* (1988), however, Susan F. Beegel convincingly demonstrates that "After the Storm" is far from a word-for-word transcription of the old guide's story. The *Valbanera* did indeed sink, and Saunders may or may not have been the first person to find her. Yet Beegel's study of the three existing manuscripts reveals that Hemingway invented at least three important elements: the diving episode, the image of the drowned woman, and the looting of the ship by Greeks (*Craft of Omission* 80–82). Hemingway's claim simply to have recorded Saunders's story, Beegel argues, was "deliberately exaggerated to support the short story's illusion of verity"

(70). Several questions thus arise: How did these changes alter the thematic concerns of the story? And do the alterations in any way call into question the biographical record established by Baker?

If Hemingway's goal had ever been to record "word for word" what had happened to Bra Saunders, he probably came closest to achieving that goal in his initial draft (item 226).[6] The setting is clearly based on the actual telling of Bra's story, with Waldo Peirce and John Dos Passos serving as the models for the characters of "Waldo" and "Dos," and Hemingway himself providing the basis for the first-person narrator. The characters are aboard a fishing boat anchored in Eastern Harbor. The draft begins with the unnamed narrator sitting in the stern beneath the moonlight, talking to "Bra," the captain of the boat, while "Waldo" and "Dos" are lying down on the forward deck, apparently asleep. Much like the earliest attempt at *The Sun Also Rises*—the first draft that features "Hem" instead of "Jake

20. Hemingway fishing with (*left to right*) Bra Saunders and Waldo Peirce, late 1920s. Saunders was the inspiration for the short story "After the Storm"—though Hemingway would deceptively overstate the influence of the local fisherman on his first Key West fiction. Ernest Hemingway Collection/John F. Kennedy Presidential Library and Museum, Boston.

Chapter 12

Barnes," "Duff" instead of "Brett Ashley," and "Niño de la Palma" instead of "Pedro Romero"—Hemingway seems to be drawing directly from real life (Reynolds, *Paris Years* 306–7).

And yet this first version of "After the Storm" seems to simplify the actual events, at least as Baker and subsequent biographers have presented them. Instead of including all of the listeners mentioned by Baker and McLendon, Hemingway includes only "Waldo" and "Dos." An alternative explanation is that only Peirce and Dos Passos were present to hear Bra's story, not Strater and Smith. If so—if, in other words, this first draft is indeed an accurate representation of that telling—then the biographical record to date has been wrong. Additionally, if Peirce and Dos Passos were with Hemingway as Saunders recounted his experience—as this draft indicates and the biographies insist—then a major question arises concerning the presumed 1928 date of the fishing trip during which Saunders related his story.

John Dos Passos's visit to Key West in 1928 was a very important event in his life. During this visit he met Katy Smith, Hemingway's old friend from his Michigan summers. Dos Passos and Smith hit it off, and by August 1929, they were married (Ludington 266). In 1928, however, Dos Passos spent only a few days with Katy, for he had left New York in mid-April to escape the pressures of his political activism and his involvement in the New Playwrights Theatre, and by early May he was back in New York preparing for his trip to the Soviet Union (Ludington 265). In fact, Dos Passos left Key West so soon that, according to Virginia Spencer Carr, he did not "meet Katy's brother, Bill Smith, in 1928 or any of Hemingway's other cronies from his Paris days. . . . Artists Waldo Peirce and Henry Strater arrived a few days after he left" (232). The fact that Dos Passos and Peirce, who both figure prominently in the first draft of "After the Storm," were not in Key West at the same time in 1928 suggests that Saunders's telling of the *Valbanera* story did not occur that year.

Baker and McLendon are quite clear, however, when they say that Saunders *did* tell Hemingway his story in 1928. This would have been while he was working on *A Farewell to Arms*. If he wrote the first draft of "After the Storm" soon after hearing the anecdote, he would have had to break away from his work on the novel, which had just reached 108 manuscript pages around the time of Dos Passos's April 26 arrival (Reynolds,

Hemingway's First War 20). Two decades later, Hemingway recalled "living in the book"—*Arms*, that is—as he followed a strict writing regimen: "Each day I read the book through from the beginning to the point where I went on writing and each day I stopped when I was still going good and when I knew what would happen next. . . . Beside it nothing else mattered" (introduction to *FTA* vii). While the intervening years may have colored his memory, Hemingway told much the same story in 1928. Writing to Maxwell Perkins on 31 May 1928 after leaving Key West to join Pauline in Piggott, he commented on the success of both his work and play during Peirce's visit: "You've probably seen Waldo. We had a grand time. I worked every morning too and did 200 pages—200 words or so to a page—in Key West" (*SL* 278). Hemingway's intense absorption in *A Farewell to Arms* suggests that he certainly did not compose the first draft of "After the Storm" at the time of Dos Passos's and Peirce's 1928 visits or even shortly afterward. His writing that summer was devoted to the novel. Nonetheless, according to Beegel, "All evidence suggests that Bra *told* Hemingway the *Valbanera* story . . . on their 1928 fishing trip" (*Craft of Omission* 77, emphasis added). As evidence, Beegel cites a letter from Hemingway to Peirce dated 15 April 1932 (*Craft of Omission* 69, 110). Unfortunately, the letter does not clarify the chronology of events, for it does not date the origin of Bra's story. Hemingway simply mentions that one of his stories will soon be published in *Cosmopolitan* and reminds Peirce, "You probably remember when Bra told it to us first" (*SL* 358). Nor is an earlier letter of much help: on 26 March 1932, Hemingway had written to Dos Passos, "Sold that After the Storm [*sic*] story for plenty," suggesting that Dos Passos would also remember the source of the story (*SL* 355). While this correspondence supports the assumption that both Peirce and Dos Passos were indeed present together the first time Hemingway heard the story from Saunders, it does not establish *when* this occurred.

The question thus becomes: if not in 1928, when? Almost exactly a year after the first Key West fishing trip, nearly the exact same cast of characters reassembled. It was time for the author to relax and indulge in masculine camaraderie. A few weeks earlier, Maxwell Perkins had departed with the completed manuscript of *A Farewell to Arms*, so Hemingway was free to gather Peirce, Dos Passos, and Strater to establish the fishing adventure as an annual event.[7] Here Dos Passos's memoirs and his biographies both clarify and cloud the timeline. According to Carr, Peirce and Dos Passos were definitely visiting at the same time during this expedition, for Dos Passos would later recall his intimidation at the hands of this imposing "Neptune out of a baroque Roman fountain," as he described Peirce (*Best Times* 200). In order to fit in with the most rugged member of the Mob, Dos Passos even "affected a blustering stance" by smoking, drinking, and cursing (Carr 253). Whatever jealousies and worries he may have had at the time about Peirce—the burly painter had known Dos Passos's wife, Katy, in Provincetown, Rhode Island—Dos Passos recalls these days fondly in his 1966 memoir, *The Best Times*: "Some of the best times in those years were with Hem and Pauline in Key West. The time that stands out was in late April and early May of 1929" (197).

Dos Passos seems here to conflate memories of his 1928 and 1929 trips. His 1928 visit had been in late April and early May; the 1929 visit came in late February and may have lasted into early March. (Hemingway biographers tend to put the visit in the last week of February; Dos Passos biographers place it in early to mid-March, after the opening of his play *Airways, Inc.* and his resignation from the New Playwrights Theatre.)[8] Even though he misremembers the specific months of his visit, Dos Passos clearly has the year right because he mentions that Hemingway's second son, Patrick, was present (*Best Times* 199), and Patrick had not yet been born when he visited in 1928.[9] Equally interesting, *The Best Times* also allusively links the sunken *Valbanera* to this 1929 visit, with Dos Passos recalling how "[w]e trolled back and forth between the wharves and an old white steamboat that had gone on a reef in a hurricane. She had lost her stack and the engines had been taken out" (*Best Times* 200). (Dos Passos also identifies Bra Saunders as the captain of their charter, although he misspells his name as "Sanders.")

With the exception of the telling of the *Valbanera* story, McLendon's version of the 1929 fishing trip features many of the same details; like Dos Passos, he tells how "[t]hey made a firm rule from the start. No champagne drinking until they caught fish" (52): "Hem had brought along a couple of bottles of champagne. . . . The rule was that you couldn't have a drink until somebody caught a fish" (*Best Times* 200). McLendon adds an interesting note that Dos Passos fails to mention, however—one I have been unable to locate in any other sources: he claims Hemingway met Carlos Gutiérrez, the future captain of his fishing boat, the *Pilar*, for the first time on this trip: "On the night before their return to Key West . . . a small motor-sailer, a Cuban fishing dinghy with a weathered canvas top, pulled alongside the Mob's dockage at the fort [Fort Jefferson]. . . . Immediately impressed by the fishing knowledge of their captain [Gutiérrez], Ernest invited both the captain and his small crew over for some rum" (52). What followed was a night of "jug passing" and storytelling, according to McLendon: "The Cuban captain told of twenty-foot rattlesnakes that swam off the Cuban coast and of crocodiles in the Gulf of Mexico, floating lazily many miles out at sea. Captain Bra matched the Cubans' stories with tales of the early white settlers in the Bahamas" (53). Notably absent among McLendon's list of tall tales is the *Valbanera* story. While it is impossible to prove that Hemingway heard the tale this particular night, he must have heard it at some point during this second fishing excursion.

Indeed, Hemingway's first draft of "After the Storm" shares much in common with the 1929 trip. For instance, one minor detail specific to the 1929 trip concerns those previously noted "bottles of good French champagne in Captain Bra's iced bait boxes" that Dos Passos (*Best Times* 200) and McLendon (52) both mention. When the fictional "Dos" wakes and joins the conversation in the first draft, the narrator gets him a drink: "I went forward. {stepping over the t} <T>wo tarpon {that} lay beside the ice box under a <stiff> canvas."[10] The two tarpon are on the deck of the boat, while the unspecified drinks—the narrator only mentions that he "poured out of the bottle"—are in the ice box (item 226).

The late-night setting of the draft also resembles McLendon's account of the 1929 trip. After Gutiérrez and his crew departed "to moor off the fort for the night," the members of the Mob "all passed a sleepless night while the spirits rolled in their stomachs" (53). Similarly, in Hemingway's first draft, neither the narrator nor "Bra" is able to sleep. "Waldo" and "Dos" are lying down on the deck and at first appear to be sleeping, but when "Bra" expresses concern about keeping "Waldo" up, "Waldo" assures him, "You arent [*sic*] keeping me awake" and encourages him to continue his storytelling (item 226). "Dos," too, soon joins in the conversation, somewhat snappishly asking the narrator and "Bra," "Dont [*sic*] you two ever go to bed?" (item 226). "Bra" explains that he cannot sleep because of his sore back, and "Waldo" immediately tries to direct him back to the story: "Go on with what happened, Bra. {Tell us the old bed time story}" (item 226). A subtle conflict, consistent with Dos Passos's concerns over fitting in with the Mob and with his potential rival Peirce, begins to emerge between the fictional "Dos" and "Waldo," who never speak directly to one another even as they lie beneath the same canvas on the deck.

Although Hemingway only superficially develops the characters in his first draft, he clearly distinguishes between their reactions to the story "Bra" tells. The embryonic relationships between the narrator and "Bra" on the one hand and "Bra," "Waldo," and "Dos" further support a 1929 setting for the actual telling of Saunders's original story. The narrator starts "Bra" on the tale and continues asking questions throughout in order to get more details, just as Hemingway himself interrogated many of the intriguing locals he met in Key West (Baker, *A Life Story* 192). "Waldo" reacts more cynically than the others and is less interested in the details of time and place than in the entertainment value of the "bed time story." "Dos," on the other hand, misses the beginning of the story and later seems taken aback by the fate of the passengers. As if concealing any annoyance he might have expressed upon waking, "Dos" accepts when "Bra" recommends a drink, saying, "Fine. That's a fine idea," and continuing when the narrator pours the drink with, "Thanks. . . . Thanks. That's fine" (item 226). His diction contains none of the "salty expletives" that Carr suggests the real Dos Passos employed in his effort to be one of the boys (254), but the character's insistence on the "fineness" of the drink clearly contrasts the narrator's silent observation of the two dead tarpon on the deck as he pours it. "Dos" then toasts "Bra" before "Waldo" harshly turns down the narrator's offer of a drink: "Hell no. . . . I want to hear what Bra did. Tell us a little story, Bra" (item 226). This request leads "Bra" to describe his discovery of the liner and his glimpse of the dead woman inside it.

Corrections made by Hemingway following the description of the woman in the first draft further indicate his efforts to maintain the distinction between the reactions of the two characters. Two cancellations indicate that Hemingway debated what comment he should use as a transition from the image of the woman to the explanation "Bra" gives about what must have happened during the final moments on board the ship:

<{Poor old Bra," Dos said.} "How did it sink there?">
{How did it sink there?"}(item 226)

Here Hemingway began with the untagged question designed simply to propel the story along before striking through it and writing above it the comment from "Dos" ("Poor old Bra"). This interjection, however, sounds more like "Waldo," or perhaps "Dos" trying to sound like "Waldo." It fits neither the tone "Dos" strikes at the previous break in the tale nor the context of the preceding description of the woman; thus, Hemingway strikes through it and rewrites the original line ("How did it sink there?"). With three significant exceptions, the rest of the questions directed at "Bra" are untagged, and the relationships between the characters implied in the first half of the manuscript are left largely unexplored. The narrator virtually disappears from the story after he pours a drink for "Dos." Instead, Hemingway focuses on the explanation "Bra" gives of how the ship sank and how the Conchs take revenge against the Greeks who loot both the ship and the Key West sponge beds.

The second half of the draft consists almost entirely of untagged dialogue, none of which is specifically assigned to the narrator. (One brief comment is attributed to "Dos"; two are attributed to "Waldo.") While most of the nineteen untagged questions in this part of the manuscript likely come from the narrator, some could legitimately be assigned to any one of the three listeners, such as when an anonymous interlocutor asks "Bra" about the jewfish now living near the ship: "Would you eat 'em Bra?" (item 226). However, even if one assumes that all of the untagged questions come from the narrator, Hemingway's loss of interest in the narrative frame is all the more pronounced. Whereas at the draft's beginning the narrator had commented on the setting and engaged in small talk unrelated to the tale "Bra" spins—in addition to asking questions about the sunken ship—the questions that appear in the second half serve merely to advance the plot in an increasingly mechanical fashion:

> "What did the Greeks do?"
> "How far is it across to Tampa?"
> "Did they ever get there?"
> "And you never got anything out of that wreck?" (item 226)

Amid these many untagged questions, the last three lines attributed to "Dos" and "Waldo" stand out all the more as the last traces of the actual telling that inspired Hemingway's story. Each comment reinforces the now abandoned attempt at characterizing the narrator's shipmates; each also offers further evidence that Hemingway first heard the original story in 1929.

In 1928, Hemingway had just arrived in Key West and was only beginning to get to know the town and its characters. He certainly did meet Bra Saunders during his first two months there, but whether they could have developed the friendship depicted in the early pages of the first draft is doubtful. Hemingway's ability to inspire loyalty and his habit of questioning the people he met are well known. But in the first draft of the manuscript, the narrator and "Bra" are clearly well-established friends. After describing the storm, for example, Bra turns his attention back to the present:

> "She's pretty near to turn," Bra said. "Ain't you sleepy?"
> "No. I drank too much coffee."
> "Coffee never kept me awake."
> {"Tell me what did you do then."}
> {"I told you all that once."}
> {"Tell me again."}
> I reached for the bottle. (item 226)

Furthermore, if Saunders told the story in 1929, Peirce and Dos Passos would each probably be meeting him for the *second* time, having met him in 1928 on their separate visits. Peirce definitely met Saunders in 1928 when he caught a record tarpon, "a silver monster that weighed 138{1/2} pounds" (McLendon 41). Thus, the last two exchanges in which "Dos" and "Waldo" are identified are more appropriate and much more believable in the context of a second meeting. Late in the first manuscript, after "Bra" recounts his attempts to loot the ship and describes the "pieces of things floating" in the water, one of the characters asks why there would be so many pieces when the woman's body remained intact. Bra explains,

> "She went right down in when she struck. . . . And {that} <the water> must have burst her boilers. That's what broke those deadlights and that would account for that other."
> "Yes," said Dos. "That would."
> "That's a good story, Bra," Waldo said. "Do you know any other good bed time stories?"
> "That's the best one I know tonight, Brother." (item 226)

The contrasting responses of "Dos" and "Waldo" once again mark the differences in their attitudes toward the story "Bra" tells: as the former maintains his somber reserve, the latter flippantly responds as if the storytelling were a joke.

At the end of the manuscript, "Bra" concludes the story by telling of how Key West Conchs wreaked revenge against the Greeks who loot the ship for raiding their sponge beds by setting the Greeks' ships on fire. The last line attributed to a specific listener reinforces the flippancy that has characterized "Waldo" throughout.

> "You havent [*sic*] any thing against us have you Bra?" Waldo asked [*sic*]
> "No, brother." Bra smiled in the moonlight. (item 226)

These comments would not be expected from an out-of-town fisherman to the stranger hired to take him fishing. But in 1929, Bra Saunders was not a stranger to Peirce; nor is the "Bra" in the first draft of "After the Storm" a stranger to "Waldo."

It seems curious that Hemingway's draft would omit an encounter like the one with the Gutiérrez boat that McLendon claims took place during the 1929 fishing trip. Several explanations are possible. Perhaps the encounter with the Cuban ship did not occur at this time. Michael Reynolds, for instance, has Carlos Gutiérrez telling similar tall tales on board Joe Russell's *Anita* in April and May 1932 (*The 1930s* 93). Another possibility is that the storytelling session with the Cubans could have occurred on a different night of the same trip. McLendon reports that the fishing on the 1929 trip was very good, and Hemingway and company quickly ran out of champagne (52). If the reference to the "ice box" in the first draft is a reference to the champagne the party stocked, then the real-life Bra must have told his story early in the trip. By the time the Cubans arrived, the Mob was drinking rum (McLendon 52). More importantly, however, the omission is consistent with Hemingway's other revisions and adds to the story's realism, as did his addition of the diving scene that Beegel describes (*Craft of Omission* 82). The truthfulness of the tale "Bra" tells is already questionable in the first draft without the addition of a fictionalized Gutiérrez to trade more tall tales. "Waldo" repeatedly refers to the tale as a "bed time story" and asks "Bra" to "[t]ell us a little story" (item 226). "Waldo" wants to be amused by what he feels is fiction, while the narrator and "Dos" seem to be intrigued by the factual tragedy. To include the tales of immense rattlesnakes that the Gutiérrez party brought to the fishing trip would destroy every element of realism. By eliminating the larger context surrounding the telling of the tale—the fishing trip in general and perhaps the encounter with the Cuban crew specifically—Hemingway takes the first step toward paring that context further and further in each successive draft, systematically eliminating anything that might detract from the credibility of the story.

Beegel's manuscript study "exposes Hemingway's assertion to Perkins that he told 'After the Storm' 'word for word as it happened to Bra' as itself a carefully crafted fiction, designed to augment his short story's compelling illusion of verity" (*Craft of Omission* 88). In the same letter to Perkins that Beegel quotes, Hemingway gives a possible reason for fibbing about the origin of his story: "I *want* them [his short stories] all to sound as though they really happened. Then when I succeed those poor dumb pricks [reviewers] say they are all just skillful reporting" (*SL* 400). In the context in which Hemingway originally encountered it, Bra Saunders's story was not believable—it did not even "sound as though it really happened" to all of the characters in the draft. It was a fisherman's tale of the one that got away, told after a long day of fishing and drinking during a trip that had its fair share of tall tales. Like the manuscript changes that Beegel observes, omitting the narrative frame bolstered the story's "verity" and increased the authenticity of the narrator's voice.

The changes in narrative structure from the first draft to the final version demonstrate this movement toward greater narrative authority. In the first draft, "Waldo" casts doubt on the truthfulness of the tale with his requests for bedtime stories. "Bra" plays along, smiling after he reassures the sarcastic "Waldo" that he has no need to revenge himself against the Mob for their incredulity as he had sought revenge against the Greeks for invading his fishing grounds. The "Waldo" and "Dos" characters do not appear in the second draft (item 226a). Instead, the narrator asks occasional questions to prompt "Bra," but he does not call into question its veracity. In the final published version, the original narrator is excised, leaving the "Bra" character, now an unnamed "I," telling his tale in the first person to an unseen and unheard audience. The narrator tells the tale straightforwardly, without interference from other characters; the storytelling context is elided, leaving readers to engage with the narrator-character directly instead of hearing the tale filtered through subsidiary characters.

The compositional development of "After the Storm" makes it clear that Saunders's tale did not have "its own intrinsic form" as Baker suggests (*A Life Story* 194), although Hemingway skillfully makes it seem so. Hemingway is solely responsible for the form of the published story, a form he discovers as he eliminates the framework that had grown out of his own experience of hearing the story. The structure that evolves from the first draft to the published version is one that increasingly develops the authenticity and credibility of the "Bra" character's voice, even as Hemingway further fictionalizes the tale.

It is impossible to know how soon Hemingway began writing "After the Storm" after hearing Bra Saunders's story, but the composition of "Wine of Wyoming," another short fiction from the same period, provides a suggestive pattern. At the end of August 1928, Hemingway and Pauline were in Sheridan, Wyoming, where they met "a French family who made and sold good wine in a neat frame house" and explored the Wyoming countryside, catching six hundred trout in a month before driving back to Piggott (Baker, *A Life Story* 196). By the time they arrived in Arkansas at the end of September, Hemingway found himself in a deep lull, having completed the first draft of *A Farewell to Arms* but resisting the urge to revise it so soon. Despite his boredom in Arkansas, he knew that he needed to gain some distance from his World War I romance before embarking on rewriting (*SL* 285). Instead, by the beginning of October, he had nearly completed his first draft of "Wine of Wyoming" (Smith 217), suggesting that the short story gave him a compact, alternative genre to continue his productivity without placing debilitating demands on his creative energies.

Hemingway completed revisions on *Arms* on 22 January 1929, and once again turned his attention to fishing (*SL* 294). As he enjoyed another break from the novel, he seems to have known that his intense work on it had drained him, and, as with the furlough that resulted in "Wine of Wyoming," he anticipated returning to his war story after recharging his powers of invention—this time to rework its conclusion.[11] Emerging from the fictional world of Frederic Henry and Catherine Barkley, he appears to have been more open to inspiration from his real surroundings—the American West in the case of "Wine," and the Keys in the case of "After the Storm." In both cases, his powers of observation proved as formidable as ever, and he began both stories with rough drafts that draw heavily on what he had actually seen and heard. Relying on recent, direct observation provided both an outlet for the energy he did have and an effective distraction from the larger task of the novel. He returned to the ending of the novel numerous times in May and June before deciding on its final version. At the end of August, he told Perkins that he was "cheerful again—have written 3 pieces" (*SL* 302). Paul Smith suggests that one was "Wine of Wyoming" (218); the first or perhaps second draft of "After the Storm" was likely another.

In both "Wine of Wyoming" and the first two versions of "Storm," a narrator based on Hemingway plays a secondary role and asks questions of his more colorful, working-class acquaintances; in both cases, the status of the narrator's relationship to these characters lies in a gray area between friend and customer. The stories take place in isolated settings, outside of mainstream America and more or less removed from the reach of its laws. From these similar starting points, however, the stories take different directions. In "Wine of Wyoming," the narrator's role grows, and his reactions to the Fontans become the focus of the fourth and final section. In "After the Storm," the narrator's role diminishes, even over the course of the first draft, before being eliminated entirely in the final draft. The stories emerged from comparable circumstances, yet Hemingway eventually ended up with two very different final products.

Perhaps more important than the different destinations, however, the two stories and the experiences that inspired them performed similar functions for Hemingway. Just as a boxer spars with a lesser partner to prepare for "going the distance" in the big fight, turning his attention to much shorter pieces that he could conceive of almost in full as he began writing enabled Hemingway to address the larger work more effectively when he returned to it. With "After the Storm" in particular, hearing Bra Saunders's story gave him a creative respite from *A Farewell to Arms* before reworking the ending. Hemingway was no doubt aware at the time that "[w]hen writing a novel a writer should create living people; people not characters" (*DIA* 191). Working on "After the Storm" allowed him an excellent opportunity to do exactly that in the character of Bra, and he approached the first draft as almost an exercise in crafting an authentic voice. His insistence after the publication of *Winner Take Nothing* that "After the Storm" was written "word for word as it happened to Bra" despite the significant changes he had incorporated by the time it was published suggests just how successful an exercise it was.

Notes

1. Hemingway had also originally intended to place "The Light of the World" first in the volume but was persuaded not to do so by Maxwell Perkins (Baker, *A Life Story* 241). Instead, he opened with "After the Storm," which Perkins suggested was "probably the most popular sort of story," and placed "The Light of the World" third after "A Clean, Well-Lighted Place" (*OTTC* 195).

2. Saunders may also be the source for certain aspects of Santiago in *The Old Man and the Sea*. As McLendon states: Hemingway "especially noticed the man's hands . . . beginning to 'freeze up' on him. . . . Captain Bra's hands became the ailing hands of another fisherman, Santiago" (44).

3. Perkins's judgment proved prescient: despite the largely lukewarm reviews of *Winner Take Nothing*, "After the Storm" received consistently favorable comments. In what became almost a refrain among reviewers, the volume as a whole was judged good but somewhat disappointing in its failure to break new ground. The *Times Literary Supplement* review was typical: "There is perhaps nothing in this collection so good as the best in *Men Without Women* and *In Our Time*. . . . But on the whole Mr. Hemingway's singular merits as a story-teller are well sustained" (90). In the most contentious review, Clifton Fadiman addressed Hemingway directly in the *New Yorker*: "As literary material, you have developed these things to the saturation point. Why not go on with something else?" (Stephens, *Critical Reception* 137). Individually, however, "After the Storm" was considered "an almost magical story, of the kind that will haunt a reader for years" (Stephens, *Critical Reception* 145), the kind of story that marked Hemingway as "one of the most skillful writers of our generation" (Canby 217).

The positive evaluations of "After the Storm" continued in the earliest critical response. In "Hemingway: Gauge of Morale" (1939), Edmund Wilson describes the story as "another of his variations—and one of the finest—on the theme of keeping up a code of decency among the hazards and pains of life" (Meyers, *Critical Heritage* 224). Wilson's comments laid the groundwork for identifying the narrator with other Hemingway code heroes. Somewhat surprisingly, despite the early attention and its importance to Hemingway's Key West years, critics largely ignored "After the Storm" in the ensuing years. Wilson's view remained the final word on the story for decades, influencing other critics' views of the narrator through the 1960s and even later in some cases. It was not until Anselm Atkins's 1967 article "Ironic Action in 'After the Storm'" that critics began to examine the story's sophisticated use of irony in more depth. Nevertheless, although the subject of a few brief notes, critical interpretation of the story remained largely static for another two decades until the appearance of Beegel's groundbreaking study of the background and composition history.

4. At one point, McLendon lists the members of the Mob as "Ernest, Dos, Archie, Waldo, and Mike Strater" (41). The Archie listed here—almost certainly Archibald MacLeish—is not mentioned anywhere else as a member of the 1928 fishing trip in McLendon's account

(or in other accounts). Apparently, McLendon substitutes Archie for "Old Bill" Smith, whom he previously lists as a member of the Mob (35). Archibald MacLeish did not visit Hemingway in Key West until the spring of 1930 (MacLeish, *Letters* 235).

5. McLendon is even more specific than Baker. He dates the beginning of the trip as "Friday afternoon of the third week in May," 1928, and adds that on Sunday night, Bra told Hemingway, Peirce, Dos Passos, Strater, and Smith the story of the *Valbanera* (41–43). Beegel also notes that Baker mistakenly refers to the ship as the *Val Banera*. The 1919–20 Lloyds Register of Shipping identifies the ship as the *Valbanera* (*Craft of Omission* 110).

6. This manuscript is numbered 226 and is part of the Hemingway Collection at the John F. Kennedy Presidential Library in Boston.

7. McLendon implies that Perkins returned to Key West after coming down at the beginning of February to pick up the manuscript of *A Farewell to Arms*. Baker and Reynolds describe two separate visits, one by Perkins alone for the first week of the month followed by the others later in February (Baker, *A Life Story* 199–200; Reynolds, *Homecoming* xiv), a sequence supported by the Hemingway-Perkins correspondence (*OTTC* 85–96). Each confirms, however, that Peirce, Dos Passos, and Katy Smith were in Key West at the same time.

8. Reynolds dates the visit 20–28 February 1929 (*Annotated Chronology* 37). McLendon also places the visit in late February. Ludington, however, in his biography of Dos Passos, states, "Dos Passos in March boarded a ship for Key West to visit the Hemingways . . . [and] in early April Dos Passos returned to New York" (277–78). Carr writes, "Dos Passos arrived in mid-March 1929 to join the group already on the scene" (253). Dos Passos wrote to Edmund Wilson from Key West in March (*Fourteenth Chronicle* 391). The visit could not have been in April and May as Dos Passos recalls in *The Best Times*; Hemingway left for Paris via Havana on 5 April 1929 (Baker, *A Life Story* 200).

9. Adding to the confusion, however, Dos Passos also clearly states that "Hem and Pauline had produced two small boys by this time, Patrick . . . and Gigi" (*Best Times* 199). Gregory was not born until November 1931. Dos Passos is in all likelihood thinking of Bumby and Patrick, both of whom were in Key West during his 1929 visit (but neither of whom was there when he visited in 1928).

10. In excerpts from the manuscripts, curly brackets {} indicate deletions, and angle brackets <> indicate insertions.

11. In Wyoming, he produced the final 107 manuscript pages in just over three weeks (Reynolds, *Hemingway's First War* 25); in January, he reported to Perkins that he was spending "6–10 hours every day" on the revisions (*SL* 292).

Why *Esquire?*

The Multiple Voices of Hemingway's Complex Public Persona

JOHN J. FENSTERMAKER

Beginning *For Whom the Bell Tolls* in 1939, Ernest Hemingway was not the same novelist who wrote *A Farewell to Arms*. The differences between the Hemingway of the 1920s and the Key West Hemingway of the 1930s find greatest expression in *Death in the Afternoon*, *Green Hills of Africa*, and the *Esquire* essays. In each, despite a range of topics, the principal subject invariably is Ernest Hemingway. Least familiar is the *Esquire* canon, significant for the breadth of personal material Hemingway addressed and for the size of his potential audience—monthly sales of nearly 200,000 in the magazine's first year and 700,000 by 1936 (Kaul 106). Even so, the question remains: Why *Esquire*, following the success of the fiction? With 80 percent of Key Westers on relief, why *Esquire*, designed for an exclusive male readership that lived largely immune to the Depression? Having abandoned journalism ten years earlier, why return to this form and this audience?

To answer, one must understand specific pressures on Hemingway during these years and his personal relationship with Arnold Gingrich. Hemingway had to face (1) the weak sales and negative reception of *Death in the Afternoon* and *Winner Take Nothing* (a continuing problem, with Scribner's printing only 17,000 more Hemingway books from 1930 to 1938 than for *A Farewell to Arms* alone); (2) the need for income to help distance himself from the largesse of Pauline's uncle Gus (e.g., in 1934, Hemingway borrowed from Gingrich and from Maxwell Perkins, his editor at Scribner's, to help buy his beloved cruiser, the *Pilar*);[1] (3) other developing interests, including travel; and, not least, (4) criticism of his artistic integrity from readers and professional critics, the latter angry over his not writing fiction addressing social issues. Yet the answer to "Why Esquire?" lay not in any single incentive, nor really in them collectively, but in a well-established Hemingway pattern finding new direction and new intensity via Arnold Gingrich's magazine.

As early as fall of 1917, in letters home exaggerating his achievements as a cub reporter in Kansas City, and later in Milan and Oak Park amid the myths surrounding his wartime wounding, Hemingway had realized the potential in language for creating a sophisticated, successful persona—an effort he refined in Toronto and later in Paris. In September 1932, Hemingway published *Death in the Afternoon*, a history and apologia for the Spanish bullfight tradition. Additionally, he presented for the first time in his published writing a carefully crafted (albeit still-in-progress) public persona: an expert on courage, death, and tragedy; literature, art, and the artist; Spanish culture, including food, wine, and travel; and more. Unfortunately, the critical and popular audiences found too many voices, too much cynicism and death. Versions of this worldly wise persona also dominate *Green Hills of Africa* and produced similarly negative reader reactions. So why turn back to journalism and to *Esquire* in particular? In major part, the answer lies with Arnold Gingrich.

In January 1933, a few months after the publication of *Death in the Afternoon*, Arnold Gingrich, editor of the fashion magazine *Apparel Arts*, initiated plans for *Esquire*, which would begin publication in the autumn. Designed as the male counterpart to *Vogue* and *Harper's Bazaar*, *Esquire* was, as Gingrich later reported, "Conceived at the darkest moment of the Depression . . . born at the dawn of the New Deal," and intended to present "everything of especial or exclusive interest to men" (*Esquire Treasury* xi).

Gingrich had been collecting Hemingway's work and corresponding with him for some months when they happened upon one another in Louis Henry Cohn's House of Books in New York. After listening to Gingrich talk up the magazine, Hemingway accepted the role of preeminent contributor, even agreeing to help solicit other writers: "[Y]ou can say I sent you" (*Nothing but People* 86). Gingrich required no contract, only a handshake. He agreed to pay Hemingway—for a monthly letter of approximately 1,500 words describing his activities wherever he might be—twice what he paid others ($500 vs. $250). He would edit only for spelling and punctuation, possible libel, invasion of privacy, and other legal issues (Grimes 21–22). Herein lay Hemingway's most immediate attraction to *Esquire*. Gingrich's desire for a broad focus and wholly uncensored topic selection offered Hemingway unparalleled opportunities, freedom beyond anything possible in works like *Death in the Afternoon* or *Green Hills of Africa*, where each volume has a specific, however expansible, subject. By exploring unlimited, handpicked subjects fleshed out with pictures and illustrations, Hemingway could, directly and immediately, *explain* and *image* his personal values, and *document* his vision of himself. He varied the voices of his persona: a contemplative, hardworking artist but also an experienced sportsman—a man of letters and of action—and sometimes, too, a man of leisure, simply and pleasantly immersed in the good life.

From October 1933 to August 1936, Hemingway produced twenty-seven pieces for *Esquire* (three of them short stories). The journalism includes the oft-reprinted "On the Blue Water" (April 1936), containing the germ of *The Old Man and the Sea*. The short story "The Snows of Kilimanjaro" (August 1936) so impressed Gingrich that he paid $1,000, double Hemingway's then usual rate; subsequently, in 1937, he helped arrange a gift of one thousand shares of stock to acknowledge the author's contribution to the magazine (*Nothing but People* 86–87). The *Esquire* essays explore literature and writing (specifically, the difficulties of being a writer in the 1930s), sports (deep-sea fishing, big-game hunting, bullfighting, boxing), travel, politics, the European economy, Hemingway's antifascism and anti-Nazism, and his predictions of the next war. They also include attacks on his critics (some, those "angleworms in a bottle" he describes in *Green Hills of Africa*).

The *Esquire* letters offer the accuracy and clarity of good feature writing and are without exception informational. A sophisticated and world-traveled Hemingway varies tone from "calm, pleasant, informative, and learned" to "lewd, coarse, and suggestive" (Grimes 6–7). His authoritative voices range among teacher, insider, sportsman, celebrity, connoisseur, and artist. His style with the letters differs from his fiction; the lead sentence in *Esquire*, for example, is often long and complex, and little dialogue occurs. The dominant voice of these personal essays is, as Robert O. Stephens observes, that of "an authoritative man talking casually, not writing and revising" (*Hemingway's Nonfiction* 332). Even so, in the sports pieces, particularly, the expert and literary artist fuse aesthetic and technical material. The poetic expression of technical detail in the struggle with a marlin offers a representative example:

> [H]e can see the bulk of him under water, great blue pectorals widespread like the wings of some huge, underwater bird, and the stripes around him like purple bands around a brown barrel, and then the sudden upthrust waggle of a bill. . . . Then when he is hooked he makes a sweeping turn, the drag screwed down, the line zings out and he breaks water, the drag loosed now, to go off jumping, throwing water like a speedboat, in those long, loping, rhythmic, pounding leaps of twenty feet and more in length.
>
> To see that happen, to feel that fish in his rod, to feel that power and that great rush, to be a connected part of it and then to dominate it and master it and bring that fish to gaff, alone and with no one else touching the rod, reel or leader, is something worth waiting many days for, sun and all. (*BL* 173–74)

So why *Esquire*? In *Esquire*, Hemingway accomplished much: he kept writing; he produced income; he described his world travels; he defined himself as a man of letters, defending his career and lifestyle to serious readers and fellow professionals, and, more familiarly as "your correspondent," to *Esquire*'s general audience. Yet, the way was not always easy. Certain pieces provoked attacks recorded in "The Sound and the Fury" section of the magazine. Among the headier complaints, readers expected polished essays as in the "big pay" magazines, the prose and voice found in his fiction, tales of the avant-garde literary world, social relevance, and explicit sexuality (Stephens, *Hemingway's Nonfiction* 332). The fishing letters angered many, including the reader who wrote describing his experience deep-sea sportfishing: "about as tough as catching flies around a garbage can with fly paper and just as sporting" (Liberman 12).

Why *Esquire*, given this open forum for attacks and for criticism of both his character and writing? The magazine provided Hemingway a platform for responding to his critics quickly and directly—at times aggressively, often dismissively, sometimes in fun: "[L]et them write letters to the magazine about how lousy letters such as this one are. It has been a long time since your correspondent could not take it and he is still able to hand a little back. He has made an extensive study of the four-letter man at home and abroad" ("He Who Gets Slap Happy" 19). The flippancy of the following regarding big-game hunting in "Notes on Dangerous Game" offers a lighter touch:

> [T]heir clients get record heads, record tusks and super lions year after year. They simply happen to be super hunters and super shots. (*There are too many supers in these last two sentences. Re-write them yourselves lads and see how easy it is to do better than Papa. Thank you. Exhilarating feeling, isn't it?*)
>
> Both mask their phenomenal skill under a pose of nervous incapacity which serves as an effective insulation and cover for their truly great pride in the reserve of deadliness that they live by. (*All right now, better that one. Getting harder, what? Not too hard you say? Good. Perhaps you're right.*) (*BL* 167–68)

Hemingway clearly relished opportunities for such sparring sessions.

Professional critics could be brutal. Edmund Wilson in the *Atlantic Monthly* is typical: "He is the Hemingway of the handsome photographs with the sportsman's tan and the outdoor grin, with the ominous resemblance to Clark Gable, who poses with a giant marlin which he has just hauled in off Key West. . . . [H]e turns up delivering Hemingway monologues in well-paying and trashy magazines; and the Hemingway of these loose disquisitions, arrogant, belligerent and boastful, is certainly the worst-invented character to be found in the author's work" (Meyers, *Critical Heritage* 304). Heywood Broun lashes out at Hemingway in his "It Seems to Me" column in the *New York World Telegram* on 18 August 1934, prompted by the latter's seeming dismissal of the greatness of Ring Lardner, who had died the previous year: "I do not like the man, and yet I must admit that I know no other phoney [*sic*] in the whole course of English letters who could write so well concerning things about which he had not the slightest comprehension [i.e., bullfighting and boxing]. . . . I feel that in the current year and in the seasons to come there is going to be an increasing demand that authors know their stuff. . . .[for example]

The Proletarian Novel" (13).[2] Joseph Koven echoes the opinions of Wilson and Broun in the clearly political *Monthly Review* (June 1934): "Artist-in-ordinary to America's pseudo-intelligenzia [*sic*] to whom the cock-and-bull struggles of neurotic adventurers are infinitely more important than the life and death conflicts of humanity" (44–45).[3]

In the *Esquire* pieces, Hemingway responded to attacks, sometimes explicitly naming his targets, and, as he claimed, giving back as good as he got. (As in *Green Hills of Africa*, Hemingway seized the opportunity to lecture, deflate, sometimes to excoriate, certain professional writers and critics. In the magazine, antagonists included William Saroyan, Alexander Woollcott, Ring Lardner, F. Scott Fitzgerald, Heywood Broun, Westbrook Pegler, and Gilbert Seldes). Additionally, he offered gratuitous evaluative remarks, occasionally proffering unexpected, even non sequitur, judgments.[4] Growing up in Oak Park, Illinois, Hemingway had much admired the Chicago journalist and sportswriter Ring Lardner and often had imitated Lardner's style in pieces for his high-school paper, *Trapeze*. Following Lardner's death and specifically responding to the encomiums by Broun, Pegler, and Seldes—the latter the editor of Lardner's collection *First and Last* (1934)—Hemingway offered a brief critique in *Esquire*:

> Ring Lardner has not been dead long enough for anyone more interested in literature than in the personality of his friends to criticize him with the impartial scalpel of the post-mortem examiner. But when it is done, and it will take a finely ground and disinterested scalpel to post him properly, for there were many places which Battle Creek, Michigan and Chicago made difficult to dissect, it will be stated that what kept Ring Lardner from being a great writer was the very thing for which Mr. Pegler praises him in his column [i.e., not using dirty words].
>
> It was not that he did not care for the human race . . . but he felt superior to the part of it he knew best [i.e., sports figures]. . . . No writer can write anything that is truly great when he feels superior to the people he is writing about, no matter how much compassion he may have. ("Defense of Dirty Words" 19, 158)

Hemingway argued that by never putting a dirty word in the mouth of his fighters, Lardner distorted "the language that they speak into a very comic diction, so there's no tragedy ever, because there is no truth" ("Defense of Dirty Words" 158).

These assertions, among others, created such furor that Gingrich invited Gilbert Seldes to write in Lardner's defense. In "The Prize-fighter and the Bull" (November 1934), Seldes's attitude toward Hemingway is as interesting as anything he says about Lardner: "Mr. Lardner despised people, if he did, because they were swine; Mr. Hemingway sneers at people because they are not bulls. I stick to Mr. Lardner, considering his attitude of mind more civilized" (174). Hemingway countered obscenely: "The magazine, it seems, is coming out early; a break for all of us who can not wait a whole month to get another shot of Gilbert Seldes, (*it's a vice with me. I tried to break it off. They said all it would bring was blindness, insanity, and death but I said no, I'd paid the fifty cents. . . . Let me read Seldes if I want to*" ("Notes on Life and Letters" 21).

We may assume that Hemingway felt the sting of professional criticism more deeply than that of the general *Esquire* reader. Regardless, he often answered both by shifting to a fundamental personal belief and enlarging the scope of the issues, as in this passage from "Old Newsman Writes":

> The hardest thing in the world to do is to write straight honest prose on human beings. First you have to know the subject; then you have to know how to write. Both take a lifetime to learn and anybody is cheating who takes politics as a way out. It is too easy. All the outs are too easy and the thing itself is too hard. . . . Books should be about the people you know, that you love and hate, not about the people you study up about. If you write them truly they will have all the economic implications a book can hold. . . .
>
> [I]f the book is good, is about something that you know, and is truly written and reading it over you see that this is so you can let the boys [i.e., critics] yip and the noise will have that pleasant sound coyotes make on a very cold night when they are out in the snow and you are in your own cabin that you have built or paid for with your work. (*BL* 183–84, 185)

This letter, like the others, is informational and educational, but its impetus is a desire to rebut criticism.

Hemingway did write about himself as an author following more positive impulses. The most detailed and eloquent of these, "Monologue to the Maestro," features the interactions between Hemingway and a young man (Arnold Samuelson) nicknamed "the Maestro" because he played the violin, who hitchhiked to Key West from Minnesota to learn from Hemingway how to become a writer. The give-and-take between Hemingway and this midwesterner, a fine night watchman for the *Pilar* but a "calamity" as crew member and writer, humanizes Hemingway, whose ironic observations are finally both generous and forgiving. The Maestro elicits helpful, and later well-known advice like "stop when you are going good and when you know what will happen next" (*BL* 216). For the general *Esquire* reader, perhaps the distinction between "reporting" (journalism) and literature was more interesting:

If it was reporting they would not remember it. When you describe something that has happened that day the timeliness makes people see it in their own imaginations. A month later that element of time is gone and your account would be flat and they would not see it in their minds nor remember it. But if you make it up instead of describe it you can make it round and whole and solid and give it life. You create it, for good or bad. It is made; not described. It is just as true as the extent of your ability to make it and the knowledge you put into it. (*BL* 215–16)

Despite his capacity to be generous, as with the Maestro, Hemingway in *Esquire* makes points about sports and, particularly literature and the literary scene, in language unacceptable in most other venues. Politics is another major subject in the letters. While Hemingway deliberately refrains from commenting in his fiction on contemporary political unrest, he is repeatedly forthcoming on political issues, expressing ideas both in language and in graphic details unlikely to be welcomed in other large-circulation publications—another answer to the question, why *Esquire?* Politics, propaganda, the next war recur as subjects in the essays from 1934 to 1936. The first appears in the second letter, "The Friend of Spain," in January 1934; in which Hemingway writes that, following revolutionary events in Spain, the number of politicians has exploded and the "spectacle of [the country's] governing is at present more comic than tragic; but the tragedy is very close" (*BL* 146). The political letters end in January 1936 with "Wings Always over

Africa," devoted to Mussolini's war in Ethiopia, but with remarks about dictators generalizable to the global conflagration Hemingway fears:

> It is a dangerous thing in a dictatorship to have a long memory. You should learn to live for the great deeds of the day. As long as any dictator controls his press there will always be great daily deeds to live for. In America as we get premonitions of dictatorship you can see in the newspapers how marvelous everything is every day in the achievements of government and looking back note how lousy is the result of any given year or period of years of governmental activity. (*BL* 234)

On political subjects, the Hemingway persona speaks as an astute (rarely, and then only ironically, humorous) insider. His experience establishes his authority; his positions develop clearly, consistently, and unequivocally. For more than a decade, Hemingway had watched European economic and political developments. For the *Toronto Star* in 1922, he had covered the results of Kemal's capture of Smyrna, the International Economic Conference in Genoa and, later that year, the Peace conference in Lausanne. In 1923, he reported on the devastating inflation in Germany and the tension between France and Germany; later, he followed, often witnessing, the rise of fascism and Nazism, the revolution in Spain, the Communist riots in Paris, the overthrow of Machado in Cuba in 1933 and the counterrevolution in 1934, the Depression in America, and Mussolini's incursion into Ethiopia in 1935. Hemingway considered Mussolini's action in Africa an unmistakable sign of the impending next war, and he savaged the Italian leader in several *Esquire* essays.[5]

In the third *Esquire* essay, "A Paris Letter" (February 1934), an urbane, albeit grim, voice details the Paris scene as a microcosm of contemporary Europe and a scene fraught with implications for America:

> This old friend shot himself. That old friend took an overdose of something. That old friend went back to New York and jumped out or rather fell from, a high window. That other old friend wrote her memoirs. All of the old friends have lost their money. All of the old friends are very discouraged. Few of the old friends are healthy. . . . The only foreigners you see are Germans. The Dome is crowded with refugees from the Nazi terror and Nazis spying on the refugees. (*BL* 155)

Ultimately, however, these details do not account for the despair: "What makes you feel bad is the perfectly calm way everyone speaks about the next war. It is accepted and taken for granted. All right. Europe has always had wars. But we can keep out of this next one. And the only way to keep out of it is not to go in it; not for any reason. There will be plenty of good reasons. *But we must keep out of it*" (*BL* 158). Twenty months later, Hemingway's theme is the same.[6] Now he fears a potentially ambitious Franklin Roosevelt, who voiced support for keeping the country out of war and signed the Neutrality Act on 31 August 1935, but averred that "he could, if he would, put the U.S. into war in ten days" (*BL* 221). Hemingway's position is unmistakable:

> [T]he fate of our country for the next hundred years or so depends on the extent of Franklin Roosevelt's ambition. . . . War is coming in Europe as surely as winter follows fall. . . . In the next ten years there will be much fighting, there will be opportunities for the United States to again swing the balance of power in Europe; she will again have a chance to save civilization; she will have a chance to fight another war to end war. Whoever heads the nation will have a chance to be the greatest man in the world for a short time. (*BL* 227–28)

Why *Esquire*? Throughout all the turbulence emanating from his premier author, Gingrich proved an able and supportive editor, an understanding and personable friend, a staunch ally:

> They can't forgive his fishing and hunting. They wish he would grow up and face the ugly facts of our changing times. They wish he would show in his writings some awareness of the pock-marked political complexion of our era. In other words, season his literary soup to the moment's taste with a sprinkling of class-consciousness, of politico-sociological salt. They forget that politics, as such, is the death of art, that nothing can more damagingly "date" a work of art for the future than preoccupation with what seem to be serious things of the moment. ("Reviving" 5)

Gingrich particularly appreciated the author's professionalism. When Hemingway ceased contributing, his editor reported: "For the first two years [Hemingway] was . . . [*Esquire's*] most conscientious contributor. He had to send his copy in from all over the world and he never let us down. He more than once chartered planes to reach a point where he could dispatch his piece in time to make a deadline" ("A Farewell" 5).[7]

Clearly Hemingway the professional differentiated between the timeliness of journalism and the timelessness of literature. Admittedly, stretches of his *Esquire* prose are unremarkable. Nevertheless, encouraged and unfettered by his editor and free to determine his topics, Hemingway produced finer writing overall than generally credited. Accusations that he "sold out," "abandoned his talent," and "compromised his integrity" are false. Desiring money, he could have sought venues like *Vanity Fair* and *Cosmopolitan* (the latter had paid him more than four thousand dollars for a story [*Nothing but People* 87]) or institutions like Hollywood, pursuing him continually after *A Farewell to Arms*.

Given more lucrative possibilities elsewhere, why *Esquire*? Put simply, in *Esquire*, Hemingway presented himself as a literary, intellectual, and sophisticated man of the world. He shared the stage (for twice the fee) with Erskine Caldwell, Clarence Darrow, John Dos Passos, Theodore Dreiser, Havelock Ellis, F. Scott Fitzgerald, Dashiell Hammett, Langston Hughes, Aldous Huxley, D. H. Lawrence, Thomas Mann, and Ezra Pound. Even the much-maligned hunting and fishing letters "enlarged his public image as an accomplished, versatile sportsman," a "technically proficient journalist," and "a man and writer who never tired of exposing the amateur, the four-letter man who failed to measure up to the professional" (Grimes 364). Most important, his ideas expressed in his own persona and voice appeared before a very large public—virtually every month.

Ultimately, Hemingway's *Esquire* canon embodies a scope and candor unavailable elsewhere. Collectively, the *Esquire* essays offer broad-canvas explorations of Hemingway's major interests (e.g., big-game sport) and most serious ideas and beliefs (e.g., writing, the role of the artist, avoiding an imminent world war). His multifaceted persona is not the exaggerated creation of earlier days in Kansas City, Milan, Toronto, even Paris, but a voice largely authentic, even down to humorous self-mockery (e.g., when, while fishing aboard the *Pilar*, he accidentally fired a pistol; the bullet splintered on impact, ricocheting and wounding him in both legs, which required an embarrassing return to shore and medical attention [see "On Being Shot Again," *BL* 198–204]). For the fan, the casual reader, and the critic alike, the letters offer, for all their casualness, enormous amounts of information and eyewitness details on an extraordinarily broad range of subjects.

Most often we see and hear in *Esquire* quintessential Hemingway, including the man of action in the natural world: "America has always been a country of hunters and fishermen. As many people, probably, came to North America because there was good free hunting and fishing as ever came to make their fortunes" ("He Who Gets Slap Happy" 19). They also foreground the man of contemplation in the world of books, as in "Remembering Shooting-Flying": "[T]his [letter] is supposed to be about shooting, not about books, although some of the best shooting I remember was in Tolstoi and I have often wondered how the snipe fly in Russia now and whether shooting pheasants is counter-revolutionary. When you have loved three things all your life, from the earliest you can remember; to fish, to shoot and, later, to read; and when, all your life, the necessity to write has been your master, you learn to remember and, when you think back you remember more fishing and shooting and reading than anything else and that is a pleasure" (*BL* 187).

Hemingway's *Esquire* canon exhibits and justifies a lifestyle and a career. It does so through the multiple voices of a complexly nuanced persona often very close to the "real" Ernest Hemingway. His key public testament in the decade of his greatest productivity, deepest personal growth, and widest range of self-expression, the *Esquire* essays merit continuing attention and a premier position among Hemingway's published writing during the Key West years.

Notes

1. Michael Reynolds says that Hemingway borrowed $3,000 from Gingrich and $2,500 from Perkins (*The 1930s* 169). In a letter to Sister Richard Mary Grimes (9 February 1965), Gingrich relates the story somewhat differently: "Very early after we got started—I believe in 1934 or early '35—Hemingway wanted some cash to buy a fishing boat of his own, the *Pilar*, and we advanced him the money he needed to complete the deal—I believe $5000 although it may have been more, but I think less than $10,000 . . . so from that point on his payments for his subsequent contributions represented credits against that advance" (Grimes 89 n. 33).

2. Hemingway knew that critics wanted him to record the tough economic times and explore revolutionary issues, but he was opposed to doing so himself and uniformly opposed critics' urging such writing upon contemporaries:

[D]on't let them suck you in to start writing about the proletariat, if you don't come from the proletariat, just to please the recently politically enlightened critics. In a little while these critics will be something else. I've seen them be a lot of things and none of them was pretty. Write about what you know and write truly and tell them all where they can place it. They are all very newly converted and very frightened, really, and when Moscow tells them what I am telling you, then they will believe it. (*BL* 184)

3. Hugh Merrill in *Esky: The Early Years at Esquire* observes that not all professional criticism involving the magazine's premier contributor concerned sport, literature, or politics, but instead issues of highbrow/lowbrow culture:

This framework of Ziegfeldian sex and comedy was not what shocked critics most about *Esquire* when it appeared in 1933. Rather, it was the mixture of those elements, which were considered low or popular culture, with literature by critically acclaimed authors, which was considered high culture. Writing in *Scribner's*, a high culture magazine of the thirties, Henry Pringle compared *Esquire* to having Thomas Mann or Ernest Hemingway read aloud from their works at a burlesque show. He called it an "unholy combination." (11)

4. The first such surprise appeared in the fourth letter written in a Nairobi hospital in January 1934 during Hemingway's two-month safari. This shortest of the letters, at eight hundred words, begins with a disquisition on amoebic dysentery—its actual and imagined discomforts and inconveniences for the author:

My own diagnosis was certainly faulty. Leaning against a tree two days ago shooting flighting sand grouse . . . after ten days of what Dr. Anderson says was a.d . . . I became convinced that though an unbeliever I had been chosen as the one to bear our lord Buddha when he should be born again on earth. While flattered at this, and wondering how much Buddha at that age would resemble Gertrude Stein, I found the imminence of the event made it difficult to take high incoming birds and finally compromised by reclining against the tree and only accepting crossing shots. (*BL* 159)

This unexpected slighting reference to Stein comes some years after Hemingway had fallen out with his early mentor but right on the heels of her unflattering comments on him in *The Autobiography of Alice B. Toklas*, serialized in the summer and published in fall 1933.

5. Hemingway interviewed Mussolini in Madrid in 1922 and wrote two negative pieces for the Toronto papers: "Fascisti Party Now Half-Million Strong" (*DT* 173) and "'Pot-Shot Patriots' Unpopular in Italy" (*DT* 174). Hemingway's attitude and concerns are obvious. (He entitled the third of these early pieces "Mussolini, Europe's Prize Bluffer: More Like Bottomley Than Napoleon.") In the second article, he describes the Fascisti Party as "extreme Nationalists, which means black-shirted, knife-carrying, club swinging, quick stepping, nineteen-year-old potshot patriots" (*DT* 173). He ends the first piece asking "what does Mussolini intend to do with his 'political party' [of 250,000 armed men] organized as a military force?" (*DT* 174). Twelve years later, writing three *Esquire* letters featuring Mussolini prominently, Hemingway has his, not unexpected, answer.

6. "France is a country and Great Britain is several countries but Italy is a man,

Mussolini, and Germany is a man, Hitler. A man has ambitions, a man rules until he gets into economic trouble; he tries to get out of this trouble by war. . . . The hell broth that is brewing in Europe we have no need to drink. Europe has always fought, the intervals of peace are only Armistices. We were fools to be sucked in once on a European War and we should never be sucked in again" (*BL* 209, 212).

7. Gingrich also proved an able critic, writing in 1970: "As a short-story writer, Hemingway was remarkably consistent. As a novelist, he was an in-and-outer. . . . [H]is big book . . . is *For Whom the Bell Tolls*. His best book is . . . *The Sun Also Rises* because it is the most perfectly realized. . . . Some of his best writing is in . . . *A Moveable Feast, Death in the Afternoon* . . . and *Green Hills of Africa*. . . . That Hemingway could still write on the master virtuoso level is proved by *A Moveable Feast*" ("Notes on Bimini" 12). Gingrich called the phrase *death in the afternoon* "the greatest four word poem in the language." Interestingly, his assessment ignores *Esquire*. Gingrich avoided comment on the part of Hemingway's achievement that had passed through his own hands.

Letters and Literary Tourism

Hemingway as Your Key West Correspondent in "The Sights of Whitehead Street"

E. STONE SHIFLET AND KIRK CURNUTT

A significant if oft-ignored fact concerning the twenty-six essays Ernest Hemingway wrote for *Esquire* between 1933 and 1936 is that all but two are either titled or subtitled "letters."[1] The label reminds us of what detractors were prone to grouse about in the mid-1930s: Hemingway's affiliation with *Esquire* had little to do with fiction, the medium that made him famous. Not only did he contribute a mere five stories to the magazine—albeit including his greatest, "The Snows of Kilimanjaro" (1936)—but his articles contain little imaginative writing. When not expatiating on the arts of hunting, fishing, and/or writing, the author admits but does not depict his increasing disillusionment with the world, usually from foreign lands, including Europe, Africa, and Cuba. Uncertain economies, encroaching civilization, and the price of fame are recurring themes in these dispatches, but the author seems willing only to discourse on the state of change they represent, not dramatize it.

In at least one case, however, Hemingway exercised his more fabulist side, and, interestingly, it would prove the *Esquire* series' most revealing treatment of both Key West and his own fame. Published in April 1935, "The Sights of Whitehead Street" is only one of four entries subtitled "A Key West Letter." While the other three—"Remembering Shooting-

Flying" (February 1935); "Sailfish off the Mambosa" (March 1935); and "a.d. Southern Style" (May 1935)—are straightforward sportsman tales, "Sights" is a literary satire on the Key West economy and its exploitation of his celebrity, written as neither journalism nor literature but as a combination of these supposedly antithetical forms. In keeping with other *Esquire* articles, Hemingway dramatizes himself as "Your Correspondent." And yet, given the absurd extremes of his fictionalizing—culminating in the claim that his three young sons actually write the works published under his name—the effect of the direct address in "Sights" differs from the rest of the pieces: it softens the supposed hectoring and posturing said to diminish their overall value. Comparing this underappreciated essay to dispatches from Paris and Spain allows us to recognize the distance the fantastic element accorded his use of the second person. In essence, the fiction spares his objections to Key West tourism from being received as mere personal complaints, allowing instead for a larger statement on what the contemporaneous commodification of travel was doing to the very notion of personal experience that was central to his literary reputation.

Obviously enough, Hemingway's initial attraction to *Esquire* was the opportunity it provided for exercising the journalistic skills that he had only recently returned to with 1932's *Death in the Afternoon* after a near decade of concentrating exclusively on fiction.[2] Hemingway had abandoned reporting by abruptly quitting the *Toronto Star* in late 1923, viewing journalism as dependent upon *timeliness* for success, as opposed to the *timelessness* to which literature aspired.[3] *Death in the Afternoon*, however, reflected his attempt to create a mode of nonfiction prose whose deep structure could transcend the transitoriness of mere opining that he associated with the editorializing "I" of personal observation. In *Death*, Hemingway describes "prose [as] architecture" instead of "interior decorations," meaning that, not unlike what T. S. Eliot derided as *sensibility* in "Tradition and the Individual Talent" (1919), the point of literature was not to convey personality through ideas, for that element of a writer's individuality was temporal and therefore bound to depreciate in intensity as readers were removed from its immediacy (*Selected Essays* 6). The point is made apropos of fiction, yet one senses Hemingway struggling to confer its import to the medium of *Death* itself:

For a writer to put his own intellectual musings, which he might sell for low price as essays, into mouths of artificially constructed characters . . . is good economics, perhaps, but does not make it literature. People in a novel, not skillfully constructed *characters*, must be projected from a writer's assimilated experience, from his knowledge, from his head, from his heart and from all there is of him. (*DIA* 191)

Hemingway goes on to create even more requirements for dealing with temporality, including an ability to engage a history (or as Eliot would say, a "tradition") of ideas: "A great enough writer seems to be born with knowledge. But he really is not; he has only been born with the ability to learn in a quicker ratio to the passage of time than other men . . . and with an intelligence to accept or reject what is already presented as knowledge" (*DIA* 191–92). Meeting these stipulations was complicated further still by his final condition for great writing, the ability to measure present phenomena against past ideas—a developmental process that, in his view, itself required time: "They are the very simplest things and because it takes a man's life to know them the little new that each man gets from life is very costly and the only heritage he has to leave" (*DIA* 192).

Another method for transcending timeliness that Hemingway had long mastered by the 1930s involved the use of setting. From the upper Michigan of his early stories to Spain's Ebro valley in "Hills Like White Elephants" and the plains of Gorizia in *A Farewell to Arms*—to name but a few—he understood how to elevate the depiction of place beyond the trendy exoticism of adventure to convey deeper spiritual and mythological meanings. *Death in the Afternoon* illuminates this method by insisting that the key to appreciating the spectacle of bullfighting is recognizing the essential timelessness of Spain itself, despite the superficial changes that modernity—and tourism specifically—inflicts on both locale and customs: "I know things change now and I do not care," he writes in the final paragraph of the famous closing chapter, a long, incantatory hymn to the country's eternal qualities. "We'll all be gone before it's changed too much and if no deluge comes when we are gone it still will rain in summer in the north and hawks will nest in the Cathedral at Santiago and in La Granja. . . . We've seen it all go and we'll watch it go again" (*DIA* 278). The guidebook moments in *Death* in which Hemingway recommends, à la Baedeker, certain hotels and restaurants mark his attempt to lead the reader to value the "things that last," which, in essence, sums up his theory of place. What he says of bullfighting is equally true of the land: "[I]t has not existed because of the foreigners and tourists, but always in spite of them and any step to modify it to secure their approval, which it will never have, is a step towards its complete suppression" (*DIA* 8).

A persistent theme of the *Esquire* essays set in Europe, however, is that its enduring qualities are increasingly "suppressed" by the travails of time and history. Suddenly, Spain is on the verge of war, and Paris is no longer a palette for painting expatriate disillusion. In fact, in "A Paris Letter" (February 1935), Hemingway describes the city as a place where "all I do is go out and get depressed and wish I were somewhere else" (*BL* 155). In effect, Hemingway's dispatch can be read as a search for an inspirational setting conducive to good writing— one that neither appeases nor panders to tourists but exists wholly unto itself, "an unexploited country" (*BL* 207) resistant to the vagaries of change.

America had never possessed for Hemingway the traditions and rituals that he found so compelling in Europe. When he moved to Key West in 1928, however, he could at least lay claim to a remote setting relatively unspoiled by modernity. The island's easy access to the Gulf Stream and the Caribbean allowed him to imagine his beloved fishing expeditions with local friends like Charles Thompson and Joe "Josie" Russell as partaking of the same sacrament of sport that he had depicted in the Burguete section of *The Sun Also Rises*, in which pursuing trout on the Irati River revitalizes Jake Barnes and Bill Gorton. Yet, as Maureen Ogle notes, much of the sparsity that Hemingway found so elemental on the island was a result of a decade-long economic crisis, not the romanticized antiquity Hemingway sought: "Of the city's sixty-nine manufacturing plants in 1919, fewer than thirty remained by 1928. Fourteen thousand jobs vanished during the decade. In 1919, the city's manufacturing workers took home more than $2 million in wages and salaries; by the late 1920s, those still lucky enough to have jobs earned just over six hundred thousand dollars. Between 1920 and 1929, the population dropped by some five thousand" (144). Even before Ernest and Pauline first set foot in Key West in April 1928, the municipality and the Chamber of Commerce were furiously trying to reverse this downward spiral by promoting the opening of the Overseas Highway, which would theoretically allow "automobilists" to drive from Miami to Key West. (In reality, motorists had to suffer a forty-mile ferry ride from Lower Matecumbe to No Name Key that added five hours to the journey.) As the *Key West Citizen* boasted that January, the opening of the highway would inaugurate an era of "unprecedented activity and growth" that would allow Key West to assume her rightful "place as one of the leading industrial and resort cities of the state" (qtd. in Ogle 140). Thus, while Hemingway believed he had discovered a realm whose rusticity was conducive to writing, he was actually relocating to a place that was already desperate to sell itself as a tourist destination—one that would show little compunction about capitalizing on his celebrity to achieve that goal.

It would take roughly a half decade and a federal intervention for Key West to recognize Hemingway's appeal as a tourist attraction. During that time, city fortunes fell even further as the massive debt incurred by the construction of the Overseas Highway crippled not only growth but its very ability to function; by the time Franklin Delano Roosevelt assumed the presidency in 1933 and immediately pushed through legislation enacting the Federal Emergency Relief Administration (FERA), the city "owed $113,000 in back pay to city employees, and another $150,000 in general operating expenses, including payments to the electric company, which had shut off the streetlights" (Ogle 153). Bonded debts alone totaled three-quarters of a million dollars. Private business fared no better. The Florida East Coast Railway, the brainchild of the entrepreneur Henry Flagler, had been a financial failure since its opening in 1912; by the mid-1930s, it was in receivership and would soon sell its property and route rights to the State of Florida for $640,000, "a sorry return indeed on a project that had required nearly $30 million, seven years, and the labor . . . of a forty-thousand-man workforce" (Standiford 254).[4] The bulk of the shipping traffic for the cigar and citrus industries moved to larger, more convenient ports, and New Orleans attracted the bulk of Cuban imports into the United States. The stagnant economy left a quarter of the island's 12,600 residents dependent on government relief to survive (Hanna and Hanna 360).

Initial attempts in 1933 by FERA and a parallel relief program, the Civil Works Administration (CWA), accomplished little more than patching potholes and building an open-air aquarium. Part of the problem was the lack of consistency in the early stages of the New Deal. By creating and dissolving federal agencies, hiring and firing administrators, designating monies only to reallocate them months later, the Roosevelt administration proved to be more desperate for immediate success than it was engaged in long-range planning. By December 1933, FERA and CWA employed nearly one thousand Key Westers; two months later, that number was slashed to four hundred as Roosevelt prepared to scrap the CWA in the face of harsh national criticism. It is doubtful that the effort to resuscitate Key West would ever have caught traction were it not for the April 1934 arrival of Julius F. Stone Jr., the newly appointed head of FERA's Florida division. An unlikely bureaucrat—he came to public service after earning a Harvard Ph.D. in chemistry and winning and losing a fortune in the 1920s stock boom—Stone hatched a plan to save the struggling island by marketing it as a tourist destination. At a 2 July 1934 meeting, both the Key West City Council and the Monroe County commissioners unanimously agreed to cede authority for the island to Florida governor Dave Sholtz, who then handed the reins over to Stone. Stone's first official act was to establish the Key West Administration, the ruling governing body that was little more than a front for the man whom newspapers would quickly dub the "Key West Kingfish" (Hanna and Hanna 361; McIver, *Dreamers, Schemers and Scalawags* 130; Ogle 158). While FERA and CWA were routinely derided as welfare agencies for "leaf-workers" and "shovel-leaners," Stone understood that his success depended on inspiring locals' sense of personal investment in the relief plan. One of his greatest accomplishments involved cajoling residents into spending over 1.5 million volunteer hours to spruce up the island. Meanwhile, the government promised to cover the losses of corporations that would serve tourists. For example, with the promise to cover a mere $15,000 dollars in losses, the Flagler Corporation successfully reopened the once-prosperous Casa Marina Hotel. Federal money touched all elements of the economy and was even used to train maids and servers. Transportation to and from Key West also fell under federal control, and FERA subsidized three weekly Pan American Airways flights to the island. The agency actually stepped in and took over operations of the ferry system as well, drastically reducing rates and increasing the ferry's schedule.

Between 1934 and 1935, Stone's plan worked, and tourist traffic increased by roughly 80 percent (Hanna and Hanna 362). Slowly but surely, Key West began making money again. Crowds invaded the once-sleepy port, and the local residents who had volunteered to return the island to prominence were now serving the flood of visitors for the small wages paid by the service industry. Despite this success, Julius F. Stone was hardly a universally adored figure, for many of his initiatives could seem invasive and controlling if not quasi-totalitarian. According to legend, he was far from offended by accusations of undue authoritarianism: "With a scratch of my pen I started this work in Key West and with a scratch of my pen I can stop it—just like that," he reputedly barked at anyone who stood in his way (McIver, *Hemingway's Key West* 65). Yet it was one thing for Stone to mandate the clearing of 55,000 cubic yards of garbage that had accumulated after sanitation workers abandoned their jobs when the city could no longer meet payroll; it was a whole other concern to dictate that KWA workers dress in Bermuda shorts, which Conchs considered only slightly less obscene than underwear. Stone was unswayable, however, and even took

21. The Key West Administration director Julius F. Stone Jr. (*white suit*)—shown here celebrating the local premiere of *The Pirates of Penzance* in February 1935—wielded such power in the Depression-plagued city that he was dubbed the "Key West Kingfish." Courtesy of the Monroe County Library, Key West.

Chapter 14

to sporting the controversial shorts himself, despite a great deal of ribbing from locals. His advocacy was rooted in the simple conviction that "resort wear [would] make Key West more attractive to northerners" (Ogle 166).

As someone who, according to legend, was most comfortable roaming the island in grubby khakis, dirty T-shirts, and either barefoot or in bedroom slippers (Samuelson 10; McLendon 106), Hemingway was not likely to cotton to Bermuda shorts. His initial reaction to Stone's arrival on the island was anti-Semitic: "Why not take kids out [on the Gulf Stream] and let them die or have fun rather than grow up in this FERA Jew-administered phony of a town[?]" he groused to *Esquire* editor Arnold Gingrich after the formation of the KWA. "If I don't give a godamn about America I can't help it" (*SL* 410). Yet the changes Stone and his underlings were imposing aroused little substantive ire, in part because Hemingway spent summer 1934 enjoying his newly acquired fishing cruiser, the *Pilar*, on an extended trip to Havana. His silence ended when he caught wind of the unsolicited role Key West planned for him to play in its tourism initiative. One of the clever aspects of Stone's campaign was to import writers and artists employed by the Works Progress Administration (WPA) to assist in promotion efforts. Their lavish paintings and lyrical treatments of the refurbished golf course, the yacht basin, and other inviting city sights formed the core of a glitzy, full-color pamphlet, *Key West in Transition: A Guidebook for Visitors*, which the KWA mailed gratis to potential guests. Among the four-dozen must-see spots the booklet lists, Hemingway's house ranks as number eighteen: "One of the older houses on the island, is now occupied by Ernest Hemingway, author and sportsman. Hemingway stopped here a few years ago, expecting to spend a day awaiting travel connections. He felt the magnetic charm of the Island City, purchased the house he now occupies, and makes this his permanent residence" (Trogdon 149). Correspondence from John Dos Passos's wife, Katy, suggests the KWA was not simply selling the opportunity to gawk at the house but the writer himself as well: "The New Dealers . . . wrote to [Broadway producer] Jed Harris['s] sister that she could have an apartment 'with a view of Ernest Hemingway,'" Katy complained to Riviera compatriot Sara Murphy in February 1935 (L. Miller, *Letters* 111).

"The Sights of Whitehead Street," written in early 1935, is Hemingway's direct response to the guidebook. It remains one of the best of the *Esquire* letters for a simple reason: it is genuinely funny. Unlike other Hemingway attempts at satire both early (*The Torrents of Spring*, 1926) and late ("The Art of the Short Story," written 1959 but unpublished until 1981), its humor never degenerates into the vituperative assaults that the author was prone to unleash on detractors when he felt backed into a corner. Significantly, the object of Hemingway's mockery is neither Julius F. Stone nor the KWA or FERA in general, nor even the tourists who invade 907 Whitehead Street wanting to know whether Hemingway was "really in Italy during the war" or whether "the background of your bestseller"—*A Farewell to Arms*—was "purely imaginative" (*BL* 193). The real target of the joke is the author whose work has become inveigled in the literary marketplace, where its value is determined by external forces such as the economics of writing and reader desires to judge his authenticity. As Hemingway implies, these commercial standards are antithetical to those of his art, whose merits should be measured solely by internal aesthetics. In this sense, "Whitehead Street" does not simply repudiate the celebrity that the KWA exploited in naming Hemingway's house a tourist attraction; on a deeper level, the essay is a product of the same identity crisis and uncertainty of purpose that would erupt more overtly the following year with the self-excoriation of "The Snows of Kilimanjaro," in which Hemingway's alter ego, the dying writer Harry Walden, rebukes himself for "destroy[ing] his talent by not using it, by betrayals of himself and what he believed in . . . by laziness, by sloth, by snobbery, by pride and by prejudice, by hook and by crook" (*CSS* 45). In other words, "Whitehead Street" reflects Hemingway's effort to reestablish his artistic reputation in the mid-1930s by relocating his writing from the timelier contexts in which it was being interpreted back to the supposed timelessness of modernist literature—a somewhat paradoxical effort given that the medium of communicating this message was a journalistic "letter" that, by its author's own estimation, was undertaken solely for *Esquire*'s initial $250 paying price, "nice money in the pocket," as Hemingway told Gingrich, "but nothing to negotiate [*sic*] about" (*SL* 384).

Appreciating the strategies by which Hemingway seeks to elevate his art over his celebrity while satirizing his new status as a tourist attraction requires understanding the reasons his critical standing had fallen by the time Stone resuscitated Key West. Perhaps the most basic reason was his supposed apoliticism. Although Hemingway would eventually cede to the proletarian push of the decade, the event that catalyzed his activism—the Labor Day Hurricane of 1935—was still a good nine months away when the KWA published *Key West in Transition*.[5] "The Sights of Whitehead Street" therefore questions the compatibility of politics and art through at least two humorous methods. The first is to ridicule the very idea of the political novel by invoking its most famous exemplar, a work that, at the time, was said to embody the pitfalls of subjugating aesthetics to a cause: Harriet Beecher Stowe's *Uncle Tom's Cabin* (1852). "To discourage visitors while he is at work your correspondent has hired an aged negro who appears to be the victim of an odd disease resembling leprosy who meets visitors at the gate and says, 'I'se Mr. Hemingway and I'se crazy about you,'" the satire reads. Unfortunately, this faux Hemingway cannot quite keep his employer's plots straight, as when he regales tourists with the story behind "De Call to Arms": "In some odd way he had confused the plot with that of another best seller, Uncle Tom's Cabin, and his description of how he wrote the passage where Missy Catherine Barkley pursues the Italian army with blood hounds over the ice would have been mirth provoking if it had not been so realistic" (*BL* 192–93).

For *Esquire* readers already familiar with Hemingway's admonitions against politicizing art—especially in his December 1934 letter, "Old Newsman Writes"—the Stowe reference was likely such an obvious example of why "books should be about the people you know, that you love and hate, not about the people you study up about" (*BL* 184) that it would have been easy to overlook the surprising parallel the author constructs while conflating *A Farewell to Arms* and *Uncle Tom's Cabin*: Catherine Barkley here is not equated with Eliza, the escaping slave whose leap across the ice floes of the Ohio River was nineteenth-century literature's most iconic political image. She is, rather, the *pursuer*, the counterpart not of the sympathetic heroine but of Stowe's loathed slave trader Mr. Haley, whose plot to sell Eliza's son is foiled by the woman's desperate jump to freedom. (Pursuing the Italian army, she is also apparently no longer an American Red Cross nurse, either, but a member of the Austrian army.) The seemingly confused equation of the abolitionists' Underground Railroad and the retreat from Caporetto places Hemingway's politics with the status quo and not with the "revolutionary mouthpieces" trying to "suck [him] into writing about the proletariat . . . just to please the recently politically enlightened critics" (*BL* 181, 184).

A second, similarly surprising act of political alignment rebukes left-ist critics even more explicitly. Hemingway describes how he himself deals with tourists who make it past the imposter hired to scare them away: he claims he does not actually author the novels that have made him famous. Escorting "Mr. Questioner" throughout 907 Whitehead Street, he reveals that his three sons generate prose that is then sold under the Hemingway name, which is "sort of a trade-mark." When his guest questions how such young minds can possibly create the stark exposés of violence for which the author is known, Hemingway admits that "the damned sad stuff" is a byproduct of "over-beat[ing] them," even though "the boys are doing fine and I'm proud of [them]. If they live I'm going to turn the business over to them." The dialogue leads to a comic indictment of specific New Deal institutions and architects:

> The N.R.A. has practically put a stop to it. . . . Johnson cracked down on us about the kids. . . . Tried to call it child labour, and the oldest boy over ten. I had to go to Washington on it. "Listen, Hugh," I said to him. "It's no skin off the ants of conscience in my pants what you do to Richberg. But the little boy works, see?" Then I walked out on him. We got the little fellow up to about ten thousand words a day after that but about half of it was sad and we had to take a loss on it. (*BL* 195)

The references here mean little unless one knows the history of the New Deal. Long before the National Rifle Association laid claim to the abbreviation, "NRA" referred to the National Recovery Administration, the industrial-relations agency Roosevelt created to facilitate the establishment of fair competition codes, minimum wages, and maximum work hours throughout commerce. Headed by retired brigadier general Hugh S. Johnson (1882–1942), the NRA rocketed to prominence only to tailspin into bureaucratic ineptitude within eighteen months of its creation when it became clear that it could not enforce its own Byzantine regulations without resorting to hardball tactics that threatened support for government relief. Johnson's rise and fall was equally rapid: *Time* magazine's Man of the Year for 1933 was replaced in September 1934 by the NRA's legal counsel, the former labor lawyer Donald Richberg, in part because of Johnson's unstable personality (fueled by his alcoholism) but also because of persistent concern that NRA policies were too reminiscent of Fascist corporativism, a resemblance that Roosevelt's long-running secretary of labor, Frances Perkins, found politically untenable in the shadow of Hitler's rise (Ohl 219–20). Given the virulent disdain for Il Duce Hemingway had been voicing in print since 1922, Johnson's reputed fascist sympathies could only confirm his suspicion that behind the socialist dressings of New Deal politics beat the heart of a Mussolini-like belief in absolute power.

The satire of Hemingway's farcical claim in "The Sights of Whitehead Street" that his sons actually write his fiction thus works on a couple of different levels. On the one hand, in depicting writing as the type of "regular business" that the National Recovery Administration would target for control (*BL* 194), the piece identifies Hemingway squarely as a *producer* of goods as opposed to a worker whose services, like those of the WPA writers Stone imported to Key West, are contracted to benefit a larger collective. Beyond this claim for the sanctity of his individualism, "Whitehead Street" suggests the further absurdity of measuring literary value by market prices, whose instability drives Hemingway to distraction: "Sometimes [we sell writing for] a dollar a word. Sometimes seventy-five cents. Sometimes you bid [editors] up to two dollars when you have something on them." The "damned sad stuff," however, brings in "only a dime a word," while "the second rate stuff" must be sold under aliases: "You've probably seen some of it around. There was quite a lot of it around at one time. Now there's not so much. We marketed it under too many names and it killed the market." Hemingway even confesses to blackmail to boost his price: "Say an editor comes down [to Key West], a married editor, we get him off to one of those—well you know—or we just surprise him in his room sometime and then of course the price goes up. But there's really no money in that anymore. The NRA has practically put a stop to it" (*BL* 195). Ridiculing fluctuating rates as artificial, Hemingway implicitly reinforces his claim throughout the mid-1930s that literature should be judged independently of the marketplace. Indeed, literary economics in "Whitehead Street" can be read as parodic proof of what Hemingway says in *Green Hills of Africa*, which he was in the process of drafting as Key West began to exploit his celebrity: "We make our writers into something very strange. . . . We destroy them in many ways. First, economically. They make money . . . [and] then they have to write to keep up their establishments, their wives, and so on, and they write slop. It is slop not on purpose but because it is hurried. Because they write when there is nothing to say or no water in the well" (*GHOA* 23). The essay also reinforces the argument of "Old Newsman Writes," in which Hemingway claims that proletarian writing, because it is a literary niche, likewise forces authors to maintain their "establishments": "A writer can make himself a nice career while he is alive by espousing a political cause, working for it, making a profession of believing in it, and if it wins he will be very well placed. All politics is a matter of working hard without reward, or with a living wage for a time, in the hope of booty later" (*BL* 183).

Politics is not the only adversary in "The Sights of Whitehead Street," however. Less overtly, the essay also seeks to insulate literature from tourism. As Jake Barnes's train trip from Paris to Bayonne in book 2 of *The Sun Also Rises* demonstrates, Hemingway was highly dismissive of modern-day travelers who indulged their restlessness by following itineraries from site to site to gawk instead of experience. As Miriam B. Mandel has written, Hemingway advocated "a kind of anti-tourism, in which the traveler 'passes' as a native in the settings he visits, changing himself from outsider to insider" (93–94). Yet, beginning with the cult popularity of *The Sun*, Hemingway had to contend with the fact that his writings could inspire the very sort of tourism he loathed. By the mid-1930s, accounts of Hemingway's travels became a routine feature in metropolitan dailies like the *New York Times* and the *New York Herald Tribune*, as well as periodicals from *Vanity Fair* to *Time*; instead of the transformative benefits of travel, however, these pieces effused over adventurous globe-trotting.

"Whitehead Street" satirizes this type of tourism through two tactics based on a distinction that Hemingway routinely made in his readership. First, the essay implicitly discourages his audience from identifying with the type of tourist who would equate literature with other attractions listed on the KWA itinerary. Hiring an "aged negro" to play the part of Ernest Hemingway would seem to set the bar of ignorance at a fairly low level; just as any "visitor who really knows much about leprosy is not at all terrified by [this surrogate] and after examining him in a cursory fashion dismisses him as an imposter," so, too, the traveler should at least know enough about Hemingway to know he is not black. Yet, significantly, *none of the tourists depicted in "Whitehead Street" do*; rather than challenge the faux Hemingway, they run "down the street toward Fort Taylor," shocked that the famous author possesses none of the heroic values celebrated in his writing (*BL* 193). As such, Hemingway insists that when tourists know nothing of the subjects they visit, they are subject to false information that impugns the authenticity of their interaction with those sites.

At the same time, the questions that the tourists pose of the imposter before they bolt from Whitehead Street reveal why they are incapable of properly appreciating his fiction: they betray a striking ignorance of Hemingway's actual work. Not only do none of the tourists question the imposter's conflation of *A Farewell to Arms* and *Uncle Tom's Cabin*; one goes so far to proffer a question that drove Hemingway to distraction in this period—namely, "why he always wrote in the first person." ("I don't write in the first person," the imposter replies. "I write on the typewriter"). Perhaps the only false perception of his work that irritated Hemingway more than this was the claim that he only wrote in dialogue, a truism bemoaned throughout *Death in the Afternoon*.[6] As "Whitehead Street" implies, visitors know about as much about Hemingway as they do the history of other sites on Key West's tourist itinerary—which is to say, nothing outside of what the guidebooks (and media) tell them. In this sense, Hemingway's repudiation of the KWA itinerary recalls his qualifications about what makes a useful guidebook for tourists in *Death*: "[Travel] being always an individual experience, there comes a place in the guide book where you must say do not come back until you have ski-ed, had sexual intercourse, shot quail or grouse, or been to the bullfight so that you will know what we are talking about" (*DIA* 62). "Whitehead Street" is thus Hemingway's way of telling visitors peppering him with questions about writing that they should not bother until they can demonstrate they know what they are talking about.

The point of depicting tourists as uninformed readers becomes clearer with the appearance of Mr. Questioner, the interlocutor who falls for Hemingway's tall tales of literature as labor exploitation. As a foil, this stock character joins a long list of fictionalized readers in Hemingway's writing, a type his contemporary audience would have recent familiarity with thanks to controversial inclusion of the intrusive Old Lady in *Death* who objects to the goriness of the bullfights. Whenever Hemingway felt defensive about his aesthetics, he parodied the reading expectations of such inquisitors. On occasion, he did invoke his ideal audience, usually a worshipful pupil such as the aspiring writer Mice in "Monologue to the Maestro," his October 1935 *Esquire* letter (a character based on Arnold Samuelson), or a studious fan like Kandisky in *Green Hills of Africa*. Interestingly, however, these disciples appear far less frequently than their resisting reader counterparts, mainly because the extreme prudery Hemingway attributed to Old Lady types allowed him to articulate his ideals without serious opposition.

In Mr. Questioner's case, the main issue is not the brutality of his prose but its monetary value. It is bad enough that this tourist ("a prominent business man and a fellow member of the Player's Club") doubts that literature is labor—"Call that work[?]" he asks—but he seems incapable of imagining any purpose to art other than remuneration: "It's a regular business," he gasps as Hemingway regales him with tales of manipulating the marketplace. "I had no idea there was that much money in it. . . . I'd like to get in on something like that" (*BL* 194, 196). Hemingway goes on to spin a tale about his sons discovering a "new angle" on the southern epic that will "[net] a million": "Bumby has the historical sense, Pat does the dialogue, and Gregory does plot. . . . It's an epic about the Civil War but the trouble with most epics is they weren't long enough but what somebody would be able to read the epic and pass the word it was lousy. We figure to run to three thousand pages" (*BL* 196). Mr. Questioner expresses no objection to this scheme to publish a book too long for anyone to read; nor does he question Hemingway's sudden reverence for the epic. Had he read *Death in the Afternoon* (which Hemingway claims six-year-old Patrick dictated to his nanny in a week), he might remember this admonition against that genre's "unrelieved turgidness": "All bad writers are in love with the epic" (*DIA* 54). Of course, Mr. Questioner is not interested in aesthetics; he does admire Hemingway's market research, however, and suddenly, with "a new respect in his tone," he voices regret for invading the author's house: "You know, I think I ought to go. . . . You must be busy" (*BL* 197). As Hemingway implies, the tourists invading Key West have no real appreciation for the purpose of literature. Their inability to experience its timeless aspects, revealed by their devotion to the transitory values of the marketplace, renders them unfit to belong to his intended audience. As such, the message of "Whitehead Street" to tourists seems fairly straightforward: stay away.

Hemingway was by no means the only modernist to employ reader-foils to assert his aesthetics. The technique is a fairly common among his literary contemporaries, indicative of modernism's insistence that true art is adversarial to the tastes of the mass audience. Yet "Whitehead Street" also invokes a third modernist ideal more specific to Hemingway's declining reputation in the mid-1930s. Even more than his supposed indifference to politics and his popular readership, critics complained about Hemingway's overbearing personality, especially in his nonfiction. As Granville Hicks surmised while reviewing *Death*: "More people will read the book because they are interested in Hemingway than will read it because they are interested in bullfighting. . . . The author, fully aware of the interest in his personality, has made a vigorous effort to put as much of himself as possible into his book" (Meyers, *Critical Heritage* 163). This line of argument would culminate in Edmund Wilson's claim while reviewing *Green Hills of Africa* that "among his creations, [Hemingway] is certainly his own worst-drawn character": "As soon as he talks in his own person, he seems to lose all his capacity for self-criticism and is likely to become fatuous or maudlin. . . . When he expounds [his] sense of life . . . in his own character as Ernest Hemingway, the Old Master of Key West, he has a way of sounding silly." Wilson attributed this defect to fame: "He is beginning to be imposed on by the American publicity legend which has been created about him and which . . . has very little to do with what one actually finds in his stories" (Meyers, *Critical Heritage* 218). For many readers, the *Esquire* essays were prima facie evidence of how that "publicity legend" permeated his prose. They were so injurious to Hemingway's reputation that by December 1935 former fans like Paul Harris in *American Criterion* were openly pleading with the author to return to fiction (13–16).

Hemingway's use of absurd amanuenses like the "aged negro" and his sons can be read as an effort to inoculate himself from such accusations. By duping tourists, he not only parodies the mass audience's desire to know the man behind the work but insists on his own disinterest in the "publicity legend." In effect, he invokes the modernist belief in the poetics of impersonality, the Eliotic idea that literature is an escape from personality rather than an expression of it. Despite Hemingway's disdain for Eliot, hints of this conviction reverberate throughout the *Esquire* pieces. "Old Newsman Writes" portrays journalism as an "I, me, my" medium that "projects . . . personality rather than goes for the facts" (*BL* 179–80). "A

Friend of Spain" likewise describes an old Spanish acquaintance who, much to Hemingway's chagrin, tries to ply him with absinthe. Hemingway is baffled by this unusual generosity until, the following day, he discovers his old friend had capitalized on his celebrity by "writ[ing] an article [for the Sunday paper] entitled Mister Hemingway, Friend of Spain" (*BL* 145).

On an abstract level then, "Whitehead Street" can be read as a parable about Hemingway's need not to succumb to celebrity and maintain his artistic ideals. He says as much in the opening paragraph upon discovering his home on the KWA itinerary: "This is all very flattering to the easily bloated ego of your correspondent but very hard on production" (*BL* 192). Interestingly, Hemingway does not satirize the public's perception of him by depicting himself as the inverse of his image: he does not reveal himself to be a homebody, a teetotaler, or an effete bookworm. Rather, every element of his farce—from employing an imposter to calling the Hemingway name a "trademark" to the claim that nowadays he only writes enough "to keep it [the business] going"—seems designed to imply that inferring a single, definable personality from the writing is a fool's errand. The point is not simply that the impressions of Hemingway that visitors glean from his books are wrong; the point is that "Hemingway" has little actual input into the content of his work and that curiosity about his personality is therefore misplaced. What matters most is the element that Hemingway is willing to take credit for: the production process. His rejection of the audience's interest in his person is ironically confirmed by his parting words to Mr. Questioner: "Details of a man's work are always interesting" (*BL* 197).

In and of itself, "The Sights of Whitehead Street" was hardly successful in resuscitating Hemingway's flagging reputation. That would not begin to happen until later in 1935 with "Who Murdered the Vets?," his angry indictment of the Roosevelt administration's responsibility for the death of several hundred itinerant World War I veterans stranded in the Labor Day Hurricane. Nor did "Whitehead Street" keep tourists away from Number 18 on the KWA's itinerary. Out of frustration, Hemingway instructed the handyman and sometime chauffeur Toby Bruce to build a brick wall around the property, a project that, according to James McLendon, at least one local official sought to foil: "A Key West City Commissioner (devoid of any official power as the city was under the KWA) had taken a dislike to the wall that he viewed as 'an eyesore,' and he used his influence to 'bar

22. Young boys performing outside the wall Hemingway erected around his house to keep tourists away, late 1930s. Courtesy of the State Archives of Florida.

the Hemingway crowd' from the city's brick sites" (134–35). Whether this commissioner felt the "eyesore" truly distracted from the natural view of Whitehead Street or whether he feared tourist complaints about obstructing their view of the Hemingway house is lost to history; what is known is that tourists continued to gather at the edge of the property despite the wall, often besieged by young beggars who sang and danced for spare change. The KWA did finally evince some sensitivity to Hemingway's wish for privacy, however: the second edition of *Key West in Transition* appends a brief note to its description of the famous writer's residence: "Closed to the public."

Before the second edition of the guidebook appeared in late 1935, the "Key West Kingfish," Julius F. Stone, had already reaped the fruits of his success: a promotion took him off the island to serve as a FERA field representative for the entire southeastern United States. By the time *To Have and Have Not* was published, he was out of government service all together, having returned to Harvard to pursue a law degree. Yet his life would continue to intersect in odd, intriguing ways with that of the man whom he helped turn into a tourist industry. In 1940—the same year that Hemingway's divorce from Pauline Pfeiffer effectively ended his tenure as Key West's most famous resident—Stone reappeared to reinvent himself as a real-estate entrepreneur. For the next two decades, as celebrity turned the Hemingway

23. The cover of the second edition of the Key West guidebook for tourists that inspired "The Sights of Whitehead Street." Hemingway's home is still listed as a city attraction, but at least this time authorities noted that it was a private residence. Courtesy of the Key West Art and Historical Society.

name into just the sort of trademark that "Whitehead Street" ridiculed, the former bureaucrat became entangled in a series of shady investment deals that, by 1960, had him deep in debt and facing an IRS lien. To avoid the law, he briefly fled to Cuba, where he discovered—just as Hemingway had when forced to abandon the Finca Vigía, his beloved Havana home—that the newly enthroned regime of Fidel Castro had little interest in coddling expatriate Americans. As Hemingway committed suicide in Ketchum, Idaho, in 1961, Key West's savior was an old man living on the lam. He died in Australia in 1967, but he had so successfully eluded his creditors that news of his passing did not make it to Key West until nearly a year later.

Before his fall from grace, Stone experienced the invasive repercussions of Key West tourism in an ironic way that Hemingway himself might have appreciated. During the 1950s, the New Deal veteran owned the Southernmost Home at the end of Duval Street, which he purchased from the novelist Thelma Strabel, whose *Reap the Wild Wind*, a hurricane melodrama set on the island in the 1840s, had been successfully adapted by Cecil B. De Mille in 1942. As Stuart McIver reports, the Stone family was flustered by tourists who knocked at their door at all hours of the day to pose a single question: "Is this really the southernmost house in the U.S.A.?" (*Dreamers, Schemers and Scalawags* 133). Had Stone remembered Hemingway's response to such interruptions, he might have employed an "aged negro" to send them packing by spinning legends. Alas, the former KWA chieftain lacked the literary imagination necessary to cope with the Mr. Questioners that tourism spawns.

Notes

1. The two exception are "Notes on Life and Letters: Or a Manuscript Found in a Bottle" (January 1935) and "There She Breaches! or Moby Dick off the Morro" (May 1936).

2. Opinion remains split over whether "Che Ti Dice La Patria?" should be classified as nonfiction or fiction. First published as a *New Republic* article in May 1927, it was subsequently included in *Men Without Women*, Hemingway's second short-story collection.

3. "Monologue to the Maestro" (October 1935) makes this aversion to *timeliness* explicit. When an aspiring writer asks how fiction differs from reporting, Hemingway responds: "If [the writing] was reporting they would not remember it. When you describe something that has happened that day the timeliness makes people see it in their own imaginations. A month later that element of time is gone and your account would be flat and they would not see it in their minds nor remember it" (*BL* 215–16).

4. The sale came about as a direct result of the 1935 Labor Day Hurricane. The railway, completed in 1913, had never been profitable.

5. Hemingway's supposed conversion to the political scene would begin with "Who Murdered the Vets?" and continue on through *To Have and Have Not* and his partisan reporting during the Spanish Civil War. By the time of *For Whom the Bell Tolls* (1940), he would return to the "separate peace" stance toward political engagement espoused during his *In Our Time* years.

6. "But, you say," Hemingway imagines readers thinking in *Death*, "there is very little conversation in this book. Why isn't there more dialogue? What we want in a book by this citizen is people talking; that is all he knows how to do and now he doesn't do it" (*DIA* 120).

Hemingway's Key West Band of Brothers

The World War I Veterans in "Who Murdered the Vets?" and *To Have and Have Not*

JAMES H. MEREDITH

Fal. But to say I know more harm in him than in myself, were to say
more than I know. That he is old, the more the pity, his white hairs
do witness it, but that he is, saying your reverence, a whoremaster, that I
utterly deny. If sack and sugar be a fault, God, help the wicked! If to be old
and merry be a sin, then many an old love host that I know is damn'd.
If to be fat be to be hated, then Pharaoh's kine are to be lov'd. No,
my good lord, banish Peto, banish Bardolph, banish Poins, but for sweet
Jack Falstaff, kind Jack Falstaff, true Jack Falstaff, valiant Jack Falstaff,
banish not him thy Harry's company, banish not him thy Harry's
company—banish plump Jack, and banish all the world.
Prince. I do, I will.

1 Henry IV, 2.4.466–81

K. Hen. We few, we happy few, we band of brothers

Henry V, 4.2.60

On 5 September 1935, Ernest Hemingway piloted his cabin cruiser, the
Pilar, into Lower Matecumbe Key, some seventy-five miles north of Key
West, and was greeted by carnage he had not seen since he was an eighteen-
year-old ambulance driver on the Italian front. Two days earlier the most

intense hurricane to hit the United States since the advent of modern re-cordkeeping had roared westward across the Atlantic, brutalizing the string of Upper Keys that led toward Miami with winds estimated at 185 miles per hour and a storm surge of nearly twenty feet (Drye 312). As part of a volunteer group organized by Monroe County sheriff Karl Thompson, Hemingway was one of the first to view what remained in the aftermath. As he wrote Maxwell Perkins on 7 September: "Nothing could give an idea of the destruction. Between 700 and 1000 dead. Many, today, still unburied. The foliage absolutely stripped as though by fire for forty miles and the land looking like the abandoned bed of a river. Not a building of any sort stand-ing. . . . Saw more dead than I'd seen in one place since the lower Piave in June of 1918" (SL 421).

The World War I analogy was not inappropriate. Among the storm's victims were 259 veterans who had been working on the island helping to build a bridge linking Lower Matecumbe Key with Jewfish Key, part of an ambitious Florida initiative to span the thirty-five-mile gap in the Overseas Highway that hampered the flow of tourism into Key West. The federal government had hired these former soldiers in order to avoid a reprise of the 1932 Bonus March on Washington, D.C., placing them in late 1934 into

Chapter 15

24a-b-c. Victims of the 1935 Labor Day Hurricane undergoing mass cremation. Ernest Hemingway Collection/John F. Kennedy Presidential Library and Museum, Boston.

three camps stretched between Lower and Upper Matecumbe. At its height, the collective camp population numbered 684, the residents representing a surprisingly diverse cross-section of America: among them were draftsmen, lawyers, high-school principals, actors, and at least one professional boxer (Drye 48). Others were, apropos of Depression-era stereotypes, itinerants. Hemingway took the veterans' deaths personally, and not merely because of his close identification with those who had witnessed combat; he had encountered at least some of these men before during their frequent furloughs in Key West, where they could prove a rowdy force when their frustrations boiled over into drunken brawls (Ogle 176). According to Carlos Baker, Hemingway himself barely missed becoming the victim of one vet who liked to summon patrons at Sloppy Joe's to his side, knock them upside the head with his crutch, and then rifle their pockets to fund his bar tab (*Writer as Artist* 207).[1]

Immediately after returning from relief efforts at Matecumbe, Hemingway wrote "Who Murdered the Vets?," a searing indictment of bureaucratic callousness that—as its title suggests—accused Franklin D. Roosevelt's administration not of reckless indifference or even manslaughter but of homicide for abandoning the veterans to the dangerous South Florida tropics:

> Whom did [the veterans] annoy and to whom was their possible presence a political danger?
>
> Who sent them down to the Florida Keys and left them there in hurricane months?
>
> Who is responsible for their deaths?
>
> The writer of this article lives a long way from Washington and would not know the answers to these questions. But he does know that wealthy people, yachtsmen, fishermen such as President Hoover and President Roosevelt, do not come to the Florida Keys in hurricane months. (Trogdon 168)

Published in *New Masses*—a leftist journal Hemingway had long disparaged—"Who Murdered the Vets?" is usually seen as inaugurating Hemingway's short-lived stint as a proletarian writer. Two years after the hurricane, that stint would culminate with the publication of the long-gestating *To Have and Have Not*, a novel whose paradigmatic distinction between the moral venality of the rich and the noble struggles of the working poor would prove one of the decade's more complex repudiations of New Deal politics. Especially in scenes that reference the Roosevelt administration, *To Have and Have Not* contains several passages whose feral tone could fit seamlessly within "Who Murdered the Vets?"

Yet for critics seeking to trace the political continuity between the essay and the novel, the latter contains some surprising differences. For starters, the Labor Day Hurricane goes unmentioned; it requires an attentive reader to realize that the action *precedes* the disaster. Even more important, the depiction of the former doughboys living on Matecumbe is—on the surface at least—far from the impassioned defense of their vulnerability in the *New Masses* essay: "You cannot interest any very wealthy people in fishing off the coast of Cuba in summer when the biggest fish are there. There is a known danger to property. But veterans, especially the bonus-marching variety of veterans, are not property. They are only human beings" (Trogdon 168). Hemingway can hardly be said to portray the veterans in *To Have and Have Not* as "human beings." Rather, their appearance in chapter 22, the novel's "Winter" section, is treated surreally, their disgruntled violence so bizarre as to border on the farcical:

> [Richard Gordon and the sheriff] were opposite the brightly lighted open front of Freddy's place and it was jammed to the sidewalk. Men in dungarees, some bareheaded, others in caps, old service hats, and in cardboard helmets, crowded the bar three deep, and the loud-speaking nickel-in-the-slot phonograph was playing "Isle of Capri." As they pulled up a man came hurtling out of the open door, another man on top of him. They fell and rolled on the sidewalk, and the man on top, holding the other's hair in both hands, banged his head up and down on the cement, making a sickening noise. No one at the bar was paying any attention.
>
> The sheriff got out of the car and grabbed the man on top by the shoulder.
>
> "Cut it out," he said. "Get up there."
>
> The man straightened up and looked at the sheriff. "For Christ sake, can't you mind your own business?"
>
> The other man, blood in his hair, blood oozing from one ear, and more of it trickling down his freckled face, squared off at the sheriff.
>
> "Leave my buddy alone," he said thickly. "What's the matter?

Don't you think I can take it?" (*THHN* 200–201)

This vignette becomes even more curious when one realizes how atypical it is compared to other portraits of wounded soldiers in the Hemingway canon. From the beginning of his career, inspired by his own 1918 wounding on the Piave River outside of Fossalta, Italy, the author fixated on the psychological plight of shell-shocked veterans. His most famous walking wounded—the "lost" refugees of the Lost Generation—may suffer from an array of undiagnosed psychological ailments, yet they are unfailingly depicted with empathy and poignancy. In the 1920s, their rendering imbued the literature of war with an unprecedented emotional depth that continues nine decades later to stand in distinct contradiction to the image of the soldier as a noble killing machine found in much popular fiction. Harold Krebs's alienation from the staid hypocrisies of the American family in "Soldier's Home" (1924), Frederic Henry's renunciation of the rhetoric of valor in *A Farewell to Arms* (1929), and Nick Adams's nervous exhaustion in "A Way You'll Never Be" (1933)—not to mention Nick's trauma in other stories such as "Big Two-Hearted River" (1924) and "Now I Lay Me" (1927)—all made it virtually impossible for subsequent writers to limn the battlefield without emphasizing its horrors and terrors and exposing the "old lie" of *dulce et decorum est.*

Yet for all the psychological intensity that Hemingway invested in his characters, before the mid-1930s he demonstrated relatively little interest in the *sociology* of soldiering. Before *To Have and Have Not*, that is, he generally eschewed the larger cultural conditions that affected veterans after the Great War. He does not delve into the fact, as a 1931 survey by the United States Veterans Administration reported, that eight hundred thouand veterans were unemployed and that well over 50 percent were chronically so despite concerted efforts to remedy the situation.[2] Nor does he plumb the postwar disenfranchisement of doughboys, who, as Jennifer D. Keene writes, returned home "in 1919 to find 'foreigners' in their factory jobs, women in clerical positions, the chance to learn a new skill gone, a postwar recession in the farming community that endured throughout the so-called 'Roaring Twenties,' an incapacitating sensitivity to noise, 'jumpy nerves,' or struggles of hard work and thrift to acquire a small house and garden . . . of losing a job, home, farm, or family after 1929" (182).

To Have and Have Not represents a first step toward this broader context inasmuch as, for the first time, Hemingway depicts the veterans *as a collective*. Gone is the famous individuation that the wounded Nick Adams asserts in *In Our Time* when he tells Rinaldi that they must make their "separate peace" (*CSS* 105). Instead, Hemingway characterizes the doughboys as a *type*, the sufferings of all standing for the sufferings of the one. Accordingly, in what follows I want to explore exactly how this approach represents a significant shift away from the modernist strain of Hemingway's most famous works toward an attempted social realism whose success by and large depends on readers' knowledge of the lamentable history of veterans' affairs in Depression-era America. What we lose in such a shift is the psychological force of Hemingway's portraits of traumatized soldiers. What we gain, however, is a better understanding of how New Deal politics demanded an alternative approach to characterization that, if flatter in its phenomenology, was more overt and more pointed in its critique of the social factors that subjected veterans to poverty and despair. Ultimately, Hemingway's Key West veterans may not be as compelling as the typical Hemingway hero in conveying the ravages of war. Yet their uniqueness invites us to consider how he struggled to balance the demands of art and politics in the 1930s. Equally important, their distinctness allows us, through the contrast they offer, to reassess that conventional Hemingway soldier-hero to better understand why his noble individuality became a representative gauge of the veteran's ability to survive not only the initiation experience of battle but the disillusionment of lost ideals.

Brothers under the Bridge: Historical Contexts of Veterans Affairs

Unlike Krebs in "Soldier's Home," Jake Barnes in *The Sun Also Rises*, or Frederic in *A Farewell to Arms*, Hemingway's Key West veterans are not only not individuals but *victims*. They lack the capacity to resist and therefore survive the degenerative, naturalistic forces attempting to crush them. As Hemingway puts it in "Who Murdered the Vets?": "Some [of these men] had been on the bum since the Argonne almost and some had lost their jobs the year before last Christmas. . . . [But] they were all what you get after a war" (Trogdon 170). Their disabilities have gone so far as to turn them into grotesque, Falstaffian figures, right down to their "old service hats" and "cardboard helmets" (*THHN* 200)—caricatures of military attire, similar to what the Cheapside merry band of brothers would have worn in a theatrical performance of Shakespeare's *1 Henry IV*. The comparison is not gratuitous: Hemingway chose as his epigraph for "Who Murdered the Vets?" a Falstaffian line from *1 Henry IV*: "I have led my ragamuffins where they are peppered; there's not three of my hundred and fifty left alive, and they are for the town's end to beg during life" (5.3.39–40; qtd. in Trogdon 168). If we use Hemingway's own everyman World War I survivor as an example, these were veterans who demonstrated that, for many demobilized men, there was no Big Two-Hearted River to turn to for spiritual recovery.[3]

The reasons for their dehumanization had much to do with the sociopolitical conditions directly responsible for the veterans being in Key West in the first place—namely, the reparation campaign that led to the 1932 Bonus March.[4] As Keene explains, "American veterans of the Great War won a major legislative battle in 1924 when their claim for adjusted compensation became law." That legislation, known as the Adjusted Service Certificate Law, awarded veterans bonus pay in the form of bonds that could be redeemed after twenty years—hardly immediate relief for unemployed doughboys, but a gesture that "aroused little complaint among veterans" amid the boom of the Roaring Twenties.[5] As the Depression set in, however, "veterans revived calls for an immediate cash payment" instead of deferred compensation (179). The campaign culminated in June and July 1932 as some thirty thousand members of the "Bonus Army" camped in a Hooverville erected on the Anacostia Flats near Washington, D.C. Under the leadership of former army sergeant Walter V. Waters, the marchers hoped to sway the U.S. Senate's vote on a bill sponsored by Texas congressman Wright Patman to require immediate disbursal of promised funds. When the bill was defeated, some marchers accepted a congressional appropriation to finance their return home, but many refused to leave the Flats. After D.C. police scuffled with the marchers, President Herbert Hoover ordered the Twelfth Infantry Regiment and the Third Cavalry Regiment to breakup the Anacostia site, a highly controversial move that failed to violate the Posse Comitatus Act that precludes the military from serving a law-enforcement function only because of a technicality: the act does not apply to Washington, D.C. since it is a federal property. (Anti-Red fervor also justified the incursion; the mission's commander, none other than General Douglas MacArthur, insisted that the Bonus Army was a Communist front.) The intervention not only killed two of the Bonus Marchers but a pair of infants who died from gas asphyxiation. The resulting public relations disaster contributed to Hoover's defeat in that fall's election, but it did little to relieve veteran woes. When Franklin D. Roosevelt assumed the presidency in March 1933, the Bonus Army returned to Washington, albeit in ever dwindling numbers: 3,000 in 1933, 1,500 in 1934 (Scott 16).

Although Roosevelt was no more inclined to pay reparations than his predecessor, he dealt with the vets more judiciously than Hoover had. One of his chief tactical tools was his wife, Eleanor, who met with the Bonus Marchers. It is Mrs. Roosevelt, in fact, who is credited with encouraging veterans to join public-service workforce projects, including the Overseas Highway initiative to Key West. Sponsored under the aegis of the Florida division of the Federal Emergency Relief Administration (FERA), the project promised vets thirty dollars a month, plus room and board. As the vets who signed on soon discovered, however, the "board" turned out to be substandard, consisting of "tents and flimsy barracks constructed literally on the beach a few yards from the surf and the tide line" (Martin, "The Storm" 76). The three camps the vets eventually grew to occupy were also unsanitary—after barely four months in the Keys, two men had already died from spinal meningitis. It did not help the veterans' plight that the director of the Florida FERA division referred to them in an interview with United Press as "derelict[s]" while describing the camps as experiments in "reconditioning" (qtd. in Drye 56). That director was none other than Julius F. Stone Jr., already an anathema to Hemingway for his ambitious plan to turn Key West into a tourist destination, an initiative Hemingway had lampooned that same April in his *Esquire* essay "The Sights of Whitehead Street."

Political posturing was not the only impediment with which former soldiers had to contend. In the relatively short nine months of the camps' existence, administrators came and went as oversight for the veterans shifted from the state highway department (which was responsible for the Overseas Highway) back to FERA (which mainly put the men to work building more living quarters for subsequent vets arriving in the Keys). The weather was also a severe handicap for men unaccustomed to the southern humidity and mosquitoes. And the mainstream press was often hostile to any New Deal program that even hinted of socialism. When the vets began protesting camp conditions shortly after their arrival, the *Washington Post* attacked them for "think[ing] Uncle Sam owes them something." According to the reporter Edward T. Folliard, employing the vets on the highway project represented a "silly, further waste of taxpayers' money" that benefited nobody but the bootleggers and hookers who rushed to Matecumbe to relieve the men of their relief pay.[6] Interviewing a vet named Bill Bevais, Folliard detailed to comic extremes the brawls arising from the vets' "booze rampage," even noting with a Hemingwayesque flourish that drinking in the camps was no mere "sissy drinking bout" but a "two-fisted alcoholic debauch" (10). A second derogatory national news story appeared in the *New York Times* that August, barely a month before the Labor Day hurricane. Blasting veterans in a sister camp in Kingstree, South Carolina, the *Times* went so far as to take credit for turning the tide of public opinion against veteran relief programs. Had the hurricane not occurred, the eleven vet camps stretching from Florida to South Carolina would have been closed that November by order of FERA director Harry Hopkins, who aimed to transfer their 2,500 inhabitants into the Civilian Conservation Corps (CCC), where the vets' threatened protests and discontented behavior would be far less conspicuous.

From "Who Murdered the Vets?" to *To Have and Have Not*

Hemingway's correspondence suggests that he originally intended to depict the Matecumbe disaster in *To Have and Have Not*. "There are two themes in it," he wrote Maxwell Perkins in a hasty prospectus dated 11 July 1936. "The decline of the individual . . . and the story of a shipment of dynamite and all of the consequences that happened from it. . . . Also have the hurricane and the vets in it" (*OTTC* 243–44). Had Hemingway been able to avoid distractions and muster the concentration to create a unified, epic narrative à la *For Whom the Bell Tolls*, the vets' place in the plot might have been more central. As it stands, we must rely on the chronological disparity between the time frame in which the story takes place (spring 1934–winter 1935) and the book's publication (October 1937) to understand the reason for the vets' appearance in chapter 22. Although *To Have and Have Not* was mostly written in the aftermath of the Labor Day Hurricane—the exception, of course, being the opening "Spring" section, which was published as the autonomous short story "One Trip Across" in 1934—the action, as previously noted, precedes the storm. Readers are thus required to look for foreshadowing of the men's impending fate, something that is not particularly easy given their rapid-fire, often nonsensical bursts of dialogue. Perhaps the most obvious clues come when a Communist organizer named Nelson Jacks lectures the faux proletarian author Richard Gordon (through whose third-person limited perspective we view the action) on just who the vets are:

> "I would like to bet you that not three men in this room were drafted," the tall man said. "These are the elite. The very top cream of the scum. What Wellington won at Waterloo with. Well, Mr. Hoover ran us out of Anacostia Flats and Mr. Roosevelt shipped us down here to get rid of us. They've run the camp in a way to invite an epidemic, but the poor bastards won't die. They shipped a few of us to Tortugas but that's healthy now. Besides, we wouldn't stand for it. So they've brought us back. What's the next move? They've got to get rid of us. You can see that can't you?"
>
> "Why?"
>
> "Because we are the desperate ones," the man said. "The ones with nothing to lose. We are the completely brutalized ones. We're worse than the stuff the original Spartacus worked with. But it is tough to try to do anything with because we have been beaten so far that the only solace is booze and the only pride is in being able to take it."
> (*THHN* 206)

There is much history to unpack here. We have already discussed Anacostia Flats and the epidemic reference vis-à-vis the unsanitary conditions at the camps when first opened. (According to Folliard, 80 percent of the Keys vets participated in the 1932 Bonus March, although there is no independent way to corroborate this claim). Hemingway also alludes to Fort Jefferson on Dry Tortugas, which since December 1934 had served as a "penal colony for vets accused of drunkenness, insubordination and theft" (Dickson and Allen 222). "Insubordination" was often a charge leveled at any vet who dared to question the horrid state of camp life: in February 1935, five vets had been arrested for forming a grievance committee that formally protested both their living conditions and the state highway department's use of outside skilled labor to construct the roadway to Key West. The men's illegal detainment sparked a strike that was quickly quelled by the intervention of the National Guard; while the protest did result in better housing and food, administrators were also quick to dismiss it as the work of Communist infiltrators (Drye 54–55). Jacks seemingly identifies himself as one such agitator when he boasts of having freshly arrived from the Dry Tortugas because "we raised enough hell so they couldn't keep us there" (*THHN* 204).

The point of Jacks's conversation with Richard Gordon is twofold: while insisting that the veterans represent the feral violence that society shuns but nevertheless calls upon to defend itself during times of war, Jacks wants Gordon to recognize how the vets are so "brutalized" that they can only find dignity in their masochistic ability to endure their own sadism. "I can take it" is the vets' common response to the beatings they inflict on each other; the phrase functions as an absurdist inversion of the stoic endurance of the typical Hemingway hero who finds his "separate peace" in his individual integrity. What Jacks wants to know from Gordon is whether the effete radical writer (whose work Jacks will shortly dismiss as "shit") believes that the vets' ferocity is innate or a product of military conditioning: "War is a noble and ennobling force," he says, sarcastically echoing Frederic Henry's denunciation of the rhetoric of valor in *A Farewell to Arms*. "The question is whether only people like ourselves here are fitted to be soldiers or whether the different services have formed us" (*THHN* 205). Ultimately, the distinction is a litmus test of reader empathy. If one agrees with the former assertion, the vets are an inherently dangerous segment of the population that must be segregated from "civilized" haves. If the latter, they are degraded by the bureaucratic system that robs them of the pretense to civilization that, in the name of patriotism, they are asked to defend.

The central line that would have most resonated with Hemingway's contemporary readers is not "I can take it," however. It is, rather, Jacks's claim that the government preferred an expedient solution to the question of why the vets are prone to drunken violence rather than wrestle with its own complicity in their condition: "They've got to get rid of us." The line evokes the unfounded yet oft-leveled charge that the Roosevelt administration *intentionally* stranded the vets in the path of the Labor Day Hurricane, supposedly to rid itself of the embarrassment the Matecumbe camps posed in the wake of the criticism by the *Washington Post* and the *New York Times*. Historians have thoroughly debunked such conspiratorial claims, demonstrating instead that the 259 veterans lost to the storm were victims of poor emergency planning and bureaucratic squabbling over unclear lines of responsibility for the men's safety. In the decades since the disaster, blame for the deaths has largely been placed on the shoulders of three men: Ray Sheldon, the Keys camp supervisor who failed to order an evacuation train early enough to relocate the vets to Miami; Fred Ghent, the former FERA director of safety who had overseen all veterans' camps in Florida since the previous March and whose responsibility it was to draw up a reliable evacuation plan; and Florida's Tallahassee-based FERA director, Conrad Van Hyning, who was apparently oblivious to the storm's danger and who failed to coordinate with Sheldon and Ghent as the hurricane bore down on the Keys. Nevertheless, accusations of malice high up in the Roosevelt administration were rampant in 1935–36, largely in reaction to the administration's hasty and sometimes glib efforts to absolve itself of blame by labeling the disaster an "act of God." Not surprisingly, that phrase was the brainchild of Hemingway's Key West nemesis Julius F. Stone.

On 17 September 1935, the *New Masses* voiced one of the blunter versions of this conspiracy theory by headlining Hemingway's irate account of recovery efforts, "Who Murdered the Vets?" While not fond of editor Joe North's editorial intervention (North deemed the original title, "Panic," insufficiently incendiary), Hemingway was hardly hesitant in the piece when it came to blurring the legalistic line between governmental negligence and outright homicide:

> During the war, troops and sometimes individual soldiers who incurred the displeasure of their superior officers, were sometimes sent into positions of extreme danger and kept there repeatedly until they were no longer problems. I do not believe anyone, knowingly, would send U.S. war veterans into any such positions in time of peace. But the Florida Keys, in hurricane months, in the matter of casualties recorded during the building of the Florida East Coast Railway to Key West, when nearly a thousand men were killed by hurricanes, can be classed as such a position. And ignorance has never been accepted as an excuse for murder or for manslaughter. (Trogdon 169)

Commenting on the article, the *New York Daily News* denounced Hemingway as "nuts," claiming that "murder . . . seems to us about the limit in the line of ridiculous accusations, but we haven't heard nothing yet" (qtd. in Dickson and Allen 246). Ridiculous or not, the "M" word appeared in numerous other editorials assessing the disaster. The American Legion even gave its independently conducted report a noirish spin by concluding that the administration's "inefficiency, indifference, and ignorance" added up to "Murder at Matecumbe" (qtd. in Drye 275). Given that the House of Representatives Committee on World War Veterans' Legislation conducted a highly contentious inquiry into the disaster in April 1936, Hemingway's original readers would have known exactly what Nelson Jacks means when he claims the government is out to "get rid of" the vets.

For as much history as Hemingway packs into the relatively short Gordon/Jacks encounter, however, there is still more that he leaves out. It is worth wondering why Jacks is seemingly the one sober, articulate resident of the Matecumbe camps at Freddy's Bar. The others are so uniformly drunk and violent it is often difficult to distinguish between them. Had Hemingway chosen to do so, he might have depicted the men more variedly by incorporating other details of camp life beyond drinking and brawling. Nowhere, for example, does he mention the popular baseball league that Sheldon's and Ghent's predecessor, interim camps supervisor William Hinchman, encouraged the men to organize in the aftermath of their February 1935 strike. (Hinchman oversaw the camps for a mere two weeks that March. The league was one reason more vets did not die in the Labor Day Hurricane: the day before the storm struck, more than one hundred of them had followed the league's all-star team to Ojus, Florida, just north of Miami, for a game against another relief camp.) Nor does Hemingway mention the camp's weekly newspaper, the *Key Veterans News*, which from March through August 1935 reported on the push for camp reforms, editorialized on ever-evolving New Deal policy, and published cartoons and humorous stories. The newspaper was even professional enough to sell advertising space to Key West bars like Sloppy Joe's that appreciated the vets' business. Finally, volunteers in nearby Homestead helped establish a makeshift library for the vets, sending books and magazines to the Matecumbe camps (Scott 49). The closest *To Have and Have Not* comes to mentioning this initiative is a fleeting reference to two contemporary pulp periodicals, *Western Stories* and *War Aces*. The vet who asks Richard Gordon if he is familiar with this escapist reading does not do so to prove he does more with his time than just drink, however—Hemingway cites the titles to demonstrate just how little relevance Richard Gordon's proletarian novels have to the vets' real life (*THHN* 210).

Hemingway's depiction of the vets is so one-dimensional that one wonders how camp residents who survived the hurricane might have reacted to their portrayal. After all, many of them objected vociferously to the public image of themselves as "psychopathic cases" (McLean 3). Several camp residents had fired off angry letters to the Roosevelt administration in the winter of 1935 complaining about their supervisors' inability to impose order and discipline in the camps by controlling access to alcohol. A central mission of the *Key Veterans News* was to critique negative coverage of the vets. While the *News*' first-ever issue "lambasted" the *Washington Post* for its "garbled" account of binge drinking at Matecumbe (Dickson and Allen 228), its last-ever issue, dated 31 August 1935 (the Friday before the Monday storm), accused the *New York Times* reporter of himself being too drunk to accurately report life in the Kingstree, South Carolina, FERA camp (Drye 75). Interestingly, reading the accounts by the *Post*'s Folliard and the *Times*' Charles McLean alongside *To Have and Have Not*, one is hard-pressed to find many significant differences in the vets' portrayal—*other than intention*.[7] Both Folliard and McLean were out to convince readers that the New Deal was a boondoggle that had accomplished little more than to provide "playgrounds for derelicts," as *Time* headlined its pre-hurricane exposé on the camps (qtd. in Dickson and Allen 233). Hemingway, by contrast, was employing the same stereotype of the "shell-shocked, whisky-shocked, and depression-shocked" (McLean 3) veteran to dramatize the men's dehumanization at the hands of an inhumane government and a country that failed to honor their wartime sacrifice.

One particular exchange between Gordon and the vets may even hint at a charge against camp life that was even more controversial (if less overtly discussed) than drunkenness. Shortly before Jacks introduces himself, a bloodied vet briefly identified as "Joey" informs Gordon that there is a "secret" reason why he is impervious to the beatings at Freddy's that leave blood running down his face. "The red-headed one put his lips almost to Gordon's ear. 'Sometimes it feels good,' he said. 'How do you feel about that?'" (*THHN* 203). Hemingway refrains from clarifying whether the masochism itself is the secret or whether something left unspoken "sometimes . . . feels good." If the reader accepts the latter interpretation, this scene hints at homosexual assault, especially when coupled with Joey's repeated insistence that he "can take it." Intertextual clues support this possibility. Whenever depicting groups of violent men, whether soldiers or those "on the bum," Hemingway so frequently hinted at the threat of rape that the danger of sexual attack is a virtual leitmotif in his writing. It is present in both *A Farewell to Arms* and "A Simple Enquiry" (1927), but perhaps the most explicit reference to it occurs in *A Moveable Feast* when Gertrude Stein quizzes a young Hemingway on his knowledge of homosexuality: "Miss Stein thought that I was too uneducated about sex and I must admit that I had certain prejudices against homosexuality since I knew its more primitive aspects. I knew it was why you carried a knife and would use it when you were in the company of tramps . . . in order not to be interfered with. . . . I could have expressed myself more vividly by using an *inaccroachable* phrase that wolves used on the lake boats, 'Oh gash may be fine but one eye for mine'" (*AMF* 18–19).

While Hemingway does not depict what *A Moveable Feast* calls "wolves" among the Key West vets, Joey's "secret" hints at this same sort of predatory violence. And while there is no evidence such assaults ever took place in the Matecumbe camps, it is worth noting that "hobosexuality" was commonly presumed among displaced male populations in the 1930s, with "outside commentators often exaggerating [homeless men's] homosexuality in order to cast disrepute on their subculture" (DePastino 85). If one interprets Joey's claim that "sometimes it feels good" as an admission that he consented to playing the "punk" role to another vet's "jocker" (DePastino 87), Hemingway actually went further than anti-New Dealers in suggesting that the relief camps were dens of iniquity. Again, however, the difference for him was a matter of environment rather than character. Folliard, McLean, and others suggested that the men were at best "shovel-leaners" and at worst degenerates. Even after the hurricane, the American Legion was stunned by administration officials who, in interviews during the Legion's investigation into the vets' deaths, casually "referred to [the men] as bums, drunkards, riffraff, and crazy men . . . [giving] the impression that they 'got what was coming to them'" (Dickson and Allen 249). Hemingway, by contrast, laid blame for the men's self-destructiveness squarely at the door of the American government. Making that charge credible, moreover, required a wholly different style than readers were accustomed to from him—one whose merits are still hotly contested.

Modernism as Memorial, Proletarian Fiction as Social Action

Exactly one month and a day after *To Have and Have Not* was published on 14 October 1937, a memorial to the victims of the 1935 hurricane was unveiled at mile marker 81.5 in Islamorada. Some four thousand to five thousand dignitaries and locals attended the ceremony, "more than four times the population of the islands outside of Key West and the largest ever to gather for an event in the Keys" (Drye 294). According to the Keys historian Jerry Wilkinson, the monument's design replicates the Thiepval Memorial to the Missing at the Somme Battlefield (1932) in France, and the Menin Gate Memorial (1927) at Ypres, in Belgium—two of the many memorials built throughout Europe a decade earlier to honor the dead and missing of World War I. The interior crypt of the Key West memorial, which is in the upper level of the eighteen-foot-high obelisk, contains the remains of some 190 of the 400-plus people, both veterans and locals, who died during the hurricane.[8] A bronze plaque commemorates the memorial in typical epitaphic style: "Dedicated to the memory of the civilians and war veterans whose lives were lost in the hurricane of September Second 1935."

Given the influence of the Thiepval and Menin Gate memorials on this structure, it is worth speculating how its construction served the same psychological need to commemorate the Great War dead by making, in Jay Winter's phrase, "remembrance [into] part of the landscape . . . [into] sites of memory" (1). As Samuel Hynes explains: "Monument-raising is an attempt by a society to deal with certain fundamental needs of those who survive a war. A monument records the dead, and so gives dignity to their undignified deaths. . . . Monuments perform other functions, too. They reassure noncombatants that the dead died willingly and do not resent or repent their sacrifice" (270).

In this sense, the Florida Keys Memorial at once honors the history of human loss while sanitizing it through the gesture of "giving dignity."

Nowhere at the site, for example, is there a narrative explanation for why "lives were lost" in the hurricane. Arguably, the linkage of civilian and veteran casualties obscures the history of the FERA camps by implying that the vets' deaths were caused by an unavoidable natural disaster (i.e., an "act of God") and not as a result of negligence. The 1937 unveiling ceremony did include at least one angry speech by the commander of the Miami American Legion post that condemned the FERA and other government agencies for failing to develop a reasonable evacuation plan; yet the imperative of recognizing that nearly half of the total storm deaths were those of longtime Keys residents distracted from criticism of the Roosevelt administration by making the site one of general mourning rather than of the vitriolic outrage Hemingway expressed in "Who Murdered the Vets?" Interestingly, Hemingway's *New Masses* essay insists that a distinction must be made between storm victims: "It is not necessary to go into the death of civilians and their families since they were on the Keys of their own

25. The unveiling of the memorial for hurricane victims, 1937. The monument elides the distinction between locals and veterans who died in the disaster, effectively attributing the loss of the latter to an act of God instead of government negligence. Courtesy of the State Archives of Florida.

free will; they made their living there, had property and knew the hazards involved. But the veterans had been sent there; they had no opportunity to leave, nor any protection against the hurricane; and they never had a chance for their lives" (Trogdon 169).

Generally, memorials commemorate lost lives symbolically rather than narratively: they evoke a feeling of solemn, dignified loss without documenting the complicated events causing it. The goal is to arrest an emotion, not offer an explanation. As such, there are many fruitful parallels between the visual art of memorials and the literary mode of modernism that help explain why Hemingway felt compelled to turn away from the style with which he depicted soldiers in the 1920s to his Falstaffian treatment of them in *To Have and Have Not*. Most definitions of modernism throughout its history employ sculptural metaphors to convey its aesthetic aim. One can trace a continuum of such metaphors in its many manifestos and treatises, from Ezra Pound's 1913 definition of imagism as "that which presents an intellectual and emotional complex in an instant of time" without the need for "voluminous" verbiage (*Literary Essays* 4), to Joseph Frank's famous 1945 description of modernism's "spatial form," to the New Critical treatment of text as a "verbal icon" (Wimsatt xi), in which the visual and the immobile are privileged above linear storytelling. In order to define the "timelessness" of literature, modernists had to impede the sequential flow of narrative to (ostensibly) fix meaning in arrested moments of action meant to be more akin to objets d'art than to stories. One sees this effort in the work of war poets like Wilfred Owen and Siegfried Sassoon, where the imagery of war horrors conveys, more than any prose account, the brutality of combat. Perhaps the most famous example is part 5 of Pound's *Hugh Selwyn Mauberly* (1920): "There died a myriad / And of the best, among them / For an old bitch gone in the teeth / For a botched civilization. . . . For two gross of broken statues / For a few thousand battered books" (*Selected Poems* 64). By describing Western civilization as statuary reduced to rubble, Pound offers his imagist aesthetic as a metatextual means of repairing the ruins of war: the iconic technique, much like monument raising, does away with the details of cause and effect, of history itself, to memorialize the sacrifice of "the best" and inspire the survivors not to "botch" the culture as the elders responsible for their going to war have.

Hemingway achieves the same effect in the interchapters of *In Our Time* and in fragments like "On the Quai at Smyrna" (1931), which offers of an interior-monologue catalogue of images of brutalized refugees from the Greco-Turkish war of 1922: "The worst . . . were the women with dead babies. You couldn't get the women to give up their dead babies. They'd have babies dead for six days. Wouldn't give them up" (*CSS* 63). In texts like this or "A Natural History of the Dead" (1933), pictures of devastation and degradation convey the inhumanity of war more than any plot with an Aristotelian beginning, middle, and end. What the reader takes away from the experience is not the narrative satisfaction of complicating action and fatal flaws or climaxes and denouements, but a more solemn recording of the gruesome tally of war. Even in early works with obvious plots and character development like *A Farewell to Arms*, Hemingway's depiction of the wounded veteran rests upon his fabled chiseled and epitaphic style, which practically imitates or even parodies the language, if not the sacrificial values, of war monuments. When Frederic Henry insists that he has always been "embarrassed by the words sacred, glorious, and sacrifice and the expression in vain," he is not rejecting the concept of valor or heroism—he is rejecting *inherited* ideas of those values in favor of personal experience, which has taught him that "abstract words such as glory, honor, courage, or hallow were obscene beside the names of villages, the numbers of roads, the names of rivers, the numbers of regiments and the dates" of battle (184–85). At such moments, the staccato style is every bit as commemorative as the rhetoric that embarrasses Frederic. Hemingway is simply memorializing the *authentic* devastation that his soldier-characters witness, as opposed to the abstraction that gives way to patriotic shibboleths and clichés.

Memorializing is not the same as social action, however, and as the high modernism of the 1920s gave way to the proletarian literature of the 1930s, suspicion was rampant that the commemorative aesthetics of the former lacked the pragmatic power to change the world upon which the latter insisted. In the same year that Hemingway was racing to complete *To Have and Have Not*, James T. Farrell wrote in *A Note on Criticism* that modernism regarded "art only as a means of producing sensations in the audience. Objects are perceived only for their own sake, and in disrelation from the process of which they are a part. The past and the future of the aesthetic object tend to become totally meaningless, for it is not the fruit of experience and the experience itself that are emphasized, but solely the latter.

The end result of such a view is the formal exclusion of the functional or objective"—i.e., "action and living" (15–16). One sees the aim of avoiding this exclusion in order to harvest the "fruit of experience" in Joe North's letter to Hemingway the day before "Who Murdered the Vets?" appeared in *New Masses*. "Everybody still remembers Anacostia Flats, and it's near election time," North wrote, calculating the political consequences of the hurricane casualties. As he surmised, the disaster would make it impossible for Roosevelt to continue opposing paying soldiers their much-needed bonus: "If we can get [legislation] moving as a result of the Key West exposure it will be a good thing" (letter 1). The prediction proved accurate: on 27 January 1936, Congress finally approved a version of the oft-defeated Patman Bonus Bill, with the Senate overriding Roosevelt's inevitable veto by an unequivocal 76–19 margin. On 16 June of that year, some 3 million checks averaging $583 were mailed to veterans of the Great War. As one newspaper exclaimed, "They're really DOUGHboys today!" (Dickson and Allen 261–62). Although few historians would claim that "Who Murdered the Vets?" was itself directly responsible for the bonus bill finally becoming reality after nearly a decade in legislative limbo, thanks to its author's fame it remains the most famous example of the posthurricane outcry that turned public sentiment against the neglect of Great War veterans. Through its aesthetic of outrage, the essay insisted on the government's responsibility to protect the soldiers who had defended its shores.

Alas, the same cannot be said for *To Have and Have Not*. By the time of its publication, the aims motivating its writing—at least those regarding the Matecumbe camps—were largely achieved or irrelevant. Not only had the surviving vets been gone from the Keys for two years already, but the construction project they were originally sent to Florida to work was near enough to completion as to no longer be an issue. The stretch of U.S. Highway 1 to Key West that had formerly required ferry service opened only a few months later on 29 March 1938, built upon the bed of the Florida East Coast Railway that was abandoned after the hurricane. The Keys of 1934–35, the time in which the novel is set, was a very different place from the Keys of late 1937, when the book finally appeared and the memorial was unveiled. This time lag is indicative of what James T. Farrell identified as the main reason that literature, despite the claims of proletarian writers, does not make for effective propaganda: "Works of literature are, generally, not quickly enough assimilated to become instruments of propaganda leading to the choice of immediate courses of action. . . . By the time a writer can assimilate material essential for a novel about a social problem, think through the potentialities of his material, arrange and write it, check his sources, rewrite it, finish it for publication, and correct the proofs—by that time one, two, or three years may have elapsed. After this, more time is needed for the distribution of the novel, and for its assimilation by readers. And, as likely as not, by that time the social and class relationships will have shifted and altered" (148–49). In the minds of the American public, the problem of veteran affairs had not only been "altered" but solved, for the 1936 bonus payment had given the Bonus Marchers exactly what they demanded.

All of which helps explain two things: (1) why Hemingway's atypical depiction of the veterans inspired so little discussion either in original reviews or in subsequent criticism; and (2) why *To Have and Have Not* is considered Hemingway's least engaging novel. Although Malcolm Cowley praised "the phantasmagorical drinking and slugging bout of the veterans on relief" as the book's best scene (Meyers, *Critical Heritage* 235), and while Carlos Baker praised it as the novel's "most vivid" episode (*Writer as Artist* 208), chapter 22 has received little attention from commentators beyond a perfunctory acknowledgment of the vets' death in the hurricane. The reason is that by eschewing the imagistic modernism by which he had previously commemorated the shell-shock of soldiers, Hemingway precluded audience empathy for the individual consciousness. Readers simply do not identify with the Key West vets in the way they do with Harold Krebs or Frederic Henry, a problem exacerbated by the fact that, while the naturalist style of the scene is meant to expose the grotesque state to which the vets had been reduced at the hands of federal abuse, that aim had already been accomplished by the time the scene was composed. As a result, the immediate historical context lacked urgency for original readers and could not effectively compensate for the loss of the modernist depth. The absence of a memorializing treatment of the vets' war wounds is even more detrimental to subsequent readers, most of whom lack any knowledge whatsoever of the FERA work camps, the hurricane, or the sad state of veteran affairs in the early 1930s. To the majority of today's audience, the vets' "phantasmagorical" cameo is merely absurd, not tragic.

To appreciate the aesthetic bind Hemingway faced while attempting to capture the political complexities of the Depression in *To Have and Have Not*, it is worth asking how differently his classic war stories might strike us had he attempted social realism earlier in his career. What if Nick Adams's shell-shock in "Now I Lay Me" or "A Way You'll Never Be" was depicted as a social problem rather than an individual struggle? What if his insomnia and disorientation were replaced with the Key West vets' alcoholic masochism? Suffice it to say the Hemingway hero would seem far less heroic; instead of an emblem of stoic endurance Nick might end up like Sir Clifford in D. H. Lawrence's *Lady Chatterley's Lover* (1928), a veteran whose paralysis in the Great War renders him an aloof, impotent emblem of pitiable victimization. At the same time, one wonders how much more satisfying *To Have and Have Not* would be had Hemingway infused more overt sympathy into his depiction of the Key West vets. What if Nelson Jacks's purpose was not merely to bash "shit" proletariat writers like Richard Gordon? What if he played a greater role in the narrative as the vets' advocate? What if Harry Morgan were revealed to be a Great War vet with a personal stake in the condition of the men congregating at Freddy's Bar? What if the hurricane itself served as a dramatic pivot as Hemingway seems to have originally intended? How much more powerful and convincing would Harry's Depression dilemmas prove were he to enter Lower Matecumbe Key two days after the disaster, much as Hemingway did, to discover "more dead than I'd seen in one place since lower Piave in June of 1918"? What if Harry learned that among the dead was his drunken charter hand Eddy, just as Hemingway learned that "Joe Lowe the original of the Rummy in that story of mine One Trip Across was drowned at the Ferry Slip"? (*SL* 421, 423). Such elements would have benefited both history and characterization. The reasons the vets were in the Keys would have been overtly explained in the narrative, and Harry's own dying declaration ("No matter how a man alone ain't got no bloody fucking chance" [*THHN* 225]) might not strike critics as such a facile blast of bravado.

Of course, such speculation is academic, but it is worth entertaining because it reveals that *To Have and Have Not* is ultimately a transitional effort that paved the way for *For Whom the Bell Tolls*, which much more successfully integrates modernist depth within the political-historical context of soldiers' lives. Here Hemingway not only widens the social and political perspective of protagonist Robert Jordan (one could argue that the novel is about the very process of an individual developing such a consciousness); he also puts Jordan into a social band of brothers and sisters, who, at times, resemble the punch-drunk veterans of *To Have and Have Not*. Despite some differences, the Key West brotherhood is similar to the Spanish band led by Pablo and Pilar: both groups irrationally quarrel among themselves, drink too much, are dislocated from their natural home, and, most importantly, are on the verge of annihilation. The Spanish guerillas are, however, portrayed less ironically than the Key West vets. As such, had Hemingway not started moving his perspective away from the individual to the social group in *To Have and Have Not*, he may not have been as successful in his group portrait of the Spanish irregulars who help Robert Jordan blow the bridge in *For Whom the Bell Tolls*. Hemingway's great Spanish novel ends up being not so much a form of social realism, which subordinates aesthetic issues to political ones, but instead seems more a form of fiction that goes beyond the transitory social issues of the time and reasserts aesthetic and spiritual primacy as a way to change the world. Jordan learns that politics is more than having the correct ideology; it is about keeping humanity alive in the face of barbarism. While some argue that Harry Morgan's deathbed proclamation about "one man alone" having no "bloody fucking chance" dramatizes a similar epiphany, it should be noted that Hemingway only included that statement during his final revision of the novel in 1937 after he had made his first and most important visit to war-torn Spain, where he learned that moral lesson firsthand.

In conclusion, the contextual factors surrounding the World War I veterans of "Who Murdered the Vets?" and *To Have and Have Not* illuminate the historical and social influences on Hemingway's literary sensibilities during the 1930s, leading to the masterpiece of his later career, *For Whom the Bell Tolls*. Quite simply, this evolving social situation of the World War I veteran in the mid-1930s complicated the value of a character type he had been developing throughout his early fiction—the wounded ex-soldier of the "Lost Generation." The portrayal of the veteran in *To Have and Have Not* is an important bridge in the emerging fabric of Hemingway's literature, a critical directional marker in Hemingway studies. The author had to revise his overall depiction of the soldier late in the 1930s, which eventually evolved into Robert Jordan, a would-be veteran in the war against fascism who is betrayed by a social cause more committed to ideology than service to the people and by a government rendered impotent by corruption and ineptitude.

Only this time the Hemingway hero was the noble leader of a band of brothers and sisters out to blow up a bridge rather than build one.

Notes

1. Hemingway tells this story himself in his *Esquire* essay "He Who Gets Slap Happy," published in August 1935, just one month before the Labor Day Hurricane.

2. For a more detailed statistical analysis, see Keene (181).

3. In his June 1935 *Esquire* article, "Notes on the Next War: A Serious Topical Letter," Hemingway took time out from his usual sportsman's commentary to speculate about the brewing world war. He comments on the plight of the common soldier: "But those who want to go to the war, the elite, are killed off in the first months and the rest of the war is fought by men who are enslaved into bearing arms and are taught to be more afraid of sure death from their officers if they run than possible death if they stay in the line or attack" (*BL* 210). This commentary, of course, was published while he resided in Key West, exactly around the time of the 1935 hurricane disaster.

4. My approach here is inspired by Trout, whose work on "Soldier's Home" demonstrates the necessity of reading Hemingway's war fiction beyond its biographical relevance.

5. In the United States, compensating veterans for war injuries goes all the way back to the Revolutionary War, when the Continental Congress and later the U.S. Congress passed legislation extending benefits to invalid veterans. In 1792, the War Department took over pension duties, and Congress created a commissioner of pensions in 1833. In 1849, the Department of the Interior took over this responsibility and, finally, in 1921, Congress created the Veterans' Bureau. To this bureau fell the duties of the Bureau of War Risk Insurance that had been created in 1914 within the Treasury Department, the Rehabilitation Division of the Federal Board for Vocational Education that had been organized in 1918, and the Public Health Service programs set up for World War I veterans (www.sos.state.il.us/departments/archives/di/955_002.htm). As an aside, Hemingway, of course, would not have had any benefits offered by these organizations since he was a veteran of the Red Cross Ambulance Corps and not the U.S. Army.

6. Folliard would regularly return to the Keys in the late 1940s as a member of the White House press corps covering Roosevelt's successor, Harry S. Truman. As the proud owner of a Key West vacation home, the thirty-third president of the United States was locally known as the "First Tourist" (Ogle 205).

7. Compare, for example, a quote from Bill Bevais in Folliard's report to "He Who Gets Slap Happy" and *To Have and Have Not*: "There were battles royal all over the streets. I saw one man hit a fellow who had just bought four bottles of beer. The guy with the beer yelled out if anybody knew him. Nobody did. Then the guy who had the beer popped the other guy over the head with a beer bottle and knocked him out cold. . . . If anybody mentioned work, some guy would be sure to say, 'aw, go to hell'" (10).

8. When the WPA began construction of the memorial in 1937, workers dug down to bedrock to form the foundation. Then, they made a 65' by 20' base on which rests the obelisk. To reach the obelisk one has to walk up five broad steps, leading to an elevated floor (Wilkinson). Covering this top floor are coral "keystone" slabs, which come from either the Windley Key or Key Largo Quarry. A later refurbishing of the memorial added artificial keystone material around the lower floor, leading to the flagpole and a concrete sidewalk and landscaping. Besides the crypt, another significant feature of the obelisk is the twenty-two-foot-long inlaid ceramic tile map of the area from Key Largo to Marathon. Key West resident Adela Gisbet was the ceramicist. Except for the obelisk, which has a design of classical origins, the memorial is a homemade creation, built of uniquely American design and material, specifically of those found on the Keys.

The Nice, the Strange, and the Wicked

Physical and Moral Landscapes in "The Strange Country"

NICOLE CAMASTRA

Controversy exists about whether Ernest Hemingway's "The Strange Country," which first became publicly available in *The Complete Short Stories of Ernest Hemingway* (1987), should be read as an autonomous short story or as the discarded first four chapters of the posthumously published *Islands in the Stream* (1970). Regardless of such debate, this narrative holds merit for Hemingway's signature use of landscape and allusion, particularly as both relate to a Florida that, for all of Hemingway's association with Key West, rarely appears in his fiction: namely, the commercialized Florida of highways, motels, and rest areas that began dominating the American vista in the 1920s. Despite the attention given to these byproducts of intra-American tourism and travel, the physical and moral nature of the story's landscape effectively function as a metaphorical representation of the protagonist Roger and his quest, much as the far more "natural" setting of northern Michigan serves as an objective correlative of Nick Adams's precarious spiritual state in "Big Two-Hearted River" (1925), and as the heather- and pine-laden forests of *For Whom the Bell Tolls* (1940) symbolize Robert Jordan's Spanish Earth political sympathies.

"The Strange Country" is an amalgam of three landscapes in particular: the nice country, the strange country, and the wicked country, each designated and named by Roger as he navigates them with his new lover, Helena. His journey demonstrates the layering of idealistic possibility in these three terrains: first, through his depiction of place and past, and second, through his inability to drive away from the reality and personal resonance that these environments imply. Ultimately, place communicates the premise that disappointment is the natural consequence of any unrealistic promise. More than the past or time, Roger hears a moral dictum at his back, implied in each "country" through which he and Helena travel.

An ostensible map of the couple's journey was provided, in part, by Hemingway's experiences in Florida. He moved to Key West with his second wife, Pauline, in early April 1928, purchasing "their first permanent house in the United States" at 907 Whitehead Street three years later with the help of Pauline's uncle Gus (Baker, *A Life Story* 221). The Hemingways most likely took their first trip across the state in 1928, when Ernest drove Pauline, pregnant with Patrick, to Piggott, Arkansas, where her family lived (Baker, *A Life Story* 194). This was the first of several such adventures traveled along a similar route taken by Roger and Helena in "The Strange Country." In 1932 Hemingway made the voyage in a new Ford V-8 roadster, which marked the introduction of that engine. He was so excited about the automobile that "he drove 654 miles in a single day" (Baker, *A Life Story* 229). Although the Hemingways were coming by way of the South, and not the East, they would still have had to cross the Everglades, taking Route 1 up from the Keys to Route 41, known as the Tamiami Trail. This road connecting Miami and Tampa was completed in April 1928, concomitant with Hemingway's arrival in Key West. The massive project, which led through what Roger terms the "nice country," inspired enthusiasm for Florida's economic potential, though that excitement disappeared by the end of the 1920s.

Appropriately then, the first or "nice" country through which Roger and Helena travel is full of promise and the memory of what was once hopeful. They begin their drive in Miami and then pass Coral Gables, a suburb of Miami that in the 1920s was a benchmark of the promise that the South Florida real-estate boom offered before the country fell into the Great Depression. The allusive "broad Coral Gables road" on which they drive indicates the wide spectrum of possibility that accompanied land speculation from about 1921 through 1925 in the "heat-stricken outskirts of Miami" (*CSS* 607). Large-scale investments and the expansive development of European-style architecture precipitated the incorporation of

Coral Gables in 1925 and marked the town's thriving economy. The enthusiasm surrounding such growth was quickly truncated by the hurricane of 1926, which devastated the southern coast of Florida and caused upwards of $100 million in damage. Rebuilding and recovery were slow as the disaster directly preceded the stock market crash of 1929. As Roger and Helena pass through the locus of destruction some ten years afterward, he notices that the road "stretched straight and heat-welted across what had *once been* the Everglades" (*CSS* 607, emphasis added). The forces of weather and economy have compromised the natural environment. Roger knows this as he looks "ahead at the road he had driven so many times in his life" and notes that even the wood ibises "used to roost much closer" to it (*CSS* 607, 612). As the couple continues down Roger's memory-laden road, Helena asks if he loves her, and he replies: "I don't know. But I'm going to damn well find out" (*CSS* 607). The beginning of this journey resembles a quest for Roger to find out if he can love in any enduring way.

Landscape suggests that Roger's search will be endangered by the erosive nature of time. He knows that on this trip, "only the car was different [and] only who was with him was different." He recalls the memory of driving through the area one winter with the mother of his son David. He remembers kissing her on this road, and her saying, "Oh Roger we're so happy and we always will be won't we?" As he continues on in the story's fictional present, however, the sun is going down, settling on "the top of the tree-tops" (*CSS* 609) and the memory of that lost love with David's mother. Not surprisingly, he "felt the old hollowness coming inside of him and knew he must stop it." In an effort to assuage the emotional anxiety over inevitable loss, Roger tells Helena, "I love you, daughter." He must suspect that this declaration will not stop the "hollowness" because "[h]e did not think it was true. But it sounded all right as he said it" (*CSS* 608).

Roger must reconcile his words and deeds in order to appease his conscience in his treatment of Helena, who tells him: "I've loved you ever since I can remember. . . . I've loved you all my life" (*CSS* 609). While he is looking for what he has lost, she is both younger and more naïve to matters of love and their great potential for mutability. Her lack of familiarity with this country, both literally and figuratively, is as significant as Roger's knowledge. When Roger tells her that "we get into some nice country now" (*CSS* 608), his tone suggests wanting to have a shared physical and emotional experience of landscape. Part of such mutual feeling is the notion that they can "throw it all away . . . beside the road" (*CSS* 611) and make a fresh start; Roger can discard disappointment in exchange for new contentment as Helena's dream of loving him becomes real. For him, the seductive desire to abandon past mistakes and create additional opportunities is denied by the reality that "everything was possible once . . . on this road. . . . That was *before*" (*CSS* 610, emphasis added). He knows that his endeavors to create prospects on a road that does not yield any will be futile.

Roger tries to arrest his emotional ambiguity with the assumption of love. He considers the lie he tells Helena about loving her, and he knows that "[e]ven if it were wrong to say them he must say [those words]. He had to say them and then perhaps he could feel them and then perhaps he could believe them. And then perhaps they would be true. Perhaps is an ugly word, he thought, but it is even worse on the end of your cigar" (*CSS* 610). The manuscript of *The Garden of Eden* contains a number of passages pertinent to this theme of romantic equivocation. Hemingway worked on *Garden* intermittently during the last twelve years of his life, including a period simultaneously spent on "The Strange Country" (as well as *Islands in the Stream*). Accordingly, the *Garden* manuscript includes a passage similar to Roger's meditation on *perhaps*: "'Spit is an ugly word' David said 'But it's even worse on the end of your cigar. That was an advertising slogan for machine made stogies out of Tampa, Florida'" (*GOE* 422.1.33.42.14).[1] David Bourne says this to Marita, his newer, and in some ways, truer lover than his gender-bending wife, Catherine. The "slogan" refers to "machine made" rather than handmade, or literally, man-made "stogies," and the major difference exists in the recognition of artificial as opposed to genuine qualities.[2]

Perhaps Roger, like David, is aware of what is fake, and he knows as Jake Barnes does in *The Sun Also Rises* that "afterward, all that was faked turned bad and gave an unpleasant feeling" (*SAR* 171). Roger is not Jake, however, and David is not Roger, but it is interesting to see that the spit on the end of Roger's theoretical cigar is equal to the "unpleasant feeling" he may have after lying to Helena regarding his love for her, though he makes no immediate effort to expiate. Roger's feelings might be described as "machine made" in that they serve a mechanical, or practical, purpose of alleviating the human frailty that comes with loneliness. Roger manufactures his sentiments in order to ease his mind that they are true. Further, the car that speeds toward Tampa serves as an objective correlative for the mechanism of his love, and their specific route, the Tamiami Trail, indicates both the mechanized triumph over terrain and the destruction of what that land possessed. As Roger leads them away from what was once the Everglades, where the memory of true love resides, toward Tampa, where "stogies" are "machine made," the tension between urban and rural landscapes points to a tenuous romantic connection.

The *Garden* passage also serves the ancillary purpose of showing thematic continuity in these two posthumously published Hemingway works, certainly more than Joseph Flora allows in "Hemingway's 'The Strange Country' in the Context of *The Complete Short Stories*." While Flora states that the story "echoes themes and situations of *The Garden of Eden*" (412), he also implies a departure from *Garden* when he says that the union between Roger and Helena "promises a great deal more than that of David Bourne and Catherine." Further, he believes that "the rhythm of the automobile ride reinforces the sense of potential" (414). It is more likely, given that the car is heading away from the Everglades and natural love, that the rhythm serves to perpetuate an illusion signaled by the ambiguity of the term "perhaps." The word conveys ambivalence, whereas conviction, it can be argued, is a central Hemingway ideal. More pointedly, the phallic imagery the cigar provides indicates the dubiety of Roger's feelings toward Helena that are dependent upon, even produced by, sexual tension.

The couple metaphorically leaves the nice country when they have their first sexual encounter. Moving beyond the terrain of idealistic promises, they enter a "strange" country of very realistic physical union. During their conversation afterward, Roger lies and tells Helena that he loves her and then thinks, "I love what we did" (*CSS* 616). Once the sexual tension dissipates, Roger's ambivalence becomes even more prevalent. Here emerges the romantic disappointment reflecting the vanishing promise of the nice country. When possibility becomes reality, Roger is no more certain of his ability to love than he was before.

To assert that the title "The Strange Country" is a euphemism for sex undermines both the vast implication of the physical act and the overall significance of the entire story, although there is an explicit association of the metaphorical landscape with it. Flora asserts that "the metaphor 'the strange country' refers to Helena as a sexual being" (416), but the matter is not that simple. There is a strangeness associated with Helena's anatomy, indicated when she asks Roger why he thinks that she is "strange" in bed, and he replies, "I'm not an anatomist" (*CSS* 630). Yet there is also the "strange" metamorphosis that takes place for Roger when he thinks: "He was not lonely after this last time as he had nearly always been. . . . He had not had the old death loneliness since the first time the night before." Roger's manufacture of emotion may have finally produced the effect of genuine feeling, though he gives the credit for this transition to Helena. He tells her that she does "something awfully good" to him (*CSS* 625). In effect, Roger says that she changes him for the better.

Here a strange alchemy takes place. Just as mercury was once considered the chemical catalyst for transforming lead into gold, Helena can be seen as the component that subdues Roger's loneliness through sex. In order to create a successful union, the chemical needs to be added to the composite; it serves to create a material change in the existing elements that, in turn, produces an entirely different element. In the same way, Helena changes how Roger feels after sex; she takes away the "old death loneliness," but not from any action of which she is aware. Instead, it is her corporeal presence and the metaphysical change that occurs when they both join physically that assuages his solitariness afterward.

The absence of the "old death loneliness" is new for Roger, and is part of the metaphorical landscape he and Helena inhabit. The general lexicon defines "strange" as unfamiliar. This description holds true for the couple in regard to their lovemaking, their conversation, and Roger's moral ambivalence. The strangeness is softened, however, with their mutual illusion of each one "holding tight" to the other (*CSS* 624). Some of Hemingway's other stories convey the importance of this image; it exists in "A Very Short Story" when the protagonist "went under the anæsthetic holding tight" (*CSS* 107). It is also in the first part of "Big Two-Hearted River" when Nick watches a big trout "under the bridge where he tightened facing up into the current" (*CSS* 164). And it is in Hemingway's later fiction as well, such as *The Garden of Eden*, in which Catherine and David and Marita all hold tight in one combination or another to brace against Catherine's mad sexual desires that threaten to pull them apart. When Roger and Helena hold tight in this terrain, they can transcend whatever reality may be awaiting them at the end of the road and live in hope for a little while longer. At the intersection of the strange country with Roger's quest to "damn well find out" if he loves Helena is the convergence of loneliness, hope, and possibility.[3]

This country is not easily navigable for either of them. Helena is "shy about it and very frightened. Always frightened" (*CSS* 630). For Roger, by contrast, it is "hard to enter, suddenly perilously difficult, then blindingly, happily, safely, encompassed" (615). This landscape is both primal, indicated by fear, and moral, indicated by how each feels afterward. The premise of hunger reinforces the primal facet of this country. There is no mention of either of them being hungry before entering the strange country. Now, Helena says, "Do you know what I am now?" Roger responds, "Hungry. . . . I'm hungry too" (616).

The theme of hunger and replenishment exists in *The Garden of Eden* as well, beginning when David Bourne thinks to himself, "There was only happiness and loving each other and then hunger and replenishing and starting over" (14). Similarly, this notion plays a substantial role in "The Strange Country." After Roger's sexual encounter with Helena, "He dressed and walked down into the village, feeling *hollow and hungry and happy*" (*CSS* 618, emphasis added). The "hollow" feeling needs to be replenished by a satiation of physical and spiritual hunger. Later, Helena says to Roger: "I found you and then all we ever had to do was eat and sleep and make love. Of course it's not like that at all" (625). It is not like that at all because primal needs are not surrogates for moral imperatives. As landscape does not remain fixed, emotions similarly change with regard to exterior demands. Although sex is the mercurial component that changes how Roger and Helena seem afterward, it does not guarantee the survival of their romance.

It is in the strange country that Roger's conscience starts to converse with him, and a moral urgency begins to make itself known. Roger thinks, "Now I've got this girl and I'll see how long my conscience holds out and when I have to go I'll go to it and not worry about it until then." Clearly, Roger feels compelled to join the fomenting war in Spain. "The Strange Country" is set in 1936 at the outbreak of that armed conflict, which troubled Hemingway immensely, and he "hated" missing it in the beginning. During its commencement, however, Hemingway "loaded the Ford car for a trip that would take him in exactly the opposite direction from Spain" (Baker, *A Life Story* 293).[4] He was, like Roger and Helena, going west, stopping in New Orleans. As his absence at the beginning of the Spanish Civil War concerned Hemingway, Roger similarly feels guilty but knows that all his excuses are "varyingly honest and they were all weak" (*CSS* 620).

Roger's personal investment in going "to it" has much to do with keeping the world safe for his children, or as he puts it, with having "to fight to keep the world so it will be O.K. for them to live in" (622). Roger also thinks that "there isn't any home," but comforts himself by appropriating a relative view of that concept when he supposes that "[t]he center line of highways was the boundary line of home" (621). The notion of a domestic sanctuary becomes fluid, adhering to the "center line of highways," and pliant boundaries transform the ostensibly rigid idea of concrete places. Fixed terrain proves to be as much of an illusion as that of "home," emphasizing the theme of displacement inherent in the emblems of the open road and the shifting Florida landscape through which Roger and Helena travel. H. R. Stoneback argues that in "The Strange Country," Hemingway "carefully constructs a symbolic landscape in the service of motifs of place and displacement" ("Et in Arcadia Ego" 196). For Roger, "home" takes on moral implications when he tells himself that "[h]ome is going to be wherever evil is strongest and can be fought. Home is going to be where you will go from now on" (*CSS* 621). But Roger tells Helena that he wants them to "get out west" (632). The war in Spain is where "evil is strongest," but that is to the east, not to the west. His choice of direction may point to his ethical weaknesses and to the seductive quality of the American West, a topography of idealistic, yet uncertain possibilities.

Roger's ambiguous moral consideration of home, war, and the West also includes his "weaknesses" that were "like streaks of fat between muscles" (620). His musings recall Harry Walden in "The Snows of Kilimanjaro," whose conscience starts to work on him because his will to write has softened, and he remembers that "they had made this safari . . . [so] he could work the fat off his soul [and] burn it out of his body" (*CSS* 44). The theme of the writer's conscience figures prominently throughout Hemingway's work, from the original ending of "Big Two-Hearted River," published as "On Writing" in *The Nick Adams Stories* (1972), to *A Moveable Feast* (1964). Particularly important for "The Strange Country," the theme is central to

The Garden of Eden, in which David Bourne struggles to write honestly while his identity is undermined through the role-reversing sexual experimentation of his marriage. It is indicative of Roger's dislocation in "The Strange Country" that he is avoiding his trade as he chases the idealistic possibility of love.

By not writing, Roger ignores the moral requisites of his art and the inevitable financial demands that come with traveling. Unlike the Bournes in *The Garden of Eden*, who honeymoon in Provence and have some money of their own, Roger and Helena more closely resemble fugitives who may eventually deplete their monetary funds. Roger knows he needs to make money, having told his conscience that he will "take good care of" Helena and "write at least four good" stories; however, "did he then . . . start one of the stories there on the table while the girl slept? He did not" (*CSS* 621). Roger does not go to the war; he does not write the stories to make needed money, and he does not necessarily take care of Helena in any moral sense. Consequently, as the narrative continues, Roger feels guilt over "destroying [Helena] and denying her" in his own mind (634).

The story's tensions are metaphorically rendered, moreover, by allusions to Florida geography, for Roger's illusion of happiness with Helena is emphasized by locating them in that Tampa region that Stoneback calls the Peace River Valley. The distance they have covered, however, provides a descriptive correlative for the instability of Roger's fantasy. The couple set out from the locus of the "strange" country with the objective of covering "a hundred [miles]," which they accomplish when they stop in Arcadia (*CSS* 626). The range most likely places their previous sojourn in Everglades City, just south of Naples. The city, known simply as Everglades prior to 1923, represents the shifting Florida values from an agrarian to a commercial-based economy, seen in the similar production of Coral Gables. Everglades, which was once a trading post where Roger and his former love, David's mother, "both bought Seminole shirts" (608), was turned into a small city by real estate mogul Barron Collier, whose name graces the enveloping county. (In a quirk of literary history, Collier was also the founder of the same advertising agency that F. Scott Fitzgerald famously quit in 1919 to write his debut novel, *This Side of Paradise*.) Conceptions of a simpler existence are supplanted by the growing need to accommodate tourism, industry, and modernity. Roger's emotional complexity signals a similar practicality. Love as a pastoral idyll becomes an arrangement that needs to be negotiated and won.

On their way to the final, "wicked" country, along the Peace River, Roger admits that they "should have stopped in Punta Gorda" (*CSS* 626), a landscape rich in both ancient and familiar allusive possibilities. This small southwestern Florida city, which is best known today for its having suffered the wrath of Hurricane Charley in August 2004, sits on the banks of Peace River, and it houses an ancient fishing enclosure built some five hundred years ago. Punta Gorda is technically along the Tamiami Trail, more specifically on Route 41, on the mouth of Charlotte Bay. Stoneback identifies the actual "town in the middle of the Florida prairie" where Roger and Helena later "linger longer than anywhere else on this segment of the trip" as Arcadia, a richly classical name evoking the aestheticized eroticism of Greek myth and legend. Arcadia, after all, houses Mount Lycaeum, one of the purported birthplaces of that most sexual of Greek gods, Zeus. Yet for Stoneback, Arcadia is less relevant to Hemingway's Florida geography for its association with Greek antiquity than with its later Renaissance-era popularity as a paradisiacal image of idyllic pastoralism. The title of his richly informative essay "*Et in Arcadia Ego*" comes from Nicholas Poussin's painting *Les Bergers d'Arcadie*, or "The Arcadian Shepherds" (ca. 1640). As *The Oxford Dictionary of Quotations* notes, the phrase refers to an "inscription on a tomb, frequently reproduced in paintings . . . by . . . Poussin, and [Sir Joshua] Reynolds. Usually translated: 'And I too [the occupant of the tomb] was in Arcadia.' But perhaps rather, 'I too [the tomb itself] am in Arcadia': even in Arcadia there am I (Death)" ("Et in Arcadia Ego" 195). For Stoneback, these seemingly conflicting translations—the first is a "romantic mistranslation" that seems to ignore that mortality inherent in the second "older, darker correct rendering"—suggests the tensions always present whenever Hemingway evokes a concrete place while dramatizing the theme of displacement: namely, conflicts between being and death, present and past, belonging and alienation, all of which preoccupy Roger during his Florida journey, a quest through seemingly familiar landscapes that render him an exile with their shifting appearance and importance.

The Hemingway-Poussin connection illuminates an ostensibly inconsequential piece of scholarly cartography. Many Hemingway readers are aware of Cézanne's relevance in Hemingway's pantheon of painters, but

Poussin holds a place there, too, if only indicated by the embedded allusion to *Les Bergers d'Arcadie*. Further, this example serves to underline Roger's ignorance of his own spiritual displacement. While the promise of the nice country seemingly endures here in the Peace River Valley, the fact that Death exists even in paradise would prove that the fantasy of unfettered happiness in paradise is, itself, an illusion. Roger's sustained chimera contradicts the very real wicked country he and Helena are about to enter.

Roger realizes that there is a choice of roads: one was "a good road through pleasant country" and the other was a "newly finished highway that might go through duller country." He concludes "the hell with maybe starting something again like I had the other night coming across the Tamiami Trail" (*CSS* 629) and goes on the newly finished road. What he does not want to commence are his memories of another time with another woman in a particular place when love seemed possible but ended in dissolution. Instead of figuratively looking back in an effort to understand, and possibly expiate for his mistakes, Roger gazes forward toward fresh beginnings, unwilling to confront the immense power of the past. When Stoneback posits that "the memory-laden road functions [in the text] in its familiar mythic character as a place of disburdenment, flight, and freedom from the past" ("Freedom" 208–9), it becomes clear that by seeking to deny the past, by choosing a "newly finished" rather than a "good" road, and sustaining an illusion in the present, the couple are indeed entering a corrupt landscape. If "wicked" points to something evil in nature, then "good" stresses an opposing, and hence, morally correct choice that Roger does not make.

Ostensibly, this is a wicked country because chain gangs work as slave labor for lumber and turpentine outfits. Roger tells Helena: "This is a wicked stretch of country. It's old and wicked with lots of law and no justice." Roger drives through the landscape only to "put it behind him" (*CSS* 631, 633), similar to the way he dismisses memories. If "nice" connotes idealism, and "strange" connotes the metamorphosis that drives away loneliness, then wicked could point to the moral implications of a selfish rejection of the past and its unavoidable influence on the present. By denying previous mistakes and residual regret, Roger becomes a *slave* of his own illusions. He wants to believe the lie of Arcadia, but despite paradise, suffering exists, and no amount of primal desire can drive it away.

As Roger drives to put the country behind him, he glimpses another vision besides his illusion. A nascent awareness of the synthesis of landscape and emotion occurs to him. Roger thinks to himself:

> You just thought you had learned something about being alone and you really worked at it and you did learn something. You got right to the edge of something. . . . [T]hen along comes this girl and you go right into happiness as though it were a country you were the biggest landowner in. Happiness is pre-war Hungary and you are Count Károlyi. (*CSS* 634)

There are two possible explanations for this odd allusion, one implicit, and the other explicit. Toward the end of the nineteenth and beginning of the twentieth centuries, the homesteaders entered southern Florida and precipitated the real estate boom of a couple of decades later, already indicated by the reference to Coral Gables. These agrarian pilgrims were successful for a time when land was abundant and making a profit from it seemed realistic. This notion proved to be idealistic, though, as seen with the example of Coral Gables's bankruptcy in the mid-1920s and the Great Depression. Promise preceded disappointment.

Hemingway's own venture into Florida followed a similar pattern. Less than two weeks after his arrival in Key West, he discovered that his parents were in St. Petersburg; they made the trip to visit their son, and he noticed his father's fragile health. Clarence Hemingway's mental anxiety was brought on, in part, by increasing uncertainty "about the wisdom of his heavy investments in Florida real estate" (Baker, *A Life Story* 193). Those "heavy investments" weighed upon Hemingway following the December 1928 suicide of his father. In a letter to his mother on 11 March 1929, Hemingway writes, "If you will send me the official location and description of *all* property—Pauline's uncle has a salesman in that territory who is interested in St. Pete[rsburg] real estate and . . . we may be able to do something about selling" (*SL* 295). Whether the land was sold remains questionable. Hemingway wrote to Maxwell Perkins in 1932 outlining some major events that occurred while writing *A Farewell to Arms* and mentioned "outside of Patrick being born only incident was my father shooting himself and me acquiring 4 new dependents and mortgages" (*SL* 351). Understandably, Hemingway felt that Florida real estate was "worthless" (Baker, *A Life Story*

199). In a poignant sense, it had come to represent a shift in emotional and familial terrain.

Hemingway's allusion to prewar Hungary and Count Mihály Károlyi may acknowledge the possibility that his father's financial illusions hastened his death and, also, that Roger and Helena's chimeric longing will precipitate defeat. Count Karolyi was the leader of the Social Democratic Party and the main catalyst for Hungary becoming a separate republic in 1918, not long before it was taken over briefly by the Communist Party, leading to internal wars throughout 1919. As idealism is a prelude to disaster, Roger and Helena similarly struggle in that their relationship cannot grow beyond their misconceptions. Roger's ambivalence gives way to the conviction of his loneliness because he knows that happiness with Helena is a Pyrrhic victory, yet, he seeks it anyway. The acquisition of land and the hopes for its literal and figurative fecundity resemble the frustrated desire for connection in "The Strange Country."

For Roger, love is a means to that attachment, though he is a very different kind of Hemingway protagonist. Whereas Frederic Henry learns that love is not a "game like bridge," Roger tries to dissociate himself from a previous possession of that knowledge. In most Hemingway narratives, the protagonist's experience and perspicacity changes him, but Roger behaves in a way that denies such things. There is very little evolution of his character. The nice country presented Roger with possibility, the strange country helped him to drive away loneliness with primal desire, and the wicked country made him a slave to his own illusion that, at once, denied the past and any moral code to which he tried to adhere. By using Helena to escape his loneliness, Roger hopes to avoid inevitable disaster, which had only begun at the end of the narrative with Helena's fragility as a possible foreshadowing of their emotional destruction.

The narrative ends with the couple having left Florida for New Orleans, where they drink absinthe in a hotel bar. The environment of the Creole city suggests a masqueradelike quality, a notion emphasized with their chosen hallucinatory libation. They both talk about writing, and Helena tells Roger that she has always made up stories to herself "and in one of them [she] save[s] [his] life." Roger says that they might be good "for each other" but not on "a basis of stories. . . . [T]he story business is bad" (CSS 642). Roger had guessed before they arrived in New Orleans that Helena was "full of illusions about [him]"; now, he is certain of it (*CSS* 634). Their respective interior insecurities and fantasies are reflected in the exterior terrain with the inherent notion that any carnival atmosphere also includes confusion and deception. As Roger must struggle with his loneliness, similarly Helena must fight with her "illusions" about Roger, who becomes visibly uncomfortable with her mention of saving him. Indeed, he admits that he is "getting scared" (643). His discomfort makes her cry, and he decides to talk about writing to appease her sadness and because he realizes that he may no longer be able to navigate this shared, alcoholically induced, psychological landscape.

Joseph Flora believes that the story ends with a "very affirmative note of healing and communion" (417) inherent in the couple's dialogue; this colloquy is indicative of the "male protagonist's sharing his most private pain with another" (419–20). Flora refers to the fact that after Helena cries, Roger relays the story of his lost manuscripts, which ended in his despair. He tells Helena that "despair would kill you in just a little time." She is curious to hear the rest of it and petitions him to "make the drink and then tell . . . what happened" (*CSS* 650). Although the act of telling can be affirming, and healing, all that is spoken is not sacred. Jake Barnes establishes a similar maxim in *The Sun Also Rises* when he tells Brett, "you'll lose it if you talk about it" (249). Memory functions as a sacred retainer for certain matters that should not be annunciated or forgotten. Roger and Helena begin to violate this rule, thereby compromising their already fragile connection. The palpable tension that exists in the dialogue prior to the "healing" divulgence suggests a difficult, perhaps impossible, resolution. Roger may ignore it by talking, but he also reproaches himself with this admonition: "What did you think could happen that would not have consequences?" (*CSS* 643). His past and present course of action illustrates that he still wants to perpetuate the illusion, despite all ostensible indications that his albatross, loneliness, will never be alleviated by any forced confession. Helena might have a better idea of what is ahead when she says: "[The absinthe] is strange and wonderful. But all it does so far is just bring us to the edge of misunderstanding" (644). One could substitute "the illusion" for "the absinthe" and the statement would yield the same realization.

If the couple is on the "edge of misunderstanding," then it is because they have traveled through the nexus of displacement, and by the end of the narrative, that concept resonates with both of them. Through allusion and metaphorical representation of landscape, Roger's banishment is made clear. There is the ironic and quiet lingering of disappointment in the nice country; there are the themes of exile, unfamiliarity, and mechanized love in the strange country, and finally, there is the notion of Arcadia, or un-fettered happiness, juxtaposed with the wicked, or slave, country. While Roger's experience smacks of all these things, Helena's does too, if only by her association with, and proximity to, Roger. Moreover, at the end of the narrative there is no clear indication that the lovers are transcending the misunderstandings between them; there is too much that is, and has been, obscured by illusion. Their relationship is a quixotic endeavor, at best.

Stoneback calls "The Strange Country" a "story, or posthumously pub-lished mutant manuscript, or discarded portion of early *Islands in the Stream* material, or intended but unfinished Great American Road Novel" ("Freedom" 207). Perhaps the narrative is "finished," with Roger holding tight to his illusion of Helena in order to avoid the things he wants not to acknowledge. It is not a very Hemingwayesque ending, but it communi-cates implied consequences and the detriment of denying responsibility. More likely, the work is not finished, and Hemingway may have written in Roger's awakening to the reality of a life that denounces idealized pos-sibility, replacing misconception with values. "The Strange Country" as a posthumously published short story does not really function as one. There are wonderful and familiar things about "The Strange Country" that echo other Hemingway works, but that alone does not create a successful work of fiction. Nevertheless, it contains some of the enduring and resonant Hemingway themes of loneliness, despair, hope, and consequences, and it is wholly unique in his oeuvre for its evocation of central and southern Florida. Paramount to these themes, though, is the notion that place con-tains memory, and holds it only as a reminder that the past is never past.

Notes

1. This passage is taken from the manuscript of *The Garden of Eden*, item 422 of the Hemingway Collection in the John F. Kennedy Library in Boston. The parenthetical refer-ence to the manuscript of *The Garden of Eden* can be understood as follows: the folder series, 422.1, is followed by the folder number, 33, then chapter number, 42, and page number, 14.

2. Incidentally, Hemingway wrote to Maxwell Perkins in 1928, shortly after his move to Key West, explaining that his night would not be too "cheerful because another cigar factory has closed down" (*SL* 277). The craft of making cigars seemed to be something that Hemingway regarded as part of a sense of place, local knowledge, that was compromised by some larger economic force, much like a lot of the topography throughout "The Strange Country."

3. In a similar way, Hemingway had dealt with these three things after moving to Key West. His new marriage to Pauline was hopeful, but his contentment was compromised by his father's suicide in 1928. The birth of Patrick proved difficult in that Pauline had to undergo a caesarean, which worried Hemingway (*SL* 280). His second novel, *A Farewell to Arms*, drew largely from some of these experiences, but mostly with the pain of loss bequeathed to Hemingway by his father's death. By 1936, the same year that Roger and Helena travel across Florida, Hemingway meets Martha Gellhorn in Key West, and the possibilities of his life and love with Pauline slowly diminish.

4. Baker cites a letter that Hemingway wrote to his friend Prudencio de Pereda in Spain that expresses his ostensible duty to go "to it" at the beginning in July 1936. He writes, "We ought to have been in Spain all this week." Baker continues to note, however, that "Ernest was still of two minds about going to Spain. . . . Yet the war troubled his conscience" (*A Life Story* 292–93). Hemingway's ambiguity over participating in the war obviously dissipated, though the same cannot be said for Roger, who gives no clear indication of what he will do.

Destination: Hemingway

Key West as Carnival

Hemingway and the Commodification of Celebrity

RUSS POTTLE

Things are rarely as they seem in Key West, including the island itself. Billed as the southernmost point in the continental United States (Davies), it is more complicated a proposition than this advertising admits. Stuart McIver comments that Key West misses being a tropical isle because it lies too far north, even if it has all the requisite elements: "heat . . . palm trees, and the beauty of the waters" (*Hemingway's Key West* 2). It misses being part of the continental United States because it is an island, one of the last in a series of geographical fragments that falls away from the Florida Everglades into the Gulf of Mexico.

Arguing for Key West's continental connection in terms of politics—that the island is possessed by the State of Florida and therefore is part of the mainland—overlooks the watery distance between where the Everglades meander into the Gulf and where Key West rises out of the water on its base of sedimentary rock. If California were suddenly to annex Hawaii, conceiving that island as part of the continental United States would be more difficult, owing to the greater distance over the Pacific Ocean, even though the political principle would be the same. In this argument, Key West is a version of Isla Navarino, the southernmost inhabited island in the Tierra del Fuego, and therefore called the southernmost inhabited island in the world. Navarino is commonly considered the southernmost part of mainland Chile, or at least it can be if one ignores the Strait of Magellan in between.

Arguing for Key West's continental connection in terms of modern industrial achievement—that the island is connected to the rest of Florida by road and therefore is materially related; or its variant, that all commodities such as food, water, gasoline, and electricity extend into the Keys from the mainland—ignores the transience of concrete structures or established supply lines. When Ernest Hemingway and his family moved to the island, the structural connection was Henry Flagler's railroad. But in 1935, the Labor Day Hurricane violently severed that continuity, turning everything between Upper and Lower Matecumbe back to fragments. Highway A1A stands now in Flagler's place, but it takes only the threat of another large storm to remind residents and tourists alike of the Keys' tenuous connection to the lower forty-eight.

Yet a perceived continental connection persists, and through it comes Key West's southernmost label, the focal point of the island's commercial appeal. On arrival, travelers are said to be as far south as they can go in the contiguous United States. And repeating "southernmost" is easy, like a habit, in Key West: the Southernmost Point, the Southernmost House, the Southernmost Motel, the Southernmost "Whatever." All such naming creates an identity, but that identity clearly is a game of language.

Geoffrey Chaucer suggested in *The House of Fame* that fame is indeed a game of language, and like the house in Chaucer's poem, Key West is a congeries of questions about identity, an appropriate place to begin discussing Hemingway, carnival, the commodification of celebrity, and how they come together south of mainland Florida. For in Key West, Hemingway's identity as a celebrity writer began to form and to pose complications.

In Key West, bankrolled primarily by his second wife's uncle, Hemingway quit being poor, laid claim to his own house of fame at 907 Whitehead Street, and almost immediately began to suffer for it. Uncle Gus Pfeiffer laid out eight thousand dollars in 1931, supplemented by Hemingway's own profits from writing, and the house, augmented by improvements and nice furnishings, placed Hemingway in an enviable position as a writer. But it also gave him fits about who he was. This tension presents itself in the notorious and, according to Carol Hemingway's essay in this collection, highly disputed swimming pool incident of 1937. That year, the second wife, trying either to please Hemingway or to keep him (Reynolds, *The 1930s* 282–83; McIver, *Hemingway's Key West* 21–22), had Gus sink twenty thousand dollars into the sand, oolite, and Key Largo limestone of their backyard to help Hemingway stay fit by swimming. Hemingway's alleged response upon hearing the cost, to fling a penny to the dirt and say, "You might as well take my last cent" (qtd. in McIver, *Hemingway's Key West* 21), whether it is true or not, enunciates a Hemingway theme of grousing disingenuously about finances. Marking an irony apparent to many, Hemingway's biographer Michael Reynolds intones:

> Actually, there was no work [for Key Westers in the early and mid-1930s] to quit, no market for fish, no money for food, but that is easy to ignore if the self-reliant strenuous life is your moral guide and your diminished bank account is in no danger of failing, not with money in Paris and New York accounts, money coming in from Pauline's trust, gift money from Uncle Gus, advance money from Scribner's. There was always money somewhere, or if things got too tight, he could write for the magazines. *Cosmopolitan* was begging for a story. (*The 1930s* 188–89)

As McIver puts it, "The plight of [Key Westers] out of work seems not to have touched him, perhaps because he knew no want. After all he had married a rich woman" (*Hemingway's Key West* 63). The novelist Thomas McGuane, a literary descendant of Hemingway's, says "Hemingway's contortions" in attempting to conceal the financial cushion he sat on in the 1930s and 1940s "were hilarious" (qtd. in Treisman 2).

Yet Walter Herbert's observation about Hawthorne, that an uneasy relationship lies between a self-made man and his money (33–34, 66–68), might well apply to Hemingway in the Key West years. Citing Mary Ryan's *Cradle of the Middle Class*, Herbert explains:

> [A] collective family strategy is put into motion to supply funds for advanced education and provide a place for the young man to live inexpensively during the early years of adulthood as he gets his career underway ([Ryan] 166–169). To refashion such a story of marked dependency into a myth of self-creation required attributing the work of tangible exterior sources to an inward spiritual potency. The denial of an indispensable support network and its absorption into the self-creating self enacted in the careers of business and professional men

were also at the heart of Emerson's vision of the selfhood from which a uniquely American intellectual and poetic achievement would spring. (60)

Move this explanation forward a few years in literary history and in the life cycle of a man, and it presents a plausible cause for resentment over money, whether Hemingway threw coins or not. No longer young, Hemingway was nonetheless starting over, leaving the Hadley Richardson years and their Parisian economics behind, beginning anew in Catholicism and career with the help of the Pfeiffers (Reynolds, *The 1930s* 21, 303). To float the new phase in Key West, a collective family strategy is put in motion to make it easy for Hemingway to write: a car, a house, a gift or three, the promise of an African safari. And here is Hemingway, legendarily transposing the Pfeiffer wealth into the product of his own inward spiritual potency, represented by the famous search for truth in the right words. His mythical explosion over the pool is Herbert's denial and absorption atomized in a penny.

Even if Hemingway did not say what legend says he did, the words remain emblematic of the difficult life of a writer, that most fragile of self-made men. Reynolds tells relentlessly of down time in the Key West decade, the spaces between writings that Hemingway filled with little projects and lots of exercise and sport and much vindictive behavior, all to distract him from his fear that once he had written the latest thing, another would not come (*The 1930s* 9, 20, 82, 258). Fourteen entries appear in Reynolds's index under "Hemingway, Ernest, biographical: mood swings" (*The 1930s* 355), and much of Hemingway's bad temper seemed provoked by his own writing process during a decade that threatened to keep him tied to the Pfeiffer purse strings. Herbert's description of Hawthorne's problems with writing and finance echoes in Hemingway's life during the Key West years:

> He now confronted a chronic male dilemma: once self-making is completed, he must settle for what he has become, and he no longer possesses a meaningful future unless the drama of self-creation can be re-enacted. What is now recognized as the crisis of "mid-life" has origins in the culture of masculine self-making, and it includes an impulse to start again at the beginning and a search for sources of spiritual regeneration. (230)

The house on Whitehead Street is simultaneously Hemingway's achievement and its mockery. It is the presence of his literary success and the harbinger of its possible absence, a time when his "Goddamned imagination" (qtd. in Reynolds, *The 1930s* 20) might not work but when he would still have the Pfeiffers to come home to, dry and washed-up but provided for. Hemingway's scheming in 1934 to buy his boat, the *Pilar*, on *Esquire* advances can be read as a need to have *something* he could pay for and control, *something* that was a significant reminder of his own progress (Reynolds, *The 1930s* 169–70). To be fair, purchase of the *Pilar* can be read a number of ways, including Hemingway's guaranteeing himself access to much-needed breaks from writing, or finding himself a vehicle for research on Gulf Stream fishing and marine life (Reynolds, *The 1930s* 92–93, 128–29, 140, 149, 170–71). But when his marriage to Pauline fell apart, he walked out of the house; he did not leave the *Pilar*. The house helped give Hemingway an identity, but equally it threatened to hem him in, and that threat pulled him apart and later pulled him away, to other places and people, to another life.

Also in the Key West years, the intensely private Hemingway developed an intensely public side, forever and for better or worse mingling the life of the mind with the image of the body. A man who enjoyed showing up underdressed and unknown, who could be mistaken for "[a] scruffy-looking bum" and who was refused banking privileges when he first came to live on the island (McIver, *Hemingway's Key West* 48), Hemingway was overcome midway through the Key West decade by a larger version of himself:

> Almost thirty-five years old, Ernest Hemingway was a newsworthy figure whose every public act was grist for the media; his broad shoulders, and his round, mustached face with its pronounced widow's peak becoming as widely recognized as some movie stars. Where once his fiction drew attention to his active life, now that life drew attention to his writing. (Reynolds, *The 1930s* 171)

Hemingway became increasingly consumed with and by his own image. A sample of his preoccupation is in the run-up to a confused struggle with the writer and political activist Max Eastman over Eastman's 1933 review of *Death in the Afternoon*. Stung by Eastman's uncomplimentary assessment, Hemingway had responded with a "sarcastic letter" to the *New Republic*,

Eastman's forum for reviewing the book (Reynolds, *The 1930s* 139). When the two men met in 1937, they came to something like blows.

Stories differ about Hemingway's altercation with Eastman, but a basic summary can be sketched. Hemingway had reacted badly to Eastman's criticisms. Virtually no writer takes poor reviews well, but Hemingway was particularly sensitive. Throughout his career, he felt underappreciated, prone to reading negative comments into even very positive notices. Eastman's review, however, nettled him into threatening violence (Reynolds, *The 1930s* 139). He took offense at such phrases as "Hemingway lacks the serene confidence that he *is* a full-sized man" and at accusations that he was writing like a self-conscious adolescent, stylistically "wearing false hair on the chest" (Meyers, *Critical Heritage* 176). After making a public statement in the *New Republic*, and after making what Reynolds calls "less restrained" statements in correspondence to friends (*The 1930s* 139), Hemingway appeared to let the matter drop.

Four years later, however, Hemingway picked it up again when he was introduced to Eastman in the office of Maxwell Perkins, Hemingway's editor at Scribner's and Eastman's friend and colleague in the publishing industry. After arguing about whether Eastman had implied in his review that Hemingway was sexually, not just stylistically, dysfunctional, the two fell literally into what Reynolds calls "a silly fight" (*The 1930s* 275). Details of the mêlée are as murky as those surrounding the swimming pool incident. Both men claimed victory in the press. Eastman said he wrestled an attacking Hemingway to the floor, and Hemingway dismissed Eastman as a "woman" who leaped, "clawing" at him (qtd. in Baker, *A Life Story* 317; see also Reynolds, *The 1930s* 275–76).

Reynolds and Carl Eby lay blame for the entire affair, from taking exaggerated offense at the review to possibly having thrown a punch in anger, squarely on Hemingway. According to Reynolds, Hemingway was "[h]igh-strung and emotionally erratic" at the time he met Eastman, a condition brought on by too much drinking, too much traveling, too much stress over work, and the impending collapse of his marriage to Pauline (*The 1930s* 268–75). Meeting Eastman provided a flashpoint for a variety of angers and anxieties. According to Eby, Eastman had blundered inadvertently into a thicket of Hemingway's neuroses, unaware that to make comments about hair, even hair on the chest, was to become tangled in "a symbolic connection between hair and potency" that had taken root in "Hemingway's psyche" (278). Thus, the sore spot Hemingway nursed for four years grew from a "misreading" invited by Hemingway's private peculiarities (Eby 278, see also 4–5, 241–75).

Carlos Baker's recounting of the dust-up shows that both Hemingway *and* Eastman had gone too far. Eastman had insensitively applied metaphors of the body to Hemingway's prose, and when faced with Hemingway's anger he had denied that metaphors can create unforeseen associations. His demand that Hemingway should "read what I *really* said" (qtd. in Baker, *A Life Story* 317) during the argument in Perkins's office is clearly an attempt to bracket the multiple levels of meaning arising from figurative language. This is, at best, a naïve action for so accomplished a writer and editor. Eastman was a poet, an essayist, the editor and publisher of two important socialist journals, and the author of books on politics and art. He must have known better than to think that cutting words might not be taken personally. Perhaps Hemingway should have ignored comments about "lack" in "a full-sized man" or about "wearing false hair on the chest." But those comments had a clear connection to the physical realm. If they had not, Eastman would not have understood the source of Hemingway's ire, nor could he have challenged Hemingway to overlook the double entendre.

Hemingway was guilty of losing himself in Eastman's metaphors. His initial reaction to the review, which Reynolds confirms as "[t]aking Eastman's jibe . . . to be a question about his sexual potency" (*The 1930s* 139), and his later behavior upon meeting Eastman, which Baker describes as Hemingway's opening his shirt to expose his own (hairy) chest, then opening Eastman's shirt to expose Eastman's (not hairy) chest, then arguing with Eastman about what the review really said, and finally, in a sudden fit of rage, whacking Eastman with a book-bound version of the review (*A Life Story* 317), indicate an acceptance, however foolish, of the association between literary style and sexual potency implied in Eastman's reckless language. Had Hemingway left his response to meeting Eastman simply at asking, "What do you mean, accusing me of impotence?" (qtd. in Baker, *A Life Story* 317), his question might be read as a witty reference to what Herbert calls the writer's inward spiritual potency. But his physical response to Eastman's review ensures that his art is indeed tied to his body, in a way that is not only the media's fault.

Eby's study of Hemingway and fetishism places the Eastman incident in a long progress of Hemingway's obsession with his own body, the real or fictional bodies of others, the color and length of everyone's hair, the depth of tan in their skins. If toward the end of his life Hemingway increasingly was driven by fetishistic behavior and increasingly was willing to write about it in the troubled manuscripts of *Islands in the Stream* and *The Garden of Eden* (Eby 155–240), the Key West years show early motions of a force that would slosh together mind and body in a cocktail that Hemingway scholars are only now beginning to pour out. The media did some of this body-mind mixing in the 1930s, but Hemingway did some himself, finishing the decade as half-man and half-myth. Reynolds tells of Hemingway's struggle in the Key West years to "keep . . . the writer separate from . . . the private man," protecting the burden of the artist from the high moralism of Catholic doctrine that attended his second marriage (*The 1930s* 148–49). But during that same time, keeping Hemingway the artist, the man of the intellect, separate from Hemingway the celebrity, the man of the body, was equally difficult. In fact, it proved impossible.

Hemingway's Key West legacy is one of tension and struggle: financial security from the Pfeiffers undermined by Hemingway's professional insecurities, a body image competing with Hemingway's literary gifts for public acclaim. It is more a series of questions about Hemingway's identity than a list of answers about who he was during this period. Small wonder, then, that attempts in the early 1980s to boost tourism in Key West by employing Hemingway's reputation, in the festival known as Hemingway Days (Davies; McIver, *Hemingway's Key West* 94), split into almost separate celebrations of Hemingway's body and mind.

Reports of early Hemingway Days festivals by McIver and Alan Davies suggest that activities in those years tilted more toward celebrating Hemingway's bodily image (McIver, *Hemingway's Key West* 90; Davies). This imbalance drove organizers to incorporate the "Hemingway Days Writers' Workshop and Conference" into the schedule to celebrate equally Hemingway's mind and talent. Unlike the activities centered on Hemingway's physical image or deeds, the workshop and conference played to Hemingway's artistic image. As one organizer put it, "We wanted to give people something of substance to take back, something more than T-shirts" (qtd. in McIver, *Hemingway's Key West* 91–92). McIver writes, in colorful explanation:

During his highly public life, [Hemingway] had emerged as two people—one a swaggering macho figure, the other a disciplined artist of
rare genius. In the alcoholic haze of Hemingway Days, the writer had
been shunted over to a table in the corner of a noisy barroom. In 1986,
the festival's founders moved to correct the problem. (*Hemingway's
Key West* 90)

Pulling the writer back out of the barroom is certainly laudable. But the
differing portions of Hemingway Days never resolved into a complementary
relationship. Uttered by an academic, the T-shirt comment above stakes a
claim on Hemingway's image in Key West, privileging literary and critical
examinations in workshops and conferences. It pushes away the foolery of
drunks and their annual spoofing on Hemingway's love for arm-wrestling
contests, or their silly Key West "Running of the Bulls," a dehydration-prone
parody of the San Fermín in Pamplona in which participants run around
dressed in bull costumes and exhaust themselves in the summer heat.

Emblematic of these latter activities is the annual Hemingway look-alike
contest, about which the novelist Russell Banks says simply, "It had come
to that" (57), indicating a degeneration, something crass with a whiff of
carney, an insult to the artist as an older man. In a twisted beauty pageant,
Hemingway imitators are brought onstage in small groups at Sloppy Joe's,
the Duval Street bar first opened as a speakeasy by Hemingway's buddy Joe
"Josie" Russell in the 1920s. They preen before a crowd of drinkers and make
short speeches, as if in a combined version of traditional evening gown,
bathing suit, and talent competitions. Approbation by the crowd and approval by a panel of judges decide the winner. The panel of judges is made
primarily from former titlists, who themselves are experts only in having
faked their own resemblance to Hemingway. The previous year's winner
gives up his crown by helping to choose a winner for the current year.

Any uncomfortable jostling between more literary and more drink-
driven celebrations in Hemingway Days is glossed over in general press
releases, which annually list intellectual and physical activities one upon
the other, with no attempt to sort out a more legitimate representation of
Hemingway's legacy ("Hemingway Days"). However, within the festival, an
official culture of Hemingway, signified by literary and intellectual activities, bumps into an unofficial culture, signified by what Banks calls "that."

26. Aspiring Hemingway look-alikes celebrate the image—not the work—
of Key West's most famous resident, 1986. Courtesy of the State Archives of Florida.

Speaking of official and unofficial cultures invokes Mikhail Bakhtin and his categories of monologic and dialogic discourse, of pronouncement and parody, of totalitarianism and its undoing. Bakhtin, writing in the early years of the Soviet Union, elucidated brilliantly the totalitarian qualities in Western European social and literary structures from the Middle Ages, only to find himself in deep trouble for having those explanations reflect too closely conditions imposed by the Soviet regime. In no way does dissent over methods of honoring a writer and bringing tourist dollars into Key West reflect the dire risks Bakhtin took in his thinking, nor does it suddenly reveal an oppressive political regime run by literary types. However, Bakhtin's thinking, particularly his work on the Western medieval carnival, is helpful in articulating how the intellectually or artistically oriented aspects of "Hemingway Days," seen in an institution like the Hemingway Home and Museum, located in Hemingway's Whitehead Street residence, and activities like the look-alike contest must coexist—even in so uncomfortable a relationship—to express properly the problematic legacy Hemingway left in Key West.

The Home and Museum is allied with Hemingway Days' more formal events, like the Lorian Hemingway Short Story Competition ("Hemingway Days"). As with other authoritative markers of Hemingway's artistic legacy, the Home and Museum helps maintain what Walter Benjamin would call Hemingway's "aura," that "presence of the original [which] is the prerequisite to the concept of authenticity" (220). Much that it presents nowadays of Hemingway may be poorly researched or perhaps deliberately false, as Carol Hemingway contends, and some of it may be truly bewildering, such as the availability of the house for weddings, given Hemingway's poor record of staying married. But the aim of the Home and Museum is to retain the singular image of Hemingway as artist, divorced from the complications of his life.

It is easy to take aim at inconsiderate commercial actions like having the Home and Museum serve occasionally as a wedding chapel. But questions about the accuracy of its exhibits or about the appropriateness of its offerings aside, the Home and Museum takes part in commodifying Hemingway by exchanging the price of admission for a brush with greatness, the *frisson* of having come into range of the original artist and brushed against what might have been, even though they probably are not, his things. Souvenirs bought in the shop are more easily identified as commodities, but as Marx explains, anything that can be exchanged for something else is a commodity, too (125), including a staged encounter with greatness. Through this action, the facility still signifies Hemingway's literary success.

By retaining Hemingway as a commodity, the Home and Museum helps maintain the Hemingway aura, the presence of the original meant to resonate in the more formal activities of Hemingway Days. As seekers of Hemingway, tourists can walk around and look at the furniture, the view, the cats, and celebrate Hemingway the artist as effectively as they might the short-story contest. These tourists do not come to visit the house in which Pauline Pfeiffer Hemingway, taken into the bosom of the Key West community after her husband's poorly managed exit, continued to live after 1939 and care well for her children (McIver, *Hemingway's Key West* 75–80; Reynolds, *The 1930s* 290–92, 302–4). They come in versions of Russell Banks's own late-1960s odyssey, a journey to find the house of the great man and, despite Hemingway's absence, find him somehow present, if only in imagination (55–57). Visitors to the house, particularly during Hemingway

Days, do come away with something more substantial than T-shirts, as they would from other events that celebrate Hemingway's mind and talent.

However, as a contrast to the Home and Museum, and to other formal activities honoring Hemingway in Key West, the look-alike contest is more than Banks's "that." It provides a carnivalesque reminder of Hemingway's dilemmas about himself and his life. Divorced from authoritative presentations of the author, the contest's emphasis on the body, and its refusal to be meaningful about Hemingway's writing, provide a counter to claims that might seal Hemingway's legacy in an artistic bell jar.

Bakhtin argues that the "[c]arnivalistic . . . is directed . . . toward a shift of authorities and truths" (*Problems* 127). It "bring[s] the world maximally close to a person and bring[s] one person maximally close to another" (160). In the sort of phrasing that so often put Bakhtin at risk, carnival "is opposed to that one-sided and gloomy official seriousness which is dogmatic and hostile to evolution and change, which seeks to absolutize a given condition of existence or a given social order" (160; see also Bakhtin, *Rabelais* 4–8). These are hard words to level at academics or working authors who wish only to give something valuable to people who travel to Key West to honor Hemingway. But the relationship between official culture and its parody resembles closely the one between substantive activities of Hemingway Days and the look-alike contest.

Housed in such sites as the Home and Museum; Casa Antigua, Hemingway's first flopping place in Key West; or the Custom House, which holds the Key West Museum of Art and History, the readings and presentations and discussions and exhibitions of Hemingway Days systematically enshrine Hemingway's literary achievements as his true legacy. Mounting the stage at Sloppy Joe's and spilling out the bar's doors, the look-alike contest interrogates this claim in the vernacular of carnival. Like medieval carnival, the look-alike contest is accessible to the vulgar public. A traditional place was "the square and the streets adjoining it," but taverns acted readily as "meeting- and contact points" for the diverse throng. Every year sees the "mock crowning and decrowning of the carnival king," the "primary carnivalistic act" (Bakhtin, *Problems* 128, 124), in the choice of a new Hemingway look-alike winner.

The contest is not meant to reproduce Hemingway, much less the version of Hemingway created by the media and the author himself during the Key

West years (McIver, *Hemingway's Key West* 98). Instead, echoing medieval carnival, it "celebrates . . . the very process of replaceability, not the precise item that is being replaced" (Bakhtin, *Problems* 125) by bringing the body forward in laughing contrast to the mind. Winners are waistline-challenged and white-haired, unlike the film-star figure Hemingway cut in the 1930s. The contest thus chooses a stand-in for Hemingway, and in choosing a version of Hemingway, its judges also choose a version of themselves. This kaleidoscopic motion emphasizes replacement, not essentiality. It elevates the arbitrary over the absolute. Hemingway is both there and not there in a way that reflects "the structural characteristics of the carnival image: it strives to encompass and unite within itself both poles of becoming, both members of an antithesis: birth-death, youth-old age, top-bottom, face-backside, praise-abuse, tragic-comic, and so forth" (Bakhtin, *Problems* 176).

Carnival posits the arbitrary nature of polarities and reveals the exchange between them. As Bakhtin writes, carnival "absolutizes nothing, but rather proclaims the joyful relativity of everything" (*Problems* 125). Taking Bakhtin at his word, terms of presence and absence can be replaced through substitution with terms of sense and non-sense. Thusly refigured in the look-alike contest, the "sense" of Hemingway becomes physical resemblance (the presence of Hemingway), joined to the "non-sense" of Hemingway, a lack of intellectual resemblance (the absence of Hemingway). The look-alike contest displays Hemingway as both sense and non-sense, as both present and absent, uniting antitheses by insisting that even as one feels Hemingway to be "there" in something, he is equally not there.

Bakhtin shows carnival parody to be "the creation of a *decrowning double*; it is that same world turned inside out" (*Problems* 127). The contest in Sloppy Joe's is the spectacular decrowning double of the formal literary events held during the Hemingway festival. To change the focus in the previous terms of substitution, the look-alike contest provides a "non-sense" of its own to double laughingly the "sense" of Hemingway perceived in exhibitions and readings and the like. Successful expressions of what one might call the talent portion of the contest, during which look-alikes address the audience in Sloppy Joe's, are not attempts to imitate Hemingway's perfect sentences. Rather, they are "calls to [the crowd] to drink up" (McIver, *Hemingway's Key West* 100).

In the small space of whatever Key West is, the incoherent body is brought maximally close to the coherent mind. Problems that surged up during the 1930s in Hemingway's public and private selves become transfigured during Hemingway Days by the contrast between celebrations of Hemingway as an artist and the cheering of look-alikes by the yawping throng at Sloppy Joe's. Authority over Hemingway's image falls into contention: is he the artist revered in Key West venues like the Home and Museum, or is he the hefty, often drunk guy at the front of the bar? As Bakhtin argues:

> [O]ne might say that carnival celebrated temporary liberation from the prevailing truth and from the established order; it marked the suspension of all hierarchical ranks, privileges, norms, and prohibitions. Carnival was the true feast of time, the feast of becoming, change, and renewal. It was hostile to all that was immortalized and completed. (*Rabelais* 10)

In 2005, the Sun Valley/Ketchum, Idaho, Chamber of Commerce and Visitors Bureau began its own annual Ernest Hemingway Festival. From a scholar's, an aficionado's, or even a general reader's perspective, the inaugural Sun Valley/Ketchum program showed a full slate of worthy panel discussions, tours, gallery exhibits, films, theater, and even a chance to shoot trap and skeet (*A Celebration*). But without the element of parody so closely associated with the Key West festival, it hosted no events that say as clearly, in the lunatic language of the look-alike contest, that the truth of a man has at least two sides. The look-alike contest is a reminder that the physical and material aspects of Hemingway's life were as meaningful and problematic for him as the intellectual or artistic ones. Perhaps one would rather remember the elegiac experiment of *Death in the Afternoon* than Hemingway worrying about his manhood and hitting Max Eastman. But both are important ways of remembering who Hemingway was and how he struggled both heroically and basely with himself for balance.

As carnival, the look-alike contest is the ephemeral that defines yet questions the eternal, the celebrity that fosters yet undermines fame, the profane without which the sacred loses its meaning. It can be condemned as just a ridiculous contest, as just Baker's "that," but it rises up annually to remind us that whichever answer we choose for the problem of Ernest Hemingway and who he was during the turbulent Key West years, Hemingway is both that answer and more, both that answer and less.

Works Cited

Aaron, Daniel. *Writers on the Left: Episodes in American Literary Communism.* 1961. New York: Columbia University Press, 1992.

Abeel, Erica. "A Winning Sort of Loser." Review of *Mile Zero* by Thomas Sanchez. *New York Times Book Review*, 1 October 1989, 7.

American Heritage Dictionary. 2nd college ed. Boston: Houghton Mifflin, 1982.

Anonymous. Review of *Winner Take Nothing*, by Ernest Hemingway. *Times Literary Supplement*, 8 February 1934, 90.

Atkins, Anselm. "Ironic Action in 'After the Storm.'" *Studies in Short Fiction* 5 (1967–68): 372–78.

Baker, Carlos. *Ernest Hemingway: A Life Story.* New York: Scribner's, 1969.

———, ed. *Hemingway and His Critics: An International Anthology.* New York: Hill and Wang, 1961.

———. *Hemingway: The Writer as Artist.* Princeton: Princeton University Press, 1963.

Bakhtin, Mikhail. *Problems of Dostoevsky's Poetics.* Edited and translated by Caryl Emerson. Minneapolis: University of Minnesota Press, 1984.

———. *Rabelais and His World.* Translated by Hélène Iswolsky. Bloomington: Indiana University Press, 1984.

Banks, Russell. "'H & I': PEN/Hemingway Prize Speech Presented at the John F. Kennedy Library, 4 April 2004." *Hemingway Review* 24 (Fall 2004): 53–60.

Barrie, J. M. *Peter Pan.* 1911. New York: Aladdin Classics, 2003.

Beegel, Susan F. "Conclusion: The Critical Reputation of Ernest Hemingway." In *The Cambridge Companion to Hemingway*, edited by Scott Donaldson, 269–99. Cambridge: Cambridge University Press, 1996.

———. "Eye and Heart: Hemingway's Education as a Naturalist." In *A Historical Guide to Ernest Hemingway*, edited by Linda Wagner-Martin, 53–92. New York: Oxford University Press, 2000.

———. *Hemingway's Craft of Omission: Four Manuscript Examples.* Ann Arbor: University of Michigan Press, 1988.

———. "Santiago and the Eternal Feminine: Gendering *La Mar* in *The Old Man and the Sea.*" In *Hemingway and Women: Female Critics and the Female Voice*, edited by Lawrence R. Broer and Gloria Holland, 131–56. Tuscaloosa: University of Alabama Press, 2002.

Bender, Bert. *Sea-Brothers: The Tradition of American Sea Fiction from Moby Dick to the Present*. Philadelphia: University of Pennsylvania Press, 1988.

Benjamin, Walter. "The Work of Art in the Age of Mechanical Reproduction." In *Illuminations: Essays and Reflections*, edited by Hannah Arendt and translated by Harry Zorn, 217–54. London: Pimlico, 1999.

Bouland, Garry. "'State of Emergency': Key West in the Great Depression." *Florida Historical Quarterly* 67 (October 1988): 166–83.

Brasch, James D., and Joseph Sigman. *Hemingway's Library: A Composite Record*. New York: Garland, 1981.

Brenner, Gerry. *Concealments in Hemingway's Works*. Columbus: Ohio State University Press, 1983.

Broun, Heywood. "It Seems to Me." *New York World Telegram*, 18 August 1934.

Browne, Jefferson B. *Key West: The Old and the New*. 1912. Gainesville: University Press of Florida, 1973.

Bruccoli, Matthew J. *Fitzgerald and Hemingway: A Dangerous Friendship*. New York: Carroll and Graf, 1994.

Burke, J. Willis. *The Streets of Key West: A History through Street Names*. Sarasota, Fla.: Pineapple Press, 2004.

Burnshaw, Stanley. "Turmoil in the Middle Ground." *New Masses* 16 (October 1935): 41–42.

Butler, Judith. *Gender Trouble: Feminism and the Subversion of Identity*. New York: Routledge, 1990.

Byrne, Janice F. "New Acquisitions Shed Light on 'The Old Man and the Sea.'" *Hemingway Review* 10 (Spring 1991): 68–70.

Cabrera, Guillermo Infante. "El primer vuelo de la generación perdida." *Filmoteca Generalitat Valenciana* 2, no. 9 (1991): 6–9.

Canby, Henry Seidel. "Farewell to the Nineties." Review of *Winner Take Nothing*, by Ernest Hemingway. *Saturday Review of Literature*, 28 October 1933, 217.

Captain Blood. 1935. Directed by Michael Curtiz. Warner Home Video. Burbank, Calif.

Carr, Virginia Spencer. *Dos Passos: A Life*. Garden City, N.Y.: Doubleday, 1984.

A Celebration of the Life of Ernest Hemingway: Sun Valley, Idaho, Ernest Hemingway Festival. Brochure. Sun Valley: Sun Valley Ketchum Chamber and Visitors Bureau, 2005.

Cobbs, John L. "Hemingway's *To Have and Have Not*: A Casualty of Didactic Revision." *South Atlantic Bulletin* 44, no. 4 (1979): 1–10.

Cohn, Louis Henry. *A Bibliography of the Works of Ernest Hemingway*. New York: Random House, 1931.

Cooper, James Fenimore. *Wyandotte, The Monikins, and Jack Tier*. Vol. 7 of *Works of J. Fenimore Cooper*. 10 vols. New York: Collier, 1892. Reprint, Westwood, Ct.: Greenwood Press, 1969.

Cooper, Stephen. *The Politics of Ernest Hemingway*. Ann Arbor: UMI Research Press, 1987.

Comley, Nancy R., and Robert Scholes. *Hemingway's Genders: Rereading the Hemingway Text*. New Haven: Yale University Press, 1994.

Cordingly, David. *Under the Black Flag: The Romance and Reality of Life among the Pirates*. New York: Harcourt Brace, 1995.

Cox, Christopher. *A Key West Companion*. New York: St. Martin's Press, 1983.

Crowther, Bosley. "Review of *To Have and Have Not*." *New York Times*, 12 October 1944.

"Cuba Dooms Kidnapper: Seventh Man Is Condemned for Abducting Railway Official." *New York Times*, 30 January 1937.

"Cuban Force Slays 3 in Kidnap Chase." *New York Times*, 15 January 1936.

"Cuba's 'New Deal,' If It Ever Enjoys One, Must Come From This Country," *Kansas City Star*, 13 May 1933.

Davies, Alan. "Florida's Hemingway Festival." *Contemporary Review* 267 (October 1995): 208–13.

De Bechevet, Lydia. *Chantey of the Keys*. Caldwell, Idaho: Claxton Press, 1936.

DePastino, Todd. *Citizen Hobo: How a Century of Homelessness Shaped America*. Chicago: University of Chicago Press, 2003.

Dickson, Paul, and Thomas B. Allen. *The Bonus Army: An American Epic*. New York: Walker, 2004.

Dollimore, Jonathan. *Sexual Dissidence: Augustine to Wilde, Freud to Foucault*. New York: Cambridge University Press, 1991.

Donaldson, Scott. *By Force of Will: The Life and Art of Ernest Hemingway*. New York: Viking, 1977.

———. "Introduction: Hemingway and Fame." In *The Cambridge Companion to Ernest Hemingway*, edited by Scott Donaldson. Cambridge: Cambridge University Press, 1996.

Dos Passos, John. *The Best Times: An Informal Memoir*. New York: New American Library, 1966.

———. *The Big Money*. Larchmont, N.Y.: Queens House, 1930.

———. *The Fourteenth Chronicle: Letters and Diaries of John Dos Passos*. Edited by Townsend Ludington. Boston: Gambit, 1973.

Doyle, Charles. ed. *Wallace Stevens: The Critical Heritage*. London: Routledge and Kegan Paul, 1985.

Drye, Willie. *Storm of the Century: The Labor Day Hurricane of 1935*. Washington, D.C.: National Geographic, 2002.

Eakins, William. *Key West 2720 A.D.* Stamford, Ct.: Knights Press, 1989.

Eby, Carl. *Hemingway's Fetishism: Psychoanalysis and the Mirror of Manhood*. Albany: State University of New York Press, 1999.

Ekstein, Modris. *Rites of Spring: The Great War and the Birth of the Modern Age*. Boston: Houghton Mifflin, 2000.

Eliot, T. S. *Selected Essays of T. S. Eliot: New Edition*. New York: Harcourt, Brace and World, 1950.

Elliott, Ira. "Performance Art and 'Masculine' Signification in *The Sun Also Rises*." *American Literature* 67 (March 1995): 77–95.

Ellis, Richard J. *The Dark Side of the Left: Illiberal Egalitarianism in America*. Lawrence: University Press of Kansas, 1998.

Engelbrecht, Helmuth C., and Frank C. Hanighen. *Merchants of Death: A Study of the International Armament Industry*. New York: Dodd and Mead, 1934.

Fadiman, Clifton. "A Letter to Mr. Hemingway." Review of *Winner Take Nothing*, by Ernest Hemingway. *New Yorker*, 28 October 1933, 74–75.

———. Review of *The Fifth Column and the First 49*. *New Yorker*, 22 October 1938, 94–95.

Farrell, James T. *A Note on Literary Criticism*. New York: Vanguard Press, 1936.

Farrington, S. Kip. *Atlantic Big Game Fishing*. New York: Kennedy, 1937.

Filreis, Alan. *Modernism from Left to Right: Wallace Stevens, the Thirties, & Literary Radicalism.* Cambridge: Cambridge University Press, 1994.

Fitch, Clarke, Ensign U.S.N. [Upton Sinclair]. *Caught in a Trap, or Clif Farady's Terrible Set-Back.* New York: Street and Smith, 1898.

Fitzgerald, F. Scott. *The Short Stories of F. Scott Fitzgerald: A New Collection.* Edited by Matthew J. Bruccoli. New York: Scribner's, 1989.

"5 More Cubans Held in an Alleged Plot." *New York Times*, 10 November 1936.

Fleming, Robert E. *The Face in the Mirror: Hemingway's Writers.* Tuscaloosa: University of Alabama Press, 1994.

———, ed. *Hemingway and the Natural World.* Moscow: University of Idaho Press, 1999.

Flora, Joseph M. "Hemingway's 'The Strange Country' in the Context of *The Complete Short Stories.*" *Studies in Short Fiction* 25 (1988): 409–20.

Folliard, Edward T. "What a Party the Veterans Had at Their 'Paradise' in Key West; But Let Bill Tell You about It, for He's an Authority; Peace Returns as Men Hail Patman Bonus Bill's Advance." *Washington Post*, 24 March 1935.

Foucault, Michel. *The History of Sexuality, Volume I.* New York: Vintage, 1980.

Fuentes, Norberto. *Hemingway in Cuba.* Secaucus, N.J.: Stuart, 1984.

Franks, Joseph. *The Idea of Spatial Form.* New Brunswick, N.J.: Rutgers University Press, 1991.

Gallagher, William. "Waldo Peirce and Ernest Hemingway: Mirror Images." *Hemingway Review* 23, no. 1 (Fall 2003): 24–41.

Gardner, Janette C. *An Annotated Bibliography of Florida Fiction, 1801–1980.* St. Petersburg: Little Bayou Press, 1983.

Gellhorn, Martha. *Selected Letters of Martha Gellhorn.* Edited by Caroline Moorehead. New York: Holt, 2006.

Gilbert, W. S., and Sir Arthur Sullivan. *The Pirates of Penzance.* Vocal Score. New edition by Carl Simpson and Ephraim Hammett Jones. Mineola, N.Y.: Dover, 2001.

Gingrich, Arnold. "A Farewell to the Lead-Off Man." *Esquire*, June 1937, 5.

———. "Notes on Bimini." *Esquire*, October 1970, 12.

———. *Nothing But People: The Early Days at Esquire, A Personal History 1928–1958.* New York: Crown, 1971.

———. "Reviving the Practice of Salutes to the Living." *Esquire*, February 1937, 5.

———, ed. *The Esquire Treasury.* New York: Simon and Schuster, 1953.

Gould, Hannah Flagg. "The Pirate of Key West." *Godey's Magazine* 32 (1846): 171–81.

"Grau Says Revolt in Cuba Is Certain." *New York Times*, 15 April 1935.

Gregory, Horace. "Highly Polished Poetry." *New York Herald Tribune Books*, 27 September 1931, 28.

Griffin, Peter. *Along with Youth: Hemingway, The Early Years.* Oxford: Oxford University Press, 1985.

Griffith, James. *Adaptations as Imitations: Film from Novels.* Newark: University of Delaware Press, 1997.

Grimes, Richard Mary, Sr. "Hemingway: The Years with *Esquire.*" Ph.D. diss. Ohio State University, 1965.

Gunter, Archibal Clavering. *Don Balasco of Key West.* New York: Routledge and Sons, 1897.

Gurko, Leo. *Ernest Hemingway and the Pursuit of Heroism.* New York: Crowell, 1968.

———. "John Dos Passos' *U.S.A.*: A 1930s' Spectacular." In *Proletarian Writers of the Thirties*, edited by David Madden, 46–63. Carbondale and Edwardsville: Southern Illinois University Press, 1968.

Hanna, Alfred Jackson, and Kathryn Abbey Hanna. *Florida's Golden Sands*. Indianapolis: Bobbs-Merrill, 1950.

Harris, Paul. "Please, Mr. Ernest Hemingway!: A Letter." *American Criterion* 1 (December 1935): 13–16.

Harrison, Jim. *A Good Day to Die*. New York: Simon and Schuster, 1973.

"Havana City Hall Robbed of $157,000." *New York Times*, 19 October 1934.

Hemingway, Carol [Mrs. John Gardener]. Unpublished letter. Vienna, Austria. 24 January 1933.

Hemingway, Carol [Mrs. Patrick Hemingway]. "907 Whitehead Street." *Hemingway Review* 23, no.1 (Fall 2003): 8–23.

"Hemingway Days' 25th Anniversary to Honor Ernest July 19–24." Stuart Newman Associates. www.flakeys.com/hemingwaymedia/2005_25th_anniversary.html.

Hemingway, Ernest. "After the Storm." Unpublished manuscript. Item 226. Hemingway Archives, John F. Kennedy Library, Boston.

———. *Anita* Fishing Log. 25 January–15 May 1933. Box 88. Hemingway Collection. John F. Kennedy Library. Boston.

———. *Anita* Fishing Log. 7–20 June 1932. Box 88. Hemingway Collection. John F. Kennedy Library, Boston.

———. "Arms and the Men." *Fortune*, March 1934, 53–57, 113–26.

———. *By-Line: Ernest Hemingway*. Edited by William White. New York: Scribner's, 1967.

———. "Call for Greatness." *Ken* 2 (July 14, 1938): 23.

———. *The Complete Short Stories of Ernest Hemingway: The Finca Vigía Edition*. Edited by John, Patrick, and Gregory Hemingway. New York: Scribner's, 1987.

———. *Conversations with Ernest Hemingway*. Edited by Matthew J. Bruccoli. Jackson: University of Mississippi Press, 1986.

———. "Cuban Fishing." In *Game Fish of the World*, edited by Brian Vesey-Fitzgerald and Francesca LaMonte, 156–60. London: Nicholson and Watson, 1949.

———. *Dateline: Toronto. The Complete Toronto Star Dispatches, 1920–1924*. Edited by William White. New York: Scribner's, 1985.

———. *Death in the Afternoon*. New York: Scribner's, 1932.

———. "Defense of Dirty Words: A Cuban Letter." *Esquire*, September 1934, 19, 158.

———. *Ernest Hemingway: Selected Letters 1917–1961*. Edited by Carlos Baker. New York: Scribner's, 1981.

———. "False News to the President." *Ken*, 8 September 1938, 17–18.

———. *A Farewell to Arms*. New York: Scribner's, 1929.

———. *The Fifth Column and Four Stories of the Spanish Civil War*. New York: Scribner's, 2003.

———. *For Whom the Bell Tolls*. New York: Scribner's, 1940.

———. *The Garden of Eden*. New York: Scribner's, 1986.

———. *The Garden of Eden*. Unpublished manuscript. Item 422. Hemingway Archives, John F. Kennedy Library, Boston.

———. *Green Hills of Africa*. New York: Scribner's, 1935.

———. "Greetings on Our Twenty-Fifth Anniversary." *New Masses* 1 (December 1936): 21.

———. "He Who Gets Slap Happy." *Esquire*, August 1935, 19, 182.

———. *Hemingway on War*. Edited by Seán Hemingway. New York: Scribner's, 2003.

———. "H. M.'s Loyal State Department." *Ken*, 16 June 1938, 36.

———. Introduction to *Atlantic Game Fishing*, by S. Kip Farrington Jr. New York: Kennedy Brothers, 1937

———. Introduction to *A Farewell to Arms*, by Hemingway. New York: Scribner's, 1948.

———. "Marlin Off Cuba." In *American Big Game Fishing*, edited by Eugene V. Connett, 55–81. New York: Derrydale Press, 1993.

———. *A Moveable Feast*. New York: Scribner's, 1964.

———. "Notes on Life and Letters: Or a Manuscript Found in a Bottle." *Esquire*, January 1935, 21, 159.

———. *The Old Man and the Sea*. New York: Scribner's, 1952.

———. *The Only Thing That Counts: The Ernest Hemingway/Maxwell Perkins Correspondence, 1925–1947*. Edited by Matthew J. Bruccoli. Columbia: University of South Carolina Press, 1996.

———. "The Snows of Kilimanjaro." *Esquire*, August 1936, 27, 194–201.

———. *The Sun Also Rises*. New York: Scribner's, 1926.

———. *To Have and Have Not*. New York: Scribner's, 1937.

———. "To Have and Have Not." Unpublished manuscripts. Item 204. Hemingway Archives, John F. Kennedy Library, Boston.

———. "The Time Now, The Place Spain." *Ken*, 7 April 1938, 36–37.

———. "Treachery in Aragon." *Ken*, 30 June 1938, 26.

———. "Who Murdered the Vets? A First Hand Report on the Florida Hurricane." *New Masses* 16 (17 September 1935): 9–10. In Trogdon, 168–71.

"Hemingway Slept Here, So the Town Cashes In." *New York Times*, 25 July 1994. http://query.nytimes.com/gst/fullpage.html?res=9E06E2DE103EF936A15754C0A962958260.

Hendricks, Vicki. *Voluntary Madness*. London: Serpent's Tail, 2002.

Herbert, T. Walter. *Dearest Beloved: The Hawthornes and the Making of the Middle-Class Family*. Berkeley and Los Angeles: University of California Press, 1993.

Hersey, John. *Key West Tales*. New York: Knopf, 1994.

Hicks, Granville. Letter. *New Republic*, 4 October 1939, 244.

Hotchner, A. E. *Papa Hemingway: A Personal Memoir*. 1966. New York: DaCapo Press, 2005.

Houk, Walter. E-mail interview by Steven Paul. 27 July 2005.

Hynes, Samuel. *A War Remembered: The First World War and English Culture*. New York: Collier, 1990.

Ingraham, Joseph Holt. *Rafael, or the Twice Condemned: A Tale of Key West*. Boston: H. L. Williams, 1845.

Johnston, Kenneth G. "Hemingway's 'Wine of Wyoming': Disappointment in America." *Western American Literature* 9 (Fall 1974):159–67.

Kaufelt, Lynn Mitsuko. *Key West Writers and Their Houses*. Englewood, Fla.: Pineapple Press, 1986.

Kaul, A. J. "Arnold Gingrich." In *Dictionary of Literary Biography*, "American Magazine Journalists, 1900–1960," 137: 106–11. Detroit: Gale, 1994.

Kawin, Bruce. "Faulkner's Film Career: The Years with Hawks." In *Faulkner, Modernism, and*

Film, edited by Evans Harrington and Ann J. Abadie, 163–81. Jackson: University Press of Mississippi, 1979.

———, ed. *To Have and Have Not*. Screenplay by Jules Furthman and William Faulkner. Madison: University of Wisconsin Press, 1980.

Keene, Jennifer D. *Doughboys, the Great War, and the Remaking of America*. Baltimore: Johns Hopkins University Press, 2001.

Kemp, Peter, ed. *The Oxford Companion to Ships and the Sea*. Oxford: Oxford University Press, 1988.

Kennedy, J. Gerald, and Jackson R. Bryer, eds. *French Connections: Hemingway and Fitzgerald Abroad*. New York: St. Martin's Press, 1998.

Kert, Bernice. *The Hemingway Women*. New York: Norton, 1983.

Knott, Toni D. "One Man Alone: Dimensions of Individuality and Categorization in *To Have and Have Not*." *Hemingway Review* 17 (Spring 1998): 78–87.

———, ed. *One Man Alone: Hemingway and* To Have and Have Not. Lanham, Md.: University Press of America, 1999.

Koch, Stephen. *The Breaking Point: Hemingway, Dos Passos, and the Murder of José Robles*. New York: Counterpoint, 2005.

Koven, Joseph. "The Liberal Literary Legion." *Monthly Review* 1 (June 1934): 44–45.

Kwon, Seokwoo. "Harry Morgan's Dismemberment and Hemingway's Critique of Violence: *To Have and Have Not*." *Journal of English Language and Literature* 46 (Winter 2000): 1041–60.

Langewische, William. *The Outlaw Sea: A World of Freedom, Chaos, and Crime*. New York: North Point Press, 2004.

Larsson, Raymond. "The Beau as Poet." *Commonweal*, 6 April 1932, 640–41.

Lawrence, H. Lea. *A Hemingway Odyssey*. Nashville: Cumberland, 1999.

Liberman, Jules. "The Sound and the Fury." *Esquire*, May 1935, 12.

Longenbach, James. *Wallace Stevens: The Plain Sense of Things*. New York: Oxford University Press, 1991.

"Love's Labor Lost: A Sketch of Key West." *Knickerbocker* 57 (January 1841): 48–51.

Lozano-Moreno, Susana. "Textos e imágenes de la generación perdida: La adaptación cinematográfica: De Hemingway a Furthman, Faulkner y Hawks." Ph.D. diss., Universidad Complutense de Madid, 2001.

Ludington, Townsend. *John Dos Passos: A Twentieth Century Odyssey*. New York: Dutton, 1980.

Lurie, Alison. *The Last Resort*. New York: Henry Holt, 1998.

———. *The Truth about Lorin Jones*. Boston: Little, Brown, 1988.

Lynn, Kenneth S. *Hemingway*. New York: Simon and Schuster, 1987.

Lyons, Nick, ed. *Hemingway on Fishing*. New York: Simon and Schuster, 2002.

MacLeish, Archibald. *Letters of Archibald MacLeish*. Edited by R. H. Winnick. Boston: Houghton Mifflin, 1983.

Mandel, Miriam B. "Configuring There as Here: Hemingway's Travels and the See America First Movement." *Hemingway Review* 19 (Fall 1999): 93–105.

Mariani, Paul. *The Broken Tower: The Life of Hart Crane*. New York: Norton, 1999.

Martin, Lawrence H., Jr. "Crazy in Sheridan: Hemingway's 'Wine of Wyoming' Reconsidered." *Hemingway Review* 8 (Fall 1988): 13–25.

———. "The Storm, the Vets, and the Author." *North Dakota Quarterly* 73, no. 1–2 (Winter/Spring 2006): 75–86.

Marx, Karl. *Capital: A Critique of Political Economy*. Vol. 1. Translated by Ben Fowkes. New York: Penguin, 1990.

Mast, Gerald. *Howard Hawks, Storyteller*. New York: Oxford University Press, 1982.

Matthews, T. S. Review of *Winner Take Nothing*, by Ernest Hemingway. *New Republic*, 15 November 1933, 24.

McGuane, Thomas. *The Bushwhacked Piano*. New York: Farrar, Straus, and Giroux, 1971.

———. *Ninety-two in the Shade*. New York: Farrar, Straus, and Giroux, 1973.

———. *Panama*. New York: Farrar, Straus, and Giroux, 1978.

McIver, Stuart B. *Dreamers, Schemers, and Scalawags: The Florida Chronicles, Vol. I*. Sarasota, Fla.: Pineapple Press, 1994.

———. *Hemingway's Key West*. 1993. Sarasota, Fla.: Pineapple Press, 2002.

McLean, Charles. "200 Veterans Build FERA Golf Course for Golfless Town." *New York Times*, 11 August 1935.

McLendon, James. *Papa: Hemingway in Key West*. Key West: Langley, 1972.

Mellow, James R. *Walker Evans*. New York: Basic Books, 1999.

Meredith, James H. "Hemingway's Multiple Voices of War: A Rhetorical Study." In *War and Words: Horror and Heroism in the Literature of Warfare*, edited by Sara Munson Deats, Lagretta Tallent Lenker, and Merry G. Perry, 197–214. Lanham, Md.: Lexington, 2004.

Merrill, Hugh. *Esky: The Early Years at Esquire*. New Brunswick, N.J.: Rutgers University Press, 1995.

Meyers, Jeffrey. "Bogart and Hemingway." *Virginia Quarterly Review* 72 (Summer 1996): 446–49.

———. *Hemingway: A Life*. 1985. New York: Da Capo, 1999.

———, ed. *Hemingway: The Critical Heritage*. London: Routledge and Kegan Paul, 1982.

———. *Hemingway: Life into Art*. New York: Cooper Square Press, 2000.

Miller, Linda Patterson. *Letters from the Lost Generation*. 1991. Gainesville: University Press of Florida, 2002.

———. "The Matrix of Hemingway's *Pilar* Log, 1934–1935." *North Dakota Quarterly* 64 (Fall 1997): 105–23.

Miller, Madelaine Hemingway. *Ernie: Hemingway's Sister "Sunny" Remembers*. New York: Crown, 1975.

Moorehead, Caroline. *Gellhorn: A Twentieth-Century Life*. New York: Holt, 2003.

Munson, Gorham. "The Dandyism of Wallace Stevens." *Dial* (November 1925): 413–17. Reprinted in *Wallace Stevens: The Critical Heritage*, edited by Charles Doyle, 78–82. London: Routledge, 1985.

Murphy, Charlene M. "Hemingway, Winslow Homer, and *Islands in the Stream*: Influence and Tribute." *Hemingway Review* 13, no. 1 (Fall 1993): 76–85.

Murphy, George, ed. *The Key West Reader*. Key West: Tortugas, 1989.

Newhagen, Jane Louise. *Sand Dollar: A Tale of Old Key West*. Parker, Colo.: Outskirts Press, 2007.

North, Joe. Letter to Ernest Hemingway. Incoming Correspondence, 1935. Ernest Hemingway Collection, John F. Kennedy Library, Boston.

Ogle, Maureen. *Key West, History of an Island of Dreams*. Gainesville: University Press of Florida, 2003.

Ohl, John Kennedy. *Hugh S. Johnson and the New Deal*. Dekalb: Northern Illinois University Press, 1986.

O'Leary, Theodore M. "Hemingway-*Esquire* Controversy Involves Rights of Republication." *Kansas City Star*, 26 August 1958.

Oxford English Dictionary. 2nd ed. Oxford: Clarendon, 1989.

Pells, Richard. *Radical Visions and American Dreams: Culture and Thought in the Depression Years*. New York: Harper and Row, 1973.

Perez, Louis A., Jr. *Cuba: Between Reform and Revolution*. New York: Oxford University Press, 1988.

Philbrick, Thomas. *James Fenimore Cooper and the Development of American Sea Fiction*. Cambridge: Harvard University Press, 1961.

Phillips, Gene D. *Hemingway and Film*. New York: Ungar, 1980.

Phillips, J. D. "Havana Swept by Gun Fire: State of Siege Proclaimed, With General Call to Arms." *New York Times*, 10 March 1935.

———. "Kidnappers Free Wealthy Cuban, 78." *New York Times* 9 June 1935, 24.

Porter, Russell B. "Batista's Army Again Makes Its Iron Felt in Cuba." *New York Times Sunday Magazine*, 27 December 1936, 6.

———. "'Cuba Libre': The New Challenge." *New York Times Sunday Magazine*, 17 September 1933, 1, 2, 16.

Pound, Ezra. *The Literary Essays of Ezra Pound*. Edited by T. S. Eliot. London: Faber and Faber, 1954.

———. *The Selected Letters of Ezra Pound: 1907–1941*. Edited by D. D. Paige. New York: New Directions, 1950.

———. *The Selected Poems of Ezra Pound*. New York: New Directions, 1957.

Prescott, Jeryl J. "Liberty for Just[us]: Gender and Race in Hemingway's *To Have and Have Not*." *CLA Journal* 37 (December 1993): 176–88.

Pyle, Howard. *Howard Pyle's Book of Pirates*. New York: Harper and Brothers, 1921.

Radosh, Ronald, and Mary R. Habeck and Grigory Sevostianov. *Spain Betrayed: The Soviet Union in the Spanish Civil War*. New Haven: Yale University Press, 2001.

Rediker, Marcus. *Between the Devil and the Deep Blue Sea: Merchant Seamen, Pirates, and the Anglo-American World, 1700–1750*. Cambridge: Cambridge University Press, 1987.

Reynolds, Michael S. *Hemingway: An Annotated Chronology*. Detroit: Omnigraphics, 1991.

———. *Hemingway: The American Homecoming*. Oxford: Blackwell, 1992.

———. *Hemingway's First War: The Making of* A Farewell to Arms. Princeton: Princeton University Press, 1976.

———. *Hemingway: The Paris Years*. Oxford: Blackwell, 1989.

———. *Hemingway's Reading, 1910–1940*. Princeton: Princeton University Press, 1981.

———. *Hemingway: The 1930s*. New York: Norton, 1998.

———. *The Young Hemingway*. 1987. New York: Norton, 1999.

Reynolds, Michael S., and Frederick Voss. *Picturing Hemingway: A Writer in His Time*. New Haven: Yale University Press, 1999.

Ritchie, Robert C. *Captain Kidd and the War against the Pirates*. Cambridge: Harvard University Press, 1986.

Robbins, Alexandra. *Secrets of the Tomb: Skull and Bones, the Ivy Leagues, and the Hidden Paths of Power.* Boston: Little, Brown, 2002.

Rockwood, Caroline Washburn. *In Biscayne Bay.* New York: Dodd, Mead, 1891.

Ryan, Steven T. "Prosaic Unity in *To Have and Have Not.*" *Hemingway Review* 4 (Fall 1984): 27–32.

Ryan, William James. "Uses of Irony in *To Have and Have Not.*" *Modern Fiction Studies* 14 (Autumn 1968): 329–36.

"The Sad Tale of the Bonus Marchers." A Doughboy Heritage Feature. Doughboy Center. www.worldwar1.com/dbc/bonusm.htm.

Samuelson, Arthur. "Beating Sharks to a Marlin." *Outdoor Life,* June 1935, 30–31, 54.

———. *With Hemingway: A Year in Key West and Cuba.* New York: Random House, 1984.

Sanchez, Thomas. *Mile Zero.* New York: Knopf, 1989.

Sanderson, Rena, ed. *Hemingway in Italy: New Perspectives.* Baton Rouge: Louisiana State University Press, 2006.

Schneider, Isidor. "The Fetish of Simplicity." *Nation,* 18 February 1931, 184–86.

Scott, Phil. *Hemingway's Hurricane: The Great Florida Keys Storm of 1935.* New York: McGraw Hill, 2006.

Seldes, George. *Iron, Blood, and Profits: An Exposure of the World-Wide Munitions Racket.* New York: Harper, 1934.

———. "The Prize-fighter and the Bull." *Esquire,* November 1934, 52, 173–74.

Seydow, John J. "Francis Macomber's Spurious Masculinity." *Hemingway Review* 1 (Fall 1981): 33–41.

Sinclair, Upton. *The Autobiography of Upton Sinclair.* London: W. H. Allen, 1963.

Smith, Paul. *The Reader's Guide to the Short Stories of Ernest Hemingway.* Boston: G. K. Hall, 1989.

Solow, Herbert. "Substitution at Left Tackle: Hemingway for Dos Passos." *Partisan Review* 4 (April 1938): 62–64.

Stam, Robert. *Literature through Film.* Malden, Mass.: Blackwell, 2005.

Standiford, Les. *Last Train to Paradise: Henry Flagler and the Spectacular Rise and Fall of the Railroad that Crossed an Ocean.* New York: Crown, 2002.

Stephens, Robert O., ed. *Ernest Hemingway: The Critical Reception.* New York: Franklin, 1977.

———. *Hemingway's Nonfiction: The Public Voice.* Chapel Hill: University of North Carolina Press, 1968.

Steinbeck, John. *Cup of Gold: A Life of Sir Henry Morgan, Buccaneer, with Occasional Reference to History.* 1929. New York: Penguin, 1986.

Stevens, Wallace. *The Collected Poems of Wallace Stevens.* New York: Vintage, 1990.

———. *Wallace Stevens: Collected Poetry and Prose.* Edited by Frank Kermode and Joan Richardson. Library of America. New York: Literary Classics, 1997.

———. *Letters of Wallace Stevens.* Edited by Holly Stevens. Berkeley and Los Angeles: University of California Press, 1996.

Stevenson, Robert Louis. *Treasure Island.* 1881. Illustrated by N. C. Wyeth. 1911. New York: Atheneum Books for Young Readers, 1971.

Stone, Julius F., Jr. "Key West Is to Be Restored by Free Labor of Her Citizens." *New York Times,* 12 August 1934.

Stoneback, H. R. "'Et in Arcadia Ego': Deep Structure, Paysage Moralise, Geomoral and Symbolic Landscape in Hemingway." *North Dakota Quarterly* 55 (1998): 186–203.

———."Freedom and Motion, Place and Placelessness: On the Road in Hemingway's America." In *Hemingway and the Natural World*, edited by Robert Fleming, 203–19. Moscow: University of Idaho Press, 1999.

Strabel, Thelma. *Reap the Wild Wind*. New York: Triangle Books, 1941.

"Sugar, the Great White Specter That Fills Cuba with Idleness and Unrest." *Kansas City Star*, 19 September 1933.

Thielen, Benedict. *The Lost Men*. New York: Appleton-Century, 1946.

Thomas, Hugh. *Cuba: The Pursuit of Freedom*. 1971. London: Picador, 2001.

Tratner, Michael. *Modernism and Mass Politics: Joyce, Woolf, Eliot, Yeats*. Stanford: Stanford University Press, 1995.

Treisman, Deborah. "All That Nature Cares About: Thomas McGuane discusses despicable characters and heroic figures." The New Yorker Online Only. 6 January 2001. www.newyorker.com/printables/online/030113on_onlineonly01.

Trogdon, Robert W. *Ernest Hemingway: A Literary Reference*. New York: Carroll and Graf, 2002.

Trout, Stephen. "'Where Do We Go From Here?': Ernest Hemingway's 'Soldier's Home' and American Veterans of World War I." *Hemingway Review* 20 (Fall 2000): 4–21.

Voyer, J. Larry. *Piratical and Privateering Books in English*. http://larryvoyer.com/piratical/pirate%20pages/pirates.htm.

Watkins, T. H. *The Hungry Years: A Narrative History of the Great Depression in America*. New York: Holt, 1999.

Watson, William Brasch. "Hemingway in Bimini: An Introduction." *North Dakota Quarterly* 63 (Summer 1996) 130–44.

Weeks, Robert P., ed. *Hemingway: A Collection of Critical Essays*. Englewood Cliffs, N.J.: Prentice Hall, 1962.

West, Ray B. "The Biological Trap." In *Hemingway: A Collection of Critical Essays*, edited by Robert P. Weeks, 139–51. Englewood Cliffs, N.J.: Prentice Hall, 1962.

Wilkinson, Jerry. "The Florida Keys Memorial." http://www.keyshistory.org/hurrmemorial.html.

Williams, Tennessee. "Authors and Critics Appraise Works." *New York Times*, 3 July 1961. www.nytimes.com/books/99/07/04/specials/hemingway-obit4.html

Williams, William Carlos. Review of *The Man with the Blue Guitar and Other Poems*, by Wallace Stevens. *New Republic*, 17 November 1937, 50.

Wilson, Edmund. "An Appeal to Progressives." *New Republic*, 14 January 1931, 234–38.

———. *The Wound and the Bow*. New York: Oxford University Press, 1947.

Wiltz, John E. *In Search of Peace: The Senate Munitions Inquiry, 1934–36*. Baton Rouge: Louisiana State University Press, 1963.

Wimsatt, William K. *The Verbal Icon: Studies in the Meaning of Poetry*. Lexington: University of Kentucky Press, 1954.

Winter, Jay. *Sites of Memory, Sites of Mourning: The Great War in European Cultural History*. Cambridge: Cambridge University Press, 1995.

Yeats, W. B. *The Plays*. Edited by David R. Clark and Rosalind E. Clark. Vol. 2 of *The Collected Work of W. B. Yeats*. New York: Norton, 2000.

Contributors

Susan F. Beegel is Adjunct Associate Professor of English at the University of Idaho and editor of the *Hemingway Review*. She has published two books on Hemingway and one on John Steinbeck, and is the author of more than fifty scholarly articles on various aspects of American literature and history.

Lawrence R. Broer is Emeritus Professor of English at the University of South Florida. He has published widely in critical collections and professional journals, and has authored or edited eight books, including *Hemingway's Spanish Tragedy, Sanity Plea: Schizophrenia in the Novels of Kurt Vonnegut,* and *Hemingway and Women: Female Critics and the Female Voice,* coedited with Gloria Holland. He is presently a Senior Fulbright Scholar and working on two books, one on Hemingway, Vonnegut, and recreation, and the other on democracy and the American Dream from Dreiser to Mailer.

Nicole Camastra is a Ph.D. student at the University of Georgia. She has presented papers at the last three International Hemingway conferences and received the James Hinkle Travel Award in 2006. She has forthcoming essays in *American Literary Realism* and *rPw: An Annual of Robert Penn Warren Studies.*

Milton A. Cohen, Professor of Literary Studies at the University of Texas at Dallas, has written books on Hemingway, Cummings, and modernism. He is presently writing a book on Stevens, Williams, Cummings, and Frost during the 1930s.

Michael J. Crowley received his Ph.D. from the University of Georgia and currently teaches in the Department of English and Fine Arts at the Virginia Military Institute.

Kirk Curnutt is professor and chair of English at Troy University. He is the author of *Ernest Hemingway and the Expatriate Modernist Movement, Coffee with Hemingway*, and *A Reader's Guide to Hemingway's To Have and Have Not*, among many other critical studies and works of fiction.

John J. Fenstermaker is the Fred. L. Standley Professor of English and a University Distinguished Teacher at Florida State University. The English Department Chair for twelve years, he is now Director of the Program in American and Florida Studies. In 2005, he served as president of the South Atlantic Modern Language Association. An active Hemingway scholar, his principal interests are Hemingway's biography and his publications between the world wars.

Mimi Reisel Gladstein is currently president of the John Steinbeck Society of America. She has won international recognition in Steinbeck studies with the John J. & Angeline Pruis Award for teaching and the Burkhardt Award for Scholarship. The Rocky Mountain Modern Language Association named her a Sterling Member in 2006, only the second such award in its history. At the University of Texas at El Paso, she has been named to the university's top award in Teaching Excellence (1988) and Service to Students (2006). The College of Liberal Arts named her Outstanding Faculty of 2003. The author of four books and coeditor of an anthology of feminist criticism, Gladstein has published articles in anthologies and scholarly journals_on subjects as diverse as Harry Potter, Ayn Rand, William Faulkner, Ernest Hemingway, and pedagogical techniques for teaching research writing.

Patrick Hemingway is the second son of Ernest Hemingway, Pauline Pfeiffer Hemingway's first-born, and a major contributor and leading expert in ongoing scholarship about and publication of his father's work. In 1999, Mr. Hemingway edited his father's posthumous novel, *True at First Light*, which spent many weeks on the best-seller list. He has written forewords for such collections as *Hemingway on War*, *Hemingway on Hunting*, the Finca Vigía Edition of the *Complete Short Stories*, and *Green Hills of Africa* (Easton Press). Mr. Hemingway was born in Kansas City, Missouri, and lived with his father in Key West, Florida, and Havana, Cuba, before attending Harvard College, where he graduated magna cum laude. For more than two decades, he lived in Tanzania, East Africa, first owning and operating a safari company and later teaching at the College of African Wildlife Management. Patrick Hemingway now resides in Bozeman, Montana, with his wife, Carol. He has one daughter, Edwina, who lives with her husband and four sons in Naples, Florida.

Carol Hemingway is a playwright whose credits include several Hemingway-related texts. In 1999, her adaptation of Ernest Hemingway's short stories, entitled *It Just Catches*, opened in Oak Park, Illinois. The play has since been performed in New York as well as in more than forty cities in Montana and received an NEA grant in 2006. Ms. Hemingway and her husband, Patrick, collaborated on a work, *Mama Jini's Lion*, based on a family safari experience led by Patrick Hemingway in his days as a white hunter. She has also written two wildlife plays, *Catch and Release* and *Talking Turkey*, focusing on her sporting life of fly-fishing and hunting. Ms. Hemingway served as a Professor of Theatre for fourteen years at City College of New York, where she taught acting, directing, playwriting, and finished as Chair of the department. She is a member of the Dramatists Guild and the Society of Stage Directors and Choreographers. A graduate of Swarthmore College, she holds an MFA from Yale Drama School and a Ph.D. from Carnegie Mellon University.

Besides his work on Hemingway, James H. Meredith has published on various writers and themes, including Andre Dubus, Henry Adams, F. Scott Fitzgerald, Stephen Crane, Edith Wharton, Robert Grave, Siegfried Sassoon, and Wilfred Owen, and the American Civil War, and World War I and II. In 2005, he was elected president of the Ernest Hemingway Foundation and Society. He also has served on the board of the F. Scott Fitzgerald Society for over two terms. He teaches online education for Troy University.

Dan Monroe earned a doctorate in history from the University of Illinois at Urbana-Champaign, where he worked with Professor Robert W. Johannsen. He received the Heiligenstein Award for Teaching Excellence and was a Fellow at the Virginia Historical Society and Lincoln Legal Papers. Monroe is the author of three books: *The Republican Vision of John Tyler* (2003); *At Home with Illinois' Governors: A Social History of the Illinois Executive Mansion* (2002); and *Shapers of the Great Debate on the Civil War: A Biographical Dictionary* (2005), with coauthor Dr. Bruce Tap. Monroe is Assistant Professor of History at Millikin University.

Mark P. Ott teaches at Deerfield Academy in Massachusetts. His book, *Ernest Hemingway and the Gulf Stream: A Contextual Biography*, was published in 2007 by Kent State University Press. Ott has presented academic papers at international Hemingway conferences in Spain, Cuba, Oak Park, Bimini, Italy, and Key West, and his scholarship has been published in the *Hemingway Review*. He has been awarded grants from the Ernest Hemingway Society, the Ernest Hemingway Collection at the John F. Kennedy Library, and the Arts and Sciences Advisory Council of the University of Hawaii-Manoa. He lives in Deerfield and Kailua, Hawaii.

Steve Paul writes for the *Kansas City Star* and was site director for the 2008 Hemingway Society Conference in Kansas City, Missouri.

Russ Pottle is Academic Dean and Abbot David Melancon Endowed Professor of Literature at Saint Joseph Seminary College, in Saint Benedict, Louisiana. His research interests are in American literature, travel writing, and cultural studies. Dr. Pottle has published work on the relationship between travel writing and the novel and on the intersection of travel writing and autobiography. He is a member of the Board of Advisors for the Society for American Travel Writing and a member of the Ernest Hemingway Society and Foundation and the International Society for Travel Writing.

Active in the development of online education products, most notably through her work with Sherecorps, E. Stone Shiflet is committed to developing the potential of distance learning in traditional humanities instruction. Her literary outreach projects include collaborative work on Hemingway with organizations in Oak Park and southern Spain. Her interests in both Hemingway's and F. Scott Fitzgerald's Florida-based literature have been the recent focus of her regional literary research. A devout resident of Tampa, she is active in several Bay Area societies that celebrate the pirate lore of the region.

Gail D. Sinclair is scholar-in-residence and executive director of the Winter Park Institute at Rollins College. She is co-editor of *War + Ink: New Perspectives on Ernest Hemingway's Early Life and Writings*.

Susan J. Wolfe is Professor of English and Professor and Chair of Languages, Linguistics, and Philosophy at the University of South Dakota. She is co-editor of several books, and her articles on the history of English, gender in English and other languages, feminist aesthetics, and the linguistic reconstruction of prehistory have appeared in several journals (*Women's Studies International Quarterly, Word, Papers in Linguistics*, and *Forum Linguisticum*) as well as books (*Gender and Discourse: The Power of Talk*; *Communication, Language, and Gender*; and *Language, Gender, and Society*). She is currently researching the representation of gender in Hemingway and in popular culture. Her first article on Hemingway appeared in the *South Dakota Review*.

Index

Catholicism, 99, 288, 292
Cezanne, Paul, 144, 276
Chambers, Canby, 36, 41
Chambers, Esther, 36, 41
Chantey of the Keys (de Bechevet), 22
Civilian Conservation Corps, 250
Cohen, Milton A., 20, 77
Cohn, Louis Henry, 207
Collier, Barron, 275
communism, 77, 83, 101–2, 124, 214, 251–52
conchs (Key Westers), 8, 39, 81, 123, 190, 198, 226
Cooper, Gary, in *Sergeant York*, 173
Cooper, James Fenimore, 5–7, 9, 11, 15, 16, 19
Corcoran, Tom, 19
Cordingly, David, 108, 111, 119
Cowley, Malcolm, 68, 78, 81–82, 93, 262
Cradle of the Middle Class (Ryan), 287
Crane, Hart, 15
Crowley, Michael J., 21, 189
Cuba, 6, 54; Cuba Libre movement, 9, 95; cuisine of, 47; revolution in, 20, 130
cummings, e. e., 88
Curnutt, Kirk, 1, 21, 103, 220

Darrow, Clarence, 216
Darwinism, 155–57
Davies, Alan, 22, 292
de Havilland, Olivia, 114, 116
de León, Ponce, 107
de Pereda, Prudencio, 282
Dietrich, Marlene, 182
Donaldson, Scott, 25, 43
Don Balasco of Key West (Gunter), 9–11, 16
Donne, John, 184
Dos Passos (Carr), 193–94, 197, 205
Dos Passos, John, 36, 53, 67, 83, 101, 166; involvement in "After the Storm," 191–97, 199, 205
Dos Passos, Katy Smith, 66, 96–97, 193
Drake, Sir Francis, 107
Dreiser, Theodore, 216
Dry Tortugas, 52, 54, 115, 190–91, 251

Eastman, Maxwell, 93–94, 289–92
Eby, Carl, 290, 292
Eleventh Biennial Ernest Hemingway Society Conference, 19
Eliot, T. S., 157, 221–22

Elliott, Ira, 158–59
Ellis, Havelock, 216
Esky: The Early Years at Esquire (Merrill), 218
Ethiopia, 90, 100, 214
Evans, Walker, 130–32
Everglades, 39, 285

Fadiman, Clifton, 76, 204
Fairbanks, Douglas, Sr., 109, 120
A Farewell to Arms (Hemingway), 1, 14, 44, 206, 228; characters in, 202, 229, 246–47, 260, 279; film version of, xix; manuscript of, 91, 194, 203; publication of, 144; settings in, 222, 229; writing of, 54–55, 190, 193–94, 203, 278
fascism, 67, 82, 214; antifascism, 88–89, 208
Faulkner, William, 21, 174; and work on *To Have and Have Not*, 172–74, 176, 178, 185
Federal Emergency Relief Administration. *See* United States Government Agencies
Fenstermaker, John J., 21, 206
Finca Vigía, 74–75, 239
Fitzgerald, F. Scott, 51, 65, 67–68, 158, 171
Fitzgerald, Zelda, 69
Flagler, Henry M., 14, 225
Flanner, Janet, 50
Flora, Joseph, 271, 280
Florida East Coast Railway, 14, 16, 56, 128, 224, 253, 286. *See also* Hurricane, Labor Day (1935)
Florida Straits, 108
Flynn, Errol, 109, 113–14, 116, 120, 127. *See also Captain Blood*
Folliard, Edward T., 250, 255–56
Fort Jefferson, 196
For Whom the Bell Tolls (Hemingway), 44, 263–64; characters in, 82–83, 167, 173, 264, 267; film version of, 173; political themes in, 82, 101–3, 130, 240; title of, 184; writing of, 55, 57, 156, 206
Fossalta, Italy, 246; lower Piave River, 242, 246, 263
Fowler, Henry W., 53
Franco, Francisco, 101–3
Frank, Joseph, 259
French Connections: Hemingway and Fitzgerald Abroad (Kennedy and Bryer), 4
Freud, Sigmund, 157

Frost, Robert, 88
Furthman, Jules, 172–73

Gable, Clark, 210
Gallagher, William, 127
Game Fishing of the World, 143
Gannett, Lewis, 72
Gardner, Carol Hemingway, 53, 62, 94
Gardner, John (Jack), 63, 94
Gellhorn, Martha, 18, 56, 72–73, 97, 282
Gender Trouble (Butler), 159, 171
*A General History of the Robberies and
    Murders of the Most Notorious Pyrates*
    (Johnson), 110
Gingrich, Arnold, 206–8, 215, 217, 219
Gladstein, Mimi Reisel, 21, 172
Gold, Mike, 78, 82, 93
Gomez, Jose Miguel, 132, 140
Gómez, Juan Vicente, 140
A Good Day to Die (Harrison), 17, 58
Gorostiza, Paulino, Jr., 138
Grau y San Martín, Ramon, 135, 137–38
Great Depression, 46, 91–95, 99, 103, 207,
    214, 268; and its relation to *To Have and
    Have Not*, 4, 108, 148, 263
Greco-Turkish War, 98, 260
Greek and Roman myth, 185, 276, 281
Gris, Juan, 34
Gulf Stream, 143–50; and its relation to *To
    Have and Have Not*, 152–57
Gutieras, Antonio, 137–38
Gutiérrez, Carlos, 57, 71, 146, 200

Hall, James, 108
Hambright, Thomas, 43
Hammett, Dahiell, 108, 216
Harmonium (Stevens), 83, 85
Havana, Cuba, 3, 150
Hawks, Howard, 113, 175, 185; Faulkner's col-
    laboration with, 21, 172–74, 176, 178, 180.
    See also To Have and Have Not (film)
Hawthorne, Nathaniel, 287–88
Hemingway, Carol (daughter-in-law), 20,
    28, 36
Hemingway, Carol (sister). *See* Gardner,
    Carol Hemingway
Hemingway, Dr. Clarence, 61–63, 278
Hemingway, Ernest, life of: as artist/family
    man, 49–50; and boxing, 31, 47, 208; and

bullfighting, 79, 93, 97, 208, 235; celebrity
status of, 66, 228, 231, 236, 238–39, 292;
and commodification of celebrity, 3–5,
21, 285, 286, 292–95, 297–98; and the
demands of art, 247; and fishing, 48, 52,
55, 57, 69, 79, 91, 93, 131, 149, 208; and
geography as metaphor, 222; and grace
under pressure, 2; as hero figure, 170, 180,
252; and hunting, 52, 71–72, 79, 93, 97,
208, 210; infidelity of, 60, 71, 73–74, 76;
injuries and illnesses of, 1, 51, 57, 216; as
journalist, 201, 207; and Key West friendships (the Mob), 53, 191, 204–5; and Key
West's relation to writing, 1, 44, 47–50,
55–56, 61, 224; macho image of, 59, 93–94,
290; and nicknames, 57, 60, 65, 182; passion for sport of, 50; suicide of, 53, 75, 239,
282; and writing truthfully, 45, 99, 144,
212–13
Hemingway, Ernest, works of: *Anita* fishing
logs, 148, 157; *The Fifth Column* (play),
74; "A Key West Girl," 20, 26, 39, 43; *The
Spanish Earth* (film), 130
—books: *The Complete Short Stories of Ernest
Hemingway: The Finca Vigía Edition*, 267,
271; *Death in the Afternoon*, 1, 44, 78, 93,
207, 221, 222, 233, 235, 289–90, 298; *The
Fifth Column and the First Forty-Nine
Stories*, 171; *The Garden of Eden*, 270–75;
Green Hills of Africa, xxiii, 44–45, 55, 68,
71–72, 78, 231–32, 235; *In Our Time*, 59,
240, 244, 247, 252; *Islands in the Stream*,
267, 281; *Men Without Women*, 204, 239;
A Moveable Feast, 256; *The Nick Adams
Stories*, 61, 274; *The Old Man and the
Sea*, 5, 144, 145, 154, 156, 184, 204, 208;
The Torrents of Spring, 228; *Winner Take
Nothing*, 44–45, 78, 99, 189, 204, 206. *See
also A Farewell to Arms; For Whom the Bell
Tolls; The Sun Also Rises; To Have and Have
Not; To Have and Have Not* (film)
—magazine and newspaper articles: "A. D.
in Africa: A Tanganyika Letter," 218; "a. d.
Southern Style," 221; "The Art of the Short
Story," 228; "Defense of Dirty Words,"
211–12; "Fascisti Party Now Half-Million
Strong," 218; "The Friend of Spain," 213,
235–36; "Hemingway Slept Here," 3; "He
Who Gets Slap Happy," 103, 210, 215,

254–56; memorial, 257–58, 266; veteran deaths, 99, 242–43, 257, 262

Huxley, Aldous, 216

Hynes, Samuel, 257

Ideas of Order (Stevens), 85, 86

In Biscayne Bay (Rockwood), 22

International Economic Conference (1922), 214

International Game Fish Association, Hemingway's contributions to, 53

Isla Navarino, 285

isolationism, 100

Italy: Hemingway's experiences in during WWI, 2, 228, 241, 246; and military action in Africa, 100, 214; and Mussolini, 214, 218; and involvement in Spanish Civil War, 101, 102

Ivens, Joris, 67, 73

Japanese invasion of Manchuria, 100

Jaycocks, O. K., 42

Jewfish Key, 242

John Dos Passos: A Twentieth Century Odyssey (Ludington), 205

Johnson, Hugh, S., 230

Joven Cuba (Young Cuba), 137–39

Jung, Carl, 157

Kansas City, Mo., 40, 216

Károlyi, Count Mihály, 279

Kashkeen, Ivan, 55, 94

Kawain, Bruce, 174, 185

Kazin, Alfred, 81

Keene, Jennifer D., 246

Kemal, Mustafa, 214

Ketchum, Idaho, 3, 239

Key, Jackie, 51

Key Largo, 108, 266

Key West, 44; history of fiction about, 5–19; as fictional pirate haven, 6–8; industries in, 9, 14, 224; outlaw industries of, 11, 46, 52; relation to writing/writers, 15–17, 58; tourism, 21, 95–97, 148, 221, 224, 249; as tropical and wild paradise 17, 19, 148

—sites: Blue Heaven Restaurant, 47; Casa Antigua, 296; Casa Marina Hotel, 15, 19, 63, 225; Duval Street, 4, 239, 293; Ernest Hemingway Home and Museum, 3, 28, 294–96; Fort Taylor, 28, 233; Key West

Art and Historical Society/Museum of Art and History (Custom House), 2, 12, 296; Key West Lighthouse, 28–29; La Concha Hotel, 45; Navy basin, 3, 28, 162; Southernmost Home, 239; Whitehead Street, 2, 28, 237

Key West, History of an Island of Dreams (Ogle), 306, 223

Key West Administration (KWA), 225, 227–29, 236–37

Key West Guidebook, 238

Key West Hemingway residence (907 Whitehead Street), 26, 28–32, 40–41, 43, 57 228, 268; brick wall, building of, 26, 28, 53, 236–37; swimming pool, 28, 30, 40, 97, 286; stories about, 39, 287; as tourist attraction, 21, 161, 227–29

Key West in Transition: A Guidebook for Visitors, 227, 229, 237

Key West 2720 A.D. (Eakins), 19

Kipling, Rudyard, 58

Klee, Paul, 34

Knott, Toni D., 22, 137

Koch, Stephen, 75

Koven, Joseph, 211

Lardner, Ring, 210–212

Latimer, Ronald Lane, 85–87, 90

Lausanne Peace Conference (1922–23), 214

Lawrence, D. H., 216, 263

L-Bar-T Ranch, Wyo., 39

League of Nations, 100

Leavens, George, 38

leftist politics, 77–89, 103

Lenin, Vladimir, 78

Leslie, John, 108

Lincoln, Barnabas, 108

Lindbergh, Charles, 148

Literature through Film (Stam), 185

Lloyds Register of Shipping, 205

London, Jack, 108

Lorimer, George Horace, 68

Lost Generation, 75, 159, 246, 264

The Lost Men (Benedict), 16

"Love's Labor Lost: A Sketch of Key West," 8

Lozano-Moreno, Susana, 185

Lurie, Alison, 18–19

Luxembourg Garden, 31

Lynn, Kenneth, 66–69

Sea Brothers (Bender), 157
Second American Writers' Congress, 73, 82, 141
S. E. Johnson and Sons, 32–34, 43
Seldes, George, 103
Seldes, Gilbert, 211–12
Serengeti Plain, 79
Service, Robert, 58
Seydow, John J., 170
Shakespeare, William, 19, 241, 248
Shames, Laurence, 19
Sheridan, Wyo., 50, 202
Shiflet, E. Stone, 21, 103
Sholtz, Dave, 225
Simons, Hi, 90
Simonton, John, 6
Sinclair, Gail D., xvii, 20, 59
Sinclair, Upton, 7–8, 15, 22
Sloppy Joe's Bar, 56, 58, 296–98
Smith, Al, 99
Smith, Bill, 53, 191, 205
Smith, Paul, 203
Social Democratic Party, 279
Solow, Herbert, 82
Southernmost House, 239, 286
Southernmost Point, 286
Soviet Union, 89
Spain Betrayed: The Soviet Union in the Spanish Civil War (Radosh and Sevostianov), 103
Spanish-American War, 9–10
Spanish bullfighting tradition, 79, 207, 222, 235. See also Hemingway, Ernest, works of: books: Death in the Afternoon
Spanish Civil War, 57, 80, 100–103, 130. See also Hemingway, Ernest, works of: The Spanish Earth (film)
Spanish Main, 107
Spanish Republic, 100–101
Stalinist directive, 102
Standard Oil, 120, 127
Stein, Gertrude, 59, 66, 218, 256
Steinbeck, John, 52; Cup of Gold: A Life of Sir Henry Morgan, Buccaneer, with Occasional Reference to History, 110
Stephens, Robert O., 98, 209
Stevens, Wallace, 15, 20, 77, 83–89
stock market, 95, 269

Stone, Julius F., Jr., (Key West Kingfish), 92, 95–97, 161, 225–26, 237–39, 249
Stoneback, H. R., 274–77, 281
Strait of Magellan, 285
Straits of Florida, 107
Strater, Henry (Mike), 52, 53, 191, 194–95, 205
Strong, John B., 6
The Sun Also Rises (Hemingway), 192, 219, 232, 280; and Brett Ashley (character), 159, 280, 193; and Jake Barnes (character), 11, 158, 170, 192–93, 223, 232, 247, 192; critical reception of, 59, 63; minor characters in, 81, 127, 159, 193, 223; setting of, 223, 232; themes in, 158–59, 162–63
Sun Valley/Ketchum, Idaho, Ernest Hemingway Festival, 298

Tamiami Trail, 268, 271
Tchitcherin, Georgi, 98
Thompson, Charles, 50–52, 54, 57
Thompson, Hunter, 58
Thompson, Karl, 242
Thompson, Smith, 6
Tift, Asa, 30
To Have and Have Not (Hemingway): Hélène and Tommy Bradley, 17, 159, 166, 169; Helen and Richard Gordon, 81, 166–67, 252, 255; influences, 108, 148–154, 157, 263–64; minor characters, 116, 122–25, 136, 159–63, 167–69; Marie Morgan, 112, 114–15, 116–17, 159, 169, 170, 180; publication of, 257; reputation as lesser work, 16, 20, 81, 262; and unpublished sections, 136
—Harry Morgan, 11, 99, 123, 135–36; amputeeism of, 111–13, 154; death of, 95, 116, 141, 156, 263; influences of, 52, 110–11; as family man, 124, 126, 165, 169, 175; as pirate/hero figure, 114, 120, 127, 159; and traits of masculinity, 115, 167–69, 171; violence and, 109, 126, 139 161
—themes: decline of the individual, 250; humanity's place in naturalistic world, 11, 148, 155–57; negative portrayal of rich, 116, 118, 124, 159, 162, 164; negative portrayal of vets, 21, 125, 245, 247–48, 250, 252, 255, 259, 263–64; political criticism, 86, 124, 129, 134, 141; proletarian sympathies, 80–81, 99, 136, 244, 260

www.ingramcontent.com/pod-product-compliance
Lightning Source LLC
Chambersburg PA
CBHW022018050726
47499CB00004BA/1201

* 9 7 8 0 8 1 3 0 6 2 3 6 5 *